Commentary on
The Gospel of Matthew
Chapters 1–7

by

Tim Hegg

TorahResource • 2007

ISBN-13: 978-0-9916639-0-3

Table of Contents

The Gospel of Matthew
Introduction
Notes by Tim Hegg

The study of the Gospels has undergone radical changes in modern times. The History of Religions, following the Darwinian concept of natural evolution, gave rise to new ways of viewing the Gospel records. Rather than receiving them as historical documents, written by specific authors to specific communities for a specific purpose, the Gospels, along with most other literary remains of ancient communities, have been subjected to various forms of criticism in order to determine source materials, literary motives, and the history of their compilation. Thus, rather than reading the Gospels for the story they tell, they have become "museum pieces"[1] presenting a kind of challenging puzzle to be unravelled by modern experts.

[1]Davies/Allison, *Matthew*, 1.1

The primary problems inherent in the current critical approach to the Gospels are several. First, much of what the modern critics purport to be the original story of the Gospels is based upon calculated speculations. One can only speculate what might have been the motivation in an author's mind for writing a particular text, unless, of course, the author explicitly reveals his or her motivation. The same may be said for compilers or redactors of a text: their motivations are something modern critics may claim to know, but they do so only on the basis of presumption. The same may be said of source criticism in the Gospels. The criteria of suspicion, for instance, is hardly verifiable. This criteria, by which some modern scholars decide what is "original" and what has been added by later generations of religious communities, is surely a matter of circular reasoning. For the criteria of suspicion suggests that when the Gospels contain "dogma" which was essential for the doctrine and practice of the later Christian Church, it certainly could not have been original, but was added via a theological motivation. Yet it is just as probable that later dogma was the result of what the Gospel writers actually said. The same may be true for the criteria of "multiple attestation." This criteria presumes that what was originally given by the Gospel writers as historical would be reiterated by more than one Gospel account. But again, it is just as possible that a true historical fact could have been included in one account, but passed by in their others.

A second problem inherent in the current discipline of Gospels Study is that of failure to abide by the very criteria that has been established. The Jesus Seminar produced a multi-colored rendition of the Gospels (*The Five Gospels*) identifying the Seminar's conclusions: what parts of the Gospels were authentic and inauthentic, and what lies somewhere in between. But scholarly assessment of the Seminar's conclusions have highlighted the fact that the criteria upon which these decisions were made were hardly historical. Hays summarizes his critique:

> The depiction of Jesus as a Cynic philosopher with no concern about Israel's destiny, no connection with the concerns and hopes that animated his Jewish contemporaries, no interest in the interpretation of Scripture, and no message of God's coming eschatological judgment is—quite simply—an ahistorical fiction, achieved by the surgical removal of Jesus from his Jewish context.[2]

[2]R. B. Hays, "The Correct Jesus," *First Things* (May, 1994), 43–48. See also Craig Evans, *Jesus and His Contemporaries* (Brill, 1995), pp. 37–40.

Thus, while we may benefit from the work of historical (or biblical) criticism, form criticism, and textual criticism, in the end, the Gospels come to us with a story of which the main character is Yeshua. It does us little good to spend our time speculating about the formation of the text within the so-called "New Criticism." Even worse is the outcome if, based upon our own speculations, we call into question the tangible text that is before us.

Since, therefore, very little verifiable data can be produced to detail the history of the formation of the Gospels, I am following the admonition of Davies and Allison, and focusing on the text of Matthew as we now have it. Of course, I also have a theological presupposition that furthers my desire to so focus this study. I believe that the Gospel of Matthew contained in our bibles is the result of the divine activity of revelation through the inspiration of God's Spirit. We all recognize, of course, that the text of Matthew we now possess has textual variants, and we do well to engage in the science of textual criticism in order to determine, as best we can, what was the original text of the Gospel writer. But in the broad stroke of things, these textual variants are peripheral to the majority of the Gospel text, which is attested without significant variation in literally thousands of manuscripts. As such, we will give ourselves in this study to understand the story of Matthew as we have it before us, and to ask the all important question in such a study: what does this story tell us about the historical figure called Yeshua, and how does our understanding of His life, teachings, and actions call us to faith and faithfulness.

While we will center our attention primarily upon the Gospel of Matthew, we cannot ignore the other synoptic Gospels if we desire to see the story in its fullest expression. So we will note the synoptic parallels, and strive to understand how the viewpoint of two other authors, who are telling the same story, help us complete or sharpen the words of Matthew's Gospel. Yet it is not my purpose to write a commentary on the Synoptic Gospels. So our primary concern will be to understand Matthew's viewpoint, and His message about Yeshua and His work.

Which Matthew?

Having determined to focus on the extant text of Matthew, and not be overly concerned with the "New Criticism" that characterizes current Gospels study, it is appropriate at this juncture to ask the obvious question, "Which Matthew?" This question is a contemporary one, however, and particularly one that has arisen among the emerging Messianic or Torah communities, based upon historical data that suggests Matthew may have originally existed in an Aramaic or Hebrew form, and only later translated into Greek. Some have suggested that the extant Greek manuscripts of Matthew, when compared with Hebrew manuscripts, show a wide divergence, and point to two (or more) distinct manuscript traditions.

In recent days, much has been made of the various copies of Matthew in Hebrew, and it has even been suggested that one of these copies, the so-called "Shem Tov," offers the best exemplar of Matthew's original Gospel. Let me first give a very brief description of the various Hebrew Matthews, and then offer my approach to the question of "which Matthew?"

The oldest extant Hebrew Matthew is that of the Even Bohan (אֶבֶן בּוֹחָן, "The Touchstone"). This was a multi-volume work produced as a polemic against Christians missionaries who were doing their work among Jewish people.[3] The *Even Bohan* was authored by Shem-Tov ben Issac ben Shaprut (sometimes called Ibn Shaprut). It is a polemical work comprising 12 sections or books (though an additional five sections were added later). It was originally written by Shaprut in 1380, and revised several times through subsequent years.

> Of the original books the first deals with the principles of the Jewish faith, the next nine deal with various passages in the Bible that were disputed by Jews and Christians, the eleventh discusses certain haggadic sections in the Talmud used by Christians or proselytes to Christianity, and the twelfth contains the entire Gospel of Matthew in Hebrew along with polemical comments by Shem Tob interspersed throughout the text.[4]

George Howard has collated an eclectic text, comparing a number of extant manuscripts, and offered the Hebrew text of Matthew first in 1987 with a revised edition in 1995.[5] The title of Howard's 1987 suggested that the Shem Tov was, in fact, a "primitive Hebrew text" of Matthew. But scholarly critiques of his work made it clear that such an assertion was not well founded. Thus, in the subsequent revision, the title was changed simply to "Hebrew Gospel of Matthew." Indeed, the reaction of the scholars to Howard's work, and thus to the value of the Shem Tov Matthew, have been predictably varied. Numbers of scholars gave strong negative reviews, but a minority were more cautious, and some have suggested that the Shem Tov Matthew should be given greater significance in the matter of textual criticism of Matthew's Gospel.[6]

This is not the place for a full evaluation of the value of Shem Tov's Matthew for text critical studies in Matthew's Gospel, and admittedly, the opinion of scholars on this matter is far from unified. Important points to consider, however, are:

1) Shem Tov's Matthew was originally interspersed with polemical comments by Ibn Shaprut. As such, it has clear tendencies toward textual corruption. For instance, an entire section (corresponding to Mark 9:20–28) is inserted following Matthew 17:17 in order to expand the single verse summary of the pericope given in Matthew's version (17:18). In other words, Matthew 17:18 is replaced by nine verses from Mark in a revised form. In other places, words and phrases are clearly missing. For example, 18:2 breaks mid-sentence: "He called a lad...," leaving out an entire section which Howard supplies from other manuscripts for his translation. Another example is 22:6, "And others [ ] and abused them and killed them." Obviously, the phrase "took his servants" is missing from the Shem Tov. Other anomalies occur in the Shem Tov text as well. In 16:16, Peter's reply to Yeshua's inquiry of "what do you say about me?" is: "You are the Messiah, that is, Kristo (קְרִיסְטֹ'וֹ), the Son of the living God, who has come into this world." Here, it appears that the Even Bohan is transliterating the Greek word Χριστός, *Christos* as a gloss, perhaps to alert the readers to the fact that Hebrew *mashiach* is called *Christos* by the Christians. But why is the final *sigma* omitted? In 24:14, the word "antichrist" is correctly transliterated. It appears that in this instance, a scribe has dropped off the final letter of christos. These few examples should be sufficient to show that the Shem Tov is far from pristine in terms of textual consistency.

2) In spite of the obvious textual problems extant in the Shem Tov

[3]For an interesting historical account of the use of Hebrew and Hebrew materials by Christian scholars in the 16th Century, see Jerome Friedman, *The Most Ancient Testimony* (Ohio Univ Press, 1983).

[4]George Howard, *The Gospel of Matthew according to a Primitive Hebrew Text* (Mercer Press, 1987), p. ix.

[5]George Howard, *Hebrew Gospel of Matthew* (Mercer Press, 1995).

[6]The following is a short list of important books & articles discussing the Shem Tov Matthew:

Pinchas E. Lapide, *Hebrew in the Church* (Eerdmans, 1984).
William L. Petersen, review of Howard, *Gospel of Matthew*, JBL 108 (1989) 722-26.
William Horbury, review of *Gospel of Matthew*, JTS n.s. 43 [1992 1166-69]
Shaye J. D. Cohen, review of *Gospel of Matthew* (Bible Review 4 (1988) 8-9).
Daniel J. Harrington, review of *Gospel of Matthew*, CBQ 50 (1988) 717-18.
Robert Shedinger, "The Textual Relationship between P45 and Shem-Tob's Hebrew Matthew," NTS 43.1 (1997), 58–71.
Robert Shedinger, "A Further Consideration of the Textual Nature of Shem-Tob's Hebrew Matthew," CBQ 61.4 (1999), 686–694.

Matthew, it still presents some unique or mostly unique readings (Shedinger finds 44 such unique readings), and these should be fully considered when engaging in matters of textual criticism. In this regard, the Shem Tov has value as we seek to study Matthew's Gospel.

Two other Hebrew Matthews are extant: the Münster and the Du Tillet. Sebastian Münster published a Hebrew version of Matthew in 1537 which he titled תּוֹרַת הַמָּשִׁיחַ, "The Torah of the Messiah." In his preface, Münster states that he used a "tattered" MS, and supplemented or altered its defective text. What is exactly meant by this notice has been debated. Some think the manuscript included many lacunae which Münster supplied from other texts (Latin or Greek). Horbury suggests that the manuscript he used was interspersed with polemical comments, which he extracted in order to make the Matthew text contiguous. Since, however, Münster did not mark his editorial work, use of the Münster Matthew for text-critical purposes is dubious. In 1551, Johannes Quinquarboreus published Münster's Hebrew Matthew with critical notes in the margin, suggesting alternate readings and corrections, but it is not always clear if these were simply his own suggestions, or if he was utilizing other manuscripts to compare with the Münster.

The history of the Du Tillet Matthew is a bit uncertain. It was published in 1555 by Bishop Jean du Tillet, bishop of Saint-Brieuc, from whom it derives its name. In the preface to the published text he writes:

> the Gospel of Matthew in Hebrew, which I would not presume to suggest Matthew wrote by divine inspiration in his own language… but yet I can affirm is clearly not in the rabbinic style, and is written in a pure form of the language that in no way resembles the writings of post-Christian Judaism.

The 1555 publication was accompanied by a Latin translation (which closely followed the Vulgate) by Jean Mercier, and was published by the firm of Martin Le Jeune (Martin the Younger). The Hebrew title page includes a note that it had been "stored until this day with the Jews and hidden in their dens," which most likely means that it was among the books confiscated under papal edict.

Both the Münster and Du Tillet texts show a far greater affinity to the Greek and Latin than does the Shem Tov. But there are also some agreements between the Shem Tov and Du Tillet against the Greek and Latin witnesses, and such affinity may therefore present an important witness to alternate readings in these few places.

But an overall assessment of the extant Hebrew Matthews indicates that the Greek text that underlies our English translations is not substantially altered by comparison. Or to put it simply: the Hebrew Matthews do not present a "different Matthew" than what we know from the Greek textual witnesses. The question, then, of "which Matthew" is moot. We are fortunate that so many manuscripts are extant that give witness to the ancient Gospel of Matthew. But these manuscripts bear a unified and singular witness to the Gospel itself, while at the same time offering variant readings in various places. Thus, we will do well to consider all of the extant manuscript evidence, and to allow the preponderance of evidence (in accordance with accepted text critical methodology) to determine the reading to be received. Surely the Hebrew Matthews have a voice in these textual determinations, but do not bear greater weight than the extant Greek manuscripts.

For a description of the textual affinities of the Du Tillet, see George Howard, "The Textual Nature of an Old Hebrew Version of Matthew," *JBL* 105/1 (1986), 49–63.

Authorship of Matthew

Like all of the Gospel accounts, the book of Matthew is anonymous, meaning that the author did not begin by identifying himself. Yet very early in the history of the Apostolic canon, our Gospel was attributed to Matthew, the tax collector who was selected by Yeshua to be among the Twelve (Matt. 9:9; 10:3; in Mark and Luke, he is called Levi). Eusebius (ca. 260–340), in his *Ecclesiastical History*, makes this comment:

> Now Matthew made an ordered arrangement of the oracles in the Hebrew (or Aramaic) language, and each one translated (or interpreted) it as he was able. (*H.E.* 3.39)

This same perspective is reiterated by Irenaeus (130–200), Bishop of Lyons:

> Matthew also among the Hebrews published a written gospel in their own dialect, when Peter and Paul were preaching in Rome and founding the church there (Eusebius, *H.E.* 5.8.2, quoting Irenaeus, *Adv. haer.* 3.1.1).

Eusebius also notes that Pantaenus, the teacher of Clement of Alexandria (ca. 150–215), "went to India, and the tradition is that he there found his own arrival anticipated by some who were acquainted with the gospel according to Matthew; for Bartholomew, one of the apostles, had preached to them and left them the writing of Matthew in Hebrew letters, and this writing was preserved until the time mentioned."

Many modern scholars have presumed that the tradition of Matthew's authorship was based entirely upon the words of Papias and not upon independent traditions. If, it is argued, Papias created the tradition, then subsequent reliance upon is words is suspect. The idea that the Papias' statement regarding Matthew's authorship is suspect relates to Eusebius' comment that Papias was a man of little intelligence. However, this derogatory remark may have more to do with the theological views of Papias (he was a chiliast) than his actual intellectual abilities.

The primary difficulties that scholars have raised in terms of Matthean authorship are:

1) the extant Greek Matthew does not read as a translation of a Hebrew original, which the traditions ascribe to Matthew. Moreover, the extant Hebrew Matthews show clear affinity to an original Greek or Latin text from which they were translated (though in some few instances, they may contain unique readings that reflect an original Hebrew *Vorlage*.)

2) if Matthew's Gospel were originally a Hebrew or Aramaic document, it is difficult to explain why such a Semitic original would have incorporated a Greek document, i.e., Mark, almost in its entirety. Of the 661 verses in Mark, 500 are essentially found in Matthew.

3) along the same line of reasoning, it is difficult to explain why Matthew, an apostle who had accompanied Yeshua, would have allowed a Greek document like Mark to determine the ordering of his material.

Yet the external evidence for a Matthean authorship seems overwhelming and very early. Less than 50 years after the writing of Matthew, the tradition is already firmly in place that the author of the Gospel was, in fact, Matthew the tax collector. Moreover, Papias was (according to Eusebius), "a hearer of John" and "companion of Polycarp" (*Adv. haer.* 3.3.4). Polycarp spoke of the "apostles who preached to us" (*Epistle* 6:4) and Irenaeus (as recorded by Eusebius) testifies that Polycarp "had familiar intercourse with John and with others who had seen the Lord" (*H.E.* 5.20.6). Their close proximity to the Apostles themselves makes their witness to the Matthean authorship that much stronger. Furthermore, the early tradition of Matthean authorship went virtually unchallenged in the early centuries of the Christian Church.

How, then, if Matthean authorship seems most likely, are we to explain the absence of early Hebrew or Aramaic manuscript evidence for the Gospel, and even more, the mixture of Semitic and Greek conventions in the Matthew text? One explanation is that the *logia* spoken of by Papias, attributed to Matthew, was actually an early Hebrew or Aramaic document of the sayings of Yeshua, and that Matthew utilized this document in the writing of his Gospel, originally in Hebrew or Aramaic. This proposed document (there is no actual manuscript evidence for such a work) has been labelled as Q (for German *Quelle* meaning "source") by recent scholars. Having based his Gospel upon Q and adding his own material, Matthew's disciples later translated the work into Greek, retaining the Semitic flavor in many cases, but putting it into native Greek for the Jewish-Christian community, which was becoming increasingly populated by Gentile believers. Hagner gives a summary:

[7]See Donald Hagner, *Matthew* in the Word Commentary, 2 vols. (Nelson, 1993), 1.lxxvi–lxxvii.

> Matthew the apostle is thus probably the source of an early form of significant portions of the Gospel, in particular the sayings of Jesus, but perhaps even some of the narrative material. One or more disciples of the Matthean circle may then have put these materials into the form of the Gospel we have today. The final editing probably was done by a Hellenistic Jewish Christian, who in transmitting the tradition addressed Jewish fellow believers who, like himself, had come to accept Jesus as the Messiah and now had to articulate that new faith in such a way as to show its continuity with the past as well as to affirm all the newness of the gospel of the kingdom.[7]

The more conventional explanation (see the exhaustive material in Davies and Allison) is that of the "two-document theory," namely, that both Matthew and Luke utilized Mark as the basic document from which they each drafted their own Gospels. This leaves the question of the common material in Matthew and Luke that is lacking in Mark, to which appeal is made to Q. There is strong evidence that Matthew knew of Mark's Gospel, and that he utilized it as the basic framework for his Gospel.

In the end, all that we can say is that 1) the earliest tradition is that the Gospel was written by Matthew the tax collector, one of the Twelve; 2) it was written within the context of a Jewish community who were followers of Yeshua; 3) that the author was aware of Mark's Gospel and utilized it in his own writing; and 4) that another source document, also known by Luke, was also used in the compilation of the Gospel, which accounts for the verbal agreement between Matthew and Luke, portions of which are lacking in Mark.

Perhaps most important is the fact that emerging from the late 1st Century were three Gospels recording and narrating the life and teachings of Yeshua. Matthew was an eye-witness, while Mark and Luke were disciples of those who were eye-witnesses (Peter and Paul). Thus, from a Torah perspective, the multiple Gospels stand as the "two or three" witnesses necessary to confirm a matter. Taken together, the synoptic Gospels offer an ancient record, confirmed by multiple witnesses, of our Master's life, teaching, death, and resurrection. As such, they form an indispensable body of literature for all who believe in Yeshua as the Messiah.

The Date of Matthew

Like most of the books of the Apostolic Scriptures, the date of Matthew is debated, with some claiming it to be as early as 40 CE while others putting it after the turn of the century, a span of 70 years or more. Since the data that would give a precise and clear picture of 1st Century Judaisms vis-a-vis emerging Christianity are scarce, it becomes all that much more difficult to identify various aspects of Matthew as "early" or "late." Moreover, we sometimes fail to remember that all of Paul's epistles were written before 70 CE. Therefore, we should not be surprised to find a developed, Yeshua-centered soteriology, ecclesiology, and eschatology in the Gospels.

Wim Weren[8] has suggested a three-phase picture of Matthew's community. The First Phase was prior to 70 CE in which followers of Yeshua formed a robust community within the multi-form Judaism of the time. The Second Phase was roughly the ten years following the destruction (70–80 CE), in which the followers of Yeshua were forced into the margin within a Jewish community that was renewing itself, especially in light of the increased Roman imperialism. The Third Phase was the next ten years (80–90 CE) in which the followers of Yeshua left the common synagogues and formed their own meetings within homes. Weren would suggest that these three phases (which are not rigid but overlap) correspond to the development of Matthew's Gospel. Though speculative, this suggestion might offer some answers to the various themes we see throughout Matthew's Gospel.

If we take the view that Matthew used Mark's Gospel, and date Mark to the late 60's (as is generally the case among scholars), then Matthew had to be written sometime after the late 60's. In seeking the latest date possible, we may note the early allusions or quotes of Matthew. We find the *Didache* using the same material as Matthew (2:2; 3:15; 5:38–42; 6:9–15; 15:13), and though some have suggested that Matthew quoted the *Didache* and not *visa versa*, most scholars maintain the view that the *Didache* utilized Matthew and place its date between 90 and 120 CE. Additionally, some would claim that reliance upon Matthew is seen in John's Gospel and Peter's first epistle.[9] Ignatius (d. ca. 107 CE) quotes or alludes to Matthew, as does Polycarp (d. ca. 156 CE) and Justin Martyr (ca. 100–165 CE).

Davies[10] has argued that some parts of Matthew reflect an awareness of the kind of rabbinic rulings formulated by the reconvened Sanhedrin at Yavneh following the destruction. If this is the case, then the final redaction of Matthew's Gospel would have occurred sometime after 90 CE.

These data would suggest, then, that the final compilation of Matthew's Gospel most likely occurred between 80 and 95 CE.

The Message of Matthew

All of the Gospels have the same basic purpose: to describe the person of Yeshua, His mission, and the manner in which He fulfilled it. Yet in this over arching purpose, each may emphasize a particular aspect of Yeshua's

[8]Wim Weren, "The History and Social Setting of the Matthean Community" in Huub van de Sandt, ed., *Matthew and the Didache* (Van Gorcum/Fortress, 2005), pp. 51–62.

[9]On John's use of the synoptics, see J. Muddiman, "John's Use of Matthew," *ETL* 59 (1983), pp. 333–7

For Peter's possible use of Matthew, cp. 1Pet 2:7 with Matt 21:24; 1Pet 2:12 with Matt 5:16; 1Pet 3:14 with Matt 5:10; 1Pet 3:8–9 with Matt 5:39, 44; and 1Pet 4:14 with Matt 5:11–12. (These references from Davies/Allison, 1.130, n. 97.)

[10]W. D. Davies, *The Setting of the Sermon on the Mount* (Cambridge, 1964), pp. 256–315.

person and work—that which would be most important to the community they each addressed. For the Matthean community (whomever they may have been), Matthew emphasizes the Royal kingship of Yeshua as the rightful heir to the Davidic throne. This (as we shall see) is clearly given in good rabbinic fashion in the opening genealogy of the Messiah. Likewise, in the entry into Jerusalem, of the Synoptics Matthew alone includes the quote from Zech 9:9, "'Behold your King is coming to you....'" Surely the other Gospels also emphasize the kingship of Yeshua. But Matthew's tracing of Yeshua's lineage through the line of Joseph, and ending with Abraham (as opposed to Luke's genealogy that goes back to Adam) emphasizes the legal right of Yeshua as the rightful heir and fulfilment of the Davidic promise. In being the fulfilment of the Davidic covenant (2Sam 7), Yeshua is likewise the One through whom the Abrahamic promise is realized.

Matthew also uses the messianic title, "son of man" (בֶּן-אָדָם, *ben adam*) more than any of the other Gospel writers (Matt, 31x; Mark, 14x; Lk, 26x; John, 13x). Of all the Gospels, only Luke mentions Adam, tracing the lineage of Yeshua to him, Who also came directly from God (τοῦ θεοῦ, "of God," cf. Lk 3:38). Is it possible that the repeated use of the "Son of Man" terminology by Matthew was also a cryptic reference to the "Abraham–David–Messiah" motif with which he begins his Gospel? ("ADaM" could be viewed as an acrostic for **A**braham, **D**avid, and **M**ashiach.)

Many attempts have been made to find an overall structure for Matthew's Gospel, but none are very successful. Perhaps Davies has given us an insight into at least one aspect of Matthew's structuring principles. He appeals to the famous saying of Simeon the Righteous, a Sage of the Maccabean era.

> Simeon the Righteous was one of the last survivors of the great assembly. He would say: "On three things does the world stand: (1) "On the Torah,   (2) "and on the Temple service,   (3) "and on deeds of loving kindness."[11]

[11]m.Avot 1:2

Davies notes that in *Avot de-Rabbi Natan* this saying of Simeon is commented on from a post-destruction perspective, for though the "Temple service" is that which is most beloved by the Holy One, the final phrase, "deeds of loving kindness" is explained as substituting for the Temple service. R. Natan does this by telling a story about Rabban Yochanan ben Zakkai (the framer of the Mishnah):

> Once as Rabban Johanan ben Zakkai was coming forth from Jerusalem, Rabbi Joshua followed after him and beheld the Temple in ruins. "Woe unto us!" Rabbi Joshua cried, "that this, the place where the iniquities of Israel were atoned for, is laid waste!" "My son," Rabban Johanan said to him, "be not grieved; we have another atonement as effective as this. And what is it? It is acts of loving-kindnss, as it is said, *For I desire mercy and not sacrifice* (Hos. 6:6).[12]

R. Yochanan goes on to show that Daniel, who also worshipped without the Temple, engaged in deeds of loving-kindness by which God delivered him. Moreover, Yochanan goes on to explain that while Daniel did not actually offer sacrifices in Babylon, his deeds of kindness and his daily prayers were accepted by God as though he had. Thus, in the post-destruction, the foundational triad given by Simeon the Righteous is reinterpreted to be: 1) the study of Torah that leads to doing the commandments, 2) daily prayers, and 3) deeds of kindness.

[12]W. D. Davies, *The Sermon on the Mount* (Cambridge, 1966).

Davies has shown how these three elements, Torah, prayer, and deeds of kindness, are regularly referenced in Matthew's Gospel, especially in the Sermon on the Mount.[12] We will do well to keep these general themes in mind as we study the words of our Master within the social context of post-destruction Judaism, and especially as we seek to understand how Matthew intended his own community to apply these words in light of the Temple's demise.

Yet even though it is obvious that various themes will be addressed throughout the Gospel, (and of course, the primary theme is the person and work of Yeshua), commentators have struggled to find a structural theme around which the book as a whole may be unified. It appears likely that Matthew, having in his possession some early gathering of Yeshua's teaching, used this along with Mark's basic outline of Yeshua's life and work to write his Gospel. As such, the structure is more literary than thematic. This will be noted in the outline that follows,[13] for in the main body of Matthew, five primary discourses of our Master are interspersed with narrative.

[13]This outline is taken from Donald Guthrie, *New Testament Introduction* (IVP, 1970), pp. 48–50.

I. THE INFANCY NARRATIVES (1:1–2:23)
The genealogy (1:1–17). The birth of Yeshua (1:18–25).
The Magi's visit (2:1–12). The flight to Egypt and the return (2:13–23).

II. THE PREPARATION FOR THE MINISTRY (3:1–4:11)
The mission of John the Baptizer (3:1–12). Yeshua's *mikveh* (3:13–17)
The temptation (4:1–11).

III. THE GALILAEAN MINISTRY (4:12–25)
The beginnings (4:12–17). Call of the first disciples (4:18–22).
A Galilaean preaching tour (4:23–25)

IV. THE FIRST DISCOURSE SECTION:
THE SERMON ON THE MOUNT (5:1–7:29)
Introduction (5:1–2). The Beatitudes (5:3–12). Illustrations from salt and light (5:13–16). Yeshua's perspective on the Torah (5:17–48). Yeshua's teaching on religious practices (6:1–7:27). The effect upon the hearers (7:28–29).

V. NARRATIVE (8:1–9:34)
Healing of the leper, the centurion's slave, Peter's mother-in-law, and others (8:1–17). Two disciples tested (8:18–22). Stilling of the waves (8:23–27). Healing of a demoniac and a paralytic (8:28–9:8). The call of Matthew (9:9–13). An enquiry about fasting (9:14–17). Healing of the ruler's daughter, the woman with a haemorrhage, two blind men and a mute demoniac (9:18–34).

VI. THE SECOND DISCOURSE SECTION:
THE MISSION DISCOURSE (9:35–10:42)
Yeshua's compassion (9:35–38). The disciples are briefed (10:1–15), warned of future trouble (10:16–25) and exhorted to be unafraid (10:26–33). They are told of division within household (10:34–39), and promised rewards (10:40–42).

VII. NARRATIVE (11:1–12:50)

Yeshua sets out to preach in the Galil (11:1). John the Baptizer's enquiry (11:2–6). Yeshua's testimony regarding John (11:7–15). His estimate of His own generation (11:16–19). Woes pronounced on cities in the Galil (11:20–24). Yeshua's thanksgiving to God (11:25–27) and call to the weary (11:28–30). Shabbat in the grain fields (12:1–8). Healing in the synagogue (12:9–14). Healing of the multitude (12:15–21). Some Pharisees criticize Yeshua, and His reply (12:22–37). Those who seek for signs, and the sign of Jonah (12:38–42). The return of an evil spirit (12:43-45). Yeshua's extended family (12:46–50).

VIII. THE THIRD DISCOURSE SECTION:
THE KINGDOM PARABLES (13:1–52)

The sower and the soils (13:1–9). The reason for parables (13:10–15), and the privileged position of the disciples (13:16–17). The first parable interpreted (13:18–23). The tares (13:24–30). The mustard seed and the leaven (13:31–33). Tanach support for the use of parables (13:34–35). The tares interpreted (13:36–43). Hidden treasure, the valuable pearl and the dragnet (13:44–51). The trained scribe of the kingdom (13:52)

IX. NARRATIVE (13:53–17:27)

Yeshua rejected at Nazareth (13:53–58). The death of John the Baptizer (14:1–12). Miracles: five thousand fed; the walking on the water; healings at Gennesaret (14:13–36). The tradition of the elders (15:1–20). More miracles: the Syro-Phoenician demoniac; healings of multitudes; four thousand fed (15:21–39). Some Pharisees demand a sign (16:1–4). Discourse on leaven (16:5–12). Peter's confession at Cesarea Philippi (16:13–20). First prediction of the passion (16:21–23) and forecast of suffering for the disciples (16:24–28). The transfiguration and the saying of Eliyahu (17:1–13). The healing of an epileptic boy (17:14–21). Second prediction of the passion (17:22–23). Discussion about the temple tax (17:24–27).

X. THE FOURTH DISCOURSE SECTION: VARIOUS SAYINGS (18:1–35)

An enquiry about greatness (18:1–5). Responsibility for causing others to stumble (18:6–10). Illustration of the lost sheep (18:11–14). Reproofs and reconciliation (18:15–22). Parable of the unmerciful servant (18:23–25).

XI. NARRATIVE: THE JUDEAN PERIOD (19:1–22:46)

Yeshua goes to Perea (19:1–2). Questions about marriage and divorce (19:3–12). Yeshua blesses the young children (19:13–15). The rich young man comes to Yeshua (19:16–22). Yeshua's comment on riches and rewards (19:23–30). Parable of the laborers in the vineyard (20:1–16). The third prediction of the passion (20:20–28). Healing of two blind men (20:29–34). Entry into Jerusalem (21:1–11). Cleansing the Temple (21:12–17). Cursing the fig-tree (21:18–22). Controversies in the Temple court (21:23–22:46).

XII. THE FIFTH DISCOURSE SECTION:
TEACHING ON ESCHATOLOGY (23:1–25:46)

Pronouncement of woes against Pharisaic leaders (23:1–36). Lament over Jerusalem (23:37–39). The apocalyptic discourse (24:1–25:46)

XIII. THE PASSION AND RESURRECTION NARRATIVES (26:1–28:20)
The preparation (26:1–19). The betrayal predicted (26:20–25). The last supper
(26:26–29). The arrest, trial, and crucifixion (26:47–27:56).
The burial (27:57–66). The resurrection, appearance to the eleven,
and farewell commission to make disciples of the nations (28:1–20)

From this brief outline of Matthew's gospel we may note a number
of important things. First, it seems clear that Yeshua is addressing His remarks primarily to the Jewish community of which He was apart, albeit, not
without the future inclusion of the Gentiles in mind. In so doing, He set the
paradigm of "to the Jew first and also to the Greek," in the matter of making
disciples. His regular rebuffs of the Pharisaic leaders read as an intramural
struggle, not as an "outsider" condemning a group of which he is not a part.
Rather, He *is* part of the community which He calls to a renewed awareness
of what true faith in God actually entails. He is not against the Pharisees *per
se*, because he considers their teachings on the Torah to an essential, high watermark of righteousness (5:20). But it is the hypocrisy of teaching one thing,
and living something else that draws the rebuke of our Master.

Secondly, we are struck with the manner in which Matthew relates
the many miraculous healings performed by our Teacher. After the First
Discourse (the Sermon on the Mount), the narrative that follows begins and
ends with a series of miraculous healings. Likewise, the narrative that follows the Second Discourse contains the healing in the synagogue as well as
the healing of the multitudes. The same pattern follows the Third Discourse,
where the subsequent narrative relates the healing of the Syro-Phoenician
demoniac and the healing of the multitudes, and the epileptic boy. As we
would expect, the narrative that follows the Fourth Discourse also contains
the story of the healing of two blind men. Up until the time Yeshua enters
Jerusalem for His final days before His crucifixion, His teaching ministry is
always followed by His healing of those who were sick. It would seem very
probable that Matthew's purpose in structuring his Gospel in this way was
to indicate that Yeshua's performance of healing miracles was done in order
to substantiate that He was the promised Messiah, and that therefore His
teaching out to be received with full acceptance. Or to say it another way, His
healing miracles were done in order to verify the authenticity of His message. If John was familiar with Matthew's Gospel, it may be that this very
structural element (teaching followed by healing miracles) is what prompted
him to include the words of Yeshua (not found in the Synoptics):

> "If I do not do the works of My Father, do not believe Me; but if I do
> them, though you do not believe Me, believe the works, so that you
> may know and understand that the Father is in Me, and I in the Fa-
> ther." (John 10:37–38)

Thirdly, the fact that Matthew includes the three predictions of Yeshua
about His impending death (as do Mark and Luke) also informs the reader
that Yeshua's message is given with His redemptive mission always in view.
He did not come as simply a wise counsellor or Sage to help people reform
themselves. He came to accomplish a work that only He could do, the work
for which the Father had sent Him. That is, to pay the penalty for sin in order

that sinners might be eternally redeemed and brought into the family of God where, by the dwelling presence of the Almighty, shalom is experienced. Even if the disciples were too close to see this over arching reality, after the fact, Matthew along with the other Gospel writers, saw it plainly, and map it out for us in their inspired words.

Fourthly, as we seek to get the whole picture of Matthew's Gospel before we embark on our journey to study it in detail, we cannot help but be greatly encouraged by the victorious Savior we serve. If our times appear to be overwhelmingly against the message of the Gospel, all the more was it so in the days of Yeshua. Even His own Jewish community was, in large measure, deafened to the message He brought. Yet this did not dissuade Him. He maintained His fervent pursuit of Torah, service to God, and the doing of kind deeds to others. This mysterious One, the very Creator become flesh, has demonstrated for us the path we too must walk, and He did so, not as the omnipotent Divine One, but as having voluntarily given up the exercise of His divine attributes, and living as a man clothed in human flesh, experiencing all of the struggles and woes we likewise experience. In doing so, His victory is our victory, because He proved that we too, even in the face of much opposition, can live out the life of faith by the power of the Spirit. Moreover, His victory over death, and His payment for our sins, assured that we too would be victorious.

As we set ourselves to study the magnificent story of our Master, we will engage in historical, social, grammatical and theological studies in an attempt to understand the ancient text. But we cannot stop our efforts at simply understanding the meaning of Matthew's words. We must strive to apply its eternal truths and concepts to our own lives, and by doing so, to walk in the footsteps of our Messiah.

Chapter One
Commentary

Matthew's Gospel begins with a genealogy of Yeshua, and apparently does so for a number of reasons. First, following the Babylonian captivity, the Jewish community was very keen on tracing genealogical records to ensure family purity, and especially as it pertained to the priesthood of the returning exiles. It is therefore very much in keeping with Matthew's Jewish perspective that he begin by showing the lineage of the Messiah. But secondly, Matthew's intention in giving us this genealogy is not merely to show that Yeshua was (and is) Jewish, but more particularly to trace His genealogy to Abraham, with whom God made an eternal covenant, culminating in the Messiah. That is, the final and ultimate blessing of the covenant made with Abraham was "in your seed all the families of the earth will be blessed" (Gen 12:3, cf. 18:18; 22:18; 26:4; 28:14), and from the viewpoint of the Apostles, Yeshua was the Seed through Whom this promise was realized (cf. Gal 3:16). Moreover, in the unfolding revelation of the Abrahamic covenant in the Tanach, the promise was continually narrowed in terms of its fulfillment. It first was given to Abraham, Isaac, and Jacob, and then narrowed to the tribe of Judah (Gen 49:10). From the tribe of Judah, the family of Jesse was chosen, and particularly David. It was to David as the chosen King of Israel that God made the eternal covenant of kingship (2Sam 7), and promised an eternal dynasty culminating in the reign of Messiah (cf. Acts 2:29f). Matthew's genealogy, then, traces Yeshua's lineage from Abraham through David, marking Yeshua as the legitimate, royal Messiah Who would sit upon the throne of David as the Messianic King.

A third purpose of the genealogical record is to dispel the accusations, which were apparently very early (cf. John 8:41, "We are not born of fornication"), that Yeshua was of illegitimate birth due to His mother's improper behavior. One such version of this slander was that Yeshua was born of a Roman soldier named Pantheras (ben Pandira/Pantira in some rabbinic literature) and Mary, who had been divorced from her husband on the basis of adultery during the betrothal period. Origen notes that Celsus (ca. 170–180) was aware of this particular slander against Yeshua, a slander that was taken up in some rabbinic literature produced in the era when Christianity had gained a formidable position against Judaism, and during which growing persecution of the Jewish community was carried out in the name of "Jesus."[1] Exactly how early this slander against the legitimate birth of Yeshua became an issue cannot be determined. But by all indications, it was quite early, and it appears certain that Matthew intends, by his genealogy, to dispel such slander.

Matthew's method of showing Yeshua's legitimacy is twofold. First, he affirms the virgin birth of Yeshua by ending the genealogy with Mary (1:16). But acceptance of the virgin birth could only be on the basis of faith. The miracle of the birth of Yeshua would be dismissed by those who were already predisposed against him. To such detractors, Matthew takes a different approach. If Yeshua's detractors deny the legitimacy of Yeshua on the basis that they accuse Mary of improper behavior, they must likewise reckon with the fact that in the legitimate and noble line of King David, no

[1]*Contra Celsum* I.28, 32, 33, 39. On the history of the slander concerning Yeshua's illegitimate birth, see:
J. Klausner, *Jesus of Nazareth*, trans. H. Danby (Macmillan, 1943), pp. 20, 23–24, 38, 40, 48, 232.
R. T. Herford, *Christianity in Talmud and Midrash* (KTAV, 1975), pp. 35ff, 103ff, 138, 344ff.
Samuel T. Lachs, *A Rabbinic Commentary on the New Testament* (KTAV, 1987), p. 2.
For Talmudic citations regarding ben Pandira, cf. b.*Shabbat* 104b; b.*Sanhedrin* 67a; Mid. Rab. *Ecc.* 10.6. Sometimes the rabbinic literature uses ben Stada as interchangeable with ben Pandira: cf. t.*Chullin* 2.23; b.*Sanhedrin* 43a, cp. 67a.

less than four women of questionable life are included. Tamar, daughter-in-law of Judah, played the harlot and bore twins by her father-in-law (cf. Gen 38:1ff). One of the twins, Perez, is listed in King David's genealogy. Rahab, a prostitute by profession, becomes the mother of Boaz (cf. Josh 2:1ff; Ruth 4:21–22). Ruth, the Moabite, whose own ethnicity would have disqualified her from being included in the Jewish community (cf. Deut 23:4), was an ancestress of David (Ruth 4:21–22). Moreover, some might question her relationship with Boaz at the threshing floor (Ruth 3:7f). Finally, Bathsheba, with whom David committed adultery, bore him Solomon, the legitimate heir to the Davidic throne. It may be that Matthew specifically includes these four woman in his listing in order to dispel those who, while unwilling to accept the virgin birth of Yeshua, were nonetheless more than willing to call David the legitimate King of Israel.

There may be, however, an additional reason for Matthew's inclusion of these four women in the genealogy of Yeshua: all of them would have been considered foreigners. Tamar was either a Canaanite or an Aramean (cf. Philo, *Virt.* 220–2). Rahab was a Canaanite, Ruth a Moabite, and Bathsheba was the wife of Uriah, a Hittite. The inclusion of Gentiles within the legitimate line of David, and ultimately in the line of Yeshua, signals an underlying motif in Matthew's Gospel: the blessing upon the nations, promised to Abraham, is fulfilled in the coming of Yeshua. The promise of the prophets, that all of the nations would be gathered to the worship of Israel's God, is foreshadowed in the genealogy of the Messiah Himself.

It is obvious that Matthew groups his genealogy in three groups of fourteen for a specific purpose, for such a grouping would otherwise seem artificial. The first group is from Abraham to David (the name David being the 14th name listed), the second is from Solomon to Jechoniah, and the third, from Shealtiel to Yeshua. The Greek manuscripts, however, list only 13 names in this last grouping, even though the notice is clearly given in 1:17 that each group contains 14 generations. For some scribes, the fact that the last group contains only 13 generations was a problem, and thus an additional name is inserted (see below). However, for the majority of manuscripts, the scribes felt no problem in having only 13 names listed. In fact, it is not uncommon in biblical lists that discrepancies between stated totals and actual totals are found (note 1Chron 3:22; Ezra 1:9–11, 2:2–64; Neh 7:7–66). Some have suggested that Mary is to be added to the final grouping in order to make the total 14, emphasizing the virgin birth of Yeshua.[1]

What does Matthew intend us to understand by his grouping of the genealogy into three groups of fourteen? A number of explanations have been offered by commentators:

1. Some have connected it to Daniel's prophecy of the 70 weeks (9:24–27), by calculating that a generation is 35 years, and that seven weeks would transpire from degree to restore Jerusalem and the coming of the anointed King, (7 X 35 = 490). But this disregards the combination of 62 + 7 in Daniel's prophecy, and the idea that a generation is 35 years is arbitrary.

2. Some have noted that the cycle of the moon is 28 days, 14 waning, and 14 waxing. In this scheme, the period from Abraham to David was that of waxing, and from David to the exile, that of waning, with the exile being the low point. Then followed the period of waxing, with the zenith

For other explanations for the fact that the final group only contains 13 names, see Allison & Davies, p. 186.

being that of Yeshua's appearance. The Midrash (Mid. Rab. *Exodus* on 12.2) uses a similar approach to the generations of Israel, but in this case marks the month as 30 days divided into two periods of 15, which hardly fits Matthew's groupings of 14.

3. Others have pointed to the fact that the number seven is prominent in the Bible, and particularly in the calculation of the *sh'mitta* (sabbatical) year and the *yovel* (Jubilee). Matthew's three groups of 14 is thus seen as six groups of seven (6 X 7), with Yeshua beginning the final group of seven, which eventuates in the dawn of the eternal sabbath, or the Jubilee. In this regard, one should also note that the Chronicler specifically emphasizes David as the seventh son of Jesse (1Chron 2:15). The weakness in this view, however, is that Matthew emphasizes the number 14, not the number seven.

4. Lachs (*Rabbinic Commentary,* p. 3) notes a reference in m.*Avot* and *Avot de Rabbi Nathan,* to the effect that 14 generations existed between Moses and the rabbinic period. He suggests that Matthew's use of 14 generations, ending in the appearance of Yeshua, was as to say: "You think that the tradition has been transmitted to you from Moses by way of fourteen generations in your literature; I say to you, on the contrary, the founder of our religion received the tradition from Abraham, and this genealogy has three times fourteen generations back to the patriarch!"

5. The most popular explanation for Matthew's three groups of 14 relates to the numerical value (*gematria*) of the name David.[1] In the Hebrew, each letter has a numerical value, *aleph* beginning as one, *bet* two, and so on. David's name (דָוִד) is therefore calculated as follows: ד = 4, ו = 6, ד = 4, 4 + 6 + 4 = 14. Moreover, David is the 14th name in the listing, and the name David is made up of three consonants, corresponding to the three groupings of 14 names.

Of these explanations, the last is the most probable. Matthew's emphasis is that Yeshua is the legitimate King, and that He is the Messiah, son of David. Thus, the genealogy itself, as well as the form and structure in which it is given, emphasizes this. If this is the case, and we are to understand a cryptic pointing to David in the manner in which the generations are grouped, then from the very beginning of this Gospel, we may note Matthew's over arching purpose: to present Yeshua as the long-awaited "son of David," the One who would reign upon David's throne as the final and ultimate King as God's Messiah.

The listing of Yeshua's genealogy both in Matthew and Luke (3:23–38) is notoriously difficult, not only because of the textual variants, but also because of the apparent discrepancies. But before we look more closely at the genealogy itself, we should try to understand the difference between an ancient perspective on history and our modern views. First, in ancient times, the telling of history, including the listing of ancestors, was done in order to make an ideological point, not merely to relate brute facts. Spelling of names, giving alternate names, etc., were not considered important.

[1] This presupposes an awareness of David's name in Hebrew. Even if Matthew's readers were receiving his words in Greek, they most likely would have been familiar with the Hebrew spelling of the name. The Greek has two spellings for David's name: Δαυείδ and Δαυιδ, which reflects the interchange between ει and ι in the *koine*. If Matthew originally wrote his Gospel in Hebrew, then the spelling of David's name would obvious fit the *gematria* suggested by the emphasis upon the number 14.

The larger picture was in view rather than the minutiae of the details. To our modern way of looking at things, this might seem irresponsible or sloppy. But the ancient way of telling a story was far less concerned with minor details and far more concerned with the overall picture.

Secondly, the writers of Scripture used sources. They doubtlessly used those sources they believed to be the most accurate, but the fact remains that they used sources. Matthew, for instance, relies upon the Lxx of 1Chronicles 1–3 for the two first groupings of 14 generations in his list, which helps explain the spelling of names, etc. Did Matthew and Luke have different sources for the genealogies they offer? Perhaps they did, and if so, this surely would help explain some differences between the two listings.

Finally, both Matthew and Luke present their genealogies as factual, not as something they have manufactured. As such, we come to these listings as likewise factual, and the seeming discrepancies between them exist, not because they were mistaken, but because we have insufficient data to understand and interpret these antinomies. Hagner puts it this way:

> In these genealogies we must not expect accuracy by our modern standards. Omissions, variant spellings, and even variant names (i.e., some persons with two names) may be expected in genealogies, with many of these alterations motivated theologically. But to admit the theological interest in and impact upon these genealogies need not lead to the conclusion that they are not in any sense meant to be taken as factual. Both Matthew and Luke are concerned to represent the facts contained in their sources; they are hardly creating lists out of thin air. These genealogies, like much of the content of the Gospels, are to be taken as interpreted history—i.e., factual and not fictional data, conceived and set forth with theological goals, these in turn informed by the eschatological fullness now inescapably present to these writers.[1]

[1]Hagner, *Matthew 1–13*, pp. 8–9.

1 The record of the genealogy of Yeshua the Messiah, the son of David, the son of Abraham:

Matthew opens his Gospel with words that echo the *toledot* of Genesis.[2] The Genesis narrative is structured around the listing of genealogies of the significant characters in the patriarchal narrative (cf. Gen. 2:4; 5:1; 6:9; 10:1, 32; 11:10, 27; 25:13, 19). Genesis 5:1 begins, "This is the book of the generations of Adam (or Mankind)" (זֶה סֵפֶר תּוֹלְדֹת אָדָם), and it seems clear that Matthew intends to mimic this language with his opening words: Βίβλος γενέσεως Ἰησοῦ Χριστοῦ υἱοῦ Δαυὶδ υἱοῦ Ἀβραάμ, literally "The book of the generation of Yeshua Messiah, son of David, son of Abraham." The Lxx of Gen 5:1 also has βίβλος γενέσεως (*biblos geneseos*), "book of the generation," found only one other time in the Lxx, Gen 2:4. In using the pattern of Gen 5:1, Matthew has taken up a line from the Torah that would have been familiar to any Jewish person of his day. But in using this well known formula for describing the genealogy of Yeshua, he has both linked Him to the fulfillment of the patriarchal promises (the covenant) as well as presented Him as the representative of mankind, even as Adam is so represented. Paul would also present Yeshua as the "last Adam" (1Cor 15:45, cf. Rom 5:14) Who had come to redeem mankind from the sin of the first Adam.

It appears most likely that this opening verse is to understood as a superscription or a heading. It is common within Jewish literature that a

[2]The DuTillet and Even Bohan have אלה תולדות ישו בן דוד בן אברהם while the Münster has אלה תולדות יֵשׁוּעַ הַמָּשִׁיחַ בֶּן דּוד בֶּן אברהם. Clearly, each of the Hebrew Matthews see the connection to the תולדות expressions used in the Torah.

book opens with superscription or titular that describes the overall purpose and message of the book.[1] Yet the use of סֵפֶר (*sefer,* "book") or βίβλος (*biblos,* "book") is used in Gen 5:1, as well as in Matt 1:18, in connection with the genealogical listings, and not specifically of the entire Gospel that Matthew is writing. The fact that "book" may be used in several ways, i.e., of the whole work of an author, as well as for a genealogical list, may actually have been in the mind of Matthew as he began his Gospel this way. One commentator has suggested this very thing:

> [1:1 is] telescopic: it can be extended to include more and more of what Matthew is beginning to write about. First, it can cover *the genealogy* which immediately follows it; then, it can refer to the account of the *birth* of Jesus…; thirdly, it can mean "history" or "life story;" finally, it can refer to the whole new creation which begins at the conception of Jesus and will be completed at his second coming.[2]

If this is the case, and it seems most probable that it is, then we should find in this opening title of Matthew's Gospel not only an introductory statement for the genealogy that follows, but also a general outline of the entire Gospel. Matthew intends to show us how Yeshua fulfilled the Abrahamic promise as well as how He is the promised son of David Who legitimately reigns as King Messiah.

The exact combination "Yeshua Messiah" (Ἰησοῦ Χριστοῦ, *Yesou Xristou*) is found only here and in 1:18 (though the versions have only Ἰησοῦ there). In Mark it is found only in 1:1, and never in Luke. John has it twice (John 1:17; 17:3). It is in Paul's writings that the combination "Yeshua Messiah" becomes so prevalent (80x).

The spelling and pronunciation of "Yeshua" changed over time. It is related to the Hebrew name יְהוֹשֻׁעַ (also spelled fully: יְהוֹשׁוּעַ, *Yehoshu'a*), which was shortened to יוֹשׁוּעַ (*Yoshu'a*) and then to יֵשׁוּעַ (*Yeshua*). Studies have shown that the even shorter pronunciation, יֵשׁוּ (*Yeshu,* in which the final *furtive patach* has been dropped), was a dialectical phenomenon in the northern Galil, and not, as many have supposed, a deliberate slur on His name by later rabbinic writers. Some have suggested that *Yeshu* is a deliberate acronym for "may his name and memory be blotted out" (יִמַּח שְׁמוֹ וְזִכְרוֹ), but though such an acronym was used in later times, it was not the reason for the shortened pronunciation, *Yeshu.* This was the Galilean pronunciation, as Flusser and others have shown.[3] In fact, the Greek Ἰησοῦς (*Yesous,* with final "s" denoting a nominative case) may itself explain the regular use of יֵשׁוּ (*Yeshu*) in the later rabbinic materials, as an assimilation to the Greek *Yesous.*[4]

Yeshua was a common name in the 1st Century. Three of the 72 who translated the Lxx had the name, and Josephus lists 20 persons by this name in his writings. The name is found in inscriptions and burial texts.[5] A pre-exilic example is found in Luke's genealogy (Lk 3:29), and in Matt 27:16, one manuscript has Barabbas called "Yesous Barabbas." In Acts 13:6 the sorcerer in Cyprus is called Bar-Yesous, and in Col 4:11, Paul's helper is "Yesous who is called Youstos." No doubt under the influence of the emerging Christian Church, by the 2nd Century, the name Yesous disappears as a proper name. According to Jastrow, the full name יֵשׁוּעַ (*Yeshua*) is found only in reference to the ninth order of the priestly courses found in 1Chron 24:7–18.

Christos (Χριστός) is related to the Greek verb χρίω (*chrio*) meaning "to

[1] See Allison & Davies, pp. 151–2 for examples

[2] J. C. Fenton, *The Gospel of Matthew* (London, 1977), p. 36, quoted from Allison & Davies, p. 154.

In m.*Yevamot* 4.13, which deals with the definition of a *mamzer* (one of illegitimate birth), an interesting notice is found: "Said R. Simeon b. Azzai, "I discovered a family register [*megilat yochasim*] in Jerusalem, in which was written: 'Mr. So-and-so is a mamzer, [having been born of an illicit union] of a married woman [and someone other than her husband]." This mishnaic notice, whether historical or not, shows that genealogical records referred to as a "scroll" (*sepher*) were not uncommon to the rabbis.

[3] See Herford, *Christianity in Talmud and Midrash,* pp. 35ff; Morris Goldstein, *Jesus in the Jewish Tradition*(Macmillian, 1950), p. 24; David Flusser, *Jesus* (Magnes, 1997), p. 24.

[4] See Foerster, Ἰησοῦς, in TDNT, 3.287.
[5] Ibid., p. 285.

anoint," and was the word used by the Lxx to translate מָשִׁיחַ (*mashiach*), "one who was anointed for a special task." The English "Messiah" is an anglicized form of "*mashiach.*" Like many titles, "Messiah" became a proper name, and we find this occurring the Apostolic Scriptures (cf. Rom 1:1; Gal 1:1; James 2:1; Rev 22:21). Yet it never lost its connection to the whole prophetic idea of "Messiah" as a title, the One promised from of old who would come to restore the fortunes of Israel, and to bring in the final redemption. Clearly, Matthew has this messianic thought in mind by his use of *Christos* (2:4; 16:16, 20; 22:42; 24:5, 23; 26:63, 68).

"Son of David" was a standard messianic title for the rabbis (cf. b.*Sanhedrin* 97a-97b). It developed, no doubt, from the messianic expressions such as "the sprout of Jesse" (Is 11:10) and "shoot (of David)" (Jer 23:5; 33:15; Zech 3:8; 6:12; 4QPatrBless 3; 4QFlor 1:11-12). In the *Shemonei Esrei,* the 15th Benediction reads:

> The sprout of David, Your servant, speedily cause to flourish and exalt His power with Your deliverance; for Your deliverance we hope all day. Blessed are You, Adonai, Who causes to sprout the power of salvation.

> The expression in Didache 9:2, "the holy vine of David your servant," is an anomoly, and is most likely explained as a combination in thought of "the shoot of David" with the vine imagery applied to Yeshua, e.g., John 15:5, "I am the vine, you are the branches...."

Thus, in the 1st Century, the Jewish expectation was that a deliverer would arise from the line of David[1] who would fulfill the promises made in 2Sam 7 to David, namely, that one of his descendants would be seated upon the throne of Israel forever. Paul stresses this in Rom 1:3-4 in which the confessional statement regarding Yeshua includes that He was " born of a descendant of David according to the flesh." It is this core issue that Matthew wishes to stress, not only in this opening genealogy, but also throughout his Gospel, namely, that Yeshua is that promised Son of David, sent by the Father at the appointed time, to bring in the final redemption of His people. Indeed, Matthew may well be reflecting the ongoing dialog with the Synagogue in which prayers for the arrival of *ben David* were offered. Matthew's message is that He has arrived, and that He has come to accomplish the salvation for which Israel was waiting, for no less than nine times does Matthew refer to Yeshua as the "son of David" (Matt. 1:1, 20; 9:27; 12:23; 15:22; 20:30-31; 21:9, 15). He also records (as do Mark and Luke) Yeshua's own dialog regarding the "son of David" title (Matt 22:42). There is no doubt that in the two opening chapters of Matthew's Gospel, he intends to demonstrate that Yeshua of Nazareth (through His father, 1:16) qualifies as the royal Messiah, the Davidic King (note especially 21:9, 15).

"Son of Abraham" was not a messianic title, but rather expressed Jewish lineage in early Jewish literature (cf. m.*BabaQama* 8:6) or one who was worthy to be named with Abraham (4Macc 6:17, 22; 18:23, cf. b.*Betza* 32b). It is possible that "son of Abraham" in Matthew's opening verse is to be connected to David rather than Yeshua. But both are possible. Obviously, if David is a son of Abraham, and Yeshua is a son of David, then He likewise is Abraham's son.

The mention of "son of Abraham" has perhaps two main emphases. Most obvious is the connection to the Abrahamic covenant. Since God promised His blessings upon Abraham "and his seed," to be noted as a "son of Abraham" means to be a chosen member of his covenant. For Matthew, the Savior must Himself be a true Israelite, a descendant of Abraham. In this regard we may note John's words: "... salvation is from the Jews" (7:22) and

[1] Cf. 4QPatrBless 2.4; 4QFlor 1:11-13; 4QpIsa[a] frags. 7–10.22; 4Ezra 12.32; Jn 7:42.

the teaching of Hebrews (2:16–17):

> For assuredly He does not give help to angels, but He gives help to the descendant of Abraham. Therefore, He had to be made like His brethren in all things, so that He might become a merciful and faithful high priest in things pertaining to God, to make propitiation for the sins of the people.

Less obvious, but yet very likely in Matthew's mind as he included "son of Abraham" as a description of Yeshua, is his interest in the salvation of the Gentiles. Abraham himself was a Gentile by birth, and it was to him that the promise of salvation for the Gentiles was made. When God changed the name Abram to Abraham, the meaning (apparently) was that he would be a "father of many nations" (Gen 17:5, cf. 1Macc 12:19–21). In rabbinic literature, Abraham is considered the first proselyte (b.*Chaggiah* 3a; b.*Sukkah* 49b), and thus it was common for proselytes to take the name "ben Avraham." Paul's teaching, that Abraham is the father both of the Jew and the Gentile who comes to faith in Yeshua (Rom 4:1–25; Gal 3:6–29), was in harmony with the viewpoint of Matthew as well, for Matthew records that "many will come from east and west, and recline at the table with Abraham, Isaac and Jacob in the kingdom of heaven" (8:11) by which he apparently means "many Gentiles." Likewise, in Matt 3:9, John the Baptizer says "God is able to raise up from these stones children to Abraham." Thus, in Matthew's dual "son of David, son of Abraham," not only is the promise of salvation to Israel fulfilled by Yeshua as Messiah, but the salvation of the chosen ones from the nations as well. For Matthew, the fulfillment of the Abrahamic promise is secure in the person and work of Yeshua.

Thus, the opening verse of Matthew's Gospel sets the stage for the entire story he intends to tell. It begins with the generation of the Incarnate One, Who has come to call the lost sheep of Israel back to God, and to the salvation that is possible only through His Messiah. Yet in the message of Messiah to Israel, there is a constant forward-looking reality to the ingathering of the nations. "In your seed all the families of the earth will be blessed" is an undercurrent throughout. And this undercurrent becomes the dominant theme at the end of the Gospel, for Yeshua sends forth the Twelve to make disciples of "all the nations," bringing them into the chosen people, and teaching them to observe "all that I have commanded you." As the "Son of David," Yeshua is the rightful heir to the throne, and both the recipient and establisher of the covenant promises. As the "Son of Abraham," Yeshua is the quintessential Israelite, the Seed of Abraham in Whom the blessing for the nations would be accomplished.

In 1:2–17, we are given the specific ancestral names of Yeshua's genealogy. It will be helpful to show the comparison with Luke's listings, as well as to note some of the more significant variants that the various manuscripts and versions offer. Obviously, a great deal of scholarly work has been done on the genealogical listings, and while we hope to summarize these findings, it is beyond the scope of these commentary notes to make an exhaustive explanation for the difficulties represented in the genealogy of Yeshua.

Matthew	Luke 3:23–38 (reversed; beginning with Abraham)	1Chronicles	Hebrew Matthews
Abraham	Abraham	Abraham	Abraham
Isaac	Isaac	Isaac	Isaac
Jacob	Jacob	Israel	Jacob
Judah & brothers	Judah	Judah	Judah & brothers
Perez	Perez	Perez	Perez
Hezron	Hezron	Hezron	Hezron
Aram (Ram)	Arni (Ram)	Ram	Ram
	Admin		
Amminadab	Amminadab		Amminadab
Nashon	Nahshon (Naasson)	Nahshon	Nahshon
Salmon	Salmon	Salma	Salmon
Boaz	Boaz	Boaz	Boaz
Obed	Obed	Obed	Obed
Jesse	Jesse	Jesse	Jesse
David the King	David	David	David
Solomon	Nathan	Solomon	Solomon
Rehoboam	Mattatha	Rehoboam	Rehoboam
Abijah	Menna	Abijah	Abia
Asa (Asaph)	Melea	Asa	Asa
Jehoshaphat	Eliakim	Jehoshaphat	Jehoshaphot
Joram	Jonam	Joram	Joram
Uzziah	Joseph	Ahaziah	Uzziah
Jotham (Joatham)	Judah (Judas)	Joash + + +	Jothan (lac. in STov)
Ahaz	Simeon	Ahaz	Ahaz (lac. in STov)
Hezekiah	Levi	Hezekaih	Hezekiah
Manasseh	Matthat	Manasseh	Manasseh
Amon	Jorim	Amon	Amon
Josiah	Eliezar	Josiah +	Josiah
Jeconiah (Jehoiachin)	Joshua (Yeshua)	Jeconiah	Jeconiah
Shealtiel (Salathiel)	Er	Shealtiel +	Shealtiel
Zerubbabel	Elmadam	Zerubbabel	Zerubbabel
Abiud (Abihud)	Cosam		Abihud
			Avner (DuTillet)
Eliakim	Addi		Eliakim (lac. in STov)
Azor	Melchi		Azor (lac. in STov)
Zadok	Neri		Zadok (lac. in STov)

Matthew	Luke 3:23–38 (reversed; beginning with Abraham)	1Chronicles	Hebrew Matthews
Achim	Shealtiel (Sala- thiel)		Achim (Stov) Ammon (DuT)
Eliud	Zerubbabel		Elihud
Eleazar	Resa		Eleazar
Mathan	Johanan		Mattan
Jacob	Joda		Jacob
Joseph	Josech		Joseph
Mary	Semein		Miriam
Yeshua	Matathias		Yeshua
	Maath		
	Naggai		
	Helsi (Esli)		
	Nahum		
	Amos		
	Mattathias		
	Joseph		
	Jannai		
	Melchi		
	Levi		
	Matthat		
	Eli (Heli)		
	Joseph		
	Yeshua		

Notes on this table:

1. Matthew's genealogy is used as the template against which the other genealogies are collated. Thus, while Luke begins with Adam and ends with Yeshua, I have reversed his order so that it could be compared with that of Matthew and have begun Lukes's list with Abraham rather than Adam.

2. It is clear from a comparison with the genealogy of the Chronicler, that his material (or versions of it) were used by the Gospel writers for the construction of the early part of their lists. Where there were clearly generations left out by the Gospel writers, I have indicated this by using the sign (+). So, for example, the Chronicler lists three additional generations between Joash and Ahaz.

3. In the Hebrew Matthews column, I have noted where the Shem Tov (STov) has left out names, and in one instance, where the DuTillet has added a name (Avner).

4. It is obvious that Matthew and Luke are essential identical up to King David. Matthew continues on with his genealo-

gy with Solomon, while Luke carries on from Nathan. It is at this point that the two genealogies diverge. It is equally obvious that Matthew continues to adhere to the list of the Chronicler as far as possible.

5. Obviously, the variants extant in the Greek manuscripts are not noted in this table. I have, however, included in parentheses some variant spellings, indicated via English. A more detailed evaluation of the Greek variants will be noted as each verse is discussed below.

Attempting to reconcile the two genealogies (Matthew and Luke) has caused many scholars to draw the conclusion that it is impossible (see Darrell Bock, *Luke* in *Baker Exegetical Commentary on the New Testament*, 2 vols (Baker, 1994), p. 919). It may well be impossible for us to reconcile the two different approaches of Matthew and Luke, but this should not be taken to mean that one of the two Gospel writers is wrong. It is more likely that we simply do not have sufficient data to assess the two different genealogies.

Moreover, there seems to be a similar divergence in the rabbinic literature. Lachs (*Rabbinic Comm on the NT*, p. 2) notes that the Targum to Zech 12:12 includes both the "house of David" (apparently through Solomon) and the "house of Nathan" as those who mourn:

> The two-line descent of the Davidic kings is not unknown to Jewish tradition. The Targum to Zech. 1:12 (sic) implies this, "and the descendants of the house of David mourn [presumably from Solomon] … and the descendants of the house of Nathan.

The prophet Zechariah, after noting that Israel will mourn for the pierced One, delineates four families: David, Nathan, Levi, and Shimeites. Baron (*The Visions and Prophecies of Zechariah* [Kregel, 1972], pp. 452-53) notes that these four family names contain two of the royal and two of the priestly line. David is the primary royal family, with Nathan subordinate, while Levi is the primary priestly family, with the Shimeites being subordinate. In this way, the entire nation is represented by her kings and priests (cf. Zech 12:14), and thus the nation as whole is in mourning. The point for our concern in regard to the genealogy of Yeshua, is that the family of Nathan appears to be connected to the royal line of David.

Bock (*Luke,* pp. 919ff) offers a listing of the various explanations for the two genealogies given by Matthew and Luke, which I summarize here:

1. The oldest explanation is given by Julius Africanus (ca 225 CE and cited by Eusebius, *Ecclesiastical History*, 1.7), that Matthew provided the natural line, while Luke provided the royal line, and that the difference in the lists was caused by the principle of levirate marriage. His explanation is thus: Matthan (Matt 1:15) had a son, Jacob, by way of his wife, Estha. Matthan died and Estha married Melchi (Lk 3:24), who had a son Heli (Lk 3:23). Heli died without children and his half-brother, Jacob, took his wife by levirate marriage, so that Jacob's sons were tied to Heli's line. Thus Joseph is linked to both: physically to Jacob, but legally to Heli. While levirate marriage was not common, it was surely extant, as the inquiry of the Sadducees to Yeshua would indicate (Matt 22:24–28).

2. A modern approach reverses the emphases of the two Gospel writ-

ers: Luke gives the physical descent and Matthew the royal descent. J. G. Machen (*The Virgin Birth* [Harper, 1930; reprint Baker, 1965]) is representative of this view. He suggests that Jacob and Heli were brothers, so Joseph was Jacob's nephew. When Jacob died childless, the nephew became the heir. Bock (*Luke*, p. 922) suggests that the use of "son" in linking Joseph as the "son" of Heli may not be denoting physical descent, but legal heritage, much the same way that Yeshua is linked "legally" to Joseph though having no physical lineage from him. Surely both Matthew and Luke affirm the virgin birth of Yeshua.

3. Another suggestion offered by some scholars is that Mary was a heiress of Eli, since she had no brothers. Eli adopted Joseph as son upon marriage, as in other cases where a father had no physical son (Ezra 2:61; Neh 7:63, see also Num 27:1–11 [which establishes lines of inheritance]; 1Chron 2:34–35). In this case, Luke's genealogy reflects adoption. On this basis, the line becomes "legal" versus physical at this endpoint.

4. Most scholars abandon any attempt in reconciling the two lists, and simply opt for a theological and literary emphasis, Matthew points to the king through David and Abraham, while Luke associates Yeshua with all of humanity through Adam.

In this regard, the rabbinic literature does refer to Abraham as a king (Mid Rab *Genesis* 55.1).

5. Many have suggested that Luke gives us the genealogy through Mary, while Matthew gives the lineage through Joseph, the legal father of Yeshua. This view dates back to Annius of Viterbo (1490). Thus, Luke says that Yeshua was "supposed the son of Joseph" (3:23), so that Joseph is actually not part of Luke's genealogy. Those who hold this position also note that the article (τοῦ) is missing from Joseph's name, showing that Luke did not intend to include him as one of the progenitors in his list. It is further noted that rabbinic literature knows of the connection between Heli (spelled Eli) and Mary (cf. y.*Hag.* 77d; y.*San.* 23c, and *SB* 2.155), though it must be admitted that the Miriam mentioned here is not specifically noted to be the mother of Yeshua, and many scholars doubt that the reference is to Yeshua's mother.

The greatest difficulty with this view is that Luke does not name Mary. Had it been his purpose to show the lineage of Yeshua through Mary, then one would expect that her name would be included in the genealogy. Moreover, legal inheritance does not necessitate physical lineage, so when Luke begins his genealogy with Joseph, he in no way is diminishing the legal inheritance that Yeshua would be accorded through Joseph. Finally, the fact that the article (τοῦ) is not found with Joseph's name (as it is with the other men listed in Luke's genealogy of Yeshua) may be explained by the fact that Joseph heads the list.

In the end, we must admit that reconciliation of the two lists illudes us. We simply do not have enough data to make clear choices. It may well be that levirate marriages, or adoption of children explain the apparent discrepancies. What we can say with some certainty is: a) neither of the Gospel writers are simply pulling their lists out of thin air. They must have followed sources that were available to them, sources they judged to be worthy; b) the theological purpose of Matthew and Luke, in the manner in which they construct their lists, seems evident. Matthew wants to emphasize the connection to Abraham and David, showing Yeshua to be the One through whom the covenant promises are realized. Luke wants to demonstrate that Yeshua is truly human, that He came, not as some aberration, but as the incarnate One who partakes of humanity as a son of Adam. In so doing, Luke represents Yeshua as the savior of mankind, while Matthew emphasizes Yeshua's role as the Messiah of Israel. Neither of these viewpoints contradict each other. The role of Israel's Messiah is not only that He will gather the "lost sheep of Israel" and save them, but that the salvation He brings to His people will also bring about the salvation of the nations.

2 Abraham was the father of Isaac, Isaac the father of Jacob, and Jacob the father of Judah and his brothers.

The beginning of Matthew's genealogy has no surprises. The listing of the patriarchs is well known. Matthew begins with Abraham because he wants to emphasize the role of Yeshua as the One who fulfills the covenant made with Abraham and his seed. Beginning with Abraham also makes a clear transition to the genealogy from the opening title (v. 1) of the his Gospel account. The title (v. 1) ends with "son of Abraham," and thus Abraham is a fitting starting point for the genealogy.

Abraham figures predominately in some of the rabbinic lists as well (m.*Avot* 5.2f; Mid Rab *Exodus* on 12:2; cf. 1Macc 2:51–60; 1Enoch 89:10; 93:5; 4Ezra 6:7–8). As noted above, placing Abraham as the first in the list also makes David's name occupy the 14th position. Likewise, Abraham was considered a king by some of the rabbis (cf. b.*San* 108b; Mid Rab *Genesis* 55.1, 6 [on Gen 22.1]). Thus, Matthew's list begins and ends with a king. Likewise, in Mid Rab *Numbers* on 13.14, Abraham heads the list of David's royal line.

Judah is singled out on the basis of Gen 49:10, where Targum Onkelos reads:

> "The ruler shall never depart from the House of Judah, nor the scribe from his children's children for evermore, until Messiah comes, whose is the kingdom, and him shall the nations obey."

Targum Yerushalami reads similarly:

> "Kings shall not cease from the House of Judah, nor scribes who teach the Torah, from his children's children, until the time of the coming of King Messiah, to whom belongs the kingdom, and to whom all dominions of the earth shall become subservient. How beautiful is he, the King Messiah, who is destined to arise from the House of Judah."

We should also note Heb 7:14, "our Lord was descended from Judah," and Luke agrees (3:33).

Matthew writes "Judah and his brothers." Why include "his brothers?" This may well emphasize that Judah was not the firstborn, and one would expect that the royal line would come through the firstborn. But this highlights a repeated motif in the early patriarchal narratives, namely, that the second born is divinely chosen over the firstborn. The point of this is that the appointed "son" does not gain his position through the natural course of events, but through the sovereign election of God. In similar fashion, Matthew mentions Zera along with Perez (1:3), and "Jeconiah and his brothers" (1:11). Again, in each of these cases, divine selection is emphasized. In this way, Matthew's listing is not merely a genealogy, but a "resúmé of salvation-history."[1]

3 Judah was the father of Perez and Zerah by Tamar, Perez was the father of Hezron, and Hezron the father of Ram [Aram].

Perez (פֶּרֶץ) and Zerah (זֶרַח) were the twin sons of Judah and Tamar (Gen 38:27–30). *Peretz* means "to split," "make a breach," "to break through or out." The name derives from the fact that though Zerah first extended his hand in the birthing process, Perez was actually born first. When Zerah's hand appeared, the midwife attached a scarlet thread in order to identify the one who had come out of the womb first. When Perez, however, actually came out ahead of his brother, it was noted that he had "broken out" in first place, and thus was given the name. *Zerach* means "to arise, shine," or "to come forth." In Is 60:3, the word means "sunrise." Thus, even though Zerah appeared first, Perez was given priority in birth. Here, once again, the motif of the second born is noted. Zerah, in having "appeared" first, was legally the firstborn, yet the chosen one through whom the promised Son would come, was legally the second born.

As noted above, the mention of Tamar in the genealogy may well stress the divine prerogative of using Gentile women in the line of the Messiah. While Matthew will emphasize the priority of Yeshua's mission to the "lost sheep of Israel" (10:6; 15:24), he nonetheless also has a strong underlying message of the ingathering of the Gentiles as a result of the Messiah's appearance and mission.

The Sages also comment on the genealogy of Messiah through Perez:

> R. Johanan replied: Scripture stated, And when Saul saw David go forth against the Philistine, he said into Abner, the captain of the host: 'Abner, whose son is this youth'? And Abner said: 'As thy soul liveth, O King, I cannot tell'. But did he not know him? Surely it is written, And he loved him greatly; and he became his armour bearer! — He rather made the inquiry concerning his father. But did he not know his father? Surely it is written, And the man was an old man in the days of Saul, stricken in years among them; and Rab or, it might be said, R. Abba, stated that this referred to the father of David, Jesse. who came in with an army and went out with an army! — It is this that Saul meant: Whether he descended from Perez, or from Zerah. If he descended from Perez he would be king, for a king breaks for himself a way and no one can hinder him. If, however, he is descended from Zerah he would only be an important man. (b.*Yev.* 76b)

Similarly, the Sages find a messianic reference in Micah 2:13—

> The breaker (הַפֹּרֵץ) goes up before them; They break out, pass through the gate and go out by it. So their king goes on before them, and Adonai at their head. (cf. Mid. Rab. *Genesis* 85.14 [on 39:29]; Mid Rab *Leviticus* 32.8 [on 24:10]).

Here, "The Breaker" is the final Messianic King who ushers in the world to come, and the connection is made to Perez as the progenitor of David.

Hezron carries the lineage of the tribe of Judah (Gen 46:12; Num 26:21; 1Chron 4:1) and should not be confused with another Hezron who gave his name to a clan of Reuben (Gen 46:9; Ex 6:14; Num 26:6; 1Chron 5:3).

It seems clear that there were different versions of the name Ram, and different lists have variations. All of the Greek manuscripts of Matthew have Ἀράμ, "Aram," but many of the English translations have "Ram" in order to conform to the usage of the MT of 1Chron 2:9 and Ruth 4:19. In 1Chron 2:9, the MT lists three sons of Hezron: Jerahmeel, Ram, and Chelubai (וּבְנֵי חֶצְרוֹן אֲשֶׁר נוֹלַד־לוֹ אֶת־יְרַחְמְאֵל וְאֶת־רָם וְאֶת־כְּלוּבָי). The Lxx adds a fourth, Aram (Ἀράμ), and makes him (not Ram) the father of Amminadab. The Lxx of Ruth 4:19 has Ar-ran (Ἀρράν), cf. Lk 3:33 which has Ἀρνὶ (Arni). It seems clear that Matthew follows the text of Lxx 1Chron 2:9, or else he had knowledge of a Hebrew text from which the Lxx was translated, which was later lost to the Masoretes.

All of the Hebrew Matthews have רָם in v. 3. The Peshitta, however, has אָרָם.

4 Ram [Aram] was the father of Amminadab, Amminadab the father of Nahshon, and Nahshon the father of Salmon.

Here Matthew follows 1Chron 2:10-11 which agrees with Ruth 4:19-20, following the Lxx spelling. Amminadab was the father of Elisheva, the wife of Aaron (Ex 6:23).

At this point in the genealogy Luke adds a name otherwise unknown. He makes Admin (Ἀδμίν) the father of Amminadab rather than Ram. This is supported neither by the MT or the Lxx of 1Chron 2:10–11 or Ruth 4:19. However, it is possible that Luke records a generation otherwise skipped by the Chronicler and author of Ruth.[2]

Nahshon (נַחְשׁוֹן) is listed as the leader of the tribe of Judah (Num 1:7; 2:3; 7:12, 17; 10:14) and 1Chron 2:10 refers to him as the "prince of the sons of Judah." The Sages taught that Nahshon was the first to enter the opened sea at the exodus (b.*Sota* 37a) when all others were fearful to proceed.

[2]See the comments of Bock, *Luke*, 1.357.

Salmon, whose name occurs only in genealogical lists, has various spellings: שַׂלְמָה (*Salmah,* Ruth 4:20), שַׂלְמוֹן (*Salmon,* Ruth 4:21), שַׂלְמָא, (*Salma',* 1Chron 2:11). The Lxx has Σαλμαν (*Salman,* Ruth 4:20–21) and Σαλμων (*Salmon,* 1Chron 2:11). Matthew uses Σαλμων while Luke (3:32) has Σαλὰ (*Sala*). The Hebrew Matthews all have שַׂלְמוֹן, and the Peshitta spells it ܣܠܡܘܢ (סַלְמוֹן).

5 Salmon was the father of Boaz by Rahab, Boaz was the father of Obed by Ruth, and Obed the father of Jesse.

The name Boaz (בֹּעַז) is spelled in the Lxx Βόος (*Boos*) or Βόοζ (*Booz*). Both Matthew and Luke have Βόος, though some manuscripts have Βοες or Βόοζ. Boaz married Ruth the Moabitess after the nearer kinsman disqualified himself.

The midrash notes that three men overcame their passions (evil inclination) through the taking of an oath: Joseph, David and Boaz (Mid. Rab. *Lev.* 23.11, cf. Mid. Rab. *Num* 15.16; Mid. Rab. *Ruth* 6.2). In the case of Boaz: "As the LORD lives, lie down until morning" (Ruth 3:13), yet he had no relations with her though they both were single and seeking a spouse. According to the Targum on 1Chron 4:22, Boaz was master of the scholars in the academy in Bethlehem.

Matthew has Salmon wed to Rahab, who was the harlot of Jericho (Josh 2 and 6). The spelling of Rahab (רָחָב) in the Lxx is Ῥαάβ (*Raab*), while Matthew's spelling (Ῥαχάβ, *Rachab*) reflects a desire to represent the sound of the medial ח, which may suggest a reliance upon a Hebrew *Vorlage*.

The rabbinic literature has Joshua as the husband of Rahab (Sifre *Numbers* 78; Mid. Rab. *Ecc* 8.13; b.*Meg* 14b–15a), not Salmon, and the Sages remark that Joshua had only one son (1Chron 7:27) but that he had other daughters (b.*Meg* 14b). In fact, there are no biblical parallels to suggest that Boaz was the son of Salmon and Rahab. Indeed, in the chronology of the Tanach, Rahab and Salmon are separated by nearly 200 years.[1] Some have suggested the possibility that ἐκ τῆς Ῥαχάβ ("by Rahab") should be understood as meaning that the line came through Rahab, not that Salmon and Rahab were husband and wife.[2] Either this is the case here, or else the Rahab mentioned here is not the Rahab of Jericho, though this seems unlikely.

The Sages reasoned that Rahab must have become a proselyte (b.*Meg* 14b). She is considered one of the four most beautiful women in the world (b.*Meg* 15a), though her beauty was used in a seductive way. Likewise, the Sages teach that the Spirit of God rested upon Rahab and that ten prophets were descended from her (Mid. Rab. *Ruth* 2.1, Sifre *Numbers* 78; cf. b.*Meg* 14b).

Ruth is likewise reckoned as becoming part of Israel by the Sages.

> R. Eleazar further stated: What is meant by the text, And in thee shall the families of the earth be blessed? The Holy One, blessed be He, said to Abraham, 'I have two goodly shoots to engraft on you: Ruth the Moabitess and Naamah the Ammonitess'.

The Sages felt the difficulty presented by the fact that the lineage of King David came through a Moabitess (Ruth), since the Torah prohibits the descendants of Moab from entering the assembly of the LORD (Deut 23:3). They solved the problem by noting that the Torah prohibits a Moabite, but not a Moabitess:

> Doeg the Edomite then said to him, 'Instead of enquiring whether he is fit to be king or not, enquire rather whether he is permitted to enter the assembly or not'! 'What is the reason'? 'Because he is descended from Ruth the Moabitess'. Said Abner to him, 'We learned: An Ammonite, but not an Ammonitess; A Moabite, but not a Moabitess! (b.*Yev* 76a; b.*Ketuvot* 7b, cf. m.*Yev* 8.3).

Indeed, the Sages considered Ruth the mother of kings, and an ancestress of the Messiah:

> So too you find with Ruth the Moabite. What did she say to her mother-in-law? "Your people will be my people, and your God, my God, where you die, there I shall die" (Ruth 1:15–17). The Omnipresent said to her, "You have not lost. Lo, kingship (הַמְּלוּכָה) will be yours in this world, and yours in the world to come" (Sifre *Numbers* 78).

> AND SHE CALLED HIS NAME SETH: FOR GOD HATH APPOINTED ME ANOTHER SEED, etc. R. Tanhuma said in the name of Samuel Kozith: [She hinted at] that seed which would arise from another source (i.e., from non-Jewish stock, Ruth), viz. the king Messiah (Mid. Rab. *Gen* 23.6 commenting on Gen 4:25).

> 'Judah is my sceptre' alludes to the Great Redeemer who is to be a descendant of the grandchildren of David. ' Moab is my wash pot.' What is the meaning of this expression? God meant to say: Even

---

[1] Rahab was encountered in the conquest of Jericho, which occured (according to conservative estimations) around 1406 BCE (those who take a late date of the Exodus would put the conquest as beginning in 1230 BCE). The book of Ruth is cast in the times of the Judges (Ruth 1:1), and most likely in the days of Gideon who ruled 1192–1152 BCE (see the comments of Keil & Delitzsch on Ruth 1:1).

Judah descended to Egypt with his brothers, meaning that Hezron, Ram, Amminadab, and Nahshon were born in Egypt, though on the basis of Gen 46:12 some conclude that Hezron was born before the descent to Egypt (but see Keil & Delitzsch, *ad loc*). Regardless, there are only four or five generations listed for the 430 years in Egypt, and this is surely not enough. We must conclude that some names were deleted from the genealogy lists, naming only those mose prominent. This must also be the case for the two generations between Nahshon and Boaz, which could not account for the span of nearly 250 years, so undoubtedly some names have been omitted.

[2] D. A. Carson, *Matthew* in *The Expositor's Bible Commentary* (Zondervan, 1984), p. 64. Yet note that the subsequent phrase, that Obed was a son of Boaz and Ruth uses the same construction, Βόες δὲ ἐγέννησεν τὸν Ἰωβὴδ ἐκ τῆς Ῥούθ.

when the aforementioned redeemers shall have come I will not offer to assist them until the Moabitess [i.e., Ruth] shall come with them. (Mid. Rab. *Num* 14.1 commenting on Ps 60:7–8 [Heb 60:9–10])

David is known as the "son of Jesse" throughout the Scriptures (1Sam. 16:18; 20:27, 30-31; 22:7-9, 13; 25:10; 2Sam. 20:1; 23:1; 1Kings 12:16; 1Chron. 10:14; 12:18; 29:26; 2Chron. 10:16; 11:18; Psa. 72:20; Luke 3:32; Acts 13:22). Moreover, the "stump" or "root" of Jesse became a messianic title, based upon Is 11:1, 10:

> Then a shoot will spring from the stem of Jesse, and a branch from his roots will bear fruit.
> Then in that day the nations will resort to the root of Jesse, Who will stand as a signal for the peoples; and His resting place will be glorious.

The Targum on Is 11:1 reads, "A king will go forth from the sons of Jesse and Messiah will increase from the sons of his sons." Likewise the midrash on Psalm 21:1–2 reads:

> *For the leader. A Psalm of David. The king shall joy in Thy strength, O Lord* (Ps 21:1–2). These words are to be read in the light of what Scripture says elsewhere: *In that day there shall be a root of Jesse, which shall stand for an ensign of the peoples; unto him shall the nations seek* (Is 11:10)—that is, seek the king Messiah, David's son, who will remain hidden until the time of redemption.

We see the use of this messianic title in the 15th blessing of the *Shemonei Esrei* (Eighteen Benedictions):

> The sprout of David, Your servant, speedily cause to flourish and exalt his power with Your deliverance. For Your deliverance we hope all day. Blessed are You, Adonai, Who causes to sprout the power of salvation.

Here Isaiah's words, "stem of Jesse" (מְגֶזַע יִשַׁי) and "root of Jesse" (שֹׁרֶשׁ יִשַׁי) are interpreted as the "sprout of David" (צֶמַח דָּוִד). In the Didache (9:2), this is interpreted further as "the holy vine of David Your servant" (τῆς ἁγίας ἀμπέλου Δαυὶδ τοῦ παιδός σου), where the messianic interpretation of the "sprout" or "shoot" imagery is specifically applied to Yeshua.[1]

6 Jesse was the father of David the king. David was the father of Solomon by Bathsheba who had been the wife of Uriah.

The Tanach refers to David as מֶלֶךְ דָּוִד, *melech David,* "king David (2Sam 6:12; 7:18; Ezra 3:10, etc. Note the variant in Lxx of Ruth 4:22 that adds τὸν βασιλέα) as well as the rabbinic literature (b.*Shab* 31a; 151b; b.*Yoma* 76a; b.*Sukkah* 51a; b.*San* 20a; Mid. Rab. *Lev* 26.9; Mid. Rab. *Deut* 5.8, etc.). As noted above, it is clearly Matthew's intention to show that Yeshua is descended from the Davidic line, for as the Messiah, He reigns upon the throne of David in fulfillment of the Davidic promise (cf. Acts 2:30ff).

Matthew has the line of Yeshua come through Solomon. It is here that the genealogy given by Luke diverges: he brings Yeshua's line through Nathan, another son of David. As noted above (p. 22), the family of Nathan was

[1] The interesting use of "vine" in the place of "sprout" or "shoot" may be influenced by John's use of the "vine" as a metaphor of Yeshua, John 15.

understood as sharing in the royal throne of David by the prophet Zechariah (12:14), and it may have been that a levirate marriage occurred between the families of Solomon and Nathan, though this is only speculative. Regardless, both Matthew and Luke list their genealogies as they knew them from their sources, and both trace Yeshua's lineage to the royal family of David.

Matthew once again brings in the matriarchal side of Yeshua's lineage, by noting that "David was the father of Solomon by Bathsheba." In so doing, he not only may be emphasizing the central role women have played in the lineage of Messiah (culminating in the virgin birth), but also the divine prerogative in using women of foreign extraction. Since Bathsheba is specifically noted to be the wife of Uriah the Hittite, this brings into question her own status as a native born Israelite.[1]

The fact that Bathsheba is listed as the wife of Uriah the Hittite also brings David's sin into the picture, for not only did David politically master the means by which Uriah was killed in battle, but he also did so for the purpose of taking Uriah's wife (2Sam 11, 12). The notice in 1Ki 15:5 makes it clear that this was a black mark in the legacy of David's reign.

The rabbis, however, are uncomfortable with the notice that "David did what was right in the eyes of the Lord … except in the matter of Uriah the Hittite" (1Ki 15:5). Since in the rabbinic theology the merit of the fathers (זְכוּת אֲבוֹתֵינוּ) figures predominately into the favor shown to Israel as a whole, there are many attempts to otherwise explain David's actions with Bathsheba. In b.*San* 56a, for instance, the conclusion is reached that David did not sin, because it was customary for soldiers to give their wives a bill of divorcement before leaving to battle, making Bathsheba legally free to marry David. Moreover, the rabbis conclude that Uriah had acted in treason against David and was worthy of death as a result. But the Scriptures themselves do not exonerate David, but rather reveal his sin, as well as his repentant heart (Ps 51). For Matthew, the line of Yeshua is comprised of fallen humanity, highlighting at once His own genuine humanity, and the very purpose for His coming, that He should "save His people from their sins" (Matt 1:21).

7 Solomon was the father of Rehoboam, Rehoboam the father of Abijah, and Abijah the father of Asa [Asaph].

Rehoboam was the first king of Judah after the division of the kingdoms. His mother was an Ammonitess, and he was known for having adopted pagan practices (1Ki 14:21–24; 2Chron 12:13–14).

Abijah, also known as Abijam, is given a negative report in Kings (15:1–8) but a more favorable assessment by the Chronicler (13:1–22).

The older Greek manuscripts of Matthew have Abijah being the father of Asaph ('Ασάφ), though the English translation correct this to Asa. The Western text family corrects the Greek to Asa.[2] It is possible that Matthew confused the ancestor of the guild of Levitic temple musicians (cf. Ps 50, 73–83) with Asa, the good king of Judah (1Ki 15:9–24), or that scribes copying the manuscripts mixed the two names. It is also possible (though less likely) that the majority text preserves the original reading.

[1]Bathsheba is listed as the daughter of Ammiel (עַמִּיאֵל, meaning "my kinseman is God") in 1Chron 3:5, though it is not certain who Ammiel is. He is also called Eliam in (2Sam 11:3) which involves a transposition of the two parts of his name. Most like this is a different Ammiel than the father of Machir (2Sam 9:4, 5). Bathsheba was thought to be the granddaughter of Ahithophel (cf. 2Sam 23:34), who was probably not of Israelite stock (cf. Lachs, *Rabbinic Comm on the NT*, p. 4).

[2]'Ασάφ: א B C 1 700 788 1071 1582* *f*1 c f g1 h q
Ασα: E K L M S U W Δ Π Ω 2c 28 33 118 124 565 579 1424 1582c *f*13 tr
All of the Hebrew Matthews have אסא.

8–9 Asa [Asaph] was the father of Jehoshaphat, Jehoshaphat the father of Joram, and Joram the father of Uzziah. Uzziah was the father of Jotham, Jotham the father of Ahaz, and Ahaz the father of Hezekiah.

Matthew follows the list of 1Chron 3:10–12. Jehoshaphat's achievements are lauded in detail in 2Chron 17–20 (cp. 1Ki 22:41–50). Joram (not to be confused with the son of Ahab) was a wicked king who reigned fro eight years (2Ki 8:16–24).

Matthew appears to skip three kings of Judah in his list.[1] 1Chron 3:11–12 has Joram (also spelled Jehoram) as the father of Ahaziah, Ahaziah the father of Joash, Joash the father of Amaziah, and Amaziah the father of Jotham, leaving out Uzziah, the son of Amaziah (cf. 2Chron 26:1). Several options have been given for why Matthew would skip three generations, but the most probable is that in his desire to arrange his list in three groups of 14, he excluded three kings whom God put to death for their idolatry (cf. 2Chron 22:1–9; 24:1–25, 28). Moreover 1Ki 21:21 records a curse put upon the house of Ahab (Ahab's daughter Athalia was Joram's wife), and Matthew may have considered the curse to have extended to the third or fourth generation. Needing to compact that genealogy to conform to the scheme of 14 generations, Matthew excluded three kings whose evil reputation was confirmed by divine retribution. We should be reminded that omission of names from a genealogy, for whatever purpose, was not uncommon in the ancient world (cf. Gen 46:21, [cp. 1Chron 8:1-4]; Josh 7:1, 24; 1Chron 4:1 [cp. 2:50]; 6:7–9 [cp. Ezra 7:3]; Ezra 5:1 [cp. Zech 1:1], etc.). This was understood by the Sages who teach that "sons of sons are sons" (b.*Qidd* 4a).

Hezekiah is known in the biblical history as an outstanding king who was faithful to the Lord in his reign (2Ki 18–20; 1Chron 29–32; Is 36–39):

> He trusted in the LORD, the God of Israel; so that after him there was none like him among all the kings of Judah, nor among those who were before him (2Kings 18:5).

The Sages also identified Hezekiah as indicative of the character of the Messiah (b.*Sanh* 94a; b.*Ber* 28b; cf. b.*Sanh* 98b–99a).

Jotham also receives a good report (2Ki 15:32–38; 2Chron 27), but Ahaz is considered an apostate (2Ki 16; 2Chron 28).

10 Hezekiah was the father of Manasseh, Manasseh the father of Amon, and Amon the father of Josiah.

Manasseh was the most wicked of the kings of Judah (2Ki 21:1–18; 2Chron 33:1–9). However, it may be that some believed he repented at the end of his life (2Chron 33:10–12), and the Sages debated whether, in fact, Manasseh's repentance was genuine, and that therefore he was received as worthy at the end of his life (cf. the Targum to 2Chron 33:13; y.*Sanh* 10.2).

For "Amon" the older Greek manuscripts have Ἀμώς, *Amos* while the majority text "corrects" to Ἀμών, *Amon*. The Lxx of Jer 1:2 and 25:3 also spells Amon as Ἀμώς, so this may have been an alternate spelling of his name within the Greek tradition.

[1]For the textual issues and variants relating to Uzziah, see the comments of Davies-Allison, 1.176.

11 Josiah became the father of Jeconiah and his brothers, at the time of the deportation to Babylon.

According to 1Chron 3:15–16, Josiah had four sons:

> 15 The sons of Josiah were Johanan the firstborn, and the second was Jehoiakim, the third Zedekiah, the fourth Shallum. 16 The sons of Jehoiakim were Jeconiah his son, Zedekiah his son. 17 The sons of Jeconiah, the prisoner, were Shealtiel his son, 18 and Malchiram, Pedaiah, Shenazzar, Jekamiah, Hoshama and Nedabiah.

Here, Jehoiakim is the father of Jeconiah, not Josiah. Jehoiakin and Coniah was an alternative name for Jeconiah (cp. 2Ki 24:8–16; 2Chron 36:9–10; Jer 22:24f). Moreover, the Lxx uses Ἰωακίμ for both Jehhoiakin (Jeconaih) and Jehoiakim (e.g., 2Ki 23:36; 24:8–16). In 1Esdra 1:41, the two names are interchanged. Further confusion of the two names results from the fact that apparently both Jehoiakin and Jehoiakim had sons named Zedekiah (cp. 2Chron 36:1–10; 2Ki 24:17). It is also of note that 1Chron 3:17 refers to Jeconiah as "the prisoner," which may be the basis for Matthew's added phrase, "at the time of the deportation to Babylon." Nebuchadnezzar bound Jehoiakim (also known as Eliakim) in chains and brought him to Babylon. Once again we see that Matthew is speaking in general terms when he states that "X was the father of Y." His sense must be that "X was the progenitor of Y," meaning that he is listing family trees without necessarily naming every generation. His motivation in doing this may have been to restrict the genealogy to 14 names in each group. Of course, there is also the possibility of scribal error, or mixup, in the listing of these names that have, admittedly, been confused as well in the earlier sources.

We may briefly refer here to the prophecy of Jeremiah (22:30) that "… no man of his (Coniah = Jeconiah) descendants will prosper sitting on the throne of David or ruling again in Judah." This has been used by some against the reign of Yeshua, since Matthew has the messianic line coming through Jeconiah. The Temple Scroll (11QTemple 59.13–15) alludes to this verse from Jeremiah:

> 11QT 59:13 and I will be their God and they My people. But the king
> 14 whose heart and eyes whorishly depart from My commandments
> shall never have a descendent sitting on the throne of 15 his fathers.
> Indeed, I shall forever cut off his seed from ruling Israel.

Jeremiah's prophecy, however, relates to the fact that following the exile, no earthly king would rule over Judah, and history has proven this to be the case. It may be that Matthew's addition of "and his brothers" refers to all of the people of Judah who were eventually taken into captivity. The Sages also considered the prophecy of Jeremiah, but concluded that the exile itself was sufficient punishment, and that as a result, atonement for the sins of Jeconiah was accomplished:

> R. Johanan said: Exile atones for everything, for it is written, Thus saith the Lord, write ye this man childless, a man that shall not prosper in his days, for no man of his seed shall prosper sitting upon the throne of David and ruling any more in Judah. [Jer 22:30] Whereas after he [the king] was exiled, it is written, And the sons of Jechoniah,

> — the same is Assir — Shealtiel his son etc. [1Chron 3:17] [He was called] Assir, [meaning "imprisoned"] because his mother conceived him in prison. Shealtiel, [the Sages considered this a second name for the same person] because God did not plant him [a play on the name: שאלתיאל is close to אל שתלו] in the way that others are planted. We know by tradition that a woman cannot conceive in a standing position. yet she did conceive standing. [for lack of room in prison, cf. Mid Rab *Lev* 19] Another interpretation: Shealtiel, [שאל אל] because God obtained [of the Heavenly court] absolution from His oath. Zerubbabel was so called because he was sown in Babylon. [זרע לבב] But [his real name was] Nehemiah the son of Hachaliah. (b.*San* 37b)

> R. Tanhum b. R. Jeremiah said: He was called Assir because he was fettered in the prison (*beth ha'asurin*); he was called Shealtiel because from him the kingdom of the house of David was replanted (*hush-telah*). (Mid. Rab. *Song of Songs* 8.5)

Thus, the Sages also recognized that the prophecy against Jeconiah was to be understood as temporal, i.e., pertaining to the fact that the throne of Judah was deposed following the exile, but that Jeconiah did have children, and that the Davidic line of the Messiah was intact.

The deportation (μετοικεσίας, used only in this chapter in the Apostolic Scriptures, but found in the Lxx to translate גלה 2Ki 24:16; Obad. 1:20; Lam. 1:7; Ezek. 12:11) was considered God's punishment upon Israel by the prophets, and so interpreted by the Sages (cf. b.*Pesach* 87b). Matthew will develop this theme more as he writes of Yeshua's descent to Egypt, and His return to the Land. The exile of God's people out of the Land is analogous to the exile of Adam and Chavah from the garden: God had promised to put His presence in the Land forever, and therefore, being exiled from the Land was to be, in measure, separated from His blessing. Conversely, to return to the Land was a restoration of the covenant blessings. Matthew's point of view is that in Yeshua, there is the inevitable restoration of Israel to her covenant, and this involves a return from exile, both in theological as well as national dimensions.

12 After the deportation to Babylon: Jeconiah became the father of Sheal-tiel, and Shealtiel the father of Zerubbabel.

The genealogies of Matthew and Luke converge in the names of Sheal-tiel and Zerubbabel, though Luke has Neri as the father of Shealtiel, and Resa the son of Zerubbabel. According to 1Chron 3:17–19 (MT), Zerubbabel was the son of Pedaiah, which might indicate there were more than one person with the name of Zerubbabel, or else a levirite marriage has taken place. The Lxx of 1Chron 17–19, however, has Zerubbabel as the son of Shealtiel, and Matthew follows this source. It is also possible that Zerubbabel is seen as the son of Shealtiel (of whom no other son is recorded) because he succeeded him on the throne.

Zerubbabel, a descendant of David, was the Persian governor of Jeru-salem following the exile (cf. Josephus, *Ant.* 11.33–78). He was viewed as a messianic figure, for his is the "servant of the Lord" and His "signet ring" (Hag 2:23). Likewise, Zechariah speaks of Zerubbabel as one through whom the Lord would rebuild the temple and re-establish the nation (Zech 4:6–10).

This was not lost on the Sages:

> For who hath despised the day of small things (Zech 4:10)? also, Who
> art thou, O great mountain before Zerubbabel (ib. 7)? Furthermore,
> the royal Messiah will be descended from the tribe of Judah, as it
> says, And it shall come to pass in that day, that the root of Jesse, that
> standeth for an ensign of the peoples, unto him shall the nations seek
> (Is 9:10). Thus from the tribe of Judah were descended Solomon, who
> built the first Temple, and Zerubbabel who built the second Temple;
> and [from him will be descended] the royal Messiah, who will re-
> build the Temple. Thus we find that these two tribes, Judah and Levi,
> are the most distinguished in their lineage of all Israel, since in them
> were royalty and priesthood. (Mid. Rab. *Genesis* 97)

13 Zerubbabel was the father of Abihud, Abihud the father of Eliakim, and Eliakim the father of Azor.

From this point on in Matthew's genealogy we have no record from the Tanach to compare, though the Greek names he lists in vv. 13–15 do occur in the Lxx. On this basis, some have suggested that Matthew just makes up his list from various names gathered together from the Tanach, but this is wrong headed. As noted above, it is illogical to conclude that Matthew and Luke constructed their genealogies out of thin air. Either they utilized sources not known by us, or they had oral traditions that maintained genealogies not recorded in the Tanach following the exile.

About 500 years lie between Zerubbabel and Joseph, and Matthew lists only nine names. Once again, it is clear that Matthew is not giving a comprehensive genealogical listing.

Abihud ('αβιούδ, which is used in the Tanach for the Abihu, the son of Aaron) is not listed as a son of Zerubbabel in 1Chron 3:19–20.

Eliakim was the name of the puppet ruler under the thumb of Pharaoh Neca (2Ki 23:24; 2Chron 36:4). Hezekiah had a royal chamberlain by the same name (2Ki 18:18, 26, 37; 19.2), of whom Isaiah prophesied:

> Then I will set the key of the house of David on his shoulder, when
> he opens no one will shut, when he shuts no one will open. (Is 22:22,
> cp. Matt 16:19)

Luke lists another Eliakim, the son of Melea, in his genealogy (Lk 3:31).

A prophet in the days of Zedekiah had the name Azzur (Jer 28:1), and Ezer (Lxx Αζουρ, *Azur*) is listed as one of the workers under Nehemiah (3:19).

The DuTillet Matthew adds a name at this point: Avner, the son of Abihud, presumably to increase the total of names in the final section of Matthew's genealogy to the desired number of 14. On what basis this name is added, however, is not known. The name Abner is well known from the time of David, and an Abner is listed as the father of Jaasiel of the tribe of Benjamin in 1Chron 27:21, but even if this family name were presumed to be carried to later generations, this would not work for Matthew's listing, since he is intent on showing lineage through the tribe of Judah.

14 Azor was the father of Zadok, Zadok the father of Achim, and Achim the father of Eliud.

The source for these names in Matthew's genealogy is unknown. Zadok is the most well known of the names, being a priest in David's court

[1]B. Z. Wachholder, *The Dawn of Qumran* (Cincinnati, 1983), pp. 99–229, quoted from Davies & Allison, 1.181.

[2]also Ματθαν, see A. T. Robinson, *Grammar*, p. 215.

[3]Note the Pseudepigraphal work, *Joseph and Aseneth*, which was probably a work done by early followers of Yeshua, that marks these parallels in a story form. See D. Thomas Lancaster, *The Mystery of the Gospel* (FFOZ, 2003), pp. 43–51.

(2Sam 8:17). There was also a Zadok who was the grandfather of Jotham (listed by Matthew in 1:9, cp. 2Chron 27:1). Some have also suggested that the founder of the Qumran community was named Zadok, whose dates were roughly 240–170 BCE.[1]

15 Eliud was the father of Eleazar, Eleazar the father of Matthan, and Matthan the father of Jacob.

Eleazar is only found here in the Apostolic Scriptures, though the name was common in the Tanach (used for at least 10 individuals). There was an Eleazar closely associated with David (2Sam 23:9–10; 1Chron 11:12–14).

Luke lists the father of Jacob, Yeshua's grandfather, as Ματθἀτ[2] (*Mathat*), and some have suggested that he and Matthew agree at this point. However, Luke and Matthew list different names for the father of Matthan.

The father of Joseph is Jacob, and it could not have been missed by Matthew and his audience that this parallels the Joseph story of Genesis. Indeed, Joseph is so much a foreshadow of the Messiah in the minds of the Sages, that they speak of "Messiah ben Joseph" to describe the suffering Messiah (b.*Sukkah* 52a–b; Mid. Rab. *Gen* 95; Mid. Rab. *Song of Songs* ii.33). The parallels between Joseph and Yeshua are also obvious: 1) he was rejected by his brothers, 2) loved by his father, 3) was considered as dead, 4) returns to life, 5) saves the world from famine, 6) reigns as a king, 7) brings in Gentiles to be co-heirs with Israel. These parallels are so close that some have suggested Matthew simply concocts the name of Yeshua's father and grandfather to make the parallel, but this, again, is illogical. Matthew is writing to a generation, some of whom could have been alive at the time of Yeshua, and doubtlessly knew His family. More on track is to see this as yet another mark of divine providence in which the story of divine redemption shows the work of a single Author Who told the end from the beginning.[3]

16 Jacob was the father of Joseph the husband of Mary, by whom Yeshua was born, who is called the Messiah.

Matthew's genealogy differs from the normal way genealogies are listed, because normally the first name in the list is the individual in view, while in this case, the last named person is the primary emphasis. Matthew's obvious purpose is to bring us to Yeshua in his list of progenitors.

Joseph was a very popular name in the 1st Century Jewish communities. At least eighteen different Josephs are named by Josephus. The name mean "he adds," (cf. Gen 30:24). If it were not for Matthew's Gospel, we would know precious little about Joseph. In the other Gospels he is only a bystander, and the husband of Mary. Even Matthew hesitates to call Joseph the husband of Mary in the ensuing narrative (cf 2:13–14, 20–21). Yet Matthew lets us know that he was of the family of David, that he was upright, a man of visions, and resolutely obedient to the Lord. Once again, Matthew's description of Joseph shows clear parallels to the Joseph of Genesis. While there is no clear evidence to say so, it is not out of the realm of possibility that the material Matthew used regarding Joseph came from Joseph himself and those who were his close companions. It is very reasonable to believe that he related his story to those to whom he was closest, and that this testimony was carried along by those who followed Yeshua as their Messiah.

The text of this verse has obviously been a point of concern as the manuscripts were copied, as the extant variants testify. This could be for a number of reasons, but perhaps the most obvious is that in this verse there is a clear change in the verb "to beget." Throughout the listing of Matthew, the text reads "And X begot Y," using the active aorist form of γεννάω, ἐγέννησεν (*gennao, egennesen*). Here, however, the verb changes to a passive form, ἐγεννήθη (*egennethe*), "was begotten." It is easy to see how scribes, after writing the active form verse after verse, might have continued to write it in this verse as well. So there are some Greek manuscripts that read: "Joseph, who was betrothed to the virgin Mary, begat Yeshua who is called Messiah" (Θ, *f*¹³). Related readings are found in a (b) c d (k) q syᶜ Ambr Aug Hipp.

Another Syriac manuscript, found in 1894, syˢ, or the so-called Sinai Syriac, which is a late 4th or early 5th Century manuscript, also attests to the reading of Θ and *f*¹³. The original Greek that lay behind the Syriac would have been Ιωσηρ, ω εμνηστευθη παρθενος Μαριαμ, εγεννησεν Ιησουν τον λεγομενον Χριστον, "Joseph, who had been betrothed to a virgin Mary, begat Yeshua who is called Messiah." This reading is also attested in a 5th Century document containing a dialog between a Christian and a Jew, called "The Dialog of Timothy and Aquila." Yet these four witnesses (Θ, *f*¹³, syˢ, Dialog of Timothy and Aquila) stand in the face of all other Greek manuscripts. It seems unwarranted, then, to presume that the many witnesses to the passive form of the verb ("was begotten") should be disregarded on the relatively small weight of these four. It is better to see how the four could have mistaken the original reading (ἐγενν́θη) for their variant (ἐγεννήσεν). As noted, the most obvious explanation is simply that scribes continued the pattern of the previous verses, neglecting to note that Matthew changed the active form to a passive, in light of the fact that Yeshua was begotten, not by the act of Joseph, but by the Holy Spirit, as he directly affirms in v. 20. There is, of course, the possibility that the variant arose from theological concerns. To a Jewish audience who had already rejected Yeshua, the virgin birth was a difficult apologetic. Moreover, it is possible that the active verb was understood in a legal sense only, meaning that Joseph was the legal father of Yeshua.

The Hebrew Matthews read several ways on this verse. The DuTillet has: יעקב הוליד את יוסף איש מרים שממנה נולד ישוע שנקרא משיח, "Jacob begat Joseph, the husband of Miriam, from whom was born Yeshua who is called Messiah." Shem Tov has: ויעקב הוליד את יוסף הוא איש מרים...הנקרא משיח ובלעז קריסטוס [, "And Jacob begat Joseph. He was the husband of Miriam [the mother of Yeshua] who is called Messiah, which in Greek is Christos." The Münster Matthew (edited by Quin.) has: יעקב הוליד את יוסף את איש מרים שממנה נולד ישוע שנקרא משיח, which is identical with the DuTillet with the exception of an added direct object particle. So all of the Hebrew Matthews affirm the vast majority of the Greek texts, in that the repetitive pattern of "X begat Y" is changed when the birth of Yeshua is noted.

The point, of course, in all of this is the virgin birth. For Matthew to change to the passive, "who was begotten," from the string of active verbs ("X begat Y"), shows a clear intention on his part to emphasize the miraculous, virgin birth of our Master, something he will explicitly relate in the following verses. That this was an early "sticking point" to those who had rejected Yeshua is evident from the rabbinic teaching that Yeshua was known as ben Pantera or ben Pandira, which some have suggested was a deliberate corruption of υἱός τῆς παρθένον (*huios tes parthenon*), "son of the virgin" (cf. t.*Chullin* ii.22, 23; b.*San* 67a). But it is difficult to see why the Greek word *parthenos* ("virgin") could not have been more clearly transliterated into

[1]Morris Goldstein, *Jesus in the Jewish Tradition* (Macmillan, 1950), p. 35; R. Travers Herford, *Christianity i the Talmud and Midrash* (KTAV, 1903), p. 39f.

[2]Quoted from Goldstein, *op. cit.* p. 38.

[3]Davies & Allison, *Matthew*, 1.184.

[3]It is not altogether certain that Jn 8:41 is a slur on Yeshua's paternity. The phrase "we are not born of fornication" in the retort of the Pharisees to Yeshua, may have to do with the degrogatory accusation that Yeshua was a Samaritan (v. 48). See my *The Messiah: An Introduction to Christology* (TorahResource, 2007), p. 131.

the Hebrew. Both Goldstein and Herford consider this enough to dismiss the suggestion.[1] Other suggestions for the name Ben Pantera (or Pandera, or Panthera, and other spellings) have yielded little of substance. Origen, in his disputation with Celsus, claims to have heard that the Jews teach the father of Yeshua to be "Panther" (*Contra Cel.* 1.32–33), a Roman soldier, but as Goldstein and others note, this seems far-fetched. There may have been an early tradition that the a family name akin to Panther was in the line of Mary. A document dated to 634 CE, called *The Teaching of Jacob*, records a genealogy of Yeshua as follows:

> his mother Mary is the daughter of Jokim, who is the son of Panther, a brother of Melchi, of the seed of Nathan, the son of David.[2]

While this is quite late, and therefore having little weight in the argument, it still might suggest that an early tradition existed that one of Mary's relatives had the family name Panther, and this was carried forward in the writing of the Sages.

There is another break in style in our verse. Not only does Matthew change from the active to the passive of γεννάω, "to beget," but he also notes a change in the manner in which he writes that "from whom (i.e., Mary) was Yeshua." In the previous list, when a women is mentioned it is in the form of "X began Y out of Z." Here the passive "begotten" has the Spirit of God in view, and thus there is no human progenitor. As Davies & Allison comment:

> But we do not read that "Joseph begat Jesus by Mary." Mary's case … stands by itself: it is an anomaly. The break in Matthew's pattern thus reflects a break in the course of history. God is about to do something new.[3]

If Matthew alone gives us what little information we have about Joseph, he does not follow suit with Mary. Mary (Maria in the Greek, for Hebrew Miriam), in Matthew's narrative has no independent identity. She is known as the mother of Yeshua, the vessel of the Ruach, and the betrothed of Joseph. She is referenced in b.*San* 67a as the mother of Ben Pandira, where the derogatory label of "adulteress" is given. This may accord with the early tradition among the Pharisees that Yeshua was of illegitimate birth (cf. John 8:41).[3]

But the fact that Matthew clearly alludes to the virgin birth in his use of the passive "was begotten" (or even "was born out of Mary") fits his purpose to show the legal heirship of Yeshua, not His physical lineage. In the ancient world, the declaration of a father that "this is my son" was sufficient to confirm legal heirship. The Mishnah states (m.*Bava Batra* 8.6), "If a man said, 'This is my son,' he may be believed." We may also reference the words of Isaiah 43:1, "I have called you by name, you are mine." We may presume that Joseph gave his name to Yeshua, and as such, Yeshua was viewed legally as Joseph's son. He would have been known, then, as Yeshua ben Yosef.

To the name Yeshua is added, "who was called Messiah." Χριστός, as noted above, is from the Greek verb meaning "to anoint." This answers to the Hebrew מָשִׁיחַ, *mashiach*, which likewise means "one who is anointed." The term Messiah is first a title, and only secondly a proper name. Here, with the addition of "who is called," the term is functioning as a title. As far as Matthew is concerned, Yeshua is the long-awaited, promised redeemer.

17 So all the generations from Abraham to David are fourteen generations; from David to the deportation to Babylon, fourteen generations; and from the deportation to Babylon to the Messiah, fourteen generations.

For comments on the three groups of 14 generations, see above, pp. 14–16.

The Virgin Birth of Yeshua[1]

18 Now the birth of Yeshua Messiah was as follows: when His mother Mary had been betrothed to Joseph, before they came together she was found to be with child by the Holy Spirit.

The genealogy having been concluded, Matthew goes on to describe in brief the circumstances that brought about Yeshua's birth. The ending of the genealogy naturally introduces this infancy narrative, and does so in a chiastic parallel. For the genealogy ends by naming Joseph, Mary, and Yeshua, in that order. The material that follows begins with Yeshua (v. 18a), then Mary (v. 18b), and then Joseph (vv. 19–20). The passive verb of v. 16 is now being explained.

Davies & Allison note a possible parallel to the Creation account of Genesis 1–2 in the structure of this first chapter of Matthew. In Genesis, the catalog of things created is given in Gen 1, while the creation of mankind becomes the more detailed focus of Gen 2. In like manner, 1:1–17 detail the ancestors of the Messiah, and vv. 18–25 concentrate specifically on the Messiah as the primary point of the story. Likewise, in both accounts, the Spirit is active in the creating/begetting process. If this parallel was in the mind of Matthew, then he is once again signalling a new beginning in the coming of Messiah.

Mary is called the mother of Yeshua, but never is Joseph called His father. Once again, the purpose is to emphasize the uniqueness of His birth as that from a virgin, and through the activity of the Spirit of God. This is not to deny that Joseph acted as Yeshua's father, and that Yeshua no doubt honored him as such, as the Torah requires. But Matthew's intention is to note the unique status of Yeshua as the divine Son of Man, whose Father is the God of Israel.

when His mother Mary had been betrothed to Joseph... The issue of betrothal in the ancient Israelite society undoubtedly went through various sociological and cultural changes, but it surely retained its primary purpose, that being to legally secure a bride for one's son.

There is some indication that marriages were arranged when children were young (b.*Yev* 62b speaks of arranging marriages when children are near the end of puberty). But arranging a marriage may not be equivalent with betrothal, which involved a legal transaction. Typically, as far as the data gives us notice, the betrothal period was for a year before the marriage was consummated. During this time, the bride-to-be lived in her father's house, even though she was legally bound to her future husband (m.*Ketuvot* 5.2; m.*Ned.* 10.5; b.*Ketuvot* 57b). There were disputes, however, how far the legal arrangement of betrothal went. For instance, could the future husband annul the vows of his betrothed? The sages say "no" (m.*Ned.* 10.5). But the future husband was required to support his betrothed wife in the event that the year was up and the marriage had not yet been finalized. So while dur-

V. 17 and the first clause of 18 is missing from the best manuscripts of the Shem Tov Matthew. Howard inserts them from other manuscripts.

[1]See my essay, "The Virgin Birth: An Inquiry into the Biblical Doctrine," (2007), available at TorahResource.com.

ing the betrothal period there were clearly legal ramifications that existed between the couple, the full responsibilities of marriage (including consummation) awaited the time when the couple came together publicly to affirm their vows, and then resided together in their own home. It is because of the legal aspects of betrothal (called שִׁידּוּכִין, *shiduchin* in rabbinic literature, as well as אֵרוּסִין, *'erusin*), that a woman legally was treated in many was as a wife (cf. Deut 20:7; 28:30; Judges 14:15; 15:1; 2Sam 3:14). If the future husband died during the betrothal period, the betrothed woman was treated, in some respects, as a widow (m.*Ketuvot* 1.2; 4.2; m.*Yevamot* 2.6; m.*Gittin* 6.2).

This explains the actions of Joseph. Though, as Matthew makes clear, Joseph and Mary had not come together (a euphemism for sexual relations), they were betrothed, and their legal relationship required an equally legal procedure for the dissolving of the betrothal contract. In cases where the betrothal is dissolved, the women (unless she is guilty of some breach of conduct) would be entitled to compensation, perhaps the retaining of the bride price paid at betrothal.

before they had come together… In the Greek papyri, the term συνελθεῖν, *sunelthein,* "to come together" also means "to marry" (see *BDAG*, "συνέρχομαι"). Thus, Mary and Joseph, though betrothed, had not yet come to the finality of their betrothal period, and as such, Mary resided in the house of her father.[1] Matthew emphasizes this in order to dissuade any notion that the child Mary was carrying was Joseph's child. Once again, the importance of the virgin birth is at the forefront of Matthew's theological purposes.

she was found to be with child by the Holy Spirit. In the structure of Matthew's narrative, the readers are given advanced insight that Joseph does not yet have. The child within Mary is the work of the Holy Spirit. Joseph will learn this through a dream given by God.

When Matthew writes that the child was "by the Holy Spirit," we should understand this to mean "by the power of God," brought about by the work of His Spirit. We should compare Lk 1:35 and the parallelism there:

> The Holy Spirit will come upon you, and the power of the Most High will overshadow you; and for that reason the holy Child shall be called the Son of God.

Here, the Spirit of God is parallel to the "power of the Most High." As in the Creation recorded in Gen 1, so here, the creative power of the Spirit of God is at work.[2] This, of course, is yet another part of the mystery of the incarnation, that Yeshua was born of a virgin. But this was anticipated by a number of things, not the least of which the giving of circumcision as the sign of the Abrahamic covenant. For like Isaac, who was born by the direct miracle of God, so Yeshua would be the promised Son Who would come by above human means.

[1]See the comments of Liddell & Scott, *Lexicon,* "συνέρχομαι."

[2]Note also that in Mid Rab *Exodus* 1.11, the Holy Spirit is involved in proclaiming to the Egyptians that the Israelite women would be fruitful with children, and that as the Israelites increased, they would grow in power.

19 And Joseph her husband, being a righteous man and not wanting to disgrace her, planned to send her away secretly.

Joseph is called "her husband" (ὁ ἀνὴρ αὐτῆς) which corresponds to the Hebrew אִישָׁהּ *'ishah*, used in the Tanach to describe the marriage relationship (cf. Num 30:8[9]f, Ezek 16:45). In Rev 21:2, the same expression is used of a bridegroom. As noted above, the betrothal period, under rabbinic law, formed a legal and binding relationship between the bride and groom, and required formal dissolution in the event that the either party failed to fulfill their obligations. Thus, for Joseph to be called "her man" (husband) reflects this betrothal arrangement.

A question arises as to the relationship of the two participle clauses: "being a righteous man and not wanting to disgrace her." To put the question simply: in what manner is Joseph described as righteous? The two possibilities are 1) that Joseph was righteous in regard to his obedience to the Torah, and thus he determined to divorce Mary privately, or 2) Joseph was seen as righteous because he wanted to spare Mary the shame of being pregnant during the betrothal period. The flow of the narrative, as well as the normal meaning for "righteous" being that of "right actions," would favor the first option. In Matthew's telling of the story, Joseph's decision to "send her away" (which is a legal way of describing divorce, cf. Deut 24:1, וְשִׁלְחָהּ מִבֵּיתוֹ□) is made before he is given the divine revelation regarding the pregnancy. He is righteous because the Torah expects that an adulteress should be exposed and punished for her lawlessness. His personal obligation was first to end the betrothal contract via the prescribed means, which would require a minimum of two witness (cf. m.*Ketuvot* 2.1–7; m.*Gittin* 9.4–8). The subsequent punishment of an adulteress was left to the judges (*bet din*, cf. Deut 22:13f). The ordeal of the bitter waters applied only to a woman in a consummated marriage (m.*Sota* 4.1).

Thus, Joseph is righteous because he intends to act, even in this most difficult situation, in accordance with the Torah. Yet he did not want to expose Mary to public shame. Here we see the combination of righteousness and genuine concern. "Love covers a multitude of sins" (Prov 10:12, cf. 1Pet 4:8). Joseph acts upon what he knows to be true (what the Torah requires) yet his love for Mary is combined with his knowledge that she (and we presume her family) were known as righteous people. Her pregnancy therefore left many unanswered questions, and as such, he determines to keep the matter as private as possible. He did not want to "disgrace her" (διεγμα-τίζω, *diegmatizo,* found only here and in Col 2:15), meaning he did not want a public condemnation. Had he rushed to judgment, the result could have been that Mary was stoned. In accordance with his righteous behavior, he wanted all of the facts (cf. v. 20) before he made a final judgment. Moreover, his affections for her remain constant in spite of what appeared to be her own unfaithfulness.

20 But when he had considered this, behold, an angel of the Lord appeared to him in a dream, saying, "Joseph, son of David, do not be afraid to take Mary as your wife; for the Child who has been conceived in her is of the Holy Spirit.

Joseph considered (ἐνθυμέομαι, *enthumeomai*) the matter, meaning that he pondered it, weighing all of the matters carefully (cf. *BDAG* on ἐνθυμέομαι), as is characteristic of a righteous man. He did not rush to judgment, but weighed the matter carefully.

It was during the days of such careful thought and meditation that Joseph received the divine revelation regarding Mary. No doubt his searching for answers was often directed toward God Himself. "In all you ways acknowledge Him, and He will direct your paths" (Prov 3:6). The interjection, "Behold" (ἰδοὺ, *idou*, which corresponds to the Hebrew הִנֵּה, *hineih*), alerts us that something out of the ordinary is taking place. The "angel of the Lord" (מַלְאָךְ יהוה, *mal'ach Adonai* which could just as well be translated "messenger of the Lord") appears to Joseph in a dream.[1] This is the first of four dreams through which Joseph receives divine revelation and instruction (cf. Matt. 2:13, 19, 22). That the Joseph of Genesis was known as "the Dreamer" (Gen 37:19) continues the parallels between the two, for both of them receive divine revelation via dreams, and both have no doubt that the dreams are from God. In our story, the angel appears only to deliver the divine message, which is clear and to the point. There is no mystical message or hidden imagery.

The messenger of God addresses Joseph as the "son of David," not "son of Jacob" as noted in the genealogy. Every other time that Matthew uses the title "son of David" he does so in reference to Yeshua (Matt. 9:27; 12:23; 15:22; 20:30-31; 21:9, 15; 22:42). This being the case, it seems obvious that his use of it here is to emphasize the legal status of Yeshua as descended from the line of David. In the very place where Joseph is informed that the child within Mary is the product of the Holy Spirit, he is addressed by a name which ties him back to the Davidic line, and thus reinforces the fact that though Yeshua is not physically Joseph's offspring, he is still legally his, and thus is likewise of the tribe of Judah, and the house of David. Moreover, it is clear that for Matthew, "son of David" has taken on messianic overtones. In 12:23f, the crowds question whether Yeshua could be the "son of David," and the Pharisee leaders attempt to dissuade them from such a conclusion by discounting the miraculous healings performed by Yeshua. Of note is the fact that they do not attempt to discredit His Davidic lineage on the basis of His family line. Furthermore, it should be noted that often the use of "son of David" in reference to Yeshua is in the context of His healing ministry, in which such miracles are given as an authentication of His messianic role.

As is often the case when God makes Himself known via direct revelation, the message is "do not fear." These are the words of the messenger of God to Joseph: "do not fear to take Mary as your wife." Joseph's desire to act righteously would not be compromised by taking Mary as his wife. The idea of "taking for a wife" (παραλαμβάνω, *paralambano*) is parallel to the use of לָקַח (*laqach*) for the legal and public transaction of marriage. In the 1st Century, this idea of "taking" may have specifically entailed taking one's betrothed wife to one's home as the final step in the marriage process (b.*Ketuvot* 17a may be referring to the procession of the bride to the *chuppah* as well as to her procession to her husband's home, to which הכנסה "leading in" most likely refers).

for the Child who has been conceived in her is of the Holy Spirit. Here is the crux of the matter. Mary is pregnant, not as the result of fornication, but by the direct act of God. As the Creator, Who fashioned the first man and woman, so in this case, the creative act of conception has been performed by divine fiat, by the Holy Spirit. Matthew refers to the Holy Spirit by the phrase "Spirit who is holy" (πνεύματός ἐστιν ἁγίου, cf. Lk 2:25 where the

[1] The DuTillet and Shem Tov have only המלאך, while the Münster has מלאך יהוה. All Greek witnesses have κυριου (of the Lord).

same construction is found). Elsewhere in Matthew (1:18; 3:11; 12:32; 28:19) the more common πνεύματος ἁγίου (or equivalent) is found.

The aorist passive participle form, γεννηθέν (*gennethen*, "was conceived") here corresponds to the aorist passive indicative of v. 16, ἐγεννήθη (*egennethe*, "was born"). The Greek γεννάω (*gennao*) means both "to be father of" as well as "to bear a child." The use of the passive voice in contrast to the consistent use of the verb throughout the previous genealogy, emphasizes the other-than-normal conception of Yeshua.

21 She will bear a Son; and you shall call His name Yeshua, for He will save His people from their sins.

This statement to Joseph in the mouth of the messenger of the Lord, prophesies the greatness of the One Who had been conceived within Mary. Its structure and form conform to a pattern not uncommon in the Tanach (cf. Gen 16:11; 17:19; Is 7:14). The name that would be given to the Child was indicative of His great work. Moreover, Matthew has been using language and patterns in the immediate context that would have been connected to the text he next will quote (Is 7:14) as proof that the messianic expectation of Israel's prophets had been fulfilled. Note the following:

Isaiah 7:14 (Lxx)	Matthew 1
ἐν γαστρὶ ἕξει (will be with child)	ἐν γαστρὶ ἔχουσα (is with child) v. 18
καὶ τέξεται υἱόν (will bear a son)	τέξεται δέ υἱόν (will bear a son) v. 21 ἔτεκεν υἱόν (she bore a son) v. 25
καὶ καλέσουσιν (καλέσεις) τὸ ὄνομα αὐτοῦ Ἐμμανουήλ (and they shall call [you will call] his name Emmanuel)	καὶ καλέσεις τὸ ὄνομα αὐτοῦ Ἰησοῦν (and you shall call His name Yeshua, v. 21) καὶ ἐκάλεσεν τὸ ὄνομα αὐτοῦ Ἰησοῦν (and he called His name Yeshua, v. 25)

The point is that Matthew has Is 7:14 in mind throughout the telling of the story, and he uses the language of Isaiah to signal that. But more to the point is that the message given by the messenger of the Lord clearly uses the language of Is 7:14, so that the matter of fulfillment of Isaiah's prophecy is from the Lord as far as Matthew is concerned: it is not something that he has manufactured.

The gender of the child in Mary's womb is specifically noted to be male, "a son." The one promised to Chavah as the solution to the trouble brought on by the enemy (Gen 3:15) has finally arrived. The Promised One has come. Further, the future ("you shall call His name Yeshua") acts as an imperative, and makes known to Joseph that he is to accept the Child as his own. The naming process will affirm that.

The name "Yeshua" (see above p. 17) is formed on the Hebrew verb יָשַׁע, *yasha'*, "to deliver, save" and akin to the noun יְשׁוּעָה, *y'shu'ah*, "salvation." The name therefore carries the primary purpose of the Child's mission: "to save His people from their sins." The deliverance He will bring will be a salvation first and foremost from the condemnation that sin brings. This forensic aspect of salvation is not devoid of physical deliverance, but the one encompasses the other. Throughout the history of Israel, as she lived out the reality of God's covenant made with her, the physical redemption of the nation is always tied to her right standing before God. This is initially made known in the promise made to Abraham, for the nation that would come from him would be known by their obedience to God's statutes, and would therefore also be the recipient of His blessings:

> Gen. 18:19 "For I have chosen him, so that he may command his children and his household after him to keep the way of the LORD by doing righteousness and justice, so that the LORD may bring upon Abraham what He has spoken about him."

It is not as though Israel's own righteousness attracts God's blessing, but that through God's mercy via the divine revelation of Himself (found ultimately in the revelation of His Messiah, Yeshua), He would make Israel righteous in order to bring upon her the blessings He desires. Ultimately, the new covenant prophesied by Jeremiah (31:31–34) has this work in mind. The Torah, written upon the heart by divine sovereignty, brings about a transformation that procures Divine forgiveness and brings about His blessing.

Thus, the promise that Yeshua would "save His people from their sins" includes not only their deliverance from the Divine condemnation of sin, but also the final blessing of their deliverance from their enemies, and the establishment of unending shalom also promised by the Prophets of old.

Who constitutes "His people" (τὸν λαὸν αὐτοῦ)? Throughout Matthew, the Greek word λαός (*laos*) refers to Israel (2:4,6; 4:16, 23; 13:15; 15:8; 21:23; 26:3, 5, 47; 27:1, 25, 64). And this is in concert with the words of the prophets that promised salvation to God's chosen people. But the prophets also teach that the nations would be drawn to Israel, and would share in her salvation through the promised Messiah (e.g., Gen 49:10; Deut 32:43; Is 42:4; 56:3–7; Zech 8:23). The point is that the locus of salvation is Israel, for it is in the Seed of Abraham (cf. Gal 3:16) that all of the nations would be blessed. This reality is what drove Paul to emphasize the fatherhood of Abraham for all believers in Yeshua, whether Jew or Gentile (Rom 4), and what explains his metaphor of the olive tree (Rom 11).

It should also be noted that the words of the messenger of the Lord to Joseph contain a clear and unequivocal purpose for which the Child has come: "to save His people from their sins." This means that if the Child is successful in His mission, His people will never be condemned for their sin. Or to put it another way: He had not come to make the salvation of His people possible but inevitable. To the extent that He fulfilled His mission, to that same extent His people would be saved. It was this reality that energized the early Apostles, for having witnessed His resurrection, they knew that He had, indeed, accomplished His mission. This, in turn, meant that a host of people beyond number were marked for eternal life. Armed with the power of this truth, they boldly proclaimed the Gospel as the means by which the elect would be summoned to God through faith in His Messiah, Yeshua.

Finally, the statement promising salvation from sin emphasizes that there is future reckoning in regard to sin. The modern notion that if there is a Divine Being, He is far to benevolent to punish sinners for their transgressions against Him and against their fellowman, is false. The God of the universe is a three-times-holy God (Is 6:3), and His justice and righteousness demand that the debt of sin be paid. There is a judgment coming. Moreover, in our post-modern world, the idea that there exist eternal and universal standards of righteousness and unrighteousness has been overturned in favor of relativism. Of course, if such were the case, there is no need for salvation from sin, since sin can only be defined by each individual. As each individual defines for himself or herself what constitutes sin, it is also within the ability of each one to overcome such "sin" and establish one's own righteousness (since this too is self-defined). In reality, this single statement summarizing the mission of the Child destroys such notions, for He came to save His people from their sins, meaning that sin has a Divine definition, and that all who bear their own sins face Divine condemnation.

22–23 Now all this took place to fulfill what was spoken by the Lord through the prophet: "Behold, the virgin shall be with child and shall bear a Son, and they shall call His name Immanuel," which translated means, "God with us."

The Divine revelation to Joseph regarding the Child Mary would bear is understood by Matthew to be in harmony with the prophetic promise of the Messiah. By using the phrase "all this took place," Matthew emphasizes the overarching Divine providence by which all of the events were set into place to bring about the incarnation of our Master. Moreover, the words of the prophet are in reality the words of the Lord Himself, spoken by Him. The prophet is but the mouthpiece of the Almighty.

The quote is from Is 7:14–

MT	Lxx	Matthew
הִנֵּה הָעַלְמָה הָרָה וְיֹלֶדֶת בֵּן וְקָרָאת שְׁמוֹ עִמָּנוּ אֵל	ἰδοὺ ἡ παρθένος ἐν γαστρὶ ἕξει καὶ τέξεται υἱόν καὶ καλέσεις τὸ ὄνομα αὐτοῦ Εμμανουηλ	ἰδοὺ ἡ παρθένος ἐν γαστρὶ ἕξει καὶ τέξεται υἱόν καὶ καλέσουσιν τὸ ὄνομα αὐτοῦ Ἐμμανουήλ
Behold, the virgin will conceive and bear a son and you will call his name "with us God."	Behold, the virgin will conceive and bear a son and you will call his name Emmanuel.	Behold, the virgin will conceive and bear a son and they will call his name Emmanuel.

It is obvious that Matthew has quoted the Lxx verbatim, with the exception that he has changed the 2nd person singular καλέσεις, "you will call" to the 3rd person plural καλέσουσιν, "they will call." But we should note that this variant is found in the Lxx texts as well, A (Alexandrinus) and B (Vaticanus) having καλέσεις, א (Sinaiticus) having καλέσει, and Γ (rescriptus Cryptoferratensis) possibly reading καλέσουσιν (though this may be an attraction to Matthew). If Matthew had a purpose for changing the verb to the plural, it may envision that more than just Joseph would call His name Yeshua, pointing to the many who would find life "in His name" (cf. Jn 20:31).

The use of Is 7:14 as a messianic text finds no clear parallels in the early rabbinic literature, and for this reason some have surmised that Matthew's use of it, as well as his emphasis upon the virgin birth, is to be traced to Hellenistic influences. It is true that pagan myths contained stories of mortal women conceiving children by the gods. Perseus, whose mother Danae was beloved by Zeus, was conceived by means of a rain of gold which descended upon her in her seclusion. Another example is Hercules, who also was the child of Zeus and a mortal woman. Other similar stories abound (see J. G. Machen, *The Virgin Birth of Christ* [Harper & Row, 1930], pp. 325f). But the most obvious telling against such a theory is that Matthew was Jewish, and could hardly have been compelled to adopt the pagan myths of idolaters as the foundation for his own story of Yeshua's birth. Moreover, the notion that the virgin birth, including the present pericope under study, was inserted by the later Christian Church into the Gospel accounts has no textual support whatsoever. As noted in the introduction, the Gospel of Matthew is known and quoted by the early 2nd Century, well before the Christological controversies of the later centuries. And the earliest manuscripts we have of Matthew show no history of significant variants that would bring the teaching of the virgin birth into question. Nor do the early versions, such as the Syriac. The fact remains that from the earliest days of Yeshua, His followers carried the story, most likely related from Mary and Joseph themselves, of His miraculous birth.

Much discussion has ensued among the commentators, both ancient and modern, over the meaning of הָעַלְמָה, *ha'almah* in Is 7:14. The word itself means "young woman," and does not necessarily denote virginity. Another Hebrew noun, בְּתוּלָה, *b'tulah* may have the meaning "virgin," (e.g., Gen 24:16; Ex 22:15; Lev 21:3,14; Judg 21:12; 2Sam 13:2, etc.) but in some cases the word may simply mean an unmarried woman without clear reference to virginity (e.g., Joel 1:8). The fact that in some cases the Hebrew text adds a descriptive phrase (such as "an no man had relations with her," Gen 24:16) might indicate that the word *b'tulah* was not of itself sufficient to describe virginity.

The Lxx of Is 7:14 utilized the Greek παρθένος (*parthenos*) to translate *'almah,* a Greek term that is most often descriptive of someone who has not yet had sexual relations. Some have suggested that *parthenos*, like *b'tulah*, only denotes "not married" without clearly suggesting virginity, but a study of the word offers a different conclusion.[1] In each place where the Lxx uses the term, the context would favor the meaning "unmarried," and perhaps a "virgin."

It may well be that the Lxx translators chose the word *parthenos* for *'almah* because the primary force of the Hebrew word is "an unmarried woman," and this is also the primary meaning of *parthenos.* For instance, Rebecca is called a *parthenos* throughout Gen 24 (and *'almah* is used in 24:43) and the context would seem to indicate clearly that she was a virgin. Isaiah's use of *'almah*, meaning "unmarried," presents a message with an obvious question: if an unmarried woman is to bring forth a son, will this child be legitimate or illegitimate? If the child were illegitimate, how would this function as a sign to Israel? Rather, the force of the prophet's words may be found in the seeming paradox that an unmarried woman would bear a son, and yet this son would be known as legitimate, not born of fornication.

This understanding of Isaiah's message fits perfectly with the message of Matthew and the situation in which Mary and Joseph found themselves. Though from a purely social perspective, Mary may have been viewed as engaging in adultery against her betrothed, for those who had received the message of God's revelation, the child she was carrying was God's appointed servant to accomplish His will. We must maintain, then, that while the virgin birth was not something anticipated in the rabbinic literature (though since we have only late representations of the Sages teachings, there is al-

[1] Lachs, in his *Rabbinic Commentary on the New Testament,* p. 7 writes: "The Lxx even uses *parthenos* for one who is not a virgin, cf. Gen 34:3." But this text describes Dinah, who had been raped by Shechem, and his describing her as a *parthenos* (in the Lxx) must be understood within the narrative. He was not about to admit his having raped her because he was asking his father, Hamor, to obtain Dinah as a legitimate wife. Thus he describes her as a "young girl" (הַיַּלְדָּה) which the Lxx translates with *parthenos.*

ways the possibility that it was expunged through an anti-Christian bias in the later years), it is anticipated (though only through suggestion) in the Tanach, and became clear when the appointed time for Yeshua's arrival dawned (cf. Gal 4:4).

In the end, we cannot base our acceptance of the virgin birth upon evidence from history. The miraculous birth of Yeshua comes to us from the pages of the Matthew and Luke, founded upon their understanding of the prophetic anticipation of the Messiah in the Tanach. We believe it to be true because we believe Matthew and Luke to be true. And it is not surprising that the mystery of the incarnation, at its very heart, can be received only by faith, based upon the words of Yeshua's trusted Apostles. For the very center of our faith is likewise without human explanation, namely, that God would send His son to redeem sinners.

How, then, does Matthew utilize Is 7:14 as indicating a prophecy fulfilled in the birth of Yeshua? He does so in the manner of midrashic haggadah, that is, in drawing obvious parallels from the prophetic message of Isaiah, parallels that also incorporate the telescoping nature of prophecy itself. The prophecies of Isaiah, contained in chapters seven through nine, incorporate the motif of children. Isaiah's own children are prophetic portends (Is 7:3; 8:3), and the birth of children (7:14; 9:6) mark the manner in which God will save and restore His people Israel. For the nation of Isaiah's day, the birth of his own children, and their names, were to be signs to the nations of God's plans for their deliverance. The name of Isaiah's son in 7:3 is שְׁאָר יָשׁוּב, "the remnant will return." The son born in chapter eight is given as an illustration of how short a time would elapse before Israel's enemies would be overcome. Before the lad would be old enough to call out for his father or mother, Assyria would plunder Damascus and Samaria (8:4). Thus, the births of the prophet's own children were to remind the people that God was with them, and that He would secure their deliverance.

This general motif is then telescoped to the distant future in the prophecy of Isaiah nine. If the current military struggles against Israel were of grave concern, how much more was there a need to see Israel's ultimate redemption? Rezin and Pekah (7:1), the enemies of Israel, were nothing more than smoldering firebrands about to be exstinguished (7:4). But how would Israel obtain her final shalom? Would she constantly be overcome by this king or that nation, always fearing for her very existence? The current struggle brought into sharper focus the promise God had made to bless her. Where were these blessings? How could God's chosen nation obtain final and lasting peace? It is to this question that the prophet's words telescope, for they look to the conclusion of the story through the lenses of the current struggle. In the same way that God had provided for the temporal deliverance from the foreign powers, so He would ultimately send His Redeemer Who would establish eternal salvation and shalom (9:6). Even as the children of Isaiah were reminders of God's presence with His people, so the coming Redeemer would be Immanuel. It is no wonder then, given this overall perspective of Isaiah's message, that Matthew and others would see its application to Yeshua.

The name given to this Redeemer in Is 7:14 is עִמָּנוּ אֵל, *'immanu el,* "God (is) with us." Indeed, throughout the Tanach, the presence of God with His people assures them of His protection and salvation (Gen 26:24; Deut 31:8; 1Chron 28:20; 2Chron 20:17; Is 41:10; 43:5; Jer 46:28). It may even be that the Sacred Name itself bears this emphasis, for in its original giving (Ex 3:14), it is אֶהְיֶה, *'eh^ey^eh*, "I will be." If we look for this same form in the Exodus narrative, we find it three times in close proximity to the revelation of God's Name in Ex 3:14, and always in connection with God's presence:

> Ex. 3:12 And He said, "Certainly I will be (אֶהְיֶה) with you, and this shall be the sign to you that it is I who have sent you: when you have brought the people out of Egypt, you shall worship God at this mountain."
>
> Ex. 4:12 "Now then go, and I, even I, will be (אָנֹכִי אֶהְיֶה) with your mouth, and teach you what you are to say."
>
> Ex. 4:15 "You are to speak to him and put the words in his mouth; and I, even I, will be (אָנֹכִי אֶהְיֶה) with your mouth and his mouth, and I will teach you what you are to do.

It may well be, then, that "I will be" is a shortened form of "I will be with you," the very meaning of Immanuel.

Thus, when Isaiah speaks of the Child given as a sign, he notes that He would be called "Immanuel." Not that He would bear this as His common name, but that in His very coming He would bear the essence of God's Name, that is, the very presence of the Almighty by which the salvation of His people is made inevitable.

This is why the fact that the name given to the son of Joseph and Mary, Yeshua, is not in contradiction to the name Immanuel, for the very meaning of "God with us" is that of salvation. In that Yeshua came "to save His people from their sins," He also proved to be Immanuel.

In quoting Is 7:14, Matthew adds an explanation of the Hebrew term Immanuel: "which translated means, God is with us." He orders the Greek to reflect the Hebrew: μεθ᾽ ἡμῶν ὁ θεός, "with us (is) God." This corresponds to עִמָּנוּ אֵל, by putting the pronoun first. The miracle, indeed, is that God should dwell with His people. But it is even more profound when the emphasis is put upon "with us." That God could dwell with holy people is at least feasible, but that He should dwell "with us," those who have rebelled against Him, and rejected His kingship—this is all the a mystery.

Why would Matthew have added the translated explanation? Even the Shem Tov Matthew includes it as does the Syriac (though the Du Tillet and Münster do not). One hardly thinks that a Hebrew audience would need such an explanation. But this may highlight the fact that the Jewish community of Matthew's day had undergone heavy hellenization, and for many, Hebrew was not their mother-tongue. Matthew is intent on making sure that his readers understand the import of Immanuel, and so he gives the translated meaning.

24 –25 And Joseph awoke from his sleep and did as the angel of the Lord commanded him, and took Mary as his wife, but kept her a virgin until she gave birth to a Son; and he called His name Yeshua.

This concluding notice is crafted after similar concluding statements in the narrative portions of the Tanach, which have 1) a verb of action, 2) notice that the action was in accordance with God's command, and 3) subsequent results. For instance, in Ex 7:10, Moses and Aaron 1) come to Pharaoh, 2) just as the Lord commanded, 3) and perform the signs (the staff becomes a snake) before him. In our text, Joseph 1) awakens, 2) does what the Lord commanded him to do, and 3) does not have relations with Mary until Yeshua is born. This "pattern of obedience" would have been familiar to any who had knowledge of Torah, particularly the book of Exodus, in which we find that each part of the Tabernacle was constructed "just as the Lord had commanded Moses." In utilizing this well-known form, Matthew is emphasizing Joseph's full obedience to the revelation he had received from God in the dream. Once again, Joseph is portrayed as a righteous man—his every action is in accordance with God's will, and this is done to highlight the fact that the child Mary was carrying was not the result of fornication.

The angel of the Lord (cf. 1:20) functions here as in the Tanach, as the messenger from God who comes with divine authority.[1] Thus, the angel of the Lord gives the command to Joseph regarding Mary, but it is understood as God's command. In fact, the angel of the Lord often takes on divine attributes in the Tanach. This may be seen in the *Akedah* (Gen 22) as well as in the revelation to Manoah (Judges 13). When Manoah asks the angel of the Lord to reveal His name, He responds, "Why do you ask my name, seeing it is wonderful?" (v. 18). Here, the use of "wonderful" (פֶּלְאִי, *phel'i*) denotes divine attributes, for the root פלא regularly denotes the miraculous.[2] In the same way, the angel of the Lord directs Joseph with divine authority.

and took Mary as his wife Normally, the betrothal period ended with a public ceremony in which the woman left the home of her father and came into the home of her husband. It was only after this ceremony that the marriage was consummated through physical union of the couple. This is why Matthew gives to us the added information that Joseph "kept her a virgin until she gave birth to a Son" (the Greek has καὶ οὐκ ἐγίνωσκεν αὐτὴν, *"and he did not know her,* which is the common Hebraic expression meaning "he did not have sexual relations with her"). Joseph no longer feared to take Mary as his wife (cf. 1:20), but the matter of a physical consummation of the marriage awaited the time following the birth of the child.

Some have suggested that the wording "and did not know her until she had birthed a son" negates the later doctrine of Mary's "perpetual virginity." But the Greek does not necessitate this. The use of ἕως (*eos*, "until") with a negative does not necessarily imply that there were marital relations later on. Still, had Matthew held to such a doctrine, he would have most likely used a less ambiguous statement, for the wording he uses would surely allow normal marital relations between Mary and Joseph following the birth of Yeshua. Likewise, Luke would have avoided the use of "first-born" (Lk 2:7) had he believed that Mary remained a virgin her entire life. It is clear from the record of the Gospels that Mary and Joseph did have children (cf. Matt 12:46; 13:55; John 7:5).[3]

and he called His name Yeshua This is a reiteration of v. 21 with only the second person ("you shall call…") changed to the third person ("he

[1] For further notes on the "angel of the Lord," see my *Messiah in the Tanach* (TorahResource, 2004), pp. 36–49.

[2] For instances of the use of פלא in connection with divine miracles, cf. Gen 18:14; Ex 3:20; 34:10; Deut 28:59; Josh 3:5; Job 5:9; 9:10; Ps 9:1; 26:7; 31:21; 71:17; 78:11; Is 28:29; 29:14; Jer 32:17,27; Mic 7:15.

[3] The earliest indication of the belief in Mary's perpetual virginity is found in *The Protevangelium of James* 19:3–20:2, a 2nd Century work.

called…"). Once again, the obedience of Joseph to the divine directive is highlighted.

Throughout this first chapter of Matthew, the overarching theme is that of promise and fulfillment. The promise revealed by God through His prophets was that One should come Who would bring salvation. He would come through the power of the Almighty, by above-human means, and He would "save His people from their sins." That the chapter ends with the simple yet profound notice, "and he called His name Yeshua," emphasizes that what had been promised was now realized in the birth of the Messiah.

Chapter Two
Commentary

Chapter one has focused on the identity of the Child ("who He is"), showing His connection to the royal line of David, and describing Him as the One promised by the prophets to bring salvation to His people. Chapter two, however, takes an interesting turn, for it describes the manner in which the King, Yeshua, would be received ("what He is"). Foreigners (the magi) come to give Him honor (vv. 1–12), while Herod seeks to take His life (vv. 13–23). From the very beginning of Matthew's story, we are confronted with the fulcrum of God's love—the person of Yeshua. Those who reject Him are left to their own demise, but those who receive Him as King, are granted entrance into His kingdom. Moreover, we are introduced to an undercurrent of Matthew's story—the ingathering of the Gentiles. Here, the first to honor Yeshua are foreigners, and at the end of Matthew's Gospel, the injunction to make disciples of the nations forms the final commission of the Master. While the primary focus of Yeshua's ministry will be "to the lost sheep of Israel" (10:6; 15:24), the fuller picture of the ingathering of the nations is consistently heard as a counter melody to the main theme.

1   Now after Yeshua was born in Bethlehem of Judea in the days of Herod the king, behold, magi from the east arrived in Jerusalem, saying,

Now after Yeshua was born The paragraph in the Greek begins with a genitive absolute[1] in the form of an aorist participle. This gives the reader notice that the events about to be described took place subsequent to the birth, with the context specifying the time-frame more precisely. That the magi enter the house (οἰκία, *oikia*) of Mary and Joseph (v. 11), makes it clear that they had taken up residence in Bethlehem, casting the narrative in a time well after the birth of Yeshua. That the magi visited the stable where Yeshua was born is the mistaken notion of later Christian tradition surrounding the celebration of Christmas.[2]

in Bethlehem of Judea Bethlehem (בֵּית–לֶחֶם), located about five or six miles south-southeast of Jerusalem, continues to link Yeshua with the lineage of David (cf. Lk 2:4; Jn 7:42), for it was David's home town and where he was anointed king of Israel (1Sam 16:1-13, cf. 17:12, 15, 58; 20:6, 28). Bethlehem was the place of Rachel's burial (Gen 35:19) as well as the city in which the story of Ruth is set (Ruth 1:19). Perhaps Matthew adds "of Judea" to distinguish the southern Bethlehem from its northern counterpart in the region of Zebulun, located seven miles northwest of Nazareth (cf. Josh 19:15). An Arab village at this location retained the name *Beit-lachm*.

Rabbinic sources contain some indication that Bethlehem was known as the place of the Messiah's appearance, though in this regard such few references may indicate a later desire to distance the tradition from the Christian use. In Mid. Rab. *Lam* 1.51 we read about the "shoot" of Zech 6:12, understood as a messianic symbol by the Sages.

> R. Judan said in the name of R. Aibu: His name is 'Comforter'; as it is said, THE COMFORTER IS FAR FROM ME. R. Hanina said: They

[1] On the syntax of the genitive aboslute, see Blass-Debrunner, *Greek Grammar*, §423 (p. 218).

[2] Christian tradition gave names to each of the magi, which they numbered as three (see Bruce Metzger, "Names for the Nameless," *NTS*, NTTS 10 (1980), pp. 23–43). The supposed relics of the magi are housed in the Cologne Cathedral (cf. Allison-Davies, p. 231, n. 17).

do not really differ, because the numerical value of the names is the same, so that ' Comforter ' is identical with ' Shoot '.

The following story supports what R. Judan said in the name of R. Aibu: It happened that a man was ploughing, when one of his oxen lowed. An Arab passed by and asked, 'What are you?' He answered, 'I am a Jew.' He said to him, 'Unharness your ox and untie your plough' [as a mark of mourning]. ' Why? ' he asked. ' Because the Temple of the Jews is destroyed.' He inquired, 'From where do you know this?' He answered, 'I know it from the lowing of your ox.' While he was conversing with him, the ox lowed again. The Arab said to him, 'Harness your ox and tie up your plough, because the deliverer of the Jews is born.' 'What is his name?' he asked; and he answered, 'His name is "Comforter".' 'What is his father's name?' He answered, ' Hezekiah.' ' Where do they live? ' He answered, 'In Birath 'Arba,[1] in Bethlehem of Judah.'

Likewise, the Targum to Mic 5:2[1] reads:

And you, O Bethlehem Ephrata, you who were too small to be numbered among the thousands of the house of Judah, from you shall come forth before Me the Messiah, to exercise dominion over Israel, he whose name was mentioned from before, from the days of eternity.

On the basis of Jn 7:27, ""However, we know where this man (Yeshua) is from; but whenever the Messiah may come, no one knows where He is from," some modern scholars have suggested that a tradition that the Messiah would be born in Bethlehem was a later Christian addition. But the words of Yeshua's detractors in this text most likely reflect the idea that the Messiah was from eternity. That Yeshua, a "local fellow," would claim to be the Messiah seemed out of sync with their idea of the eternal status of the promised redeemer.

in the days of Herod the king   Twice Matthew refers to Herod as king (cf. v. 3), contrasting him with the "King of Jews" about whom the magi inquire. Herod, the son of Antipater (murdered in 42 BCE), was born in the late 70's BCE, and ruled the Jewish regions of Israel from 37–4 BCE. He was officially granted the title "king of Judah" in 40 BCE by Antony and Octavius. According to Josephus (*Ant.* 14–18) from whom we glean the majority of evidence for this period, Herod died shortly before Pesach in 4 BCE. This being the case, most scholars put the birth of Yeshua between 7 and 4 BCE.[2] Josephus also mentions an eclipse of the moon shortly after Herod's death (*Ant.* 17.167), which has been calculated to have happened March 12-13, 4 BCE. Ernest L. Martin (*The Birth of Christ Recalculated* [FBR, 1978]), however, has given evidence that the eclipse occurred January 10, 1 BCE, and he proposes a date for Yeshua's birth of September, 2 BCE. The difficulty presented by the fact that Josephus gives 37 years of Herod's reign (34 years from the time of his effective reign) is countered by Martin by suggesting that Herod's successors antedated their reigns to 4 BCE, but this may not be convincing.[3] While a good deal of debate continues over the year of Yeshua's birth, there is no good reason to discount Matthew's notice that it was during the reign of Herod the Great. At the end of Herod's reign, he fell into physical and mental anguish, and history substantiates his penchant for executing people at will. His own final demise may be linked to his having executed his own wife, Miriamme.[4]

[1] In *y.Ber* 5a the reading is "in the royal capital of Bethlehem."

Targum Pseu-Jon. on Gen 35.21 has וּנטל יעקב ופרס למשכניה מן להלא למוגדלא דעדר אתרא דהתמן עתיד ד{א}יתגלי מלכא משיחא בסוף יומייא, "Then Jacob traveled and pitched his tent further on toward the tower of Eder, the place where King Messiah would be revealed in the end of days."

[2] The discrepancy with the numbering of years, putting Yeshua's birth BCE, results from an error of the 6th Cent. scholar Dionysius Exiguus, who moved the Western world away from dating according to the year after the foundation of Rome.

[3] For a critique of Martin's proposals, see Carson, *Matthew*, p. 84.

[4] For a good summary of the life and reign of Herod the Great, see L. Levine's article in *The Anchor Bible Dictionary*, "Herod the Great."

It seems likely that Matthew's notice, that Yeshua was born in the days of Herod the king, have more than chronology in mind. The parallels to the Exodus story, in which Pharaoh attempted to put to death all male children (Ex 1:15f), are obvious. Midrash Rabbah *Exodus* 1.18 gives even closer parallels. There, the reason provided for Pharoah's genocidal decree, is that his astrologers had informed him that the mother of Israel's future deliverer was already pregnant with him. Moreover, the midrash notes that Moses was born amid great light:

> AND HIS SISTER STOOD AFAR OFF (II. 4). Why did Miriam stand afar off? R. Amram in the name of Rab said: Because Miriam prophesied, ' My mother is destined to give birth to a son who will save Israel'; and when the house was flooded with light at the birth of Moses, her father arose and kissed her head and said: 'My daughter, thy prophecy has been fulfilled.' This is the meaning of: And Miriam the prophetess, the sister of Aaron, took a timbrel (Ex. XV, 20) [Mid. Rab. *Ex* 1.22].

Though this midrash is admittedly late, it may well reflect an earlier tradition, and may have given Matthew his link to the decree of Herod. If this were the case, then Matthew is clearly using the redemption motif of the Exodus as a fitting portend of the birth of the final Redeemer. Even as Moses was born to lead Israel out from her slavery, so the Messiah came to "save His people from their sins."

behold, magi from the east arrived in Jerusalem   The NASB leaves out the word "behold," as do the NIV and NRSV, no doubt because they understood the particle as that which simply introduces a story (cf. ἰδού in *BDAG*). It doubtlessly function here in this capacity, but it also is given to heighten the awareness of the reader that something extra-ordinary is about to be seen.

The Greek term μαγός (*magos*) usually refers to a "wise man or priest, who was an expert in astrology." The word always connotes some connection to magic or sorcery. The Du Tillet and Münster have מכשפים ("sorcerors") while the Shem Tov has חוזים בכוכבים ("star gazers," "astrologers"). The Peshitta has the more common מְגוּשֵׁא (*megushei'*) which corresponds to the common term for magicians/sorcerors in the rabbinic literature, אַמְגּוֹשָׁא (*'amgosha'*, e.g. b.*Yoma* 35a, b.*Chullin* 62b, b.*Sanh* 98a). Often, *magos* is connected to the priestly class of astrologers connected with Zoroastrians of the Medes and Persians who were known for their ability to interpret dreams, but in later years became a common term for all who engage in astrology, sorcery, and soothsaying.

It is not clear from which region the magi came. "From the east" might include Arabia, Babylon, or Persia. If they came from Babylon, did the magi have an ancient tradition based upon Daniel's visions? One can not be certain, but the idea is intriguing. Regardless, Matthew gives us the sense that even the pagan idolaters of the Gentile nations recognize the importance of this Child, and come to pay Him homage. This may also be an early indictment by Matthew upon the many Israelites of his day, who, though having known of the prophesies concerning the Messiah, still rejected Yeshua. Like the story of Jonah, in which the pagan sailors give worship to the God of Israel from Whom the prophet was fleeing, so here the magi, who represent the populations of the nations enslaved by the darkness of the evil one, come to the One Who is the true light, even though He is rejected by His own kindred.

2 "Where is He who has been born King of the Jews? For we saw His star in the east and have come to worship Him."

These are the only words the magi speak. Their opening query regarding "where" the Promised One was, is taken up by Matthew in this chapter. To the question "where was He born," Matthew appeals to Micah 5.2—"in Bethlehem." As to where He went after His birth, Matthew quotes Hosea 11.1, "out of Egypt I have called My son." And regarding where He lives, Matthew responds with "Nazareth," and "He shall be called a Nazarene."

The grammar of the opening phrase makes it clear that the meaning is not, "Where is He who had been born, King of the Jews?" but that this One is the new-born King. He has come for the purpose of reigning as King. The title "King of the Jews," found often in the Gospels (Matt 2:2; 27:11, 29, 37; Mark 15:2, 9, 12, 18 ,26; Luke 23:3, 37-38; John 18:33, 39; 19:3, 19, 21), is only uttered by Gentiles. Jews use the phrase "King of Israel" (Matt 27:42; Mark 15:32; John 1:49; 12:13).

How was it that the magi referred to Yeshua by this title? Apart from the possibility (if they were from Babylon) that a tradition based upon Daniel's prophecy was known to them, it may have been that the astrological phenomenon they had observed was of such a magnitude as to be applicable only to the appearance of royalty. This was not uncommon in the ancient world.[1] For example, Tacitus (*Ann.* 14.22) remarks that "the general belief is that a comet means a change of emperor," so much so that "when a brilliant comet now appeared…people speculated on Nero's successor as though Nero were already dethroned." Even the Sages remark that "every righteous man has his star and it shines according to the brightness of his deeds" (*Mid. Ps.* on 148:3).

[1]See the examples given by Allison-Davies, 1.233–34.

There is little doubt that the prophecy of Balaam (Num 24:17) informed the Jewish perspective that a star would accompany the appearance of Messiah: "A star will come forth out of Jacob, and a scepter will rise out of Israel." Both Onkelos and Ps. Jonathan understand this text as referring to Messiah, as do the midrashim (Mid. Rab. *Ex* 30.24; Mid. Rab. *Lam* 2.4). Likewise, the Qumran society interpreted Num 24:17 as a prophecy of the levitical Messiah (CD 7.18–26, cf. 4QTestimonia; 1QM 11.6). Finally, the fact that Akiva attributed this prophecy to Bar Kosiva, changing his name to Bar Kokhba ("son of the star") in order to proclaim him "messiah," witnesses to its early and strong messianic interpretation.

This being the case, one might wonder why Matthew did not incorporate it into his story, especially since he alone of the Gospel writers gives us the notice of the magi and the star they had seen. The answer must be that at this point in Matthew's narrative, he is focusing on geographical information (each of the quotes from the Tanach include a place name), something Num 24:17 does not have. He will spend the remainder of his efforts in the Gospel account to show that Yeshua fulfills the "star/scepter" prophecy.

Various suggestions have been given as to what star the magi may have seen. Jupiter (the "star of kingship") and Saturn (the "star of the Jews, Tacitus, *Hist* 5.4) were in conjunction three times in 7 BCE. A comet appeared in 5 BCE.[2] The fact that the magi refer to the star as being "in the east" may also be understood to mean "rising." The Greek word ἀνατολή (*anatole*) has a technical use in astronomy, meaning "at its rising. This is confirmed by the fact that points of the compass in Greek never take the article, which is found

[2]See Colin Humphreys, "The Star of Bethlehem," *Science and Christian Belief* 5.2 (1993), 83–101. For further ideas on the star, see Robert S. McIvor, "The Star of Messiah," *Irish Biblical Studies* 24 (2002), 175–183.

here. We can only speculate the possibility that Matthew has the rising star of Num 24 in mind by using this language. According to Matthew's further account, the star "went on before them until it came and stood over the place where the Child was" (v. 9). Whatever the star was, then, it was the result of a divinely appointed sign, marking the appearance of the Promised One.

and have come to worship Him.   Here Matthew has the pagan magicians giving honor in worship to Yeshua. The language parallels the common Hebrew הִשְׁתַּחֲוָה, "to prostrate oneself" (e.g., Gen 18:2; 19:1). Matthew has no problem, from the very beginning of his Gospel, describing the manner in which people worship Yeshua. In fact, Matthew will use the same word 12 more times, and always in connection with proper worship, and especially the worship of the Messiah (2:8,11; 4:9-10; 8:2; 9:18; 14:33; 15:25; 18:26; 20:20; 28:9, 17). Thus, for Matthew, worshipping Immanuel is the proper response of those who meet Him.

Prostrating oneself before a king or dignitary was common practice in the ancient Near East, and thus one could understand this phrase as "and they paid homage to Him." Yet, as noted above, Matthew regularly uses the Greek verb προσκυνέω (*proskuneo*) of worship, and it seems fitting to give the word this same sense here. As such, the magi portray in a figurative sense the manner in which the nations, eventually, will all bow to worship the Messiah.

> so that at the name of Yeshua every knee will bow, of those who are in heaven and on earth and under the earth, and that every tongue will confess that Yeshua Messiah is Lord, to the glory of God the Father (Phil 2:10–11).

3 When Herod the king heard this, he was troubled, and all Jerusalem with him.

We may note similar language in 2Sam 4:1,

> Now when Ish-bosheth, Saul's son, heard that Abner had died in Hebron, he lost courage, and all Israel was disturbed.

Herod's reign was tenuous from the beginning. His political office was constantly being challenged. It was primarily his strong loyalties to Rome, and his own cunning, that allowed him to remain in power as long as he did. Granted, he was known for his wide and grandiose building projects, chief among which was the expansion of the Jerusalem Temple, and this gave him favor with the people. Yet his unstable character (especially toward the end of his reign) left him vulnerable to his enemies, both external and particularly internal. The fact that "all Jerusalem" was also troubled reflects the historical fact that the Jewish leaders did all in their power to prevent uprisings of the people, since history had proven that acts of insurrection were almost always met with sudden and wide disaster. The notion that one had arisen who would declare Himself "King of the Jews" suggested the undercurrent of revolt, and the Jewish leaders would have taken such a notice very seriously. Moreover, the fact that foreigners were coming with such knowledge would have been unnerving. We should understand "Jerusalem" in this context to stand for the leaders of the Jewish community (and perhaps the Sadducean priesthood) and not as a metonymy for the Jewish people as a whole.

4 Gathering together all the chief priests and scribes of the people, he inquired of them where the Messiah was to be born.

The "chief priests and scribes" were two separate classes of leaders, though Matthew and Luke have them together in several places (Matt 16:21; 20:18; Luke 9:22; 22:66). More often, Matthew combines the scribes with the Pharisees (5:20; 12:38; 23:13-15, 23, 25, 27, 29). The chief priests (ἀρχιερεύς, *arxiereus*) comprised more than merely the high priests, present and past. They comprised an established college which included the current high priest and his predecessors, the captain of the temple, the heads of the weekly courses, the directors of the daily courses, the temple overseers, and the temple treasurers.[1] Scribes, on the other hand, were the teachers of the Torah (later referred to as "sages," כחמים), the lawyers who interpreted the legal aspects of the Torah, and administered justice (all functions that at one period in Israel's history belonged to the priesthood). The Scribes functioned as an independent body of leaders, but always in connection with either the Sadducees or Pharisees.

That Herod would have had ready access to the "chief priests and scribes" is obvious, since history records that he had taken it upon himself to appoint several of the high priests (Josephus, *Ant.* 15.22–41, 319–22). Thus, Herod held plenty of political clout in connection with the temple leadership, and it was only natural that he would seek information from them. Some have suggested that Herod gathered the Sanhedrin, but this is unlikely, since his relationship with the Sanhedrin was tenuous. When Herod came to power, one of his first actions was to execute the standing Sanhedrin (Josephus, *Ant.* 14.175, cf. b.*BavaBatra* 3b).

Herod's question was quite simple. He wanted to know, according to Jewish tradition, where the Messiah (χριστός, *xristos*) would be born. But as one would expect, his motives for gaining the information were nefarious.

5–6 They said to him, "In Bethlehem of Judea; for this is what has been written by the prophet: 'And you, Bethlehem, land of Judah, are by no means least among the leaders of Judah; For out of you shall come forth a Ruler Who will shepherd My people Israel.'"

The question of Herod is answered by the group rather than by a designated spokesman, indicating that they had formulated their answer after discussing it together. No doubt they wanted to be careful in how they answered since political intrigue was the warp and woof of Herod's reign.

They base their answer upon the words of Micah 5:2, that the Messiah would be born in Bethlehem of Judea, the tribal allotment of Judah. The older notion that the Sadducees relied entirely upon the five books of Moses (the Torah) and gave no credence to the Prophets, has been shown to be in error. Here, both the chief priests and the scribes base their answer to Herod upon Micah, and show that they considered the Prophets to be included in the canon of their authoritative scriptures.

The quote is from Micah 5:2[1]:

[1] G. Shrenk, *TDNT*, 3.265–283.

MT	Lxx	Matthew
וְאַתָּה בֵּית־לֶחֶם אֶפְרָתָה צָעִיר לִהְיוֹת בְּאַלְפֵי יְהוּדָה מִמְּךָ לִי יֵצֵא לִהְיוֹת מוֹשֵׁל בְּיִשְׂרָאֵל וּמוֹצָאֹתָיו מִקֶּדֶם מִימֵי עוֹלָם But as for you, Bethlehem Ephrathah, too little to be among the clans of Judah, from you One will go forth for Me to be ruler in Israel. His goings forth are from long ago, from the days of eternity.	καὶ σὺ Βηθλεεμ οἶκος τοῦ Εφραθα ὀλιγοστὸς εἶ τοῦ εἶναι ἐν χιλιάσιν Ιουδα ἐκ σοῦ μοι ἐξελεύσεται τοῦ εἶναι εἰς ἄρχοντα ἐν τῷ Ισραηλ καὶ αἱ ἔξοδοι αὐτοῦ ἀπ' ἀρχῆς ἐξ ἡμερῶν αἰῶνος And you, Bethlehem, house of Ephratha, are few in number to be reckoned among the thousands of Judah; yet out of you shall one come forth to me, to be a ruler of Israel; and his goings forth were from the beginning, even from eternity.	καὶ σὺ Βηθλέεμ, γῆ Ἰούδα, οὐδαμῶς ἐλαχίστη εἶ ἐν τοῖς ἡγεμόσιν Ἰούδα· ἐκ σοῦ γὰρ ἐξελεύσεται ἡγούμενος, ὅστις ποιμανεῖ τὸν λαόν μου τὸν Ἰσραήλ. And you, Bethlehem, land of Judah, are by no means least among the leaders of Judah; For out of you shall come forth a Ruler Who will shepherd My people Israel.

It can be readily seen that Matthew's quote is neither directly from the MT nor from Lxx, which is, by-and-large, an accurate translation of the Hebrew. Some have suggested that Matthew, rather than quoting Mic 5:2, gives a rather free, interpretative midrash. Instead of "Ephrathah," which would have had little connection to Matthew's readers, he substitutes "land of Judah," which would have had direct bearing upon them, and further connects the Messiah to the tribe of Judah. Moreover, where the MT and Lxx emphasize Bethlehem's insignificance, Matthew says the opposite: "by no means least among the leaders of Judah." Most obvious is Matthew's complete reinterpretation of the final clause, which attributes to the Ruler a shepherding role over the people of Israel, while both the MT and Lxx emphasize the eternal (and thus authoritative and even divine) rule or reign of the prophesied One. It is possible that Matthew has combined a phrase from 2Sam 5:2 (=1Chron 11:2), where God addresses Saul through the prophet Samuel: "You will shepherd My people Israel, and you will be a ruler over Israel," or else he has paraphrased the Lxx of Mic 5:4, "And the Lord shall stand, and see, and feed his flock with power…."

But one wonders if this should be construed as Matthew's interpretive quotation (as most commentators take it), or whether the quote as he gives it reflects the manner in which the chief priests and scribes presented it to Herod. If it is their paraphrase, one could see a desire to soften the idea of "ruling" to leading like a shepherd, though admittedly, the role of a king in the ancient Near East was often compared to that of a shepherd. Moreover, if the chief priests and scribes were concerned that Herod be pleased and not distracted with their answer, they may have desired to cast Judah, the domain of his political power, as great rather than least among the clans of Israel. Regardless, the use of the quote in reference to the birth of the Messiah reflects the wider tradition among the Judaisms of the 1st Century, that connected the prophecy of Mic 5 to the coming Messiah (see above).

7 Then Herod secretly called the magi and determined from them the exact time the star appeared.

Herod has put together two pieces of information, one from the magi, that a star appeared as a portend of a change in rulership, and one from the chief priests and scribes, that the prophets had predicted a ruler for Israel who would be born in Bethlehem. But he wants to know the timing of the event, so he inquires of the magi "the exact time" the star appeared (began to shine, τοῦ φαινομένου ἀστέρος). There is no indication that the Jewish leaders are aware of the presence of the magi, nor that the magi know of Herod's inquiry of the chief priests and scribes. This all adds to the clandestine plot ("Herod secretly called the magi") being formulated against the Child.

Moreover, the "exact time" of the star's appearance is necessary because Herod has already determine to affect a mass slaughter of Jewish boys. He needs to know how wide to make his massacre (cf. 2:16). The fact that he eventually determines all males two years old and younger were to be destroyed would indicate that the initial appearance of the star had occurred some time earlier, but we cannot say that it was necessarily two years earlier. One would expect a mad-man like Herod to have cruelly chosen an excessively wide margin of time to assure that the Child was no longer a threat.

8 And he sent them to Bethlehem and said, "Go and search carefully for the Child; and when you have found Him, report to me, so that I too may come and worship Him."

A number of questions arise from this verse. First, is it possible that the magi were unaware of Herod's sinister reputation? Perhaps so, but it brings into question their ability to know secrets (the very occupation in which they were engaged). Secondly, why would Herod rely upon foreigners when he had a whole police force at his disposal? Perhaps the answer to this question lies in the fact that toward the end of Herod's reign, he was able to trust no one in his court. Had it become known that Herod was "running scared," it would have offered an opportune time for his enemies to seize the throne.

He tells the magi to "search carefully for the Child" (παιδίον, *paidion*, a diminutive form of παῖς, *pais*, and thus "young child") emphasizing the exigency of the matter, just as he had inquired about the "exact" time the star appeared. He further explains that when they have found the Child, they should inform him so that he too could "come and worship Him." This lets the reader know beyond doubt that the magi are not complicitous in the plot, but must be "tricked" in order to do Herod's bidding. Again, it seems strange that Herod would trust their ability to discern hidden things on the one hand, while thinking that they were unable to see through his scheme on the other. But the same power that corrupts also makes fools.

9 After hearing the king, they went their way; and behold the star, which they had seen in the east, went on before them until it came and stood over the place where the Child was.

"Hearing" may have its Semitic sense of "obey," so that they went on their way in obedience to Herod's instructions (though see Allison-Davies, p. 246).

The star seems to appear, disappear, and reappear. Apparently it appeared to magi while they were still "in the east," and now it reappears in order to guide them to the location of the Child. This is indicated by the use of "behold" (ἰδού, *idou*), which once again the NASB, NIV, and NRSV omit. The Greek does not require an interpretation such that the star hovered precisely over the house where Mary and Joseph lived. Rather, the star reappeared and directed the magi to Bethlehem (they were probably travelling at night, contrary to early Christian tradition), where they doubtlessly made discreet inquiry about the birth date of a boy that coincided with the original appearance of the star. Moreover, since according to Luke's account, the shepherds did not keep silent about the event they had witnessed (cf. Lk 2:18), it is reasonable to presume that the town as a whole was aware of the birth.

10 When they saw the star, they rejoiced exceedingly with great joy.

The star, which the magi had seen while still in their country, reappeared while they were in Jerusalem. There is nothing in the text to indicate that the star had originally led them to Jerusalem, so we should presume that they came to the capital city because they had interpreted the star as indicating the birth of a king. When they saw the star once again, they took it as a confirming sign of their original interpretation, and thus they rejoiced exceedingly (ἐχάρησαν χαρὰν μεγάλην σφόδρα, literally, *"they rejoiced with great joy exceedingly"*).[1] Apparently the star was in the direction of Bethlehem, offering them further direction as to where they might find this newly born king.[2]

Why does Matthew include this notice? We wonder why the magi would have had such joy at knowing that a king had been born in Israel, especially when we have just read that all of Jerusalem was troubled over the matter (v. 3). Whatever the case, we may once again note the sub-theme of Matthew in regard to the ingathering of the Gentiles to the worship of Israel's God. Here, Gentiles have come from a foreign nation, and express joy at the birth of the Messiah. Whatever the cause of rejoicing may have been for the magi themselves, in Matthew's retelling of the story, this highlights the fact that the birth of the Messiah signalled the time foretold by the prophets, when the nations would come to Israel's light, and offer worship to her God.

11 After coming into the house they saw the Child with Mary His mother; and they fell to the ground and worshiped Him. Then, opening their treasures, they presented to Him gifts of gold, frankincense, and myrrh.

The notice that they entered a house alerts us to the fact that Mary and Joseph had taken up residence in Bethlehem, something that would have been reasonable given the fact that infant mortality was high in the ancient world, and traveling long distances with a newborn would have been avoided if possible. It would also seem likely that Joseph had relatives living in Bethlehem, so remaining there would not have been difficult. There is no discrepancy with Luke's account (*contra* Allison-Davies, 1.248), in which he describes a stable as a temporary dwelling where Mary gave birth to Yeshua. Matthew fills out the picture by alerting us to the fact that after the birth, Joseph found more permanent housing in Bethlehem.

Having previously seen only the star, the magi now come to gaze upon the King they were seeking. The "Child" is listed before Mary, since He is

[1] The Shem Tov and Du Tillet have שמחו שמחה גדולה עד מאד. The Münster and Peshitta have שמחו שמחה גדול מאד.

[2] Josephus notes that a star appeared over Jerusalem, interpreted as a portend of the city's destruction: "Thus there was a star resembling a sword, which stood over the city, and a comet, that continued a whole year." (War 6.5.3)

the center of attention. Indeed, Mary is known primarily as His mother, and when the magi offer their worship and gifts, they do so only to Yeshua, not to Mary. Moreover, Joseph is not even mentioned, stressing the fact that Yeshua had no earthly father. We may also note the repeated use of the phrase "the child and *Mary* His mother" (with slight modifications) in 2:13, 14, 20, 21, where Joseph is not listed. In each case, "the Child" is listed first because this is Matthew's focus.[1]

and they fell down to ground and worshiped   The combination of "falling down" and "worshiping" is not uncommon, and is generally the meaning of the Hebrew verb חָוָה (*chavah*, always in the *hishtafel*, הִשְׁתַּחֲוָה). Commonly in the Tanach, the use of חָוָה is combined with a locative, such as "to the ground" (e.g., Gen. 18:2; 19:1; 24:52; 33:3; 37:10; 43:26; Ruth 2:10), indicating a prone position. Such a posture was not reserved only for worship in a religious sense, but could be used when giving honor to royalty, or to someone of high importance (1Sam 25:23, where Abigail lays prone before David; 2Ki 2:15, where the people bow to Elisha; Ruth 2:10, where Ruth is prostrate before Boaz). However, the early strata of rabbinic literature evidences that bowing in the presence of an idol was prohibited, indicating that bowing had become a recognized form of worship:

> All places which are called by names complimentary to idolatry does one rename with euphemisms insulting to idolatry .... He whose coins were scattered in the direction of an idol should not bend over before it to pick them up, because it looks as if he is bowing down to an idol. But he turns his back on the idol and collects the coins. (t.*AvodaZarah* 6.4)[2]

Even if Matthew is simply relating a social custom of the magi in prostrating oneself before royalty, it may well be, in light of the importance attached to bowing as an act of worship among the Jewish community, that he wishes to stress the legitimacy of worshiping the Messiah, something that in formative Judaism was proper only for God.

Having given honor through prostrating themselves before the Child, the magi open their treasures (θησαυρός, *thesauros*, probably some kind of box or chest which could be locked) to present Him gifts. Once again, as far as Matthew is concerned, their gifts are for the Child, not for His mother or father. The later Maryology of the Roman Catholic Church is entirely lacking from the biblical text.

gold, frankincense, and myrrh   The gifts listed (there may have been more) were all costly in the ancient world. Frankincense (λίβονον, *libonon*, a Semitic loan word, cp. לְבוֹנָה) is a fragrant gum resin from various trees used primarily in cultic worship in the ancient Near East, being difficult to obtain and thus quite expensive. It was also used by perfumers, as well as for medicinal purposes (as a pain killer, cf. b.*Sanhedrin*43a). It is doubtful that it was cultivated in Israel. We know that frankincense was imported from Arabia, where the trees from which it was collected grew in abundance (cf. Is 60:6; Jer 6:20). Frankincense was one of the ingredients in the incense of the Tabernacle and Temple (Ex 30:34-38), and was added to the Bread of Presence (Lev 24:7). It was also added to the grain offering (Lev 2:1–2, 14–16; 6:14–18).

Myrrh (σμύρνα, *smurna* = μύρρα, *murra*; Latin, *murra*; Heb מֹר, *mor*) is a fragrant gum resin from the *balsamodendron myrrh* or *commiphora kataf* trees which are particularly abundant in Arabia and north Ethiopia. It was used

[1] cp. the Lxx of Ex 4:20, τὴν γυναῖκα καὶ τὰ παιδία ("his wife and children"), which is the normal order.

[2] cp. also Philo, *Leg. Gaius* 116; *Decalogue* 64.

for perfumes, cultic ceremony, and as a burial spice. Myrrh was used in the holy anointing oil (Ex 30:23) of the Tabernacle and Temple services, and is repeatedly mentioned in Song of Songs (as is frankincense) as a component of incense or perfume (Song 1:13; 3:6; 4:6, 14; 5:1, 5, 13). Myrrh, like frankincense, was quite costly.

Commentators, both ancient and modern, have taken the three gifts as symbolic in one way or another. The early Church Fathers considered gold to be a symbol of Yeshua's kingship, frankincense as indicative of His divinity, and myrrh as a portend of His sacrificial death.[1] While such interpretations may be useful for homiletical midrashim, they hardly find support in the text itself. For instance, Matthew does not list myrrh in connection with Yeshua's death, but uses "gall" instead (27:34, cf. Ps 68:22 Lxx). And gold and frankincense would have been a well-expected gift for royalty, so they needed no further connection in Matthew's mind. As Carson notes regarding the common interpretation among the Church Fathers (and those who follow them):

> This interpretation demands too much insight from the Magi. The three gifts are simply expensive and not uncommon presents and may have helped finance the trip to Egypt.[2]

If we were to search for an extended meaning of the gifts in Matthew's perspective, we might consider the suggestion by some that the gifts themselves represent an eschatological anticipation of the ingathering of the nations.

> A better guess as to what the gifts mean is this: the magi's worship and presentation are the firstfruits of the eschatological pilgrimage of the nations and their submission to the one true God.[3]

Isaiah 60 and Psalm 72 both are texts that spoke to this end-time reality. In Is 60:5, the "wealth of the nations" comes to Israel, and v. 6 mentions frankincense and myrrh, while v. 9 lists silver and gold. In Psalm 72:9, the "nomads of the desert" bow before Israel's king, and v. 10 speaks of the kings of Tarshish, Sheba, and Seba, along with the remote nations, bring gifts to the king, and scene (v. 11) in which "all kings bow down before him, all nations serve him." The apocalyptic literature stresses this same scenario. Ps. Sol. 17.31 has the heathen nations coming to present gifts to the "Son of David," and Enoch (1Enoch 53.1) foresees the time when all those dwelling on the earth and sea and islands will bring to the Righteous and Elect One, the Son of Man, gifts and presents and tokens of homage. Likewise, the later rabbinic midrashim offer the same emphasis. Note the comments of Mid. Rab. *Gen* on Gen 49:10:

> UNTIL SHILO COME. This indicates that all the nations of the world will bring a gift to Messiah Son of David, as it says, *In that time shall a present be brought unto the Lord of hosts* (Is 18:7).

From the very beginning of Matthew's Gospel, Yeshua is set forward as the rightful heir to the Davidic throne, and the Messiah Who would redeem Israel and gather the nations to her as the prophets foretold. Moreover, the revelation of His arrival is not limited to Israel, but through the appearance of the star, is broadcast to the nations as well. The magi and their gifts, then, may well have been understood by Matthew as a symbolic representation of

[1] Irenaeus, *Adv. haer.* 3.9.2; Clement of Alexandria, *Paed.* 2.8.63f; Origen, *Contra Cels.* 1.60; Theodotus of Ancyra, *Hom.* 1.5 [references from Allison-Davies, 1.249].

[2] Carson, *Matthew* in *The Expositors Bible Commentary*, 12 vols. (Zondervan, 1984), 8.89.

[3] Allison-Davies, 1.249.

[1]The Greek word translated "warned," χρηματίζω, *xrematizo,* is used elsewhere only of divine revelation (Matt. 2:22; Luke 2:26; Acts 10:22; 11:26; Rom. 7:3; Heb. 8:5; 11:7; 12:25.

the dawning of the final days of redemption.

12 And having been warned[1] by God in a dream not to return to Herod, the magi left for their own country by another way.

This emphasis of Matthew's, that foreigners receive divine revelation in concert with the appearance of God's Messiah, is continued here. The Magi are specifically warned by God in a dream not to return to Herod with the information regarding the Child. And, once again, the foreigners are obedient to the divine revelation. They depart to their unknown country without traveling on the main roads which would have, most likely, taken them through Jerusalem.

The Flight to Egypt

The second section of Chapter Two deals with the flight to Egypt by Joseph, Mary, and Yeshua, in order to escape the persecution perpetrated by Herod. It divides neatly into three sections, each ending with a quote or allusion to a Tanach reference: 1) vv. 13–15, the warning in the dream and the flight to Egypt, Hos 11:1, 2) vv. 16–18, the slaughter of the innocent ones, Jer 31:15, and 3) vv. 19–23, the return to Israel and settling in Nazareth, with an allusion (perhaps) to Is 11:1.

For further linguistic parallels between Matthew's story and the exodus narrative, see Hagner, *Matthew,* 1.34.

The parallels of this section of Matthew to the story of the exodus seem apparent, and have been noted by commentators throughout the centuries.

Exodus Story	Matthew
The slaughter of male children	The slaughter of male children
Flight of Moses out of Egypt	Flight of Joseph, Mary, Yeshua out of the Land
Israel is delivered at night (Ex 12:29)	Joseph, Mary, and Yeshua flee to Egypt at night (Matt 2:14)
Moses returns after the death of Pharaoh	Joseph, Mary, & Yeshua return after the death of Herod
"for all those who have sought your life have died" (Ex 4:19)	"for those who sought the Child's life are dead" (Matt 2:20)

As the paradigm for redemption, the exodus is here brought forward by way of type and anti-type. The anti-type of Pharaoh is Herod, while Moses stands as a type of Messiah. Even as Moses mediated the covenant for Israel, and led her out of her bondage, so Yeshua would be the mediator for His people, and redeem them from the slavery of sin.

But it is not as though Matthew has contrived his story in order to conform it to the pattern of the exodus. The sources upon which he drew related the history of Yeshua's birth and early years, including the events that parallel the exodus. Matthew is simply telling his story in such a way as to highlight these parallels.

13 Now when they had gone, behold, an angel of the Lord appeared to Joseph in a dream and said, "Get up! Take the Child and His mother and flee to Egypt, and remain there until I tell you; for Herod is going to search for the Child to destroy Him."

Once again God communicates to Joseph via a dream. Matthew's use of "behold" (ἰδου, *idou*, cf. vv. 1, 9) signals a significant event in the unfolding of the story. He also casts the word "appeared" in the so-called "historical present," (φανέται, *phanetai*) bringing the reader into the scene as though it were now taking place: "Look (behold), an angel of the Lord appears in a dream." The divine providence, expressed in the dream given to the magi, is now at work in leading Joseph and his family away from the coming disaster. Like Abraham who was called to go from his family, and to wait upon God for further revelation, so Joseph was to go to Egypt, and to remain there until God instructs him to return. The path of obedience is also one of faith. The future of Joseph's family, and particularly of the Child, is dependent upon God's faithfulness to reveal His will.

In the Torah, decent to Egypt or connection to Egypt spells trouble. Abraham descends to Egypt because of famine, and puts Sarah in jeopardy (Gen 12); Hagar is an Egyptian; Isaac is commanded not to descend to Egypt (Gen 26:2); the Midianite traders to whom Joseph was sold were on their way to Egypt (Gen 37:25, 28); Joseph is enslaved in Egypt prior to his rise to power; ultimately, the nation of Israel is enslaved in Egypt as well. Thus, Egypt became a symbol of trouble and slavery.

In Matthew's story, however, Egypt is a place of protection away from the murderous decree of Herod. This may parallel the life of David in which he too retreated to the land of Israel's enemies to escape those seeking his life. In 1Sam 21:10f, David flees from Saul to the land of Achish, king of Gath, and feigning insanity, takes refuge there. In a similar fashion, the Son of David is taken to a foreign land in order to escape His enemies.

The rabbinic sources are aware of the "flight to Egypt," but most likely they have taken this from the Gospel sources. We therefore gain little historical value in their mention of this event. The purpose for including Yeshua's flight to Egypt, however, seems clear: wanting to portray Him as a magician whose powers were not from God and who led Israel astray, some notices in the rabbinic literature describe Yeshua's magical arts as having been learned in Egypt. For instance, in b.*Sanhedrin* 107b, the accusation against Yeshua is linked to the fact that His father, called Joshua ben Parahyah, had taken Him to Egypt. But Joshua ben Parahyah lived nearly two generations before the time of Yeshua, showing that this notice, like the others, were put forward as a polemic against Yeshua and His followers.[1]

But Matthew is clear in relating the facts of his sources: Joseph took Mary and Yeshua to Egypt on the basis of divine instructions, and remained there until God instructed him to return to the Land. The "flight to Egypt" is entirely the plan of God.

14 So Joseph got up and took the Child and His mother while it was still night, and left for Egypt.

Joseph's obedience is precise and immediate. He does not wait, but believing the revelation he has received, and knowing that Herod is intent on

[1] For other rabbinic references to the "flight to Egypt," see b.*Sota* 47a; Origen, *Contra Celsum* 1.28, 38, and the comments of Sachs, *A Rabbinic Commentary on the New Testament*, pp. 11–12.

harming Yeshua, he leaves at night. Like the Israelites of old who left Egypt at night (Ex 12:29), so Jacob and his family flee from Herod at night. But even more important is the notice, once again, that Joseph was entirely obedient to the divine word he had received. The earlier notice that Joseph was a righteous man (1:19) is confirmed in the story time and again.

Egypt fit the circumstances well. It was close, and a well established Roman province outside of Herod's jurisdiction. Moreover, it had a large Jewish population. According to Philo (*Flaccus* 43), a million Jews lived in Egypt.

15 He remained there until the death of Herod. This was to fulfill what had been spoken by the Lord through the prophet: "Out of Egypt I called My Son."

[1]Carson, *Matthew*, p. 91

The death of Herod brought relief to many. Carson[1] notes that following the death of Herod, the Qumran covenanters returned to rebuild their center which had been destroyed in 31 BCE. The death of Herod also made it possible for Joseph and his family to return safely to the Land.

The return to the Land is said by Matthew to fulfill a prophecy of the Tanach, introduced by the common formula. The quote is from Hosea 11:1, but the manner in which Yeshua's return to the Land was its fulfillment requires further discussion.

MT	Lxx	Matthew
כִּי נַעַר יִשְׂרָאֵל וָאֹהֲבֵהוּ וּמִמִּצְרַיִם קָרָאתִי לִבְנִי:	διότι νήπιος Ισραηλ καὶ ἐγὼ ἠγάπησα αὐτὸν καὶ ἐξ Αἰγύπτου μετεκάλεσα τὰ τέκνα αὐτοῦ	ἐξ Αἰγύπτου ἐκάλεσα τὸν υἱόν μου.
When Israel was a youth, I loved him; and from Egypt I called My son.	for Israel is a child, and I loved him, and out of Egypt have I called his children.	out of Egypt I have called my son.

Matthew quotes from the Hebrew rather than the Lxx, for he follows the reading לִבְנִי, "my son" rather than the Lxx τὰ τέκνα αὐτοῦ, "his children." The phrase in the context of Hosea 11 is clearly a reference to the exodus. As the prophet bemoans the waywardness of Israel in regard to her marriage covenant with God which she has despised, he reminds her that God had loved her and had proven His love through redeeming her from the slavery of Egypt. Her exodus was not the result of her own strength, but was entirely the work of the Almighty Who stretched forth His hand to redeem h er (Ex 6:6, cp. Deut 4:34; 5:15; Ps 136:12; Jer 32:21). It is this demonstration of His redeeming love that is the point of the prophet in his bringing the judgment against Israel for her faithlessness.

Thus, the quote in Matthew's story is given to parallel the exodus event as the demonstration of God's covenant faithfulness to Israel which resulted in her redemption, with the coming of Yeshua as His Messiah Who would effect eternal redemption. In that Yeshua represents Israel, He does so as her Redeemer, as the One through Whom she receives her promised reward.

But the question we immediately confront is how Matthew could say that the flight to Egypt by Joseph and Mary, taking Yeshua out of harm's way, could be the fulfillment of Hosea's prophecy, when in the original context of the prophetic oracle, the reference is obviously to the historical event of the exodus.

First, it is clear that Matthew understood Hosea's original meaning, and its connection to the exodus events. It is not that he was naïvely unaware that "out of Egypt I have called my son" referred to historical Israel in Hosea's prophecy. If the original context and meaning of Hosea's words are apparent to us, they were likewise apparent to Matthew. Secondly, the common explanation given by many Christian commentators, that Matthew is here teaching a "New Israel" with a "new exodus" that replaces the "Old Israel" and reinterprets the historical exodus, is wrong-headed. Though the notion that Matthew's message is supersessionistic has been often repeated throughout Christian interpretation, it does not stand in the face of Matthew's message. Why would he clearly related Yeshua's instructions to His disciples, that they were not to go to the Gentiles, but only to the "lost sheep of Israel" (Matt 10:6; 15:24), if his intention was to show that the new community of Yeshua's followers had replaced unbelieving Israel? Moreover, the consistent sub-theme of Matthew's Gospel, that relates to the manner in which Gentiles received Yeshua, carries the message that Gentiles are brought into Israel, not that they replace her. The commission to make disciples of the nations (Gentiles) that concludes Matthew's Gospel (Matt 28:18f), incorporates the ritual of the *mikveh* (ritual immersion), would certainly have been connected to the proselyte ritual by Matthew's audience, something that portrayed Gentiles joining Israel, not replacing her. So we must seek other explanations for Matthew's fulfillment interpretation of Hosea's prophecy.

Some have suggested that Matthew's use of Hosea 11:1 is based upon *gezera shava* (literally, "an equal or identic category," see Jastrow, p. 232), a rabbinic hermeneutic whereby texts that contained similar verbal components were linked together as speaking of the same subject (e.g., b.*Pesachim* 66a). If this is the case, we must seek to find the verbal links that led Matthew to utilize Hosea's prophecy as he did. We may first note Num 24:8, of the Balaam oracles, and the phrase "God brings him out of Egypt" (אֵל מוֹצִיאוֹ מִמִּצְרַיִם). In the previous verse (24:7), where the MT has "water will flow from his buckets" (יִזַּל־מַיִם מִדָּלְיָו), the Lxx translates "a man will come forth from his seed" (ἐξελεύσεται ἄνθρωπος ἐκ τοῦ σπέρματος αὐτοῦ). The Peshitta (Syriac) has "a mighty man shall proceed from his sons" and Targum Onkelos interprets the phrase as "a king shall grow great, who shall be reared from his sons." Thus, it is understandable how these verses would have been interpreted messianically by those (like Matthew) who were familiar with the Lxx and Targumim. Interestingly, in the margin of Codex Sinaiticus, at Matthew 2:15, a scribe has written in the margin that the quote is from Num 24:8, indicating the early connection between the two texts. The verbal linkage to Hosea 11:1 for Matthew, then, would have been the word "Egypt," strengthened by the Targumic use of "sons." Linking the two texts together allowed Matthew to also link the messianic interpretation of Num 24:7–8 to Hosea 11:1.

Moreover, the use of "son" (and particularly "son of God" and "son of man") as applied to Yeshua by Matthew carried a messianic flavor. It is notable that the Davidic covenant as given in 2Sam 7 uses the term "son" in a covenant sense.

Note 2Sam 7:12–16:

> 12 "When your days are complete and you lie down with your fathers, I will raise up your descendant after you, who will come forth from you, and I will establish his kingdom. 13 "He shall build a house for My name, and I will establish the throne of his kingdom forever. 14 "I will be a father to him and he will be a son to Me; when he commits iniquity, I will correct him with the rod of men and the strokes of the sons of men, 15 but My lovingkindness shall not depart from him, as I took it away from Saul, whom I removed from before you. 16 "Your house and your kingdom shall endure before Me forever; your throne shall be established forever."

(For the use of "son" in connection with the Davidic throne, see also Ps 2:7; 89:26–27).

The fact that the Davidic covenant included "father/son" language is foundational for the "son of God" and "son of man" terminology that was understood messianically in the 1st Century (cf. 4Q246; 4QpsDanA[a]), as well as for Matthew's use of the titles. Indeed, "son of God" terminology is repeatedly used in Matthew's Gospel (4:3, 6; 8:29; 26:63; 27:40, 43, 54), the final reference being the affirming words of the centurion: "Truly this was the Son of God!"

Furthermore, the idea that a messianic figure could represent the whole of Israel as the quintessential Israelite, is seen in Isaiah, where the "servant of Adonai" is used both of the nation as a whole (Is 41:8-9; 42:19; 43:10; 44:1-2, 21, 26; 45:4; 48:20; 49:3) as well as of the promised Redeemer and Messiah (Is. 37:35; 42:1; 49:3, 5-7; 53:11). This double use of the "servant" language furthered the idea that the promised Redeemer would represent all of Israel, and that His victory would be theirs. This idea of "corporate solidarity" within a redeemer is not something new for Isaiah. David himself represented Israel as he fought Goliath, the Philistine representative. And each year the High Priest represented all of Israel as he entered the Most Holy place on Yom Kippur. In this sense of corporate solidarity, the one represents the many, and may thus be viewed as constituting the whole. Indeed, Israel is viewed as a single individual when God declares that "Israel is My son, My firstborn" (Ex 4:22), which parallels Hosea's words: "Out of Egypt I have called My son."

We may now tie these strands of thought together in reconstructing Matthew's use of Hosea 11:1—

    a. from Num 24:7–8, the idea was presented that Israel's deliverance from Egypt could be summed in an individual (interpreted messianically)
       "a man shall come forth from his seed" (Lxx and Targum)
       "God brings him out of Egypt"

    b. from 2Sam 7:12ff, the idea that the Davidic king has a "father/son" relationship with God, so that Israel as God's firstborn (Ex 4:22) could be summed in the Davidic King Who is also God's Son.

    c. the "Lord's servant" in Isaiah strengthens the dual concept of the nation in corporate solidarity with the Messiah.

    c. Hosea 11:1 - "out of Egypt I have called My son" could therefore apply both to Israel as the nation, as well as to the representative of Israel, the Davidic King, the Messiah.

Given these lines of connectivity, Matthew's use of Hosea 11:1 gathers together the strands of messianic expectation with the redemption of Israel. He applies the prophecy of Hosea 11:1, "out of Egypt I have called My son" to Yeshua, because, like the exodus from Egypt which formed the paradigm for redemption itself, it is in Yeshua that Israel's ultimate and final redemption would be realized. Even as Yeshua would be taken to Egypt by Joseph and Mary, and would return to the Land at the appointed time, so Israel as a nation, God's firstborn son, would find her redemption from slavery in the person and work of God's Son, the Davidic King Messiah. Far from wresting Hosea's prophecy from its context, or misusing it for his own theological purposes, Matthew has brought it forward within the overall messianic promise of the Tanach, appropriately applying it to Yeshua.

16 Then when Herod saw that he had been tricked by the magi, he became very enraged, and sent and slew all the male children who were in Bethlehem and all its vicinity, from two years old and under, according to the time which he had determined from the magi.

The word of the angel given to Joseph has come true (v. 13). Herod, realizing that the magi had failed to cooperate with his plan (ἐμπαίζω, *empaizo*, "to mock, dupe, deceive"), became enraged (like Pharaoh in the exodus story, and exactly the opposite of the joy expressed by the magi), and initiates his plan to massacre all male children in the environs of Bethlehem in hopes of destroying Israel's infant king. The exact time frame is not given, but we should reason that sufficient time had elapsed for Herod to realize the magi had refused to further his murderous plot.

Herod's later years were marked by massacres of innocent people. Not only is he remembered for murdering his own wife, but he also slew his two sons, Alexander and Aristobulus (6 or 7 CE), and thereafter his son Antipater. He further ordered that upon his death, a member of every prominent Jewish family under his rule should be executed, in order that there would be sufficient mourning for his passing.[1]

The author of the *Testament of Moses* likewise "prophesies" of "powerful kings" who would arise over Israel, usurping the office of High Priest, and who would "exterminate them in secret places so that no one will know where their bodies are. He will kill both old and young, showing mercy to none… He will impose judgments upon them as did the Egyptians, and he will punish them."[2] So the connection of Herod's reign with the oppression of the Pharoah of the exodus is something already in place by Matthew's time.[3] For Herod (like Pharaoh), only the male children are murdered: Matthew gives no room for a female king.

How many male children were massacred is not known, but given the fact that the population of Bethlehem and its environs was most likely around 1,000, and given the birth and mortality rates of the time, it is likely that the number would be in the neighborhood of 20. The tradition in the Christian church exaggerated the number to 14,000 or even 64,000.[4]

As note above, Herod expanded his execution order both geographically and chronologically: "in Bethlehem and all its vicinity, from two years old and younger." Given the age of the victims, it is reasonable to presume that the birth of Yeshua (calculated by the original time the star appeared to the magi) had most likely occurred at least a year and a half earlier.

[1] See Josephus, *Ant.* 15.5–7, 50–87, 232–6, 247–52, 260–6, 289–90; 16.361–94; 17.42–4, 167, 182–7 [noted in Allison-Davies, 1.234-5].

[2] *The Testament of Moses* in Charlesworth, *The Old Testament Pseudepigrapha*, 2 vols. (Doubleday, 1983), 1.930 (quoting to 6:4–6). The translator (J. Priest) adds a note: "The bulk of this chapter (6:2–7) almost certainly reflects the reign of Herod the Great (37–4 BCE)."

[3] Note the parallels above, p. 51, in Mid. Rab. *Ex* 1.22 for Pharoah's attempt to kill the baby Moses; cp. b.*Sota* 12a.

[4] See Hagner, *Matthew*, 1.37.

[1]The typical quotation forumla is not followed here by Matthew. Instead of the common use of ἵνα, "in order that what was spoken … might be fulfilled," Matthew uses the temporal τότε, "Then what was spoken … was fulfilled." Hagner (1.37) suggests that Matthew did not want to ascribe the massacre to God's hand, and thus uses a different quotation forumla here. Davies-Allison offer the same explanation, 1.266.

17–18 Then what had been spoken through Jeremiah the prophet was fulfilled:[1] "A voice was heard in Ramah, Weeping and great mourning, Rachel weeping for her children; And she refused to be comforted, Because they were no more."

The appeal to Jeremiah 31:15 once again requires explanation for Matthew's use of the Tanach in his narrative. Clearly, Matthew has made a connection between the death of children spoken of by Jeremiah, and the situation in Bethlehem at the time of Yeshua's infancy. If we look more closely at Jer 31, we will see some remarkable parallels to Matthew's story. Moreover, it is clear that Jer 31 was understood eschatologically as speaking of the time of Yeshua, for the New Covenant passage (vv. 31–34) was regularly interpreted as being accomplished by the salvific work of Yeshua (cf. Heb 8:8, 10:16; cp. Luke 22:20; 1Cor 11:25; 2Cor. 3:6).

Jeremiah 31	Matthew
vv. 4, 21 - O virgin of Israel	1:23 - the virgin shall be with child
v. 9 - I am Israel's father, and Ephraim is my firstborn son	11:25 - You…have revealed them to infants
v. 8 - See, I will bring them…among them will be … expectant mothers	1:18 - she was found to be with child by the Holy Spirit
v. 7 - O Lord, save Your people, the remnant of Israel	1:21 - He will save His people from their sins.
v. 17 - Your children will return to their own land	2:20–21 - go into the land of Israel; Joseph got up, took the child and His mother, and came into the land of Israel.
v. 35 - He appoints … the stars to shine by night	2:2 - For we saw His star in the east
v. 25 - those who hunger and thirst will be filled	5:6 - blessed are those who hunger and thirst for righteousness, for they shall be satisfied
vv. 31–34 - a New Covenant to be established with Israel	26:28 - for this is My blood of the covenant

As Allison and Davies point out (1.267), knowing the story of Yeshua's birth and infancy, and then re-reading Jeremiah 31, Matthew would have seen these verbal parallels as significant, and would have naturally concluded that the prophet's promise of a coming New Covenant with Israel must have come to fulfillment in the appearance of Yeshua. The fact that Jeremiah 31 also includes a notice of weeping over the loss of children therefore fits the scenario perfectly. Even if the completion of Jeremiah's prophecy remained for the yet eschatological future, in Matthew's mind, the appearance of the Messiah sealed the prophecy as inevitably fulfilled by Him. Furthermore, since some of what Jeremiah foresaw had already taken place in a representative way in Yeshua (as noted above in the discussion of Hosea 11:1), then Matthew could reason that the rest of Jeremiah's prophetic message would also be accomplished by Him.

Matthew's quote from Jeremiah 31:15 aligns with the Hebrew text, and is not a direct quote for the Lxx as we have it, though the Lxx does generally capture the sense of the MT:

MT	Lxx	Matthew
קוֹל בְּרָמָה נִשְׁמָע נְהִי בְּכִי תַמְרוּ־רִים רָחֵל מְבַכָּה עַל־בָּנֶיהָ מֵאֲנָה לְהִנָּחֵם עַל־בָּנֶיהָ כִּי אֵינֶנּוּ׃	φωνὴ ἐν Ραμα ἠκούσθη θρήνου καὶ κλαυθμοῦ καὶ ὀδυρμοῦ Ραχηλ ἀποκλαιομένη οὐκ ἤθελεν παύσασθαι ἐπὶ τοῖς υἱοῖς αὐτῆς ὅτι οὐκ εἰσίν	φωνὴ ἐν Ῥαμὰ ἠκούσθη, κλαυθμὸς καὶ ὀδυρμὸς πολύς· Ῥαχὴλ κλαίουσα τὰ τέκνα αὐτῆς, καὶ οὐκ ἤθελεν παρακληθῆναι, ὅτι οὐκ εἰσίν.[1]
A voice is heard in Ramah, mourning and great weeping, Rachel weeping for her children and refusing to be comforted, because her children are no more.	A voice was heard in Rama, of lamentation, and of weeping, and wailing; Rachel would not cease weeping for her children, because they are not.	A voice was heard in ramah, weeping and great mourning, rachel weeping for her children; and she refused to be comforted, because they were no more.

The historical background of Jer 31:15 is that of the deportation of Israelites to Babylon (most like of the deportation of Judah and Benjamin) under the reign of Nebuchadnezzer, by the hand of the commander of his imperial guard, Nebuzaradan. He gathered the captives at Ramah before taking them to Babylon (Jer 40:1–2). Rachel's tomb lay north of Jerusalem at Zelzah in the same vicinity (1Sam 10:2), for Jacob buried her "on the way to Ephrath" (Gen 35:19). Jeremiah's prophecy thus envisions the captives of Judah going past Rachel's tomb, and her crying out from her tomb as her "children" are taken away. (Rachel was idealized as the mother of Israel, even though more of Jacob's sons were born by Leah.)

But how does this fit Matthew's story? The weeping in Bethlehem is not for the One who is being exiled to Egypt, but to those who remained and were slaughtered. The answer may be found in the context of the Jeremiah quote. Jer 31 is a chapter of hope, for even though there are tears in connection with the exile, there is hope because the Almighty intends to reverse the exile and regather His people, renewing them in their obedience to Him, forgiving and wiping away their transgressions, and establishing them forever as His people in the Land. In the same way, the anguish at the needless slaughter of children will give way to hope for the coming redemption, for the Redeemer has come. Furthermore, Matthew has already noted that the exile has ended (1:11–12), and that the Davidic King has arrived. The One who would establish the New Covenant has come, and the tears will be wiped away. Gathering the hopeful tone of Jeremiah, writing in the face of the exile, Matthew brings this hope to rest squarely upon Yeshua, Immanuel. As Carson concludes:

> The tears of the Exile are now being "fulfilled"—i.e., the tears begun in Jeremiah's day are climaxed and ended by the tears of the mothers of Bethlehem. The heir of David's throne has come, the Exile is over, the true Son of God has arrived, and he will introduce the new covenant (26:28) promised by Jeremiah.[2]

[1] The longer reading in the Majority Text (KJV) which includes "lamentation, and weeping, and great mourning" is most likely an assmilation to the Lxx. The Hebrew has only two elements: בְּכִי תַמְרוּרִים being literally "weeping of bitterness."

[2] Carson, *Matthew,* p. 95.

19–20 But when Herod died, behold, an angel of the Lord appeared in a dream to Joseph in Egypt, and said, "Get up, take the Child and His mother, and go into the land of Israel; for those who sought the Child's life are dead.

Herod's death is recounted in Josephus (*Ant.* 17.168–69), and apparently he died of some disease that ate away at his vital organs. Though given every manner of cure from physicians, he died of his sickness, only after he had given the order to have his son Antipater executed and given an ignoble burial at Hyrcania. It was Herod's death that signalled the time for Joseph's return. Even though the news of Herod's death would have been immediately broadcast in the local region, it would have taken some time to reach Egypt. Accordingly, the angel of the Lord (this is the third mention in Matthew) gives yet another dream to Joseph, assuring him that it is safe to return to the Land.

How long were Joseph, Mary, and Yeshua in Egypt? The biblical text gives us no answer. The apocryphal gospels supply various reckonings: 3Infancy 1:3 and Latin Gospel of Thomas (1–3) have one year, while the Arabic Gospel of the Infancy (25–6) has three years. But these are all speculation.

The message of the angel notes a plural: "*those* who sought the Child's life are dead." Were there more than Herod in on the plot to destroy the infant Yeshua? While it is possible that Herod's father, Antipater, may have been involved in the decree to slaughter the Hebrew boys, it is more probable that Matthew's plural is a generalizing or categorical stylization. Besides, Herod had enlisted his troops to carry out the decree, and so the plural is understandable. Some have suggested that Matthew employs the plural in order to strengthen the parallel to Ex 4:19, "Go back to Egypt, for all the men who were seeking your life are dead."

21–22 So Joseph got up, took the Child and His mother, and came into the land of Israel. But when he heard that Archelaus was reigning over Judea in place of his father Herod, he was afraid to go there. Then after being warned by God in a dream, he left for the regions of Galilee,

Once again, Joseph is fully obedient to the word of God given by the angel in a dream. He and his family return to the Land as God has instructed. But on arriving, he receives the information that Herod's successor was Archelaus. Previously, Herod had decreed that Antipas (referred to simply as Herod the tetrarch in Matt 14) should be his successor over Judea, but at the time of Herod's death, he changed his mind, assigning Antipas to be tetrarch of Galilee and Berea, and named Archelaus as successor to his throne (Josephus, *Ant.* 17.188). He named his son Philip tetrarch over Iturea, Trachonitis, and some other territories (in the north, Transjordan region). Of the three, Philip was the best, and Yeshua frequented the region under his control (Matt 14:13; 15:29; 16:13). Both Archelaus and Antipas, however, were ruthless, and Archelaus was the worst of the pair. "His short reign was marked by scandal, by brutality, and by tyranny."[1] So foul was his reign that complaints lodged by a Jewish and Samaritan envoy to Rome succeeded in having him deposed and exiled to Gaul in 6 CE.

Though it appears as though Joseph would have chosen to settle in Judea, had the conditions been favorable, having been warned by God (once again, in a dream), he travelled to the north and settled his family in Galilee.

[1]Allison-Davies, 1. 273.

23 and came and lived in a city called Nazareth.[1] This was to fulfill what was spoken through the prophets: "He shall be called a Nazarene."

Joseph takes up residence in the city called Nazareth. Nazareth is situated in the Lower Galilee, just north of the Valley of Jezreel, approximately 64 miles north of Jerusalem, and 20 miles southwest of Capernaum. The population of Nazareth in the early 1st Century is estimated at approximately 480 people, calculated on a 60 acre land area.[2] The village was apparently founded in the 3rd Century BCE, though it was not until the late Hellenistic period that it grew to the size of a small city. Its economy in the 1st Century was entirely based on the surrounding agriculture.

It was well known that Yeshua came from Nazareth, a city of low esteem to some (Matt 21:11; 26:71; Mk 1:24; Lk 18:37; Jn 1:45-46). Nathanael is credited with the statement, "Can any good thing come out of Nazareth?" (Jn 1:46).

Once again, Matthew wants his readers to know that each part of Yeshua's life is in direct fulfillment of the prophetic message regarding the Messiah. Thus, His living in Nazareth becomes the fulfillment of the prophets: "He shall be called a Nazarene." Yet, as we quickly discover, no prophet of the Tanach makes such a statement, and we are left wondering exactly what text Matthew appears to be quoting. However, we should note that, unlike Matthew's other quotes, here he attributes the saying, not to a particular prophet, but to "the prophets" (plural). This is important, because it alerts us to the fact that Matthew is not giving us a verbatim quotation of one particular Scripture from the Tanach, but he is rather appealing or alluding to a general perspective gleaned from the wider voice of the prophets. Similar to this, in 26:54, Yeshua appeals to the "Scriptures" (plural) which must be fulfilled, rather than to a single text. Here, again, the fulfillment of the Scriptures is seen in that the events taking place agree with the overall message of the Tanach.

Secondly, it seems likely that our text has to do with a word-play on two words that have similar sound, namely, the word נָזִיר, *nazir*, "a nazirite" and the word Nazarene (someone from the city of Nazareth). A nazirite was a person who dedicated himself or herself to the service of God by taking a special vow which required abstinence from anything related to the vine, and letting one's hair grow uncut.[2] The first step in this subtle word play is to understand that a "nazirite" was considered "holy" (separated) unto God. In fact, in Judg 13:7, where Samson's mother relates the words of the "man" who visited her and gave her notice of the coming child, we read:

> "But he said to me, 'Behold, you shall conceive and give birth to a son, and now you shall not drink wine or strong drink nor eat any unclean thing, for the boy shall be a Nazirite to God (ναζιραῖον θεοῦ) from the womb to the day of his death.'"

However, in the other Lxx version of this text (the B text), ναζιραῖον θεοῦ (*naziraion theou*, "Nazirite of God") is changed to ἅγιον θεοῦ (*hagion theou*, "holy one of God"). We discover the same phenomenon in Judg 16:17. Once again, the Lxx A text has ναζιραῖος θεοῦ while the B text has ἅγιος θεοῦ. Nowhere in the B text of the Lxx is Samson referred to as a "Nazirite," but only as one separated ("holy") to God. This tells us that from a very early period, well before the 1st Century, the idea of "holy one of God" and "Nazirite of God"

[1]The spelling of Nazareth in the Greek manuscripts varies. Some have Ναζαρετ (ℵ B D L 33 700 892 1241 1424). Others have Ναζαρεθ (C K N W Γ [Δ] 0233ᵛˡ *f*⁽¹⁾ ¹³ 28 565 lat co). P⁷⁰ᵛⁱᵈ has Ναζαρα.

[2]James Strange, "Nazareth" in the *Anchor Bible Dictionary*.

[2]On the laws of the Nazirite, see Num 6; Judg 13:5–7; 16:17; Amos 2:11–12; 1Macc 3:49–52; Acts 18:18; 21:17–26; m.*Nazir*.

were linked through the concurrent translations of Judges into Greek.

To this we may add Mk 1:24. In Mark's story, Yeshua has entered the synagogue on Shabbat, and while He was teaching, a man with demon spoke out and said:

> "What business do we have with each other, Yeshua of Nazareth? Have You come to destroy us? I know who You are—the Holy One of God!"

Here, "Yeshua of Nazareth" is paralleled by "Holy One of God," utilizing the same Greek words found in the B text of Lxx which substituted for "Nazirite." This helps us tie the two similar sounding words together (נָצְרִי [*natzri*, Nazarene] and נָזִיר [*nazir*, Nazirite]) with the very meaning of Nazirite, i.e., "holy one of God."

Moreover, in Luke's account, he alludes to Scripture relating to Samuel (who was a Nazirite), applying them to Yeshua. The Magnificat of Mary is modelled after the prayer of Hannah (1Sam 2:1–10; Lk 1:46–55). Also note this parallel:

> 1Sam 2:26 Now the boy Samuel was growing in stature and in favor both with the LORD and with men.
> Luke 2:52 And Yeshua kept increasing in wisdom and stature, and in favor with God and men.

Further, Yeshua's words at the last Pesach, that He would not drink of the fruit of the vine until He came into His kingdom, are reminiscent of the Nazirite prohibition regarding eating or drinking anything from the vine. The same may be said of Yeshua's refusal to accept the wine while on the cross.

Finally, with these data in mind, we may note Is 4:2–3, where the prophecy of the "Branch of the Lord" is given, understood as pertaining to the Messiah by the Targum. In v. 3, the text reads: "…he who is left in Zion and remains in Jerusalem *will be called holy*…." Once again, in the Jewish tradition of the 1st Century, there is evidence that the Messiah would be called "holy" was well in place, as was the idea that a Nazirite was "a holy one of God."

It seems, then, that Matthew has given us a subtle play on words, linking *natzri*, *nazir*, with "the Holy One of God." And since the Lxx had made a clear connection between a *nazir* and "the Holy One of God," then it was easy to apply the equation to Yeshua, especially if at the last Pesach, His words were interpreted along the lines of a Nazirite vow.

A second suggestion given by many is that Matthew is alluding to Is 11:1, and the prophecy of the "Branch" (נֵצֶר, *netzer*): "Then a shoot will spring from the stem of Jesse, and a branch from his roots will bear fruit." In this case, the sound-alike words would be *natzri* (Nazarene) and *netzer* (Branch). This suggestion also has merit, for: 1) Is 11:1 was interpreted messianically by the Jewish Sages (Targum, Mid. Rab. *Gen* 2.4,; 97; 98.9; Mid. Rab. *Num* 13.11; Mid. Rab. *Ruth* 5.6; b.*Sanhedrin* 93b; Rashi on Is 11:1–2), so an allusion to the "branch" in the sound of *natzri* is possible; 2) Is 11 is very Davidic, and this fits with the opening genealogy of Matthew; 3) Other Apostolic writers appeal to Is 11 (Rom 15:12; 1Pet 4:14; Rev 5:5); 4) since צֶמַח "shoot" is also used in Is 11, as well as other prophets in a messianic way (cf. Jer 23:5; 33:15; Zech 3:8; 6:12), this could help explain Matthew's use of "prophets" (plural);

and 5) it is possible that נֵצֶר may have been pronounced as νάζαρ (*nazar*) in 1st Century Hebrew, which is strikingly close to the form of Nazareth (ναζαρά) as found in Matt 4:13 and Lk 4:16.

Yet the connection with *nazir,* "Nazirite," and the substitution of "holy one of God" in the Samson narrative of the Lxx, seems particularly compelling. Of course, it is always possible that Matthew found more than one key word or text for his Nazarene midrash.

To summarize then: Matthew finds a general message in the prophets regarding the Messiah, a message that is connected with the word "Nazarene" (*natzri*). By a play on the word, Matthew connects to "Nazirite" (*nazir*) by way of assonance (similar sound). The primary characteristic of a Nazirite is that he or she was separated to God by way of a specific oath. This overarching idea of the Nazirite separated ("made holy") unto God was strong enough that in the two versions of the Lxx, in the story of Samson, "Nazirite" is replaced by "holy one of God." That strong connection between "Nazirite" and "holy one of God" is the point Matthew is making. In the same way that a Nazirite is separated unto God (holy), so Yeshua, in all of His life lived out the quintessential meaning of a Nazirite vow, for He was the Holy One of God in every way. Thus, that by God's providence, Joseph would settle in Nazareth, and Yeshua would be known as *Yeshua haNatzri* was sufficiently close for Matthew's midrash. He is *Yeshua haNatzri, Yeshua haNazir,* and *Yeshua, haKodesh Adonai.*

Chapter Three
Commentary

Chapter three introduces Yochanan HaMatbil (יוֹחָנָן הַמַּטְבִּיל) or John the Baptist, as he is known through our English translations. The word translated "Baptist" is a noun based upon the verb "to immerse" (βάπτω, *bapto*). For instance, in Mark 6:24, the participle of βάπτω is used (yielding "John the baptizer"), which is how the name should be understood throughout.

3:1–17 divides easily into three sections: vv. 1–6 introduces John the baptizer, vv. 7–12 reports John's encounter with the Pharisees and Sadducees, and vv. 13–17 describe the baptism of Yeshua.

1–2 Now in those days John the Baptist came, preaching in the wilderness of Judea, saying "Repent, for the kingdom of heaven is at hand."

Matthew's story now skips ahead, shifting the focus of the narrative from the birth of Yeshua to His *mikveh* at the hands of John. Only Luke gives us any information about the intervening years. He writes of Yeshua's circumcision and naming on the eighth day (Lk 2:21), of Mary's observing the days of purification following the birth of a son (Lev 12, cf. Lk 2:22), and the redemption of the firstborn (Ex 13:2; 34:20; Num 18:15, cf. Lk 2:23), all of which were prescribed in the Torah. The completion of the days of purification, as well as the redemption of the firstborn required offering sacrifices at the Temple. And since Luke specifically mentions the alternative offering of a pair of turtledoves or two young pigeons in the place of a lamb and a pigeon for the burnt offering and sin offering respectively (Lk 2:14), we know that Joseph and Mary were not economically able to afford the more expensive sacrifice. Luke also describes the occasion of Yeshua's interchange with the Sages in the Temple courts when He was twelve years old and had traveled to Jerusalem with His family for Pesach (Lk 2:41ff). Except for these notices by Luke, the Gospels are silent about Yeshua's childhood and adolescent years.

We may ask ourselves why this was the case. Why did the Gospel writers put little or no emphasis upon the years that intervened between Yeshua's birth and His public appearance as a teacher in Israel? We know that the same question was asked in the centuries immediately following His appearance, because the apocryphal gospels and other works produced during this time do their best to "fill" in the missing information. The answer may be that the Gospel writers lacked the information in the sources they utilized, or that the sources had only scanty information regarding these years of Yeshua's life. It may also be that detailing the years of Yeshua's childhood and adolescence did not fit their purposes. After all, we would expect that Yeshua's upbringing was quite normal. A Jewish father bore five responsibilities toward his son: 1) circumcise him on the eighth day, 2) pay the redemption for the firstborn, 3) teach him Torah, 4) find a wife for him, and 5) teach him a trade. The first two Joseph did, as Luke makes clear. We may presume that if Yeshua confounded the Sages at the age of 12, Joseph and Mary had taken seriously the requirement to teach Him Torah. Marriage, while highly prized, was not considered absolutely

[1] See the comments of Travers Herford, *Pirke Avoth* (Schocken, 1962), p. 97, and the legend regarding ben Azai in b.*Ketuvot* 63a.

[2] See the reference in *BDAG*, "τέκτων."

necessary for every man. For example, Shimon ben Azai, a renown disciple of Akiva, and companion of Shimon ben Zoma, was never married[1] and is regularly quoted as an authority in rabbinic literature. As to Yeshua's occupation, in Mk 6:3 people refer to Him as a τέκτων (*tekton*) which means a "carpenter" or "craftsman." According to Epictetus, Joseph made "plows and yokes," which would have been made out of wood obtained locally.[2] Thus, Joseph apparently trained Yeshua in his own craft.

Since the people are surprised at Yeshua's wisdom, ability to teach, and the miracles He was performing (Mk 6:3, "Is this not the carpenter?"), it may well be that in His years of growing up, He was viewed as simply one of the community, without the character of a "boy wonder" that the later apocryphal works attribute to Him. Though He doubtlessly had proven Himself to be a righteous young man with full integrity, His membership in the local community of Nazareth may have been more or less lackluster when compared with the myths and fairy tales that grew up in the later centuries. In fact, Luke's short notice, "The Child continued to grow and become strong, increasing in wisdom; and the grace of God was upon Him" (Lk 2:40), may be a comprehensive description of the years intervening His birth and His public appearance at the shores of the Jordan. While such a description does not produce the religious fervor needed to build cathedrals, it does fit the highly praised description of the Wisdom Literature that considers character of far greater value than charisma. And it reminds us that the life of Torah is not impressed with the trinkets of religion that may sparkle, but sets itself to obtain gold that endures the refiner's fire (cf. 1Pet 1:3–9).

In those days, John the Baptist came, preaching … The opening words "in those days" (εν δὲ ταῖς ἡμέραις ἐκείναις) are often used by Israel's prophets to designate the messianic era and the time of Israel's restoration (Is 38:1; Jer 3:16, 18; 5:18; 31:29; 33:15-16; 50:4; Joel 2:29; 3:1; Zech 8:6, 23). Some have therefore suggested that Matthew's use of this same phrase signals that he wanted his readers to understand that the eschatological era had dawned, and that Israel's salvation was at hand.

[1] so Allison-Davies, 1.288.

When the text says that "John the Baptist came," it most likely means "he made an appearance."[3] Matthew gives no formal background to the person of John the Baptist, so we may presume that his readers already know about John, or else Matthew's sources gave him little or no information about John's background to incorporate into his story.

John came "preaching" using the Greek κηρύσσω, *kerusso*, found in the Lxx as the most common translation of קָרָא (*qara'*), "to call, summon." While Yeshua proclaims the same message of repentance (cf. 4:17), Matthew regularly connects the Gospel with Yeshua's "preaching" (4:23; 9:35; 24:14; 26:13). In contrast, John the Baptist is never said to "preach the gospel." Yet the content of John's proclamation is clearly in concert with, and preparatory to, the Gospel, for his was a message of repentance.

[4] For additional information on the geographical location of John's activities, see David Flusser, *Jesus* (Magnus Press, 1998 [2nd edition]), pp. 42–3, 258, n.2.

The location of John's activities is stated to be "in the wilderness of Judea," which is the Judean wilderness in the lower Jordan valley, between the Judean plateau and the Dead Sea and the lower Jordan river. Contrary to the popular tourist attractions in Israel today, the precise place where John administered *mikveot* in the Jordan is not known.[4] The Gospel of John places his activities in the trans-jordan (Jn 1:28, cf. 10:40), and perhaps in the minds of some, Judea was enlarged to include areas in the Transjordan. But it may also be that the Transjordan desert dwelling of John was to emphasize a re-entry of the Land at the time of the approaching kingdom, as a re-enactment

of Israel's original conquest of the Land, but in this case, with a full awareness of the eschatological redemption that was dawning. It may also have
been to make the comparison with Elijah more concrete. Elijah found refuge
in the desert, and it was from the desert that he was taken up in a chariot,
near the Jordan (1Ki 17:3; 19:3–18; 2Ki 2:1–12). Later tradition had it that
Elijah was a Tishbite "from the land of the Arabs," that is, from the Trans-
jordan.[1]

John's activity and message are obviously complimentary. That is,
his calling people to repentance in view of the imminent appearance of the
kingdom of heaven, was matched with the administration of a baptism or
mikveh. Once again, Matthew presumes that his readers need no explanation
about what a *mikveh* entails, and what it signified. However, in order for us
to understand what John was doing and why, we must look into the historical method and significance of the Jewish immersion ritual.

Excursus: Mikveh in Ancient Judaism

In matters of ritual purity prescribed by the Torah, bathing in water
often concludes the period of uncleanness and returns the person to a state
of ritual purity. This is applied to those who become unclean through a skin
disorder (הַמְּצֹרָה, *ham'tzorah*, Lev 14), who were unclean through a bodily
discharge (Lev 15), to the High Priest on Yom Kippur and to those who led
away the scapegoat (Lev 16), to anyone who ate meat from an animal that
had been killed by predators or had died on its own (Lev 17:15), to the priest
who administers the ashes of the red heifer as well as the one who burns the
carcass of the red heifer (Num 19), and anyone made unclean through corpse
defilement (Num 19:11f). In some cases, vessels which had acquired ritual
impurity could be immersed in water in order to be returned to state of purity (Num 31:22–23).

The Torah, however, never fully describes the particulars of the ritual
bath. In Lev 15:13, the ritual bath described for a man unclean through a
bodily discharge must be in living water (מַיִם חַיִּים), that is, "running water."
Since other notices requiring a ritual bathing use similar words and phrases,
it seems warranted to agree with the Sages, and apply the requirement of
Lev 15:13 to all ritual baths, meaning that they all must be done in "running
water." It may be further implied from the use of the phrase (Lev 14:9) וְרָחַץ
אֶת־בְּשָׂרוֹ בַּמַּיִם, "bath his flesh (i.e., body) in water," that sufficient water for a
complete bathing is implied in the biblical text. As we shall see, the rabbinic
halachah for a *mikveh* required sufficient water for a full immersion.

The word *mikveh* (מִקְוֶה, also spelled מִקְוֵה in Is 22:11) is found four times
in the Tanach. In Gen 1:10, it describes the "gathering of the waters" to form
the sea. In Ex 7:19 and Is 22:11, it means a "reservoir of water," and in Lev
11:36 it denotes a "gathering of water" in a cistern (בּוֹר, *bor*). In the biblical
text, it is never used to describe a place of ritual bathing, but the rabbis adopted the term from its biblical setting, and utilized it to describe a gathering
of water sufficient for a ritual immersion. The noun is derived from the verb
קָוָה (*qavah*), "to gather," and thus "a gathering place for water." In Jer 14:8
and 17:13, *mikveh* means "hope," and may derive from the fact that those living in arid regions of the Middle East always considered places of abundant
water (oasis) the anticipated intermediate resting place along a journey.

The rabbinic *halachah* that developed regarding the physical requirements of a *mikveh* as well as its proper use, is found primarily in the sixth

[1]This if found in the 1st Century work, *The Lives of the Prophets,* according to Allison-Davies, 1.291.

tractate of the order of the Mishnah and Tosefta called *Mikvaot*. Though the rabbinic *halachah* on *mikvaot* is very involved, we may briefly summarize the rabbinic requirements here:

Physical requirements of a mikveh according to rabbinic halachah:

1. ponds, pools, rivers, or larger bodies of water are valid (in most cases) because water is continually coming in and going out. Any natural body of water that contains less than 40 *se'ahs* (approx. 120 gallons) is invalid.
2. water for a *mikveh* must flow from a natural source, and may not be "drawn." "Drawn water" (מַיִם שְׁאוּבִים, *mayim she'uvim*), defined as water that does not flow, invalidates a *mikveh*. Rain water, however, if directed into a *mikveh* without being collected in a vessel (thus constituting *drawn water*) is valid for a *mikveh*. Once a *mikveh* has the minimum amount of water needed (40 *se'ahs*), adding drawn water does not invalidate the *mikveh*.
3. water from a natural source must be pure, that is, not discolored by an admixture.
4. water directed to a *mikveh* from a natural source may not flow through pipes made of materials susceptible to ritual impurities (metal, wood). Since clay was not susceptible to ritual impurity, this became the material most often used for directing water to *mikvaot*. Additional rabbinic *halachah* ruled that pipes attached to the ground are not susceptible to ritual impurities.
5. two *mikvaot* that utilize the same natural water source may not have water from one flowing to the other unless the upper one is able to maintain the minimum amount of water needed from the natural source. However, since the Sages ruled that once a *mikveh* has the minimum amount of water needed, adding "drawn water" does not invalidate it, sufficient water for a lower *mikveh* was virtually assured.
6. the minimum size of the *mikveh* must accommodate the needed water, and allow for a person to be fully immersed.

While this general summary is of the later rabbinic *halachah* in regard to a *mikveh*, the many *mikvaot* uncovered in archaeological digs in the Land substantiate that in many regards, significant aspects of the later *halachah* reflect the earlier practice. Thus, elaborate systems for the flow of water from natural sources are known, and the enclosures themselves are clearly large enough to accommodate the minimum water requirements established by the Sages. Moreover, the common steps that descend into the *mikvaot* uncovered in the Land indicate that full immersion was the common practice.

Requirements for performing a mikveh according to rabbinic halachah:

1. since a *mikveh* is not a washing for cleanliness but in order to fulfill a Torah commandment, the body must be entirely clean before descending into the *mikveh*. It became custom-

ary, then, to bathe before undergoing a *mikveh*, and to thoroughly clean oneself, including the finger nails and hair.

2. The person or object must be completely immersed in the water of the *mikveh* and the water must come into contact with the entire body or surface of the object. In order to assure that this requirement has been done, it became customary to immerse three times (though one immersion fulfills the *halachah* if done properly). It also became customary to have an attendant watch to make sure a complete immersion was done.

3. The question of "intention" (*kavvanah*) was debated among the Sages. Some ruled that a *mikveh* is invalid if the one immersing did not do so in regard to the specific commandment to bathe. Others disagreed, and ruled that the immersion was valid regardless of one's intentions.[1]

[1] See discussion below on the need for intention in performing a *mikveh*.

After the destruction of the Temple, ritual purity laws were suspended, for the obvious reason that the need to be ceremonially clean related to the Temple and its services. However, among the Sages, the *mikveh* was enjoined upon the people in three cases: for the *niddah* (menstruant), for the proselyte, and for vessels purchased from Gentiles. Since the Torah prohibits sexual union during the time of a wife's menstruation, and since the penalty attached to this commandment was that of *karat* (being cut off from one's people, cf. Lev 20:18), it was considered proper for a woman to mark her return to purity by performing a *mikveh*. The *halachah* of immersing dishes or vessels received or purchased from Gentiles was most likely given as a curb against assimilation. Proselyte immersion will be discussed below.

Mikveh in the 1st Century CE

While a good number of *mikvaot* have been uncovered through archaeological excavations in the Land, we have very little information about their use during the days of the 2nd Temple. It is clear that the purity of the Temple and its courts was strictly guarded (cf. Acts 21:26ff), and the number of *mikvaot* discovered on the south of the Temple mount as well as on the mount itself attest to this as well.

The rabbinic literature describes the ritual of the proselyte as concluding with a ritual immersion:

> Our Rabbis taught: If at the present time a man desires to become a proselyte, he is to be addressed as follows: 'What reason have you for desiring to become a proselyte; do you not know that Israel at the present time are persecuted and oppressed, despised, harassed and overcome by afflictions'? If he replies, 'I know and yet am unworthy', he is accepted forthwith, and is given instruction in some of the minor and some of the major commandments. He is informed of the sin [of the neglect of the commandments of] Gleanings, the Forgotten Sheaf, the Corner and the Poor Man's Tithe. He is also told of the punishment for the transgression of the commandments. Furthermore, he is addressed thus: 'Be it known to you that before you came to this condition, if you had eaten suet you would not have been punishable with kareth, if you had profaned the Sabbath you would not have been punishable with stoning; but now were you to

eat suet you would be punished with kareth; were you to profane the Sabbath you would be punished with stoning'. And as he is informed of the punishment for the transgression of the commandments, so is he informed of the reward granted for their fulfillment. He is told, 'Be it known to you that the world to come was made only for the righteous, and that Israel at the present time are unable to bear either too much prosperity, or too much suffering'. He is not, however, to be persuaded or dissuaded too much. If he accepted, he is circumcised forthwith. Should any shreds which render the circumcision invalid remain, he is to be circumcised a second time. As soon as he is healed arrangements are made for his immediate ablution, when two learned men must stand by his side and acquaint him with some of the minor commandments and with some of the major ones. When he comes up after his ablution he is deemed to be an Israelite in all respects.[1]

[1] b.*Yevamot* 47a–b.

[2] *Sifre* §108, cf. b.*Keritot* 9a.

We may also note the commentary on Numbers 15 (*Sifre*), where we read: "Rabbi says, 'Just as an Israelite did not enter the covenant except by means of three things– circumcision, immersion, and the acceptance of a sacrifice – so it is the same with the proselytes (*gerim*).'"

However, exactly what the *mikveh* was thought to accomplish in the ritual of the proselyte is not precisely clear. The idea that the *mikveh* some how "washed away" Gentile uncleanness does not seem to be substantiated by the later rabbinic texts. For instance, in b.*Pesachim* 92a we read:

MISHNAH. AN ONEN PERFORMS TEBILLAH AND EATS HIS PASSOVER-OFFERING IN THE EVENING, BUT [HE MAY] NOT [PARTAKE] OF [OTHER] SACRIFICES. ONE WHO HEARS ABOUT HIS DEAD [FOR THE FIRST TIME], AND ONE WHO COLLECTS THE BONES [OF HIS PARENTS], PERFORM TEBILLAH AND EAT SACRED FLESH. IF A PROSELYTE WAS CONVERTED ON THE EVE OF PASSOVER, — BETH SHAMMAI MAINTAIN: HE PERFORMS TEBILLAH AND EATS HIS PASSOVER-OFFERING IN THE EVENING; WHILE BETH HILLEL RULE: ONE WHO SEPARATES HIMSELF FROM [THE STATE OF] UNCIRCUMCISION IS LIKE ONE WHO SEPARATED HIMSELF FROM A GRAVE.[3]

[3] See also m.*Eduyot* 5.2.

GEMARA: …

A PROSELYTE WHO WAS CONVERTED etc. Rabbah b. Bar

Hanah said in R. Johanan's name: The controversy is in respect of an uncircumcised heathen, where Beth Hillel hold: [He is forbidden to eat in the evening] as a preventive measure lest he become defiled the following year [by the dead] and he argues, 'Did I not perform tebillah last year and eat [of the Passover offering]? So now too I will perform tebillah and eat.' But he will not understand that the previous year he was a heathen and not susceptible to uncleanness, whereas now he is an Israelite and susceptible to uncleanness. While Beth Shammai hold: We do not enact a preventive measure. But with regard to an uncircumcised Israelite all agree that he performs tebillah and eats his Passover-offering in the evening, and we do not preventively forbid an uncircumcised Israelite on account of an uncircumcised heathen. It was taught likewise, R. Simeon b. Eleazar said: Beth Shammai and Beth Hillel did not differ about an uncircumcised Israelite, [both agreeing] that he performs tebillah and eats his Passover-offering in the evening. About what do they differ?

About an uncircumcised heathen, where Beth Shammai rule: He performs tebillah and eats his Passover-offering in the evening; while
Beth Hillel maintain: He who separates himself from uncircumcision
is as though he separated from a grave.

The apparent conflict between Hillel and Shammai does not pertain to an
Israelite who is circumcised on the eve of Pesach, but only to the *halachah*
pertaining to a Gentile convert who is circumcised on the eve of Pesach. But
the point that is interesting for our discussion of *mikvaot* is that Hillel holds
that a Gentile is not susceptible to uncleanness because the laws of purity in
the Torah do not apply to him. But once he becomes a proselyte, the laws of
purity do apply, and Hillel fears that admitting the proselyte immediately to
the Pesach seder might cause confusion in his mind about his newly acquired need to become ceremonially clean before eating the Pesach sacrifice.

> The Tosefta adds a notice: "R. Eliezer
> b. Yaacov says, "There were Roman
> soldiers and guards in Jerusalem
> who immersed and ate their Pesach-
> offerings in the evening [of the day
> on which they converted and were
> circumcised." (t.*Pesach* 7.14).

While some of the Sages may have held that the *mikveh* of the proselyte
did, in some way, physically remove impurities of idolatry and other pagan
uncleanness, it seems most likely that the *mikveh* was considered simply the
final step in the proselyte ritual, as a symbol of a change of status. When the
proselyte comes up from the waters of the *mikveh*, he is regarded as an Israelite in every way. According to the Bavli, "… one who has become a proselyte
is like a child newly born,"[1] meaning that all ties to one's former life have
been severed. The symbolism of death and resurrection dramatically performed in immersion demonstrated the end of his existence as a Gentile, and
the beginning of his life as a *bona fide* covenant member of Israel. It is this
symbolism that most likely stands behind the command to bring Gentiles
into the *mikveh* in the discipleship process enjoined upon the twelve at the
conclusion of Matthew's Gospel.

[1] b. *Yevamot* 22a.

But it is clear that John's baptism was not that of proselytes. Those who
came to him were from the Pharisees and Sadducees (Matt 3:7). So we must
inquire about the use of the *mikveh*, not as means of regaining the status of
ritual purity, but as enjoined by John to those who were coming out to him
in the desert.

The spiritual significance of performing a mikveh

The issue of intention in performing a *mitzvah* was clearly taught by
some of the Sages, and this pertains to the performance of a *mikveh* as well.
Rambam wrote:

> It is plain and manifest that the laws about uncleanness and clean-
> ness are decrees laid down by Scripture and not matters about which
> human understanding is capable of forming a judgment; for behold,
> they are included among the divine statutes. So, too, immersion as
> a means of freeing oneself from uncleanness is included among the
> divine statutes. Now "uncleanness" is not mud or filth which water
> can remove, but is a matter of Scriptural decree and dependent on
> the intention of the heart. Therefore the sages have said, if a man im-
> merses himself, but without special intention, it is as though he has
> not immersed himself at all.
>
> Nevertheless we may find some indication (for the moral basis)
> of this: just as one who sets his heart on becoming clean becomes
> clean as soon as he has immersed himself, although nothing new has

befallen his body, so, too, one who sets his heart on cleansing himself from the uncleanness that besets men's souls—namely, wrongful thoughts and false convictions—becomes clean as soon as he consents in his heart to shun those counsels and brings his soul into the waters of pure reason. Behold, Scripture says, "And I will sprinkle clean water upon you and you shall be clean; from all your uncleanness and from all your idols will I cleanse you" (Ezek. 36:25)

May God, in His great mercy, cleanse us from every sin, iniquity, and guilt. Amen. (*Yad haHazakah* [Mishneh Torah], Mikvaot, 11:12).

He who says, "I shall sin and repent, sin and repent"— they give him no chance to do repentance. "I will sin and the Day of Atonement will atone," - the Day of Atonement does not atone (Yoma 8:9)

Indeed, the Sages of the Mishnah teach that the purpose of the *mikveh* was to become "holy," and this should not be construed as pertaining only to the physical or the non-physical, for there was no such clear bifurcation in the mind of the Sages. In the same mishnah (Yoma 8:9), R. Akiva is quoted:

R. Akiva said: Happy are you, Israel! Who is it before whom you become clean? And who is it that makes you clean? Your Father which is in heaven, as it is said: And I will sprinkle clean water upon you and you shall be clean (Ezek. 36:25). And it further says: You, Hope (*mikveh*) of Israel, the Lord! (Jer. 17:13). Just as the *mikveh* renders clean the unclean, so does the Holy One, blessed be He, render Israel clean.

The main point to be gleaned from this is that though the performance of a *mikveh* was the ceremony which rendered a person ritually clean, some of the Sages recognized that one's heart intention was a necessary prerequisite. This accords with the view of the Qumran sect, which (owing to the *mikvaot* discovered at Qumran) were very keen on ritual immersion. The Community Rule (1QS 5:1–2) gives the purpose of the *Yahad* (community):

This is the rule for the men of the Yahad who volunteer to repent from all evil and to hold fast to all that He, by His good will, has commanded. They are to separate from the congregation of perverse men.

In the same context (1QS 5:13–14) we read:

None of the perverse men is to enter purifying waters used by the Men of Holiness and so contact their purity. Indeed, it impossible to be purified without first repenting of evil, inasmuch as impurity adheres to all who transgress His word.

Regarding one whose *halachah* did not match that of the Qumran sect, and whose life therefore remained (from their perspective) disobedient to the Torah, we read in 1QS 3:3–8,

Yet he cannot be justified by what his willful heart declares lawful, preferring to gaze on darkness rather than the ways of light. With such an eye he cannot be reckoned faultless. Ceremonies of atonement cannot restore his innocence, neither cultic waters his purity. He cannot be sanctified by baptism in oceans and rivers, nor purified by mere ritual bathing. Unclean, unclean shall he be all the days that he rejects the laws of God, refusing to be disciplined in the Yahad of His society. For only through the spirit pervading God's true society can there be atonement for a man's ways, all of his iniquities; thus only can he gaze upon the light of life and so be joined to His truth by His holy spirit, purified from all iniquity.

The parallels to John's *mikveh* for repentance are remarkable, for there is both a call for repentance from sin (evidenced by how one lives) required before one undergoes the *mikveh* of initiation into the *Yachad,* as well as the work of the רוּחַ הַקוֹדֶשׁ (Holy Spirit) in connection with the *mikveh* and the cleansing of iniquities.

Summary

This brief excursus on the use of *mikvaot* in the 1st Century has provided the following points of interest:

1. Though there is a paucity of data from the earliest strata of rabbinic literature concerning the precise meaning of the *mikveh*, it is clear from both literary and archaeological evidence that ceremonial immersion (*mikveh*) was well known and generally practised by a wide spectrum of Jewish sects in the early centuries.
2. The Torah commandment requiring "living water" for a *mikveh* was of central concern for the rabbis as they developed the *halachah* for *mikvaot.*
3. While some (perhaps many) may have viewed the water of the *mikveh* as a "cleansing agent" for removal of ritual impurities, it is clear that some of the Sages recognized the need for cleansing of the soul (repentance) as the highest meaning of the *mikveh* ceremony.
4. The fact that a *mikveh* concluded the proselyte ritual, and that the general ruling of the Sages was that a Gentile was not under all of the laws of purity (which pertained only to Jews), would indicate that the *mikveh* in this case signified a change of status more than a cleansing process for ritual impurity. However, since vessels procured from Gentiles were also required to undergo immersion, the proselyte *mikveh* may have functioned in both spheres, i.e., cleansing of ritual defilement *and* change of status.
5. While there was a debate among the Sages regarding whether a *mikveh* done without proper intention was valid, there is significant evidence to show that at least some of rabbinic authorities stressed the need for heart-felt repentance that preceded the performance of a *mikveh*.
6. From the Qumran scrolls (particularly *The Rule of the Community*, 1QS), we see that at least one sect of Judaism considered the *mikveh* as an entrance requirement into their community, and that it was construed as evidence of one's soul/heart commitment to righteousness as the sect

----

2 "Repent, for the kingdom of heaven is at hand."

The first words we hear from John HaMatbil are a call for repentance in light of the soon coming of the kingdom of heaven.[1] Repentance (μετανοέω, *metanoeo*) is conveyed by the verb שׁוּב (*shuv*, "to turn, return") in the Tanach (cf. 1Kings 8:47; 2Chron 6:37; Is 59:20; Jer 3:22–4:2; Ezek 33:9, 11; Zech 1:3;), as well as נָחַם (*nacham*, in the nifal, "to regret, relent," used mostly of God, cf. Ex. 32:14; Jer 18:8, 10; 26:3, 13, 19; Amos 7:3; Jonah 3:10, but also of people, cf. Ex. 13:17; Job 42:6; Jer 8:6; 31:19). The import of שׁוּב in conveying repentance is (1) turning from evil and (2) turning toward God, which means (a) admitting one's wrong doing (confession of sin), (b) accepting God's standards of righteousness, (c) forsaking the sin, (d) and adhering to new conduct.

In the Lxx, the Greek μετανοέω (found in our verse), which literally means "to change one's mind or thinking," usually translates נָחַם ("to regret, relent," 15x), and only once translates שׁוּב ("to turn, return," cf. Is. 46:8, "recall it to mind"). But by the time of the 1st Century, שׁוּב had become the common verb meaning "to repent," and the noun תְּשׁוּבָה (*teshuvah*) (itself coined by the Sages) had become the commonly used word for "repentance." We see this clearly in the rabbinic literature:

> Be not like the fools who, when they sin, bring an offering, but do not repent. They know not the difference between good and evil, and yet venture to make an offering to God. (b.*Berachot* 23a)

> "And Cain went out" (Gen. 4:16). On his way Cain met Adam, who said to him, "What has happened as regards the judgment passed upon you?" Cain replied, "I repented, and I am pardoned." When Adam heard that, he smote his face and said, "Is the power of repentance as great as that? I did not know it was so." (Mid. Rab. *Lev.* x.5)

> If a man were to come and say that God does not receive the penitent, Manasseh would come and testify against him, for there was never a man more wicked than he, and yet, in the hour of his repentance, God received him, as it is said, "He prayed unto God, and God entreated of him." (2Chron 33:13, Mid. Rab. *Num.* xiv.1)

> Who is a penitent man? R. Judah said, "The man who, when the same opportunity for sin occurs once or twice, refrains from sinning." He added, "the same woman, the same season, the same place."

> R. Judah Nesiah said in the name of R. Judah b. Simeon, "If a man shoots an arrow, it may reach one field's length or two, but greater is the power of repentance, for it reaches unto the throne of glory." (*Pesiqta Kahana* 163b)

> Sin offering and guilt offering and death and the Day of Atonement, all of them together, do not expiate sin without repentance. (t.*Yoma* 5.9)

[1]Because these exact words are found on the lips of Yeshua (4:17), some (e.g., Allison-Davies, 1.292) consider this phrase redactional on the part of Matthew.

Josephus (*Ant.* 18.116–19) gives a description of John and his message, and though he does not mention "repentance" explicitly, he does indicate that John "commanded" the Jews in terms of virtue and righteousness with God and man: "[116] Now, some of the Jews thought that the destruction of Herod's army came from God, and that very justly, as a punishment of what he did against John, that was called the Baptist; [117] for Herod slew him, who was a good man, and commanded the Jews to exercise virtue, both as to righteousness towards one another, and piety towards God, and so to come to baptism; for that the washing [with water] would be acceptable to him, if they made use of it, not in order to the putting away [or the remission] of some sins [only], but for the purification of the body; supposing still that the soul was thoroughly purified beforehand by righteousness."

In the Synoptic parallels (Mk 1:4, 15; Lk 3:3), the message of John includes (1) forgiveness of sins, (2) the time is fulfilled, and (3) believe in the gospel. Matthew's summarization of John's message in the single phrase "Repent, for the kingdom of heaven is at hand," fits the immediate need of his context. The other aspects of John's message will be given in the teachings of Yeshua as Matthew's gospel progresses.

God says, "My hands are stretched out towards the penitent; I reject no creature who gives me his heart in penitence." Therefore it says, "Peace, peace to the far and to the near. To all who draw near to me I draw near, and I heal them." (Mid. *Psalms* on 122:7)

R. Simeon says, "If a man was righteous his entire life but at the end he rebelled, he loses the whole, since it is said, *The righteousness of the righteous shall not deliver him when he transgresses* (Ezek. 33:12). If a man was evil his entire life but at the end he repented, the Omnipresent accepts him, as it is said, *And as for the wickedness of the wicked, he shall not fall by it when he turns from his wickedness* (Ezek. 33:12)." (t.*Quiddushin* 1.15–16).

These few quotes only give a brief glimpse at what is a central theme in much of the rabbinic literature, i.e., the fruit of repentance. In fact, the mark of a righteous person is that their life is marked by repentance (itself a paradox). Yet these few quotes should be sufficient to indicate that the call to repentance was not foreign to the message of Judaism, nor even to the Judaisms extant in the days of Yeshua. John's message, then, rings in concert with what many of the teachers of his day were saying. And as we shall see, repentance was a core element of Yeshua's teaching as well.

Though repentance was a familiar subject in the teachings of the Sages, John's call for repentance emphasized an urgency since the "kingdom of Heaven" was "at hand." "At hand" (ἐγγίζω, *engizo*) means "to come near." The kingdom of Heaven was about to be established, and it was this eschatological dawning that energized the message of John.

But what is meant by the "kingdom of Heaven" (מַלְכוּת שָׁמַיִם)? First, the use of heaven, as often in the rabbinic literature,[1] is a circumlocution for the ineffable Name (and thus in English translations that capitalize names referring to God, it should be written "kingdom of Heaven"). Thus, the "kingdom of Heaven" is equivalent to "the kingdom of God." Once again, Matthew has indicated that he is telling his story within a Jewish context, for the use of a substitute word for the sacred Name was common among the Judaisms of his time.

The phrase "kingdom of Heaven" is used exclusively by Matthew (32x)— it is not found elsewhere in the Apostolic Scriptures. The equivalent phrase, "kingdom of God" is also used by Matthew (12:28; 19:24; 21:31, 43), and it is the phrase used by the other Gospel writers as well as in the epistles. Thus, the notion that "kingdom of Heaven" denotes something different than the phrase "kingdom of God" is without substance.[2]

In short, the "kingdom of Heaven" is the rule of God, the place and time in which His kingship is both established and received. It therefore was part of the apocalyptic message of the prophets who foresaw the regathering of Israel, the defeat of her enemies, her return in obedience to the Torah, and the blessings that would be come as a result, not only upon the nation of Israel itself, but also upon all nations. At the heart of the prophetic promise of God's rule at the end of days was the appearance of the Messiah Who would bring God's redemption for His people, and establish justice upon the earth.

[1]For example, in *Pirkei Avot*, "Heaven" is used as a circumlocution: ""And let the fear of Heaven be upon you" (1:3, cf. 1:11; 2:2, 12; 4:4, 11-12; 5:17.

[2]"Kingdom of heaven" (מַלְכוּת שָׁמַיִם) is found twice in the Mishnah (m.*Ber.* 2:2, 5), as well as in the Bavil (b.*Berchot* 10b, 13a-b, 14b, 15a, 21a; b.*Chagigah* 5b; b.*Shavuot* 35b) as well as in the Midrash Rabbah (e.g., *Gen.* 9.13; 68:14; *Exod.* 20:13; *Deut ii.*31; *Lamm* 1.43).

Excursus – The Kingdom of Heaven

The Kingdom of Heaven or the Kingdom of God is a dominant theme throughout the Gospels. As noted above, Matthew alone uses both the designation "Kingdom of Heaven," where οὐρανός (*ouranos*, "heaven") represents the common Hebrew circumlocution שָׁמַיִם (*shamaim*) for the divine name, and the phrase "kingdom of God." That the kingdom theme is dominant in the Synoptics is evident from the repeated use of the term itself (βασιλεία, *basileia*): Matthew, 55x; Mark, 20x; Luke, 45x. John only uses the term 5x in his gospel. The "Kingdom of God" continues as a dominant theme in Luke's second volume (Acts), where the opening verses refer to it, and the book concludes with the notice regarding Paul that he continued "preaching the kingdom of God and teaching concerning the Lord Yeshua Messiah with all openness, unhindered." In the Pauline epistles, the kingdom theme continues (14x), while the remainder of the epistles use the term "kingdom" in reference to God's rule 10x. Beyond the explicit use of the term "kingdom" with its various added descriptive terms, the concept of the reign of God is also implicit in many other contexts and in the overall message of the Apostles.

This dominant theme of the reign and rule of God among the affairs of mankind is based upon the prophetic message of the Tanach. It was not a new teaching brought by our Master and His Apostles, but was spoken of by Israel's prophets and anticipated throughout the generations of Israel. The nation of Israel was viewed as a kingdom of priests, and thus a nation set apart to God: "… you shall be to Me a kingdom of priests and a holy nation" (Ex 19:6). When God established the throne of a reigning king, beginning with Saul, the fact is clearly established that He intended Israel's kingdom to be eternal. Samuel informs Saul that had he obeyed the commandments of God, "the LORD would have established your kingdom over Israel forever" (1Sam 13:13). It is this aspect of an enduring, unending kingdom that formed the eschatological expectations of the prophets. In the promise made to David, God foretells that David's son, Solomon, would build the Temple, and that He would "establish the throne of his kingdom forever" (2Sam 7:13). Indeed, in the Davidic covenant, God says of David, "Your house (dynasty) and your kingdom shall endure before Me forever; your throne shall be established forever" (2Sam 7:16).

This Davidic promise is thus the foundation for the eschatological expectation of the later prophets, who anticipated and spoke of the establishment of Israel's kingdom at the end of days, in which Israel would be planted forever in the Land, and would never again be disrupted by the nations. Such a reality would be the result of Israel's return to the Lord, and her full obedience to His commandments. But the kingdom's establishment would be the work of the Promised One, the ultimate Davidic King, that is, Messiah. He would bring Israel to repentance, regather her from exile, and rule over her as the final and eternal righteous King.

> There will be no end to the increase of His government or of peace, on the throne of David and over his kingdom, to establish it and to uphold it with justice and righteousness from then on and forevermore. The zeal of the LORD of hosts will accomplish this. (Is 9:7).

Likewise, it was this promise of a future Davidic kingdom that became the foundation for the apocalyptic message of the later prophets, in which the Messiah would wage war against the nations that had come against Israel, defeating them, and establishing Israel's dominance forever.

> In the days of those kings the God of heaven will set up a kingdom which will never be destroyed, and that kingdom will not be left for another people; it will crush and put an end to all these kingdoms, but it will itself endure forever. (Dan 2:44)

In Daniel's vision of the Ancient of Days (Dan 7), the Messianic ruler comes from heaven and establishes His eternal kingdom upon the earth:

> I kept looking in the night visions, and behold, with the clouds of heaven One like a Son of Man was coming, and He came up to the Ancient of Days and was presented before Him. And to Him was given dominion, glory and a kingdom, that all the peoples, nations and men of every language might serve Him. His dominion is an everlasting dominion which will not pass away; and His kingdom is one which will not be destroyed. (Dan. 7:13–14)

It is upon this background of the prophetic notice of the eschatological kingdom and reign of Messiah that John's words take meaning. Obviously, he does not explain what he means by "Kingdom of Heaven," nor would he have needed to, since those who heard his words would have been very familiar with the concept. The Pseudepigrapha is replete with references to the "kingdom of God" and similar terms (e.g., Sybl 3.767; 3Bar 11.2; Ps Sol 17.3; Apoc Abraham 8.3; cp. 1Enoch 46.1–6; 48.2–6; 62.5–7; 4 Ezra 13.32-38). Likewise, the Targumim use the phrase "kingdom of God" to describe the rule or reign of God.[1]

Moreover, the rabbinic literature refers to the "kingdom" in a number of ways, indicating that the concept was well in place in the 1st Century. In the halachah of reciting the Shema, the question is posed as to why the Shema precedes the command of the blessings. The answer comes: "So that one may first accept upon himself the yoke of the kingdom of heaven[2] and afterwards may accept the yoke of the commandments" (m.*Ber* 2.2). In the same context we learn that R. Gamliel recited the Shema on his wedding night, even though the Sages had ruled that a bridegroom was exempt from the command to recite the Shema until after the first night. R. Gamliel's reason is given: "I cannot heed you to suspend from myself the kingdom of heaven [even] for one hour" (m.*Ber.* 2.5). Indeed, so dominant was the kingdom theme in the rabbinic mind that the phrase "Blessed is the Name of the glory of His kingdom for ever and ever" was appended to the reciting of the opening phrase of the Shema (though to be said in a whisper or silently lest it be construed as equal with Scripture). According to b.*Ber* 15a,

> R. Johanan also said: If one desires to accept upon himself the yoke of the kingdom of heaven in the most complete manner, he should consult nature (use the latrine) and wash his hands and put on tefillin and recite the Shema and say the tefillah (prayers): this is the complete acknowledgment of the kingdom of heaven.

In other words, the establishment of the Kingdom of Heaven in the rabbinic mind is seen in the obedience of His people to the ways of Torah.

But the return of Israel to Torah obedience, though it begins with each

[1]See B. D. Chilton, *God in Strength: Jesus' Announcement of the Kingdom* (SNTU B/1. Freistatdt, 1979), pp. 87–88.

[2]For other references to the "yoke of the kingdom of heaven," see b.*Ber* 10b, 13a–14b.

individual, still was considered eschatological by the rabbis. The future reign of the Messiah would result in the subjugation of Israel's enemies, her return to the Land, and thus a return to righteous living. The midrash on Song of Songs ties this all together with the appearance of the Messiah:

> THE RAIN IS OVER AND GONE (2:11): this refers to the subjection of Israel. THE FLOWERS APPEAR ON THE EARTH: the conquerors have appeared on the earth. Who are they? R. Berekiah said in the name of R. Isaac: As it is written, And the Lord showed me four craftsmen (Zech 2:3), namely, Elijah, the Messiah, Melchizedek, and the War Messiah. THE TIME OF THE ZAMIR (pruning) IS COME: the time has come for Israel to be delivered; the time has come for uncircumcision to be cut off; the time has come for the kingdom of the Cutheans to expire; the time has come for the kingdom of heaven to be revealed, as it says, And the Lord shall be king over all the earth (Zech 14:9). AND THE VOICE OF THE TURTLE IS HEARD IN OUR LAND: Who is this? This is the voice of the Messiah (Mid. Rab. *Song* II.3).

The Dead Sea Scrolls also contain numerous references to the reign of God, in which the wicked will be destroyed and the righteous of Israel will be exulted (cf. 1QM 15–17). In the Rule of the Community we read:

> [For] He chose you [...] and to place you at the head of the Holy Ones and with you to bl[ess ...] by your hand the men of God's council, rather than by the hand of the prince of [...] one another. May you [abide forever] as an Angel of the Presence in the holy habitation, to the glory of the God of host[s. May you] serve in the temple of the kingdom of God, ordering destiny with the Angels of the Presence, a Council of the Yahad [with the Holy Ones] forever, for all the ages of eternity! (1QSb 4:1f).

We see by these few examples that the concept of God's reign upon the earth by the hand of His Messiah was well in place during the 1st Century, and that therefore John's use of the phrase "Kingdom of Heaven" needed no explanation. Indeed, the Kingdom of Heaven was understood to be the rule of God upon the earth by His Messiah by which wickedness is abolished and the righteousness prevails. Since the prevailing rabbinic viewpoint of the 1st Century was that only Israel was righteous, by extension, the establishment of righteousness upon the earth also meant the establishment of Israel over her enemies.

Yet when we consider the "Kingdom of Heaven" in the teachings of Yeshua and His apostles, we are immediately confronted with a tension, one that has been the focus of an exorbitant amount of scholarly labors in the past century. This tension is apparent when the kingdom passages are examined, and may be simply stated as a question: is the Kingdom of God present in the coming of Yeshua, or is it yet future? If the rule of God among men means that wickedness has been abolished, then how is it possible to say that "the kingdom of God has come" (Matt 12:28) in light of the fact that wickedness remains?

The explanations offered by scholars to this apparent dilemma may be grouped around several dominant perspectives (many of which overlap in meaning). (1) Yeshua turned the concept of the Kingdom of Heaven from one of territorial dimensions to that of ethics. In other words, the rule of God would be seen not by conquering Israel's enemies and placing her as the dominant peoples of the earth, but as an ethical reality in which the Kingdom of God would be seen in the righteous behavior of those who submitted to His rule. Thus, the Kingdom of God is seen as the "organization of redeemed humanity, whose actions are inspired by love."[1] Thus, the expectations of the Jewish people, that the Kingdom of the God would result in victory over their enemies, was replaced by Yeshua as the Kingdom of God that ruled in the hearts of men. This non-eschatological explanation of the kingdom (given initially in the work of A. Ritschl, and furthered by that of A. von Harnack) became a dominant force in the social gospel movement at the turn of the 20th Century, for the Kingdom of God was not to await the return of Yeshua to rule and reign but was already extant in the reality of the Gospel. The Kingdom would thus be realized by the reformation of society into one holy community.

(2) In opposition to this non-eschatological view was that of J. Weiss, Ritschl's son-in-law, who reacted strongly against the non-eschatological view of Ritschl, and emphasized the future apocalyptic character of the kingdom.[2] A. Schweitzer, building on the work of Weiss, read the message of Yeshua as thoroughly eschatological, understanding His words to mean that He expected the end to come during the mission of the Twelve. When Yeshua realized that He was mistaken, He decided to cast Himself "headlong to death in a final, heroic attempt to force God to set up His kingdom."[3] The impact of Schweitzer may be seen in that his interpretation of the "historical Yeshua"[4] became the dominant position among German scholarship in the early 20th Century.

(3) In reaction to Weiss and those who followed him, R. Bultmann, who also considered that Yeshua was mistaken about the realization of the kingdom in His lifetime, taught that the kingdom was supra-historical, that is, existing out of the confines of earth's history (*heilsgeschichte*, "salvation history"). The kingdom of God exists at the point of decision, when mankind is confronted with the divine and with the need to accept what is righteous and shun the evil. In this way, Yeshua came as the supreme example, and "redemption" comes from following His example. Yeshua, though mistaken about the kingdom's arrival, nonetheless provided the best example of how the supra-historical kingdom of God could be realized in the lives of people, for in giving His life, he demonstrated the way of love.

(4) C. H. Dodd[5] presented a strong christological view of the kingdom of Heaven, holding that it became present at the coming of Yeshua. Indeed, Dodd's view may be a near equating of the Kingdom of God with the person of Yeshua Himself. Particularly in His performing of miracles, and especially in the casting out of demons, Yeshua showed that He personified the rule of God upon the earth, a rule that subdued the kingdom of darkness. For Dodd, the "kingdom of God has come" in the person of Yeshua, and is therefore a timeless reality. In this sense, the only futuristic aspects of the Kingdom of God relate to eternity or the world to come.

(5) In reacting to these various interpretations of the Kingdom of Heaven/God in the Gospels, evangelicals and neo-evangelicals recognized some measure of truth in most of them. It is clear (as we shall see) that Yeshua proclaimed the arrival of the Kingdom. Yet it is equally clear that He also taught its future reality. This led scholars like Kümmel, Jeremias, and G. E. Ladd[6] to suggest that the appearance of Yeshua in His first coming brought both the reality of the Kingdom, as well as the means for its future fulness in

[1] C. C. Caragounis, "Kingdom of God/Kingdom of Heaven" in *Dictionary of Jesus and the Gospels,* Green & McKnight, eds. (IVP, 1992), p. 420, describing the work of Ritschl.

[2] J. Weiss, *Die Predigt Jesu vom Reiche God,* 1892 (English: *Jesus' Proclamation of the Kingdom of God,* 1971).

[3] Caragounis, *Op. cit.*

[4] A. Schweitzer, *The Quest for the Historical Jesus* (1910).

[5] See particularly his *The Parables of the Kingdom* (1935).

[6] G. E. Ladd, *The Presence of the Future* (Eerdmans, 1974).

[1]Quoted from Caragounis, *Op. cit.,* p. 421.

the eschatological reign (whether of the millennium or of the eternal state). In the words of J. Jeremias, the Kingdom of God is an "eschatology in process of realization."[1] This view (utilizing Ladd's terminology) has been labeled as "realized eschatology." It incorporates the idea of "already–not yet" in terms of how the Kingdom of Heaven/God is manifest. This is more than simply saying that we have a "foretaste" of the future and full kingdom. The idea of "already–not yet" is that the Kingdom is fully manifest in the lives of believers today, but awaits its fulness in the future. It is qualitatively extant now, but in quantitative terms will be fully realized at the end of days.

The Kingdom of Heaven in Matthew

When we consider the various teachings of Yeshua and His Apostles, we will understand the tension that exists between the present reality of the kingdom, and its futuristic manifestations.

Jochanan HaMatbil proclaims that the Kingdom of Heaven is approaching (Matt 3:2), and Yeshua reiterates these words (4:17). In His Sermon on the Mount, the Kingdom is described as yet future, when those who are righteous will be vindicated (5:3, 10). Moreover, only those with genuine righteousness will even enter the Kingdom (5:19–20). In describing His pattern from prayers, Yeshua teaches His talmidim to say "May Your (i.e., God's) kingdom come" (6:10), and to rejoice in the inevitable victory of God's reign (6:13, note textual variants). In 7:21, Yeshua speaks about "entering" the Kingdom, casting it as yet future. This future Kingdom includes Abraham, Isaac, and Jacob (8:11–12) with whom the citizens of the Kingdom will dine, meaning that the resurrection has occurred. The gospel that Yeshua proclaimed is designated as the "gospel of the Kingdom" (9:35), which He was teaching in the synagogues. Indeed, the imminent arrival of the Kingdom was the core message of the Gospel with which He commissions His talmidim (10:7, cf. 13:19), and it will be that when the "gospel of the Kingdom" is preached throughout the world that the end will come (24:14). The essence of this gospel message is that the Kingdom of God is approaching (10:7). In 18:3, Yeshua admonishes a child-like faith, without which one will not enter the Kingdom of Heaven. Moreover, entrance into the Kingdom is not dependent upon one's social status, but upon genuine repentance and faithfulness. Even the tax collectors and prostitutes who repent and do the will of the Father will enter the Kingdom (21:31). It seems quite possible that the transfiguration was a special revelation of the future Kingdom, for Yeshua promised that some of His talmidim would not die until they had seen the Son of man coming in His kingdom (16:28). Finally, at His last Pesach, Yeshua states that He will not drink of the fruit of the vine until He comes in His Father's Kingdom (26:29). These are examples of how the Kingdom was portrayed as yet future.

Still, in other places, the Kingdom of Heaven/God is spoken of as already present. Most markedly is the statement of our Master in 12:28, "But if I cast out demons by the Spirit of God, then the kingdom of God has come upon you." In Luke 17:21 Yeshua states that the "kingdom of God in in your midst." In 16:19 Yeshua gives the "keys of the Kingdom" to His Apostles, allowing them authoritative voice in kingdom matters. In 19:12, Yeshua speaks of those who "make themselves eunuchs for the sake of the Kingdom," which would suggest that the Kingdom already existed. In Yeshua's critique of some of the Pharisees, He judges them because they have "shut off the kingdom of heaven from people" (23:13), indicating that real access to the Kingdom existed in their time.

In the parables of the Kingdom (Matt 13), there are strong indicators that the kingdom had arrived. In offering the parable of the sower, Yeshua's talmidim question Him regarding His use of parables in general. His answer is that the mysteries of the Kingdom had been revealed to those whom God had chosen and hidden from the others. In the next parable, in which the enemy sows tares among the wheat, the implication is that the wheat represents the Kingdom of God which, though with an admixture of tares, is nonetheless present and not merely future. The same may be said of the mustard seed and leaven parables. In each of these, the primary point is that the Kingdom of Heaven will continue to grow until it envelopes the whole world. Finally, the parables of obtaining objects of value (treasure hidden in a field; a merchant seeking fine pearls; a net in the sea catching fish) emphasize that the obtaining or getting is going on now by those who are citizens of the Kingdom, but that the judgment of those things awaits the future.

We see, then, that in Matthew's Gospel, the descriptions of the Kingdom of Heaven/God portray it as both a current reality as well as something that is yet coming in the future.

John's Gospel contains an oft quoted text regarding the Kingdom of God:

> Yeshua answered, "My kingdom is not of this world. If My kingdom were of this world, then My servants would be fighting so that I would not be handed over to the Jews; but as it is, My kingdom is not of this realm." (John 18:36)

Though often interpreted as meaning that the Kingdom of God is not connected to the physical world, this is hardly the meaning of the text. Yeshua's point is that the nations will be brought into subjection to His reign, not by the efforts of man but by the direct, sovereign work of God. His Kingdom comes about by super-natural, that is, divine means.

Examples of the Kingdom of God in other Apostolic Texts

Paul uses the phrase "Kingdom of God" in the conclusion of His chapter about forfeiting one's rights for the sake of another community member (Rom 14). He concludes "for the kingdom of God is not eating and drinking, but righteousness and peace and joy in the Holy Spirit" (Rom 14:17). In other words, the demonstration of one's citizenship in the Kingdom of God is best done through how we treat each other rather than our strict adherence to extra-biblical *halachah*. This is not a negation of traditions, but a putting of them as secondary to the genuine needs of others. In a similar vein, Paul writes that "the kingdom of God does not consist in words but in power" (1Cor 4:20), meaning that walking in righteousness by the power of the Spirit is the true demonstration of God's rule and reign. This is evident among those who have been rescued from the domain of darkness and have been transferred to the "kingdom of His beloved Son" (Col 1:13), something that is apparently a present reality as far as Paul was concerned. Indeed, he mentions by name some "who are workers for the Kingdom" (Col 4:11).

Yet Paul clearly teaches the coming of a yet future, eschatological Kingdom of God. He speaks of "inheriting" the Kingdom (1Cor 15:50; Gal 5:21;

Eph 5:5) and he recognizes that the present suffering for righteousness sake will be judged as worthy for those who enter the Kingdom (2Thess 1:5), and that his own suffering would never cause his demise, but that God would rescue him out of every trouble, and bring him safely "to His heavenly Kingdom" (2Tim 4:18). This phrase "heavenly Kingdom" should most likely be understood in light of the "Kingdom of Heaven" terminology, i.e., the Kingdom that is known by the rule of God.

This future arrival of the Kingdom is spoken of by John in the Apocalypse, for it is when the "kingdom of the world has become the kingdom of our Lord and of His Messiah" that the reign of God is known to be eternal (Rev 11:15). The full realization of the Kingdom is when the "accuser of the brethren" has been cast down, when the "salvation, and the power, and the kingdom of our God and the authority of His Messiah have come" (Rev 12:10).

It is clear, then, when we take a survey of the kingdom language in the Apostolic Scriptures, that the Kingdom of Heaven is, indeed, "already and not yet." The Kingdom has arrived in that the King has come, and in His coming, He has accomplished all that is necessary for the complete and full realization of the reign of God upon the earth. Yet such application of the accomplished reality is being worked out in the course of human history. In each person and each place where the righteous reign of the Messiah is seen, there the Kingdom of God is known. But the fulness of His reign will be marked by the salvation of Israel (cf. Rom 11:25f), for the Kingdom, in its most basic sense, is the fulfillment of the covenant promises to the covenant people. The current expression of the Kingdom of God, then, is likened to the first fruits which anticipates the final harvest. The first fruits are valid fruit! They are not a reasonable facsimile, but the genuine thing. Yet in terms of the complete harvest, this awaits the future when Messiah returns and reigns.

We must conclude, then, that the Kingdom of Heaven/God was taught by our Master and His Apostles as already existing yet having future dimensions as well. In terms of God's all-pervasive providence, the Kingdom was assured because the King had appeared, and would accomplish everything necessary to bring about the Kingdom's final and full expression. Yet the complete realization of the Kingdom in all of its dimensions would await the end of days. All who would receive the King would enter the Kingdom, but those who reject Him would be cast out. In this way, the Kingdom of Heaven incorporates both the physical restoration of Israel and those who would join her through faith in her reigning King, Messiah, for in the end, Israel comes to repentance on a national scale, confessing the pierced One to be their King. The Kingdom of Heaven is thus neither entirely internal (ethical) nor external (political, geographical) but both, for the return of Israel to her Land is in conjunction with her repentance and the establishment of the covenant on her behalf. The rule and reign of God is thus seen in its fulness when the Torah is written on the heart, which results in outward obedience to the word of the King (Jer 31:31–34). What is future is the national expression of this new covenant in the descendants of Jacob. The present expression of the Kingdom of Heaven is the believing remnant who have participated in the new covenant already, as the first fruits of the eventual harvest.

Practical Implications of The Kingdom of Heaven

It should, first of all, arrest our attention that the Gospel proclaimed by Yeshua, and commissioned to His Apostles, is the "Gospel of the kingdom" (Matt 4:23; 9:35; 24:14; Mark 1:15; Luke 16:16). From this we should understand that the "good news" proclaimed by Yeshua and His talmidim was, at its core, kingdom centered. This has vast implications for our understanding of what the Gospel is, and what it entails. First, contrary to the primary emphasis in our day, the Gospel is not ultimately an individual reality. That is to say, while the salvation procured by Yeshua through His death, resurrection, ascension, and intercession is indeed a salvation of individuals from the condemnation of their sins, and comes to each individual on the basis of having been individually chosen to salvation and given the gift of personal faith, this salvation nonetheless brings each individual into a kingdom under the rule and reign of the Messiah. Thus, acceptance of the good news is at the same time an acceptance of a new citizenship, which brings the believer into a covenant relationship with God as well as with all other members of the kingdom. All who are born from above through the work of the Spirit in the life-changing regeneration of the soul become members of an established Kingdom of Heaven in which the present reign of Messiah is evident through their obedience to Him. The notion that salvation is merely a personal, individual soul response to God leaves out the ultimate goal of God's saving grace, that is, His intention to establish a kingdom of people who have a corporate identity as His loyal subjects. The Kingdom of Heaven is not restricted, then, to the vertical relationship of the individual to his Savior, but equally finds expression in the relationship between each other.

Secondly, the Kingdom of God as the primary expression of the Gospel cannot ignore the fact that the national expression of the people of Israel is both the first expression of this kingdom and the foundation of it. That Yeshua expressed His intention to go first to the "lost sheep of Israel" shows that any definition of the Kingdom of God that excludes the divine prerogative to remain faithful to the physical seed of Jacob is wrong headed. Rather than forsaking Israel, or redefining "Israel" in platonic overtones of the ideal, Yeshua and His Apostles consider the covenant promises made to the physical offspring of Jacob as the foundational elements of the Kingdom of God. Indeed, the presence of the *Shekinah* in the Tabernacle was the expression of God's rule and reign as Israel's King. That the Cherubim are designated in terms reminiscent of a throne upon which the King sits (Num 7:89; 1Sam 4:4; 2Sam 6:2; 2Ki 19:15; 1Chron 13:6; Ps 80:1; 99:1; Is 37:16) shows that His throne was integral to His covenant presence among the chosen people of Israel. And we see that the eschatological victory of God as promised by the prophets incorporates this same imagery. God reigns forever in Zion (Ps 146:10; Is 24:23; 52:7; Mic 4:7), for He has placed His Name, His eyes, and His heart there forever (1Ki 9:3). It is from Jerusalem that His future reign in the millennial kingdom via His chosen Messiah emanates, and it is thus in the context of a regathered, united Israel, worshipping in accordance with Torah of Moses, that His kingship is ultimately seen. The Kingdom of Heaven therefore cannot be separated from the chosen people of Israel and her inevitable future blessing by the sovereign hand of God. Any message of the gospel that fails to incorporate God's clear intention to save Israel at the end of days is therefore vastly deficient. Moreover, that the Gospel of the Kingdom would go to all the nations (Matt 28:19–20) makes it clear that the salvation of those chosen from nations does not eventuate in a second kingdom, or one that replaces God's reign in Zion. Rather, the redeemed ones from the nations join Israel as members of God's established kingdom. Yeshua emphasized this when He taught that "many will come from east and west, and recline at the table with Abraham, Isaac and Jacob in the kingdom of heaven" (Matt 8:11), and that He had many sheep who were not presently part of His flock, but that He would bring them nonetheless, and they would all form one flock with one Shepherd (John 10:16). The Gospel of the Kingdom is therefore a call to join an entity already in existence, not a call to initiate and construct a new kingdom which had not previously existed.

Thirdly, the message of the Gospel of the Kingdom incorporates the message of the King's established and revealed commandments. The good news is not merely that of escape from condemnation (though this is a most wonderful and foundational aspect of the Gospel) but also a call to submit to the King's teachings (Torah). The Apostles are instructed to teach the future members of the kingdom "to observe all that I commanded you" (Matt 28:20). Membership in the Kingdom of Heaven requires submission to the rule and reign of the King. Thus, the message of the Gospel must include not only the glory of forgiveness based upon the infinite and unfailing grace of God in Messiah, but also the message of sanctification, that is, the requirement to pursue holiness as befits those who claim kingdom identity and who are endowed with the sanctifying presence of the Spirit. This is because the Gospel of the Kingdom is, at its heart, a message incorporating a covenant relationship with the King. All too often in our day, the Gospel is truncated to include only the message of forgiveness without mention of what characterizes the lives of true citizens of the Kingdom. Such a synthetic "gospel" fails to produce members of the Kingdom because it is not the message of the King. Rather, this anemic "gospel" has resulted in the establishment of man-made "kingdoms" where the rule of Messiah is hardly evident or is entirely eclipsed in the bright lights of Hollywood Christianity.

Fourthly, the fact that the Gospel is kingdom centered is a source of great confidence. The King is the One who establishes He kingdom, and it is therefore an inevitability. This is portrayed in the kingdom parables of Matthew 13, where what appears to be something insignificant or small (mustard seed; pinch of leaven) eventually grows large and encompasses the whole. When Yeshua stated that "I will build My *kehilah*" (ἐκκλησία, *ekklesia*, "assembly," Matt 16:18), He is proclaiming that He is the One Who will establish His kingdom. While He graciously assigns to His disciples the task of proclaiming the Gospel, the success of its message is in His hands. The Father is the One Who draws the elect into the fold; the Spirit is the One Who opens the eyes and ears, and plants the seeds of faith in the heart to receive the good news; Yeshua is the One Who secures the success of His redeeming sacrifice through His High Priestly intercession. The Kingdom is already established, and its success and victory over all other rulers and kingdoms is secure. Yeshua demonstrated this by casting out demons (Matt 12:28), showing that no obstacle can stand in the way of His ultimate and final reign as God's rightful King. Therefore, as His servants and disciples, we may proclaim the message of the Kingdom without fear, for the gospel is itself the power resulting in salvation to all who believe (Rom 1:16), for it is the good pleasure of the Father to use the message of the Gospel to accomplish His sovereign design in establishing His Kingdom upon the earth.

Finally, that the concept of a "kingdom" is at the heart of the Gospel message helps us define the ultimate destination of our spiritual existence and journey. We are not in the process of preparing for some ethereal existence in a celestial city, but we are rather anticipating the rule of Messiah in Jerusalem. Our focus upon living in accordance with God's Torah today is a fitting preparation for life in the physical presence of the reigning Messiah in Zion. The Kingdom of Heaven will find its ultimate expression in the physicality of a Temple on a well-known piece of real estate called "the Temple mount" in the city of Jerusalem. Realizing that the kingdom is the core element of the Gospel dismisses the idea that the goal of our salvation is to escape from this world. Rather, our purpose as citizens of the kingdom is to prepare ourselves for the future reign of our Messiah in this world. In this regard, our message is the same as that of Yochanan HaMatbil: "repent, for the Kingdom of Heaven is at hand." But we send forth this message not only in word, but also in deed. Our business is to sanctify His Name upon the earth—to let everyone, everywhere know Who the King actually is, and to admonish them to submit to His present reign, and prepare for His future appearance as the enthroned King. While we basque in the blessings of our own citizenship and the benefits afforded us as subjects of the King of Kings, we nonetheless realize that as citizens of the Kingdom of Heaven, it is not ultimately about us, but about Him. It is therefore our primary desire that His Name be magnified through our words and our actions.

---

3 For this is the one referred to by Isaiah the prophet when he said, "The voice of one crying in the wilderness, 'Make ready the way of the Lord, Make His paths straight!'"

The work of Yochanan HaMatbil is here explained as fulfilling the prophetic words of Isaiah the prophet. Matthew names Isaiah six times in his gospel (3:3; 4:14; 8:17; 12:17; 13:14; 15:7), and except 3:3, all are in connection with the ministry of Yeshua. Three of the quotes from Isaiah (4:14; 8:17; 12:17) pertain to Yeshua's role as the suffering servant of the Lord Who brings salvation, while the final two (13:14; 15:7) are given as a rebuke for Israel's blindness to the message of the Gospel.

The current text is the sole example of a quote from the Tanakh in Matthew that is not introduced with a "fulfillment" formula. Some have suggested that this is to indicate that Matthew did not see Yochanan as the fulfillment of the Isaiaic prophecy, but only as aligning with the general thrust of it. But Carson is right when he says:

> It goes too far, however, (contra Gundry), to say that the omission of fulfillment language means that for Matthew, John the Baptist does not fulfill Scripture but serves merely as a "protypical Christian preacher." If Matthew had wanted to say so little, he would have been better off eliminating the OT passage.[1]

The language Matthew employs is that of a *Pesher*: "This is that…," meaning that one commonly held application of the prophetic text was to apply it to Yochanan's ministry. For instance in 1QS 8:12–14, those of the Qumran society, who have left the "perverse" society of Jerusalem and taken up residence in the "desert," are reckoned as the fulfillment of Isaiah 40:3,

[1]Carson, *Matthew* in *The Expositors Bible Commentary*, 8.101.

> When such men as these come to be in Israel, conforming to these doctrines, they shall separate from the session of perverse men to go to the wilderness, there to prepare the way of truth, as it is written, "In the wilderness prepare the way of the Lord, make straight in the desert a highway for our God" (Isaiah 40:3).

The parallel account in Mark (1:2–3) combines Mal 3:1 and Ex 23:20 with the quote from Is 40:3–

> As it is written in Isaiah the prophet: "Behold, I send My messenger ahead of You (Ex 23:30), Who will prepare Your way (Mal 3:1); The voice of one crying in the wilderness, 'Make ready the way of the Lord, Make His paths straight (Is 40:3).'"

Matthew and Luke also use a similar combination of Mal 3:1 and Ex 23:30 later on in their gospels (Matt 11:10; Lk 7:27) in connection with the appearance of Yochanan.

Matthew's quote of Is 40:3 conforms exactly to the wording of Mark, which likewise follows the Lxx (with a few slight modifications):

MT	Lxx	Matthew
קוֹל קוֹרֵא בַּמִּדְבָּר פַּנּוּ דֶּרֶךְ יְהוָה יַשְּׁרוּ בָּעֲרָבָה מְסִלָּה לֵאלֹהֵינוּ A voice is calling, "Clear the way for the LORD in the wilderness; Make smooth in the desert a highway for our God."	φωνὴ βοῶντος ἐν τῇ ἐρήμῳ ἑτοιμάσατε τὴν ὁδὸν κυρίου εὐθείας ποιεῖτε τὰς τρίβους τοῦ θεοῦ ἡμῶν The voice of one crying out in the wilderness, "Prepare the way of the Lord; Make straight the paths of our God."	φωνὴ βοῶντος ἐν τῇ ἐρήμῳ· ἑτοιμάσατε τὴν ὁδὸν κυρίου, εὐθείας ποιεῖτε τὰς τρίβους αὐτοῦ. The voice of one crying out in the wilderness, "Prepare the way of the Lord; Make straight His paths."

As can be readily seen, the Lxx has understood the MT a bit differently, though in so doing the primary thrust of the Hebrew is not missed. In the Hebrew (according to the Masoretic accentuation, which places the *zaqef gadol* over בַּמִּדְבָּר) בַּמִּדְבָּר, ("in the wilderness") is adverbial, modifying פַּנּוּ,"Prepare," describing the location in which the way of the LORD is to be made straight. In the Lxx, however, ἐν τῇ ἐρήμῳ, "in the wilderness" modifies φωνὴ βοῶντος, "a voice crying out," indicating the location of the one making the proclamation. However, the Targum, Old Peshitta, and Vulgate all take "in the wilderness" as modifying "a voice crying," which might indicate that there was an earlier, pre-Masoretic understanding of the syntax. But the parallelism of the Hebrew supports the MT accentuation: "Clear the way…in the wilderness// Make smooth…in the desert."

The other minor differences are 1) that Matthew (who follows Mark) substitutes the masculine pronoun "his" (αὐτοῦ) for "our God" in the final clause: "the highway for our God" vs. "His paths," and 2) the singular מְסִלָּה, "highway" is made plural in the Lxx (which Matthew follows), τὰς τρίβους, "the paths."

The original context of Isaiah 40 is one of comfort to the Babylonian exiles. They are to take courage and be hopeful, for God has not abandoned them but is making a way for their return to the Land. The obstacles that stand in their way are being removed, and the road home is being prepared. But the Book of Comfort, which begins with Isaiah 40, does not only have the

The Du Tillet has מְסִלָּה לֵאלֹהֵינוּ, conforming to the MT. The Peshitta, however, follows the Greek of Matthew, and Mark, with לִשְׁבִילוֹהִי. The Münster has מְסִלּוֹתָיו, "his paths."

immediate needs of the exiles in view, for it foresees not only the rebuilding of Jerusalem and the cities of Judah (43:26) as well as the restoration of the Temple (44:28), but also the gathering of the nations who anxiously await the Torah of God (42:4). Moreover, Isaiah's prophecies contain the promise of the suffering Messiah, by Whose stripes Israel is healed (53:5) for He would bear upon Himself their transgressions. The regathering of the exiles is thus just the beginning of an eschatological restoration of Israel that would never again be exiled (55:13), and everlasting peace would be realized (60:15–20).

It is this overarching picture of Isaiah's Book of Comfort that is the background for Matthew's use of Is 40:3, for the covenant blessing that would come upon Israel are all based upon the work of the Servant of the LORD Who would accomplish Israel's final redemption, bringing upon her the covenant blessings, and Yochanan was functioning as the prophet, proclaiming His arrival.

Interestingly, Mid. Rab. *Deut* iv.11 utilizes Is 40:4 in the same way. Commenting upon Deut 12:20 and the phrase "When the LORD your God extends your borders," the Sages wonder how the Land could be enlarged. They compare it to a Torah scroll which, when full unrolled, looks much larger. Similarly, the Land consists of many hills and valleys, but when "every valley is lifted up, and every mountain and hill made low," then the full extent of the Land will be realized. Having quoted Is 40:4, the midrash goes on to quote Mal 3, Zech 1 and 9, referencing the timing of these events to be in the days of the Messiah. The Gospel writer's use of the Isaiah text in this manner, then, is not a later "Christianization" of the Tanakh, but falls in line with a common understanding of how the prophetic promises were to be fulfilled in the coming of Messiah.

Obviously, for Matthew and the other gospel writers, the dawning of this eschatological time of fulfillment had arrived with the appearance of Yeshua. And Yochanan's message of repentance in light of the coming Kingdom signalled the beginning of the eschaton. That millennia have passed since the days of Yochanan and the Messiah does not diminish the reality of Yochanan's message. For the Almighty, a thousand years is as a day (Ps 90:4; 2Pet 3:8). Yeshua came as the suffering Servant to accomplish everything necessary to bring about the eternal redemption of His people. Though from a human perspective, time languishes in anticipation of the fulfillment, but from God's point of view, the redemption of His chosen ones is right on schedule (2Pet 3:9–10).

We should also note, in regard to Matthew's use of Is 40:3, that while in its original context it applies to the work of יהוה (the LORD), its application to Yochanan and thus to Yeshua as the One Whose way is being prepared, marks a common theme among the Gospel writers and Apostles, namely, that Yeshua is Immanuel, God with us. They neither try to explain this mystery, nor do they deny it or seek to diminish its force. As Carson notes:

> In Isaiah 40:3 the way [the LORD] is being "made straight"…; in Matthew 3:3 it is the way of Jesus. This sort of identification of Jesus with [the LORD] is common in the NT (e.g., Exod 13:21 and 1Cor 10:4; Is 6:1 and John 12:41; Ps 68:18 and Eph 4:8; Ps 102:25–27 and Heb 1:10–12) and confirms the kingdom as being equally the kingdom of God and the kingdom of Jesus. While the deity of Messiah is only implicit in such texts, it certainly goes beyond Jesus' being merely a royal envoy.[1]

[1]Carson, *Matthew* in *The Expositors Bible Commentary*, 8.102.

How is it that the way for the Coming One would be prepared in the desert? The imagery of Isaiah 40 is the arrival of the Holy One coming through the desert Who would affect the salvation of Israel. As the King, only a perfect road would be fit for His travel. The preparation is understood by Matthew (and apparently by Yochanan) as that of people, not of roads. Personal preparation (meaning repentance and sanctification) is the preparation befitting the King.

4 Now John himself had a garment of camel's hair and a leather belt around his waist; and his food was locusts and wild honey.

From this point on, Matthew refers to Yochanan without the adjective HaMatbil ("the baptizer"). His familiarity among Matthew's readers was sufficient, along with the preceding context, to warrant the shorter reference.

The use of camel's hair for clothing is not widely attested in the sources. Apparently some *soft* camel hair was used for luxurious clothing,[1] but other than that, its use as a description for Yochanan's garments is most likely given to emphasize that he was clad in the most basic of attire. Matthew is contrasting Yochanan with the later description of those who lived in king's palaces and wore expensive clothing (Matt 11:8). Yochanan lived in a self-sufficient manner, subsisting on what could be found in the desert itself. In this, there may well be a parallel to Elijah. In 2Ki 1:8 we read the description of Elijah: "He was a hairy man with a leather girdle bound about his loins." Matthew wishes us to see that Yochanan was a portend of the final days when Elijah would herald the final arrive of the Messiah, not as the suffering servant, but as the reigning King (Mal 4:5).

Some have suggested that by "locusts" (ἀκρίδες, *akrides*) is meant the fruit of the "locust tree," i.e., the carob pod. But this is not supported either by linguistic evidence nor by probability (so *BDAG*, ad loc.). The large grasshopper is still eaten by bedouins to this day, and are specifically noted to be kosher (Lev 11:21–22) and were not considered "meat" by the Sages (m.*Chul* 8.1). Wild honey (μέλι ἄγριον, *meli agrion*) is distinguished from the honey taken from hives that were tended by a beekeeper. It is not to be understood by these descriptions that he only ate these two foods, but that these were a common part of his diet. The point of these descriptions is to cast Yochanan as living a simple and self-sufficient life. He was not out to bilk the masses of their offerings in order to amass personal wealth. And, as the next verse indicates, his demeanor bespoke integrity and sincerity, and as a result, attracted the masses.

5 Then Jerusalem was going out to him, and all Judea and all the district around the Jordan;

Jerusalem is personified here, meaning that it stands for the population of the city and the immediate surroundings. Judea broadens the geographical reference. The "district of Jordan," while contained in the broad term "Judea," is most likely given to indicate that Yochanan's influence had extended eastward beyond the Jordan, e.g., in Perea. Here, again, we see the thought of coming into the Land at the same point as Israel initially entered at the time of the conquest. If later in the life of Yeshua, the masses turn against Him, here, in the opening chapters, the masses are receiving Yochanan's message, and presumably anticipating the coming of the Messiah he proclaimed

[1] John Nolland, *Matthew* in *NIGTC*, p. 139, who notes a reference in *Applonius Paradoxographus* 20 of luxury clothing made of soft camel hair.

(cp. 4:24–25). It seems to be a general phenomenon that the people are easily persuaded by the message of the truth until they are led in another direction by their teachers. One could suggest that this is true whether the message is valid or not, that the masses are generally naïve and easily led this way or that. But given the opportunity to assess the Scriptures on their own, it is interesting to see how often people are ready to follow what appears evident to them, and how just as easily they turn back to follow teachers who inform them that they need not obey what the Scriptures plainly state.

6 and they were being baptized by him in the Jordan River, as they confessed their sins.

On the question of the *mikveh* in ancient Israel, see the Excursus above. The question that is often asked is what role Yochanan played in the ceremony of the *mikveh* in the Jordan river. Traditionally, one goes into the *mikveh* without assistance, while the text before us appears to indicate that Yochanan was active in the sense of "plunging" or "dipping" the people into the water. However, the Greek does not necessarily require this. The verb (ἐβαπτίζοντο) is a middle form, meaning that it could just as well be understood as "they were baptizing themselves." If this is the case, then we would understand the following "by him" to mean "under his supervision," which would conform to the tradition that required witnesses of a *mikveh* in order for it to be considered valid.

That the *mikveh* in ancient Israel pertained to more than ritual purity, but also included the intention of one's heart, has been discussed above (see pp. 79–81). Thus, the *mikveh* administered by Yochanan, which is here connected to the confession of sins, is not (contrary to some commentators)[1] an innovation on the part of Yochanan. Indeed, the words of the Prophets that connect the imagery of the *mikveh* with repentance and renewal, would have formed obvious parallels in the minds of those coming to the Jordan.

> Then I will sprinkle clean water on you, and you will be clean; I will cleanse you from all your filthiness and from all your idols. (Ezek 36:25)

Moreover, the renewal of Israel in the end of days incorporates the metaphor of water in connection with pouring out of the Spirit:

> For I will pour out water on the thirsty land And streams on the dry ground; I will pour out My Spirit on your offspring And My blessing on your descendants… (Is 44:3)

Since the common practice of doing a *mikveh* was in view of visiting the Temple precincts, it only stands to reason that it was likewise connected to one's desire to worship and honor the God of Israel. As Yochanan announced the soon appearance of the Messiah, it was only natural that those who heard and received his message would want to prepare themselves, both in terms of ritual purity as well as one's inner life.

The present participle, ἐξομολογούμενοι (from ἐξομολογέω, *exomologeo*, "to confess") need not indicate that they were confessing their sins as they were performing the *mikveh*. It's primary emphasis is that the confession of sins was vitally linked with the performance of the immersion.

[1]Samuel Lachs, *A Rabbinic Commentary*, p. 37, writes: "Neither biblical nor rabbinic Judaism knows of this type of baptism. In Jewish sources there are only two kinds of immersion—for purification from ritual uncleanness and proselyte baptism." Hagner, *Matthew*, 1.49, suggests that the those Jewish people who were coming for a *mikveh* in the Jordan were humbling themselves in that they were submitting to the ritual of a proselyte, but this seems hardly warranted.

Nor does the participle necessitate that they were publicly confessing their personal sins, or that they were confessing their sins to Yochanan. Rather, their performance of the *mikveh* was itself the public demonstration of their confession. Moreover, in the language of the Torah, in which wayward Israel is promised God's faithfulness to the covenant, the language is striking:

> If they confess their iniquity and the iniquity of their forefathers, in their unfaithfulness which they committed against Me, and also in their acting with hostility against Me—I also was acting with hostility against them, to bring them into the land of their enemies—or if their uncircumcised heart becomes humbled so that they then make amends for their iniquity, then I will remember My covenant with Jacob, and I will remember also My covenant with Isaac, and My covenant with Abraham as well, and I will remember the land. (Lev 26:40 –42).

As the people listened to Yochanan, and realized that the Messiah was close at hand, they may well have connected Yochanan's message with that of Moses, and realized that confession of their iniquities was the necessary requirement for God's returned blessings upon them.

Moreover, confession of sin is specifically commanded in the Torah (Lev 5:5; Num 5:6–7) in connection with making the proper restitution for one's error. Yeshua Himself taught that the giving of a sacrifice was moot if one knew that he had sinned against his brother, and had not followed the Torah in making restitution. Rather, one was to forego offering a sacrifice until the matter was made right (Matt 5:23–24). In other words, the rituals involved in worship were to be preceded by a cleansed heart and conscience.

Taking all of these factors together, Yochanan's call for repentance, and his administration of *mikvaot* in the Jordan, fit well into the Judaisms of his day. From Qumran we know that at least some of the Judaisms were expecting the imminent arrival of the final redemption. As such, it is reasonable to presume that many were preparing themselves in light of these expectations. That the Torah required confession of their iniquities, and the iniquities of their forefathers to occur before a restoration to covenant blessings could be achieved, confession of their sins in connection with Yochanan's call to repentance (*teshuvah*) makes perfect sense.

7 But when he saw many of the Pharisees and Sadducees coming for baptism, he said to them, "You brood of vipers, who warned you to flee from the wrath to come?

As Yochanan encouraged and oversaw the *mikvaot* of those who were receiving his call to repentance, many (πολύς, *polus*) of the Pharisees and Sadducees also came to the Jordan to participate. This paragraph (vv. 7–10) is one of only three instances in Matthew where the Pharisees and Sadducees are linked together (cf. 16:1–12; 22:34). More often, Matthew associates the Pharisees and the scribes together (5:20; 12:38; 15:1; 23:2, 13-15, 23ff). In Mark and Luke, the Sadducees are only mentioned once (regarding their rejection of a resurrection, Mk 12:18; Lk 20:27) and never in connection with the Pharisees. Mark associates the Pharisees with the scribes three times (Mark 2:16; 7:1, 5) while Luke makes this association five times (Luke 5:21, 30; 6:7; 11:53; 15:2). It might be that Matthew's repeated mention of the Pharisees indicates the close association of himself and his community with the Pharisaic sect, and thus a more "insider's" view of their practice, and especially, the rejection of Yeshua as Messiah by the sect's prominent leaders.

While Matthew regularly notes the Pharisaic opposition to Yeshua, it is clear that he does not dismiss them as altogether unrighteous. In 5:20, Matthew reports Yeshua's assessment that "unless your righteousness exceeds that of the scribes and Pharisees, you will not enter the kingdom of Heaven." Moreover, Matthew relates how Yeshua honored the authority of the Pharisees who sat in the "seat of Moses" (Matt 23:2), given credence to their role as teachers of the Torah, even though He warned His disciples not to follow the manner in which they themselves failed to live out their own instructions.

Yet the majority of the time in Matthew's gospel, the Pharisee leaders are opposed to Yeshua and His teaching, and plot against Him, seeking to discredit Him. At first they wonder why Yeshua and His disciples are not conforming to their established *halachah* (not to associate with certain people [9:11]; to fast twice weekly [9:14]; to accept added restrictions on the Sabbath [12:2]; to wash one's hands before eating [15:1f]). But as Matthew's gospel unfolds, the Pharisaic leaders turn from questioning Yeshua's lack of halachic conformity to opposing Him and seeking to discredit Him. They accuse Him of using satanic powers to cast out demons (9:34; 12:24) and conspire to destroy Him (12:14). Their plan was to trap Him by asking questions that presented a "no-win" scenario. They ask Him to provide proof of His greatness by manifesting a "sign from heaven" (16:1f, cp. 12:38) and seek to entangle Him in the *halachic* discussions regarding divorce (19:3f). They likewise sought to embroil Yeshua in the controversy over payment of taxes to Rome (22:15ff). The Sadducees also test Him by presenting a scenario that seemed sure to undermine His teaching regarding the resurrection (22:23f). Such tactics, however, come to an end when Yeshua Himself asked the Pharisaic leaders about the identity of the Messiah, and how He could be the son of the David while, at the same time revered by King David as his Master (22:41f, quoting Ps 110:1). After this, "no one was able to answer Him a word, nor did anyone dare from that day on to ask Him another question" (Matt 22:45).

It is clear, then, that while the Pharisees as a whole may have presented a worthy benchmark for attention to Torah observance,[1] some of the leaders were nonetheless better known for their political prowess than their consistent lives of piety. This may be reflected in the rabbinic notice that marks seven kinds of Pharisees. In m.*Sota* 3.4, it speaks of the "blows of the *perushim* (Pharisees), and the Gemara (b.*Sota* 22b) expands on this phrase as follows:

> Our Rabbis have taught: There are seven types of Pharisees: the *shikmi* Pharisee, the *nikpi* Pharisee, the *kizai* Pharisee, the 'pestle' Pharisee, the Pharisee [who constantly exclaims] 'What is my duty that I may perform it?', the Pharisee from love [of God] and the Pharisee from fear. The *shikmi* Pharisee — he is one who performs the action of Shechem.[2] The *nikpi* Pharisee — he is one who knocks his feet together.[3] The *kizai* Pharisee — R. Nahman b. Isaac said: He is one who makes his blood to flow against walls.[4] The 'pestle' Pharisee — Rabbah b. Shila said: [His head] is bowed like [a pestle in] a mortar.[5] The Pharisee [who constantly exclaims] 'What is my duty that I may perform it?' — but that is a virtue! — Nay, what he says is, 'What further duty is for me that I may perform it?'[6] The Pharisee from love and the Pharisee from fear…

[1]Now, for the Pharisees, they live meanly, and despise delicacies in diet; and they follow the conduct of reason; and what that prescribes to them as good for them, they do; and they think they ought earnestly to strive to observe reason's dictates for practice. They also pay a respect to such as are in years; nor are they so bold as to contradict them in anything which they have introduced; 13 and, when they determine that all things are done by fate, they do not take away the freedom from men of acting as they think fit; since their notion is, that it hath pleased God to make a temperament, whereby what he wills is done, but so that the will of men can act virtuously or viciously. 14 They also believe that souls have an immortal vigor in them, and that under the earth there will be rewards or punishments, according as they have lived virtuously or viciously in this life; and the latter are to be detained in an everlasting prison, but that the former shall have power to revive and live again; 15 on account of which doctrines, they are able greatly to persuade the body of the people; and whatsoever they do about divine worship, prayers, and sacrifices, they perform them according to their direction; insomuch that the cities gave great attestations to them on account of their entire virtuous conduct, both in the actions of their lives and their discourses also. (Josephus, *Ant* 18.12f)

[2]He performs Torah duties for unworthy goals, such as the men of Shechem were circumcised in order to obtain wives.
[3]He walks with exaggerated humility. The Yerushlami adds, "he says, 'spare me a moment that I may perform a commandment.'"
[4]In his anxiety to turn away from looking at a woman, he dashes his face into the wall. The Yerushalmi adds that he thinks he can offset an evil deed with a good one.
[5]He tries to look humble to everyone, i.e., he wears his humility on his sleeve.
[6]In other words, he is certain that he has fulfilled the *mitzvot* perfectly and therefore has nothing more to do.

In light of the fact that the Bavil was written and compiled by the remnant of the Pharisees (the basis for "rabbinic Judaism"), it is all that more remarkable that such clear denouncement of Pharisaic short-comings are included. But we should understand that even the Pharisees themselves judged each other on the basis of sincere piety, and condemned (as did Yeshua) outward actions of holiness that were not matched by inward piety.

The words of Yochanan judging the hypocrisy of the Pharisees and Sadducees, then, are not something unfamiliar to the college of Sages. He knew that their coming to participate in the *mikveh* of *teshuvah* (repentance) was not consistent with their actions. Such religious fakery had no place in the kingdom of Heaven, but besmirches the very essence of *teshuvah* itself. Repentance is a humble admission of one's sin in light of the unchanging standard of God's holiness. What is more, the Messiah, Who is the central focus in the coming kingdom, requires true holiness of heart, which inevitably produces evident obedience to God's commandments (cp. Matt 12:34).

Yochanan uses the phrase "brood of vipers" (γεννήματα ἐχιδνῶν,[1] "offspring of vipers"), used also by Yeshua in reference to the hypocritical leaders of the Pharisees (12:34; 23:33). While the viper is poisonous, that is not the primary emphasis here. Rather, the viper lurks in unsuspected places, and presents a real danger to those who might accidentally happen upon it. Interestingly, the rabbinic literature mentions the danger of snakes hiding in privies (b.*Berachot* 62a), a fitting picture of uncleanness and danger.

Yochanan questioned the Pharisees and Sadducees: "who warned you to flee from the wrath to come?" The emphasis could be upon the word "who," meaning "it surely was not I who warned you, because you failed to accept my teachings." Or the emphasis could be upon "you," meaning that coming to the Jordan to do a *mikveh* of repentance would have been entirely out of character for such as these. But regardless, the point is that John's message of imminent kingdom included a warning of the judgment that such a kingdom would render upon the unrighteous. Since these Pharisaic and Sadducean leaders doubtlessly projected a confidence in their status of righteousness, their coming was entirely out of character.

8–9 "Therefore bear fruit in keeping with repentance; and do not suppose that you can say to yourselves,[2] 'We have Abraham for our father'; for I say to you that from these stones God is able to raise up children to Abraham.

Yochanan's admonition is straight to the point: true *teshuvah* is marked, not by mere outward ritual, but by a turning from the sin as the initial fruit of repentance, and then engaging in honest, humble obedience before God. The metaphor of "fruit" to indicate something that is the consequence or product of one's thoughts and decisions is common in the Tanach.[3] When one wishes to determine the nature of a tree, he looks not at the root but at the fruit. Yeshua will likewise utilize this metaphor in His teaching (cf. 7:17-19; 12:33; 13:23; 21:43).

Apparently the prevailing theology of the Pharisees and Sadducees (and most likely other Jewish sects) was that physical lineage to Abraham, which granted covenant status, was the basis for a guarantee of God's blessing and protection, and thus a place in the world to come (escape from the final judgment against the wicked). We see this in m.*Sanhedrin* 10:1[4]

All Israelites have a share in the world to come, as it is said, Your

---

[1]ἐξιδνα is used only in Matt. 3:7; 12:34; 23:33; Luke 3:7 and in Acts 28:3. It is not found in the Lxx.

[2]"say to yourself" represents the Semitic idiom אמר בְּלֵב "speak to the heart." E.g., Gen 8:21; Ps 10:6; Ecc 2:1.

[3]For the metaphor of "fruit" to describe the outward reality of one's heart, cf. Ps 1:3; 92:14; Prov 11:30; 12:12, 14; 13:2; 18:20; Is 3:10; 10:12; Jer 32:19; Amos 6:12; Mic 7:13.

[4]Note also *Test. of Levi* 15: 1 Because of these things the temple, which the Lord shall choose, will be desolate in uncleanness, and you will be captives to all the nations. 2 And you will be an abomination to them, and you will receive reproach and everlasting shame from the righteous judgment of God, 3 And all who see you will flee from you. 4 And if not for Abraham, Isaac, and Jacob, our fathers, one of my seed should not be left upon the earth.

people also are all righteous, they shall inherit the land forever; the branch of my planting, the work of my hands, that I may be glorified (Is. 60:21).

If Is 60:21 was, in fact, taught by the Pharisaic Sages of Yochanan's day as the foundational text for trusting in one's Israelite status, then it is all the more significant in light of Yochanan's call to "bring forth fruit corresponding to repentance," for the righteousness of God's people as prophesied by Isaiah, is parallel to God's having *planted* them in the land, with the idea that the work of the supreme husbandman would inevitably produce good fruit.

Of course, in the rabbinic understanding, one could forfeit one's covenant status through egregious sin (which received the penalty of *karat*), as the remainder of the mishnah quoted above makes clear. Yet it seems quite certain that in the 1st Century (and probably dating to times much earlier), the prevailing theology of Israel's Sages was the covenant status, given to ever Israelite, was the means by which one would escape the final judgment and be assured of a place in the world to come. From this it is easy to see why the ritual of becoming a proselyte (by which a Gentile was accorded the status of an Israelite) was considered the only way into the covenant for Gentiles. Moreover, since circumcision was the primary and most significant element of the proselyte ritual (at least for males), it is understandable how the term itself became synonymous with covenant status. When some were teaching the Gentiles that "unless you are circumcised according to the custom of Moses, you cannot be saved" (Acts 15:1), it must be understood in light of the prevailing theology that accorded covenant status ("son of Abraham") as the basis for right standing before God and a place in the world to come. This also informs the perspective of Paul, that 1) believers in Yeshua are children of Abraham (Rom 4; Gal 3) and 2) that those who rely upon circumcision (i.e., Israelite status gained through becoming a proselyte) will inevitably be condemned (Gal 5:2f).

But Yochanan has already judged these Pharisees and Sadducees who were coming to him as the "offspring of vipers" (note the parallel in John 8:44 where Yeshua labels the Pharisees He is confronting as the offspring of the devil). One's deeds give evidence of one's lineage: "If you are Abraham's children, do the deeds of Abraham" (John 8:39). To such a charge, they would have apparently retorted, "we are Abraham's offspring," that is, we already are guaranteed God's favor. Yochanan's assessment is that their lives do not match their pedigree.

Yochanan goes to say that God is able to raise up children of Abraham through a miraculous creative event: "from these stones[1] God is able to raise up children to Abraham." The phrase "to raise up from" (ἐκ τῶν λίθων τούτων ἐγεῖραι) is a semitic idiom meaning "to cause to be born" (cf. Deut 18:15, 18; 2Sam 7:12). The picture is of God giving rocks the ability to bring forth people. The point is that God is not limited in terms of His covenant blessings to those who are the physical offspring of Jacob. Neither Yochanan nor Yeshua deny the rightful place of the physical offspring of Jacob to the covenant promises made to the fathers. But the point is that the covenant promises were never predicated entirely nor exclusively on the basis of physical lineage. Since Abraham is characterized by his having "believed in God" (Gen 15:6, cf. Rom 4:11ff), those who are his offspring will likewise be so characterized. Those who participate in Abraham's faith will bring forth the deeds of Abraham, and this is the mark of covenant status, nor merely

[1]Some have suggested that there is a play on words between Hebrew בָּנִים, "sons" and אֲבָנִים, "stones." Aramaic would be בְּנַיָא/אַבְנַיָא. While there may be some similarity in assonance, it seems a bit far fetched to suggest that he was making a word play that would have been readily recognized by his audience. The sounds are not that close, since the ב would be stopped in one form, and spirantized in the other. Moreover, he may have used the more common *kepha'* when referring to "stones," as reflected in the Greek λίθων.

one's pedigree.

Furthermore, if one considers the manner in which Isaac as the "promised son" came, the emphasis of Yochanan upon God's miraculous ability to raise up offspring for Abraham is all the more poignant. For Isaac himself was the result of a miraculous move of God's hand whereby He overcame the inability of Sarah to conceive and gave her a son in her old age. This very point, using a similar metaphor, is made by Isaiah (51:1–2):

> Listen to me, you who pursue righteousness, who seek the LORD: Look to the rock from which you were hewn and to the quarry from which you were dug. Look to Abraham your father and to Sarah who gave birth to you in pain; When he was but one I called him, then I blessed him and multiplied him.

In a very real sense, Abraham and Sarah were as "rocks" when it came to having children: Sarah had ceased having her monthly cycle, and thus was physically incapable of conceiving children. Yet the miraculous birth of Isaac was forever to stand as a witness that God's covenant children were the result of His mighty hand. Yochanan therefore cuts the ground out from under the Pharisees and Sadducees who claimed to stand on the basis of their own flesh (i.e., physical lineage) rather than upon God's miraculous and gracious favor.

Once again, we may see (even if only very subtly) Matthew's awareness of the Gentile inclusion into the covenant. While covenant nomism[1] may have been the prevailing theology of the Sages, and thus an effective way to exclude the Gentiles, Matthew already knows that many Gentiles have been drawn into covenant relationship with God through faith in Yeshua. Their status is secure, not on the basis of their having been born to Jewish parents, but on the basis of their having been born again by the Spirit through a living and abiding faith in the Messiah. Thus, God's purpose to bless the seed of Abraham is not thwarted by Israel's disobedience. God is able both to change the heart of stone into a heart of flesh, and to write the Torah upon the heart in order to affect genuine obedience and faithfulness. Israel will be what God created her to be. What is more, God is able to bring chosen ones from the nations and give them the same heart. Therefore, Israel's disobedience cannot frustrate God's plan—He will have a people that honors Him, and through whom His power and grace is made known to the whole world.

10 The axe is already laid at the root of the trees; therefore every tree that does not bear good fruit is cut down and thrown into the fire.

Having given the imagery of "bearing fruit," the "wrath to come" as the judging hand of God as the King of the kingdom, is pictured as the husbandman clearing trees that have ceased to produce fruit. There is little time left because the "axe is already laid at the root." The imminent coming of the kingdom of Heaven means that the judgment is close at hand. Such a picturesque metaphor is appropriate on several accounts. First, the prophet had already given the picture of God leveling trees with an axe as part of His judgment and wrath (Is 10:33–34; Jer 46:22). Secondly, a saying of R. Eleazar b. Azariah, contained in *Perkei Avot*, might indicate that the metaphor of trees was something already used by the Sages:

[1]"Covenant nomism" has become a term that describes the belief of 1st Century Judaisms, that one's place in the world to come was based upon covenant membership granted through birth (or conversion) and maintained by adherence to the Torah.

He would say, "Anyone whose wisdom is greater than his deeds-to what is he to be likened? To a tree with abundant foliage, but few roots. "When the winds come, they will uproot it and blow it down, "as it is said, He shall be like a tamarisk in the desert and shall not see when good comes but shall inhabit the parched places in the wilderness (Jer. 17:6). "But anyone whose deeds are greater than his wisdom-to what is he to be likened? To a tree with little foliage but abundant roots. "For even if all the winds in the world were to come and blast at it, they will not move it from its place, "as it is said, He shall be as a tree planted by the waters, and that spreads out its roots by the river, and shall not fear when heat comes, and his leaf shall be green, and shall not be careful in the year of drought, neither shall cease from yielding fruit (Jer. 17:8). (m.*Avot* 3.17)

Thirdly, Yochanan's admonition to the Pharisees and Sadducees was that they should "bear fruit in keeping with repentance." Thus, his continued use of the tree/fruit metaphor in relationship to the coming judgment fits his message perfectly.

The emphasis upon the root (ῥίζα, *hriza*) pushes the metaphor to the final judgment. It is not merely unproductive branches that are pruned, but the entire tree is cut down. A parallel is found in the parable of Yeshua about the unproductive fig tree (Lk 13:6–9). There, a tree that had not produced fruit for three years is marked for destruction by the owner: "Why does it even use up the ground?" The worker, however, pleads for more time: "Let it alone, sir, for this year too, until I dig around it and put in fertilizer; and if it bears fruit next year, fine; but if not, cut it down." The point of the parable is that the judgment is coming, and those without fruit will be destroyed. However, some mercy is being shown by calling Israel to repentance and the fruit of righteousness. Yochanan's message is that the time of mercy is drawing to a close. The owner of the trees will require that the unproductive ones be destroyed, and He is currently making a distinction between those with and without fruit.[1]

Adding to the finality of the coming judgment, the trees that are cut down are "thrown into the fire." This metaphor of the final judgment as a consuming fire comes from the prophets (cp. Is 66:24; Joel 2:30) and became a common figure in the early Jewish literature (cp. 4Macc 9:9; Jub 9:15; 1QpHab 10.5, 13; 1Enoch 10.6; 54.1–2; 90.24–5). Interestingly, Malachi includes both roots and branches in his prophetic vision of the final judgment:

> "For behold, the day is coming, burning like a furnace; and all the arrogant and every evildoer will be chaff; and the day that is coming will set them ablaze," says the LORD of hosts, "so that it will leave them neither root nor branch." (Mal 4:1)

The point is that the coming judgment is final. Those trees that are cut down and thrown into the fire will forever be lost. There is coming a time when repentance will no longer be possible, and thus the message of Yochanan is made that much more urgent. This urgency is not only highlighted by the opening ἤδη (*ede*, "already") but also by the fact that all of the verbs ("laid," "bearing," "cut down," "thrown") are in the present tense. In the coming of the Messiah, the judgment of God has begun, since He is the touchstone of true righteousness, and He is the One to Whom the Torah has always pointed (Rom 10:4).

[1] The majority of English versions (KJV, NKJV, NASB, NIV, ESV, NRSV) translate πᾶν οὖν δένδρον as "Therefore every tree...," but a more precise translation is "Therefore any tree...," since anarthrous πᾶς followed by an anarthrous noun often means "each, any," akin to the Hebrew כָּל/כּוֹל followed by a singular noun (but not a collective singular). Note the remarks of Turner, *Syntax,* p. 199f.

11 As for me, I baptize you with water for repentance, but He who is coming after me is mightier than I, and I am not fit to remove His sandals; He will baptize you with the Holy Spirit and fire.[1]

Yochanan's baptism was the *mikveh* in water, and it was with a view to (εἰς, *eis*, literally "unto") or connected with repentance, in that it demonstrated in an outward way what was to be an inward reality.[2] The point is that Yochanan's call to repentance was combined with a desire for personal purity, as demonstrated in the *mikveh*. Yochanan could only call people to repentance in light of the imminent kingdom of Heaven. He could not, however, affect the necessary repentance. This inner work is the result of divine activity.

He who is coming after me surely alludes to the "coming one" language prevalent in the messianic expectations of late 2nd Temple Judaism.[3] The phrase from Ps 118:26, בָּרוּךְ הַבָּא בְּשֵׁם יהוה, "Blessed is he who comes in the name of Adonai," was understood messianically by the Apostles (Matt 11:3; 21:9; 23:39, cf. Heb 10:37). In Midrash Rabbah on Gen 49:10, "until Shilo comes" was interpreted as referring to the Messiah, and Onkelos translated the phrase "until the Messiah comes, whose is the kingdom, and him shall the nations obey." Likewise, in Mid. Rab. *Song* ii.22, the phrase of 2:8, "Listen, my beloved! Behold, he is coming…," is interpreted as referring to the coming Messiah. In presenting himself as the forerunner of the Messiah, Yochanan takes up the role of Elijah as the harbinger of the Messiah at the end of days.

Yochanan describes the Coming One as "mightier than I," that is, with greater strength and power. This no doubt refers to the powerful impact of the kingdom which the Messiah would bring. But His greater strength is not only in His ability to bring the kingdom of Heaven to reign upon the earth, but also in His own honor and majesty. Yochanan considers himself unworthy to act as His servant to carry (βαστάζω, *bastazo*, "to bear, carry," so NIV) His sandals, while Mark and Luke have Yochanan saying he is unworthy to "untie" (λύω, *luo*, "loose") His sandals.[4] It may be, however, that *bastazo* may also have the meaning "untie."[5] Regardless, Yochanan uses the hyperbole to heighten the majesty of the Coming One, Who is the Davidic King.

It was commonly held by the Sages that the duty of a Gentile servant or slave, as well as one's son or pupil, included that of carrying his master's shoes (particularly in connection with the bathhouse). In *Mechilta* on Ex 21:2 we read:

> …the Sages said: A Hebrew slave must not wash the feet of his master, nor put his shoes on him, nor carry his things before him when going to the bathhouse, nor support him by the hips when ascending steps, nor carry him in a litter or a chair or a sedan chair as slaves do. For it is said: "But over your brethren the children of Israel you shall not rule, one over another, with rigour" (Lev 25:46). But one's son or pupil may do so. (cf. b.*Ketuvot* 96a; b.*Eruvin* 27b; b.*BavaMetzia* 41a)

Yochanan thus puts himself in the lowest of status when compared with the Coming Messiah.

While Yochanan's activity related to the water *mikveh*, the Coming One would "baptize you with the Holy Spirit and fire." The figure of immersion, so well demonstrated in the *mikveh*, was already linked metaphorically to the

[1]Matthew and Luke (3:16) are parallel in the manner in which the two baptisms (Yochanan's and Yeshua's) are connected, i.e., with Yochanan's interspersed description of his inferior status when compared to that of Yeshua. Mark (1:7–8), however, juxtaposes his baptism and that of Yeshua without intervening words: "I baptized you with water; but He will baptize you with the Holy Spirit."

[2]Only Matthew has εἰς μετάνοιαν, "for repentance." Mark and Luke have only "I baptize you with water."

[3]Some have suggested that the Afikomen (אֲפִיקֹמֶן) of the Pesach Seder is actually derived from the Greek ἀφικόμενος, "the One who comes." For further insights on this possibility, see Paul Sumner, "He Who is Coming (The Hidden Afikoman)," *Yashar* 24 (Apr, 1993), pp. 1–2; David Daube, *He That Cometh* (London, 1966), pp. 6–14; "The Earliest Structure of the Gospels," *NTS* 5 (1959), 174–87. Whether the Afikomen was a part of the 1st Century Pesach Seder is debated, however. (Note the Kaufman Mishnah at *Pesachim* 10:7f, which includes notice of the Afikomen, and also the remarks of Jastrow on אֲפִיקֹמֶן).

[4]Of the Hebrew Matthews, the Du Tillet and the Münster follow Matthew's Greek, having לָשֵׂאת אֶת נְעָלָיו while Even Bohan has להתיר שרוך נאלו, following Mark and Luke.

[5]See *BDAG* and *Moulton-Milligan*, "βαστάζω."

outpouring of the Spirit by the prophets (Ezek 36:25f; Jl 2:23 [3:1]), so that the picture of being immersed in the Spirit (in the sense of being entirely overtaken by His presence) was a ready figure of speech for Yochanan.

But what does a "baptism in the Holy Spirit" mean for Yochanan and those who heard him? Matthew and Luke (3:16) have the additional "and fire," lacking in Mark (1:8). The Du Tillet and Even Bohan seem to conflate the Synoptic witness with the interpretive יטבל אתכם באש רוח הקדש, "He will baptize you in the fire of the Holy Spirit." The Münster follows the Greek (as does the Peshitta): והוא יטבל אתכם ברוח הקודש ובאש, "and He will baptize you with the Holy Spirit and with fire."

It would seem that the couplet "with the Holy Spirit and with fire" may well be a hendiadys, formed on the background of the prophetic visions of judgment that often linked water and fire. In Dan 7:10 we read of a "river of fire" that comes forth from the throne of the Ancient of Days, and in Ps 50:3 combines fire with tempestuous waves. In the Apocalypse, the abyss is designated as a "lake of fire" (Rev. 19:20; 20:10, 14-15). Moreover, the prophets combine the idea of "wind" (*ruach*) and "fire" in their oracles of judgment. For instance, in Is 30:27–28 we read:

> Behold, the name of the LORD comes from a remote place; Burning is His anger and dense is His smoke; His lips are filled with indignation and His tongue is like a consuming fire; His breath is like an overflowing torrent, which reaches to the neck, to shake the nations back and forth in a sieve, and to put in the jaws of the peoples the bridle which leads to ruin.

Here, the fire that comes forth from the mouth of the Almighty is also an overflowing torrent. The combination of wind and fire was well in place as a symbol of judgment in the early Jewish literature as well (cf. 4Ezra 13:8–11). Thus, the baptism of Yeshua as foretold by Yochanan is not a two-fold baptism (one with the Spirit, and another with fire), but one that is characterized by the judging and purifying work of the Spirit.[1] For those who are righteous, the baptism of the Holy Spirit and fire will function to purify them as citizens of the kingdom. For those who are unrighteous, the baptism will be one of judgment and condemnation. In either case, the judging or proving work of the Spirit will reveal the true nature of each one, as the following metaphor of wheat and chaff gives further elucidation.

12 His winnowing fork is in His hand, and He will thoroughly clear His threshing floor; and He will gather His wheat into the barn, but He will burn up the chaff with unquenchable fire.

The mini-parable provides a well-known picture for Yochanan's audience. The practice of taking a wooden fork with a long handle and scooping up the beaten sheaves of grain to allow the wind to separate the chaff from the wheat was a common sight in Israel. Moreover, the metaphor of winnowing had already been used by the prophets as pertaining to judgment. Isaiah speaks of the breath of God consuming the chaff and stubble (33:11) and the Psalmist speaks of the wicked who are like chaff blown away by the wind (1:4). Indeed, Yochanan may have had Mal 4:1[3:19] in mind, for it combines the metaphor of the uprooted tree with that of the threshing floor:

[1]This may also be seen in that there is only one preposition that governs both nouns: ἐν πνεύματι ἁγίῳ καὶ πυρί. Interestingly, in the Münster, the preposition is repeated in accordance with normal Hebrew syntax.

"For behold, the day is coming, burning like a furnace; and all the arrogant and every evildoer will be chaff; and the day that is coming will set them ablaze," says the LORD of hosts, "so that it will leave them neither root nor branch."

Here, it is יהוה Who is the Judge, yet for Yochanan the judgment comes from the hand of the Messiah. The winnowing fork is in His hand and the threshing floor belongs to Him. He is the executor of the Almighty's vengeance against the wicked, as well as the One Who gathers in the grain. Indeed, in the Targum on Is 33:11, the *memra* (word) of God is the one who destroys the chaff as a whirlwind.

Note carefully that the wheat belongs to Him ("He will gather *His* wheat") but not the chaff. Yochanan's concluding remarks continue to emphasize the need to prepare oneself for the Coming One.

This same metaphor of chaff and wheat as a picture of judgment is found in the rabbinic literature. In Midrash *Psalms* we read:

> R. Chanina commented on what R. Simeon ben Lachish said: Why are the children of Israel likened to wheat? The parable of the householder and his steward will tell you. When the steward comes to cast up his accounts with the householder, the householder does not ask: "How many wicker baskets of straw are you bringing into the storehouse?" or "How many bundles of stubble are you bringing into the granary?" Instead, he lets the steward consign the stubble to the fire and scatter the straw before the wind. What, then does he say? "Take heed! Take the sum of the measures of wheat you bring into the granary, for it is life for the world." (In the ensuing context, God is the householder, and Moses is the steward, Mid. *Ps.* 2.13)

13   Then Yeshua arrived from Galilee at the Jordan coming to John, to be baptized by him.

The Synoptic accounts of Yeshua's *mikveh* at the hands of Yochanan bear numbers of differences, but many of the commentators have, it seems to me, exaggerated the problems.

Matthew 3:13–17	Mark 1:9–11	Luke 3:21–22
13 Then Yeshua arrived from Galilee at the Jordan coming to John, to be baptized by him. 14 But John tried to prevent Him, saying, "I have need to be baptized by You, and do You come to me?" 15 But Yeshua answering said to him, "Permit it at this time; for in this way it is fitting for us to fulfill all righteousness." Then he permitted Him. 16 After being baptized, Yeshua came up immediately from the water; and behold, the heavens were opened, and he saw the Spirit of God descending as a dove and lighting on Him, 17 and behold, a voice out of the heavens said, "This is My beloved Son, in whom I am well-pleased."	9 In those days Yeshua came from Nazareth in Galilee and was baptized by John in the Jordan. 10 Immediately coming up out of the water, He saw the heavens opening, and the Spirit like a dove descending upon Him; 11 and a voice came out of the heavens: "You are My beloved Son, in You I am well-pleased."	21 Now when all the people were baptized, Yeshua was also baptized, and while He was praying, heaven was opened, 22 and the Holy Spirit descended upon Him in bodily form like a dove, and a voice came out of heaven, "You are My beloved Son, in You I am well-pleased."

It can be immediately seen by this comparison that Matthew alone has vv. 14–15, in which Yochanan's hesitancy to administrate Yeshua's *mikveh* is voiced, and Yeshua's answer is given. Luke does not even specifically name Yochanan, so some have suggested that Yeshua underwent the *mikveh* on His own, which is why the interchange between Yochanan and Yeshua is lacking in Mark and Luke. But the contexts of all the Synoptics at this point is that of Yochanan's baptism, so there is really no problem identifying Yochanan as directly involved in Yeshua's *mikveh*. The other minor differences are more than likely stylistic for each of the Gospel authors.

Matthew begins with "then" (τότε, *tote*) which corresponds to Mark's "in those days" and Luke's "now when all the people were baptized." The time frame is merely noted to be when many people were coming to Yochanan at the Jordan to undergo *mikvaot*.

14 But John tried to prevent Him, saying, "I have need to be baptized by You, and do You come to me?"

How did Yochanan recognize Yeshua? In John 1:29f, it might appear as though Yochanan was unacquainted with Yeshua ("I did not recognize Him," v. 31). But to suggest that Yochanan, a relative of Yeshua, had not been informed by his mother about Yeshua's miraculous birth, or that he was ignorant of Yeshua altogether, is hardly likely. Far more likely is that Yochanan was well acquainted with Yeshua, but that the statement of John should be understood to mean that Yochanan had not recognized Yeshua as the Messiah. In fact, the words of John inform us that Yochanan came to realize who Yeshua actually was only after His *mikveh*, the descent of the Holy Spirit in the form of a dove, and the heavenly voice. "I did not recognize Him, but so that He might be manifested to Israel, I came baptizing in water" (John 1:31). He realized after the fact that the very purpose for his ministry of baptism in view of repentance was so that Yeshua Himself could be openly shown to be the Messiah.

Moreover, it seems likely that it was Yochanan's close familiarity with Yeshua that caused him consternation when asked to baptize Him. Yochanan's baptism was a *mikveh* in view of repentance. As a humble man, he would have been fully aware of his own shortcomings, and as someone well acquainted with Yeshua, he would have known of His sterling character and His utter righteous life within the community (not to mention His vast understanding of Torah, even at an early age). Putting himself next to Yeshua, Yochanan could only imagine that in terms of a *mikveh* reflecting repentance, he was the one in need and not Yeshua.

The idea that Yochanan desired for Yeshua to administer a *mikveh* on his behalf, because he thought in doing so he would receive a greater measure of the Spirit, is far-fetched. As noted above, the baptism with the Holy Spirit and fire is eschatological as far as Yochanan is concerned. This had far more to do with proving those who were righteous and those who were not, than endowing individuals with special gifting or power.

> Matthew does not present Jesus as bestowing his Spirit-and-fire baptism on anyone: the Cross and Resurrection are focal for him; and, writing after Pentecost (Acts 2), Matthew doubtless believes Jesus' baptism was bestowed on his people later than the time he is writing about.[1]

Matthew has ἐπὶ τὸν Ἰορδάνην while Mark has εἰς τὸν Ἰορδάνην. The difference in prepositions is that Matthew views the Jordan as a destination, while Mark is describing Yeshua's actually going *into* the Jordan. Matthew's use of ἐπί may reflect Hebrew עַל sometimes used as equivalent to אֶל (see *KB*, עַל). Both the Du Tillet and Münster have עַל.

[1]Carson, *Matthew*, p. 107.

15 But Yeshua answering said to him, "Permit it at this time; for in this way it is fitting for us to fulfill all righteousness." Then he permitted Him.

Here we have the first words of Yeshua recorded by Matthew, and they contain two important words that will continue to characterize much of His teaching: "fulfill" and "righteousness." Indeed, His appearance as the incarnate One was in fulfillment of the prophets' words, and the means by which sinners may become righteous. But in these first words of our Master, we are met with more questions than answers. What exactly does His explanation to Yochanan mean?

We empathize with Yochanan's quandary as to why Yeshua would seek his assistance in a *mikveh* of repentance. In what way was Yeshua's *mikveh* in the Jordan a means by which all righteousness would be fulfilled? Numbers of suggestions to this dilemma have been offered:

1) that Yeshua's *mikveh* was anticipatory of His own "baptism of death," by which He would secure "righteousness for all." Often those who opt for this interpretation rely upon Is 53:11 ("by His knowledge My righteous servant will justify many") and read Matthew's use of "righteousness" forensically, in line with Paul's use of the term.

2) that Yeshua's *mikveh* was undertaken in light of the Torah commandment to wash oneself with water as a means of regaining ritual purity after becoming unclean. He did this as a necessary first step of consecration in light of the mission for which He had come.

3) that Yeshua offered an example in His baptism for all would become His followers, and thus as they also were baptized as Christians, they would be reckoned as righteous. In this view, when Yeshua says that "it is fitting for <u>us</u> to fulfill all righteousness," He includes all those who would undergo Christian baptism.

4) Yochanan was calling the people to repentance and righteous living ("fruits of repentance"). Yeshua undergoes a *mikveh* in order to declare to them that the righteousness demanded by Yochanan would be fulfilled by Him and all who followed His righteous life.

5) Yeshua did not actually need a *mikveh*, but He underwent one in the sight of the people in order not to offend them, and in order to win them to His point of view. Like paying taxes to Caesar, the *mikveh* was done so that others would not be offended, and in order to "get along in the world."

6) On the basis that the word "fulfill" (πληρόω, *pleroo*) is almost exclusively used by Matthew in connection with fulfillment of Tanach prophecy (cf. 1:22; 2:15, 17, 23; 4:14; 5:17; 8:17; 12:17; 13:35; 21:4; 26:54,56; 27:9), Yeshua undergoes the *mikveh* in order publicly to be seen as the Messiah who fulfills Scripture and therefore proves God to be faithful and righteous in keeping His promises.

Of course, a number of commentators consider our text to be entirely redactional by Matthew, and influenced by the later ritual of Christian baptism, so for these, the whole matter of "fulfilling righteousness" relates entirely to the later Christian Church, and was read back into the history of Yeshua to give substantiation for the Christian ritual. But this anachronistic approach is not necessary. As we have already shown, the use of the *mikveh* was common in Yeshua's day, and by all the data we have, the activity of Yochanan in calling the people to repentance, marked by undergoing a *mikveh*, would not have been seen as something out of the ordinary.

As to #1, it does not square with Matthew's use of the word "righteousness" (δικαιοσύνη) which always means "moral conduct in accord with God's will."[1] In order to accept this interpretation, one would need to understand "righteousness" as entirely forensic, which seems out of place in this context. Moreover, it is questionable that Yeshua would have included Yochanan ("it is fitting for <u>us</u> to fulfill all righteousness") if His *mikveh* was specifically a prophetic foreshadowing of His own sacrificial death.

#2 has much to commend it, though its short-coming is that it does not fit with the specific purpose of Yochanan's baptism, i.e., a call to repentance and confession of sins. If Yeshua had come in order to demonstrate His ritual purity in light of His coming self-sacrifice on behalf of sinners, one wonders why He chose Yochanan's baptism. Nevertheless, ritual impurity could, in general, be considered symbolic of sin in the broadest sense, since ritual impurity was always connected (even if only remotely) to death, and death was the result of sin in the world. In this case, Yeshua could be seen as the "sin bearer" and thus the *mikveh* would have foreshadowed the cleansing He would bring for sinners through His own death. Moreover, it may be that the words "to fulfill all righteousness" does not pertain entirely to the act of receiving a *mikveh*, but views the *mikveh* as a beginning point for the whole of Yeshua's coming passion:

> "It is not the baptism alone which 'fulfills all righteousness'; rather, the baptism constitutes the opening move of an unfolding sequence designed (building on John's existing efforts) 'to fulfill all righteousness'."[2]

#3 may be immediately rejected on the simple basis that, though the emerging Christian Church of the 2nd and 3rd Centuries considered Christian baptism as a salvo for sin, it was not so taught either by Yeshua or His Apostles.

#4 suffers from the same problem as #1, for if Yeshua is declaring that Yochanan's call to repentance and confession, that is, to righteous living, will be fulfilled in His own baptism, there seems to be no good explanation for why the plural "us" (which includes Yochanan) is used.

#5 does not give sufficient reason why the descent of the Spirit and the proclamation of the Heavenly Voice would accompany a ritual undertaken to comply with the people's expectations. Moreover, the messiahship of Yeshua was confirmed to Yochanan (cf. John 1:30–34) through the *mikveh* and subsequent descent of the Spirit and proclamation of the Father, and it was thus a far greater event in the minds of the Gospel writers than simply one which complied with conventional expectations.

#6 has its merits, for it takes seriously the use of the word "fulfill" in Matthew's Gospel. Yet its weakness is that it takes the word "righteousness" to mean God's righteousness, which is not generally how Matthew uses the term. Rather, "to fulfill all righteousness" should, in context, mean "to

[1]The following are the places were δικαιοσύνη / δίκαιους / δικαιόω, "righteousness / righteous / declare righteous" are used in Matthew: 1:19; 3:15; 5:6,10,20,45; 6:1,33; 9:13; 10:41; 13:17, 43, 49; 21:32; 23:28-29, 35; 25:37, 46; 27:19.

[2]John Nolland, *The Gospel of Matthew* in *The New International Greek Commentary* (Eerdmans, 2005), p. 153.

do what is righteous in accordance with God's commandments." In other words, while this explanation recognizes that Yeshua's public ministry, here initiated by His *mikveh* at the hands of Yochanan, was in fulfillment of the words of Israel's prophets, and thus a demonstration of God's faithfulness to His own covenant obligations, it fails to give a valid explanation for why Yeshua would give the reason to Yochanan as "it is fitting for <u>us</u> to fulfill all righteousness."

It may be that a combination of the above suggestions would best explain the *mikveh* of Yeshua and the manner in both He and Yochanan fulfilled all righteousness in it. First, if we presume that the word "righteousness" is to be understood as it generally is in Matthew's Gospel, i.e., as "moral conduct in accord with God's will," then we should understand that Yeshua's *mikveh* was in direct response to something commanded in the Torah or otherwise understood to be necessary in terms of obedience to God. Secondly, since the word "fulfill" (πληρόω) is everywhere used by Matthew to mean the fulfillment of prophetic Scripture, we should likewise seek to find an explanation for Yeshua's *mikveh* as related to the prophetic message about Messiah.

Is it possible that the consecration of priests as given in the Torah formed the background for Yeshua's *mikveh*? In Exodus 29 we read of the laws given to Moses in regard to the consecration of Aaron and his sons as priests who would attend the altar and fulfill the office of priest and high priest. After offering sacrifices of a bull and two rams, together with a grain offering of unleavened bread, cakes, and wafers mixed with oil, Moses is commanded to wash the priests:

> Then you shall bring Aaron and his sons to the doorway of the tent of meeting and wash them with water (Ex 29:4)

Interestingly, the washing with water would have been understood as a *mikveh*, but it is Moses who is instructed to do the washing. In other words, like the *mikveh* of Yochanan, the *mikveh* of the priests included Moses as a necessary attendant.

Following the *mikveh*, Aaron was to be clothed in his sacred garments (the tunic, the robe of the ephod, the ephod itself, the breastplate and the turban with its golden crown) and then anointed with oil:

> Then you shall take the anointing oil and pour it on his head and anoint him (Ex 29:7).

The pericope in Exodus 29 concludes with the statement "So you shall ordain Aaron and his sons" (v. 9). The ordination of Aaron as high priest and his sons as priests involved sacrifice, donning the sacred garments, a *mikveh*, and anointing with oil. Only then were they duly ordained for their service as priests.

It seems very possible, then, that Yeshua, recognizing His role as the Suffering Servant, and thus as a priest who would bear the sins of Israel and atone for them (cf. Num 18:23; Is 53:6, 11), likewise recognized that at the initiation of His priestly work it was necessary to undergo a *mikveh*. Yochanan's attendance at His *mikveh* symbolically fulfilled the role of Moses when he initiated the priesthood upon Aaron and his sons, and gives the reason why Yeshua would have said "it is necessary for <u>us</u> to fulfill all righteousness."

Furthermore, the subsequent descent of the Spirit in the form of a dove matches the anointing with oil also required for the ordination of the high priest.

Thus, Yeshua's *mikveh* as presented by Matthew may well be drawn against the Torah background of the consecration of priests for their duties. If this is the case, then the point of Yeshua's *mikveh* is to emphasize that He is now entering into the duties of a priest (and particularly the high priest) on behalf of the people as the Suffering Servant of Isaiah 53. The "righteousness" which He and Yochanan fulfill in the *mikveh* was in the sense of type and anti-type in the foreshadowing of the Aaronic priesthood, pointing to the ultimate High Priest, the Messianic Servant of Adonai.

16 After being baptized, Yeshua came up immediately from the water; and behold, the heavens were opened, and he saw the Spirit of God descending as a dove and lighting on Him

Having immersed Himself in the waters of the Jordan, Yeshua came up *immediately* from the water. Here Matthew includes Mark's often used term,[1] which emphasizes the direct and purposed divine action in connection with Yeshua's words and deeds. In Mark's account, the "immediately" is not necessarily connected with Yeshua's coming up out of the water, but with the events that transpire, i.e., the descent of the Spirit and the voice from heaven. Though Matthew has a different syntax,[2] the general sense must be the same. The subsequent giving of the Spirit and divine proclamation are tied to the *mikveh* event of Yeshua. This strengthens our previous suggestion that the *mikveh* was symbolical of Yeshua's initiation as a priest.

Matthew uses "behold" (ἰδοὺ) here and also to introduce the divine proclamation in v. 17. These are both emphatic introductions to the two events, not only emphasizing their importance, but also showing them to be coordinated and connected.

the heavens were opened The idea of the heavens opening was a way of identifying the privilege of chosen prophets to receive the direct revelation of God, as though the curtains of the divine dwelling were pulled aside (cf. Ps 104:2; Is 40:22) and thus special (and otherwise hidden) knowledge about God and His activities are made known. We see this in Ezekiel 1:1,

> Now it came about in the thirtieth year, on the fifth day of the fourth month, while I was by the river Chebar among the exiles, the heavens were opened and I saw visions of God.

We see similar verbiage in the account of the stoning of Stephen (Acts 7:56) and in Peter's vision (Acts 10:11). John's Apocalypse also utilizes this motif (Rev 11:19; 19:11). In the present text, the revelation is given to the people rather than to Yeshua, as Yochanan's testimony (John 1:30f) makes clear. The heavens were opened in order to make known to Israel that her Messiah had come. But had they understood the import of the *mikveh* as initiating Yeshua's priestly role, they might have better understood His role as the Suffering Messiah rather than demanding His immediate role as the Royal Messiah (cf. Lk 24:25–26).

and he saw the Spirit of God descending Matthew's text is ambiguous as to the antecedent subject of the verb "he saw" (εἶδεν). Does he mean that Yeshua saw the Spirit descending, or that Yochanan did? Yochanan's own

[1] For "immediately" (εὐθύς) in Mark, see 1:10, 12, 18, 20-21, 28-30, 42-43; 2:8, 12; 3:6; 4:5, 15-17, 29; 5:2, 29-30, 42; 6:25, 27, 45, 50, 54; 7:25; 8:10; 9:15, 20, 24; 10:52; 11:2-3; 14:43, 45, 72-15:1.

[2] The phrase in Mark 1:10 should be translated as: "And immediately, having come up out of the water, he saw the heavens opened ...," the present participle ἀναβαίνων coming after the adverb εὐθύς. Matthew has the aorist indicative ἀνέβη, with εὐθύς modifying the verb.

witness is that he saw the Spirit descend in the form of a dove:

> John testified saying, "I have seen the Spirit descending as a dove out
> of heaven, and He remained upon Him" (John 1:32).

We should conclude that, along with Yeshua Himself, Yochanan (and perhaps others) witnessed the visible descent of the Spirit.

The Spirit is described as "coming down" (καταβαίνω, *katabaino*) and "lighting on Him" (literally, "coming upon Him," ἔρχομαι, *erxomai*). The use of *katabaino* in the sense of "descending" may well reflect the Lxx of Ps 133, which parallels the joy of congregated Israel at the festivals with the anointing of Aaron as the high priest:

> It is like the precious oil upon the head, coming down (καταβαίνω)
> upon the beard, even Aaron's beard, coming down (καταβαίνω) upon
> the edge of his robes.

For references to the descent of the Spirit of God in the Tanach, see Num 11:17, 25; Judg 14:19; Is 63:14.

Once again, if our suggestion that Yeshua's *mikveh* was to be seen as part of the ordination ceremony for a priest, then the subsequent descent of the Spirit upon Him fulfills the meaning of the anointing of the high priest with oil, which concluded his ordination. It was through the ordination ceremony, that the Aaronic high priest was made fit for his duties. In like manner, our Messiah was made ready by the empowering Holy Spirit for the priestly duties in which He would soon engage. Surely it was this "anointing" by the Spirit that was foundational for Yeshua's proclamation in the synagogue at Nazareth. He was given the scroll of Isaiah for reading the *haftarah*, and He stood and read from Is 61:1–2,

> The Spirit of the Lord GOD is upon me, because the LORD has anoint-
> ed me to bring good news to the afflicted; He has sent me to bind
> up the brokenhearted, to proclaim liberty to captives and freedom to
> prisoners; to proclaim the favorable year of the LORD…

His commentary on the portion was short and to the point: "Today this Scripture has been fulfilled in your hearing."

The Gospel writers all contain the notice that when the Spirit descended upon Yeshua, He came in the form of a dove. The explanations offered for the use of the dove are legion.[1] Some make a connection to Noah's dove, sent from the ark, which returns with the olive branch as proof that the flood has subsided. Those who connect this with the Spirit in the form of a dove at Yeshua's *mikveh* emphasize that Yeshua's appearance marked the end of God's judgment in that Yeshua would Himself take the divine judgment due to God's people. They likewise note that the olive branch had messianic portends (based upon the "branch" as a messianic symbol, and the play on words between *netzer*, "branch" and *Natzri*, "Nazarene," cf. 2:23).

Others have noted that in the later rabbinic literature, the *bat kol* (voice of God) is sometimes connected with the dove (b.*Berachot* 3a). In the Targum on *Song of Songs* 2.12, the "voice of the turtle dove" is translated "the voice of the Spirit of salvation."

Some have suggested that the text suffers from an early scribal error, in which an original Hebrew יָנוּחַ, "rest upon" was read as יוֹנָה, *yonah*, "dove." Such a suggestion notes the language of Num 11:27, in which the Spirit of God "rests" (נוּחַ) upon the 70 elders. But there is no extant textual evidence to

[1] In summarizing various suggestions for the dove symbolism, we need not include the many attempts to show a dependence upon pagan motifs from magical texts using birds and doves as messengers or magical portends. For a description of these, see Allison-Davies, *Matthew*, 1.331f.

warrant such a claim. The Peshitta has יָנָה and all of the Hebrew Matthews have יוֹנָה. If such a mix-up had occurred, one would expect that some textual evidence for the original reading would remain, especially in the semitic versions or translations.

Some note that Israel (Ephraim) is called a dove in Hos 7:11, and that in *Mechilta* on Ex 14:13, the Holy Spirit rests upon Israel as she crosses the Red Sea. Likewise, in *Mechilta* on 15:2, the voice of the Holy Spirit is heard as Israel crosses through the sea. Those who note these parallels suggest that Yeshua is thus marked out as the "renewed Israel," or the One Who stands as the quintessential Israelite, Who will bring Israel back to her God. This explanation, however, suffers from the fact that the Spirit descends as a dove, so that the dove imagery is of the Spirit, not of Yeshua. Moreover, the Hos 7:11 parallel speaks of Ephraim as a "silly dove," using the symbol in a negative sense.

Still others take the phrase "as a dove" in an adverbial sense, describing the manner in which the Spirit descended, not the form. They note that the rabbinic literature (b.*Chagigah* 15a) describes the "brooding of the Spirit" in Gen 1:2 as the "fluttering of a dove." They then suggest that what the Gospel writers are describing is the power of creation attributed to the Spirit, particularly in the work of Messiah Who would affect a "new creation" by bringing salvation to Israel.

Allison and Davies (along with others) take this final view but disregard the notion that "as a dove" is adverbial. Thus, a dove did descend upon Yeshua as the visible representation of the Spirit of God, and the closest and most obvious parallel is that of Gen 1:2, in which the Spirit of God "hovers" (מְרַחֶפֶת, *merachefet,* "to brood," "hover as a bird") over the waters in the work of creation. Thus, in Gen 1:2 three elements are parallel with the *mikveh* of Yeshua: 1) water, 2) a bird, 3) the Spirit of God. The import for the Gospel writers, then, would be that Yeshua is marked as the One through Whom a new creation would occur:

> We are, accordingly, encouraged to conclude that the Spirit as dove originally meant—and meant also for Matthew—that the events of Gen 1 were being recapitulated or repeated in the Messiah's life: the eschatological creation had commenced.[1]

and lighting upon Him   Neither Mark nor Luke have this added verb. Apparently Matthew wants to emphasize the remaining presence of the Spirit upon Yeshua. Though descending in the form of a dove, of which one would expect that the presence of the Spirit was only momentary, Matthew adds that the Spirit "was coming (ἔρχομαι) upon Him." It may be that Matthew has a text like Num 11:17f in mind, in which God promises Moses to "take of the Spirit" Who was upon him, and put Him upon the 70 elders chosen to assist him. The presence of the Spirit upon the 70 elders is evidenced by their engaging in prophesying, but the text is clear that this was a one-time phenomenon:

> ...and He took of the Spirit who was upon him and placed Him upon the seventy elders. And when the Spirit rested upon them, they prophesied. But they did not do it again (Num 11:27).

The fact that the Spirit "rests" upon the elders, but that the ability to proph-

---

[1] Allison-Davies, *Matthew,* 1.334.

esy is only temporary, may have prompted Matthew (if such a text was indeed in his purview) to emphasize the opposite in the case of Yeshua. The Spirit Who came upon Him remained. As the anointed Messiah and the Servant of Adonai, He is endowed with the power and presence of the Spirit (cf. Matt 12:18, quoting Is 42:1) in order to accomplish His mission of salvation.

17 and behold, a voice out of the heavens said, "This is My beloved Son, in whom I am well-pleased."

Matthew uses the exclamation "behold" once again, to indicate both that the sound of the heavenly voice is separate from the descent of the Spirit in the form of a dove, but connected with it as a second attestation of Yeshua's messiahship. As to the fact that Yeshua is the long-awaited Messiah, two witnesses confirm the reality: the Spirit and the Father.

Throughout the rabbinic literature, notice is found of the audible voice of God. Yet by the time of the rabbinic Sages, the need to separate the Almighty from the fallen world prompted them to adopt the terminology בַּת-קוֹל, *bat qol* to describe the heavenly voice. This "daughter of a voice" describes an "echo," and though it can at times describe the very voice of God, more often is seems to make the audible sound as secondary and therefore once removed from the Almighty. This desire to make a separation between the Holy God and His created universe is also seen in the Targumim, in which the *memra* ("word") of God is that which enters the realm of human existence rather than God Himself. It may be that the use of *bat qol* was adopted in direct opposition to the followers of Yeshua, and emphasis upon the incarnational status of God in Messiah. For quite often (though not always), the *bat qol* is an inferior representation of the divine will or revelation. One example will suffice to illustrate this. Involved in *halachic* disputes, the follow story is told about the Sages:

> It has been taught: On that day R. Eliezer brought forward every imaginable argument, but they did not accept them. Said he to them: 'If the halachah agrees with me, let this carob-tree prove it!' Thereupon the carob-tree was torn a hundred cubits out of its place — others affirm, four hundred cubits. 'No proof can be brought from a carob-tree,' they retorted. Again he said to them: 'If the halachah agrees with me, let the stream of water prove it!' Whereupon the stream of water flowed backwards — 'No proof can be brought from a stream of water,' they rejoined. Again he urged: 'If the halachah agrees with me, let the walls of the schoolhouse prove it,' whereupon the walls inclined to fall. But R. Joshua rebuked them, saying: 'When scholars are engaged in a halachic dispute, what have you to interfere?' Hence they did not fall, in honour of R. Joshua, nor did they resume the upright, in honour of R. Eliezer; and they are still standing thus inclined. Again he said to them: 'If the halachah agrees with me, let it be proved from Heaven!' Whereupon a Heavenly Voice cried out: 'Why do you dispute with R. Eliezer, seeing that in all matters the halachah agrees with him!' But R. Joshua arose and exclaimed: 'It is not in heaven'(Deut 30:12f). What did he mean by this? — Said R. Jeremiah: That the Torah had already been given at Mount Sinai; we pay no attention to a Heavenly Voice, because You have long since written in the Torah at Mount Sinai, After the majority must one incline (Ex 23:2). (b.*Bava Metzia* 59b)

Here, even the Heavenly Voice (בת קול) is not sufficient to settle the argument. One cannot help but wonder if this story was given particularly to discredit the testimony of the followers of Yeshua, who claimed divine prerogative on behalf of Yeshua, based upon the voice from heaven at His *mikveh*.

Still, the rabbinic literature gives evidence that God did make His will known at times through audible communication, and particularly in terms of marking out worthy individuals:

> When the latter prophets died, that is, Haggai, Zechariah, and Malachi, then the Holy Spirit came to an end in Israel. But even so, they made them hear through a *bat qol*. Sages gathered together in the upper room of the house of Guira in Jericho, and a *bat qol* came forth and said to them, "There is a man among you who is worthy to receive the Holy Spirit, but his generation is unworthy of such an honor." They all set their eyes upon Hillel the elder. And when he died, they said about him, "Woe for the humble man, woe for the pious man, the disciple of Ezra."
>
> Then another time they were in session in Yabneh and heard a *bat qol* saying, "There is among you a man who is worthy to receive the Holy Spirit, but the generation is unworthy of such an honor." They all set their eyes upon Samuel the Small. At the time of his death what did they say? "Woe for the humble man, woe for the pious man, the disciple of Hillel the Elder." (t.*Sota* 13:3–4).

For other references to the *bat qol*, see b.*Sota* 21a; 48b; b.*Sanhedrin* 11a; 104b; b.*Ta'anit* 24b; b.*Chagigah* 14b.

Thus, the sound of the Heavenly Voice at the time of Yeshua would have been understood as giving divine authority and approval to Yeshua. Moreover, it was clearly the voice of the Almighty and not an echo. Indeed, in Immanuel the Divine One had come to dwell with man.

It seems highly likely, as well, that the Heavenly Voice at Yeshua's *mikveh* would have immediately caused the people to draw parallels to the well known narratives of the Tanach in which God spoke audibly, and particularly to passages like the *Akedah* (Gen 22) in which the voice of God played such a central role.

The message proclaimed was emphatic: "This is My beloved Son, in Whom I am well-pleased." Many have considered this a conflation of Is 42:1 and Ps 2:7, while others deny any connection to these texts.

Isaiah 42:1

MT	Lxx
הֵן עַבְדִּי אֶתְמָךְ־בּוֹ בְּחִירִי רָצְתָה נַפְשִׁי נָתַתִּי רוּחִי עָלָיו מִשְׁפָּט לַגּוֹיִם יוֹצִיא	Ιακωβ ὁ παῖς μου ἀντιλήμψομαι αὐτοῦ Ισραηλ ὁ ἐκλεκτός μου προσεδέξατο αὐτὸν ἡ ψυχή μου ἔδωκα τὸ πνεῦμά μου ἐπ᾽ αὐτόν κρίσιν τοῖς ἔθνεσιν ἐξοίσει
"Behold, My Servant, whom I uphold; My chosen one in whom My soul delights. I have put My Spirit upon Him; He will bring forth justice to the nations.	Jacob is my servant, I will help him: Israel is my chosen, my soul has accepted him; I have put my Spirit upon him; he shall bring forth judgement to the nations.

Psalm 2:7

MT	Lxx
אֲסַפְּרָה אֶל חֹק יְהוָה אָמַר אֵלַי בְּנִי אַתָּה אֲנִי הַיּוֹם יְלִדְתִּיךָ	διαγγέλλων τὸ πρόσταγμα κυρίου κύριος εἶπεν πρός με υἱός μου εἶ σύ ἐγὼ σήμερον γεγέννηκά σε
I will surely tell of the decree of the LORD: He said to Me, 'You are My Son, Today I have begotten You.	declaring the ordinance of the Lord: the Lord said to me, You are my Son, today have I begotten you.

We should also note the quote from Is 42:1 in Matt 12:18, for Matthew's quote is somewhat changed from the Lxx text:

ἰδοὺ ὁ παῖς μου ὃν ᾑρέτισα,
ὁ ἀγαπητός μου εἰς ὃν εὐδόκησεν ἡ ψυχή μου·
θήσω τὸ πνεῦμά μου ἐπ' αὐτόν,
καὶ κρίσιν τοῖς ἔθνεσιν ἀπαγγελεῖ.

Behold, My Servant whom I have chosen;
My Beloved in whom My soul is well-pleased;
I will put My Spirit upon Him,
And He shall proclaim justice to the Gentiles.

We may compare these now with our text in Matthew:

καὶ ἰδοὺ φωνὴ ἐκ τῶν οὐρανῶν λέγουσα·
οὗτός ἐστιν ὁ υἱός μου ὁ ἀγαπητός,
ἐν ᾧ εὐδόκησα.

and behold, a voice out of the heavens said,
"This is My beloved Son,
in whom I am well-pleased."

We see that there are some similarities but hardly close parallels. The phrase in Ps 2:7, "you are My son" is surely reminiscent of "This is my beloved Son," but only in subject matter, not as a verbal parallel. The fact that Matthew's quote of Is 42:1 (in 12:18) substitutes "beloved" for "chosen" may show an influence from the Targum, which has "beloved" (אִתְרְעֵי): "Behold My Servant Messiah whom I bring near, My chosen one, My beloved, My word is in Him." This does tie our text together more closely with Is 42:1. That the proclamation of the Heavenly Voice included "My beloved" would surely have drawn a link to the targumic reading of Is 42:1. We may also note that the idea of "beloved" may denote "unique." For instance, in the Lxx of Gen 22:2, we read: "Take your son, your beloved one, whom you love, and go into the highland ...." Here, the Lxx substitutes "your beloved one" for "your only one" (יְחִידְךָ) of the Hebrew. It can be seen, then, how the phrase "chosen one" of Is 42:1 could easily be construed as "beloved one" in the sense of the Servant's unique, chosen status before the Almighty. It may be, then, that the proclamation at Yeshua's *mikveh* gathers together a number of messianic themes well embedded in the Tanach, and perhaps Ps 2:7 and Is 42:1 are chief among these. The use of ἀγαπητός (*agapetos*, "beloved") in the Lxx of Gen 22:2, 12, 16 would also indicate that "My beloved Son" would draw obvious parallels to the *Akedah* which was well recognized as having many messianic themes and overtones.

Here, at Yeshua's *mikveh*, is the first public announcement of His fulfilling the "Son of God" role. The role of Yeshua as the Son will continue to be a central messianic theme for Matthew (cf. 11:27; 16:16; 17:5; 26:23; 28:19), for through His words and deeds, He shows Himself to be the Promised One of Israel, i.e., Messiah, Son of David, Son of Man, and Servant of Adonai.

in Whom I am well-pleased   We should note the same declaration from Heaven in the Transfiguration pericope (17:5): "This is My beloved Son, with whom I am well-pleased; listen to Him!" Here, the added "listen to Him!" is understood (though not explicitly stated) at the *mikveh*. The obvious point of the divine pleasure in the person and work of the Messiah is that what He accomplishes will be fully acceptable before the Almighty. Moreover, the verbiage emphasizes the familial, covenant relationship that exists between the Father and the Son. The Son is "beloved" in the sense of chosen and unique in His relationship to the Father. As such, the Father will assist Him and enable Him to accomplish the divine mission of salvation. Moreover, from the standpoint of the Son, He has come to do the Father's will (Jn 8:28; 14:31), and in so doing demonstrates His covenant loyalty and love for the Father.

The fact that Yeshua is marked as the One in Whom the Father is well-pleased also reinforces the Davidic connection. In 2Sam 22:20 (cp. Ps 18:19) we read:

> He also brought me forth into a broad place; He rescued me, because
> He delighted in me. (ὅτι εὐδόκησεν ἐν ἐμοί)

Here, in a Psalm of thanksgiving for deliverance from the hand of Saul and his enemies, David, the rightful King, recognizes that his success and salvation was the result of the sovereign and beneficent grace of the Almighty. That the same language would be used in regard to Yeshua must certainly emphasize the messianic connection to David.

Thus, the beginning of Yeshua's public work as the promised Messiah of Israel is announced in connection with His *mikveh* at the hands of Yochanan. He did not declare Himself to be the Messiah, but was proclaimed to be so by the evident and visible presence of the Holy Spirit, and the audible testimony of the Almighty. The *mikveh*, connected as it was with the ordination of the high priest, marked the kind of work in which Yeshua would engage, that is, the bearing of the people's sins in order to affect atonement for them. Likewise, the coming of the Holy Spirit upon Yeshua was reminiscent of the oil of anointing given to high priest on his ordination day. And the statement of the Father, affirming the unique and privileged status of the Son, assured the success of His priestly endeavors.

Here, then, is the historical record regarding our Master. We know the end of the story, for He stands before us today as the exalted, risen Savior Who has won the victory for us, and has secured eternal redemption (cf. Heb 9:12), Who ever lives to make intercession for us before the Father (Heb 7:25). We may trust that His work on our behalf is sufficient, for the Father announced from the beginning that He is beloved, and that the Father is well-pleased with Him. It is His worthiness, not ours, that affects our salvation, for He has satisfied the Divine justice completely, and has thus made full payment for our transgressions. It is by His stripes that we are healed.

But Matthew's story has just begun. This One, beloved and accepted by the Father, will not long be accepted by many of His peers. He will face the onslaught of the Tempter, the disapproval of the religious leaders of His day, the abandonment of those who had pledge their loyalty, and the scourge of death at the hands of those who would not and could not acknowledge the mystery of His incarnation.

We can only imagine what the reaction was of those who stood that day on the banks of the Jordan, many of whom doubtlessly had themselves undergone a *mikveh*. Did they see the descent of the Spirit upon Yeshua? Did they hear the Heavenly Voice proclaiming the divine pleasure in our Master? We would have to believe that some were forever changed as they recognized Yeshua as the Messiah, and pledged themselves to Him as loyal disciples. But one could also imagine that others were skeptical, and some perhaps dismissed the entire event as of little or no consequence.

In a similar way, we are confronted today with the words of Matthew, for we too must decide whether we agree or disagree with his witness of Yeshua and the events that happened that day. If He is truly the Messiah as Matthew says He is, then He is our only hope of salvation—the only means of obtaining forgiveness of our sins. He is the beloved One in Whom the Father is well-pleased.

Chapter Four
Commentary

The Temptation

Chapter Four opens with the Temptation of Yeshua by the devil, who is also called "the tempter" (v. 3) and Satan (v. 10). That Yeshua combats the tempter by quoting three times from Deuteronomy casts the whole pericope as a parallel to the wanderings of Israel in the desert for 40 years, and may well be written with Deut 8:2–3 specifically in mind:

> Deut. 8:2 "You shall remember all the way which the LORD your God has led you in the wilderness these forty years, that He might humble you, testing you, to know what was in your heart, whether you would keep His commandments or not. 3 "He humbled you and let you be hungry, and fed you with manna which you did not know, nor did your fathers know, that He might make you understand that man does not live by bread alone, but man lives by everything that proceeds out of the mouth of the LORD.

Thus, the temptation of Yeshua is put in direct contrast to Israel, who grumbled over the lack of food and gave into idolatry in the sin of Baal Peor (cf. Num 31:16; Josh 22:17). In each place where Israel failed, Yeshua is victorious. Likewise, that the Temptation comes after Yeshua's *mikveh* may also signal the parallel with Israel's having gone through the Red Sea in her exodus from Egypt.[1] Having gone through the waters of a new exodus, Yeshua enters the desert to undergo a time of testing, His forty days of fasting analogous to Israel's forty years of wandering. He is tested through hunger and by "relief" through idolatry, but in each case He models the true heart of faith and obedience which gains the victory.

We may also note a rabbinic source (dealing with how true and false prophets are to be discerned) in which a story is told of Satan's tempting of Abraham on his way to sacrifice Isaac on Mt. Moriah. While the legend is found in the later talmudic literature, it may reflect an earlier (and well-known) story:

> On the way Satan came towards him [Abraham] and said to him. *'If we assay to commune with thee, wilt thou be grieved? . . . Behold, thou hast instructed many, and thou hast strengthened the weak hands. Thy words have upholden him that was falling, and thou hast strengthened the feeble knees. But now it is come upon thee, and thou faintest.'* (Job 4:2–5) He replied, *'I will walk in mine integrity.'* (Ps 26:2) *'But'*, said Satan to him, *'should not thy fear be thy confidence?'* (Job 4:6) *'Remember'*, he retorted, *'I pray thee, whoever perished, being innocent?'* (Job 4:6) Seeing that he would not listen to him, he said to him , *'Now a thing was secretly brought to me.'* (Job 4:12); thus have I heard from behind the Curtain, "the lamb, for a burnt-offering but not Isaac for a burnt-offering." (cp. Job 4:7) He replied, *'It is the penalty of a liar, that should he even tell the truth, he is not listened to.'* (b.*Sanhedrin* 89b)[2]

The similarities to the Temptation are obvious: 1) Satan argues by quoting

[1] Luke inserts the genealogy between Yeshua's *mikveh* and the temptation, thus highlighting a parallel to Adam, where he was tempted and fell, but Yeshua remains obedient and thus righteous.

[2] As referenced in Allison-Davies, 1.352–53.

Scripture, 2) Abraham rebuffs by quoting from Scripture, but especially by showing that Satan misquotes or misinterprets the Scripture, and 3) that even when Satan correctly quotes Scripture, he is not to be believed since he is a known liar (thus explaining the criteria for discerning a false prophet).

Moreover, the rabbinic perspective, based upon Ps 11:5, was that God tests the righteous, not the wicked.[1] *Pirkei Avot* 5.4 reads, "Ten trials were inflicted upon Abraham, our father, may he rest in peace, and he withstood all of them, to show you how great is His love for Abraham, our father, may he rest in peace."

We may therefore understand Matthew's retelling of the Temptation as a clear message of Yeshua's greatness, that He was chosen as a righteous man to accomplish God's will. This is seen in His superior knowledge of Scripture (and thus of God) and His strength in withstanding the tempter. As such, He stands as the quintessential Israelite Who maintains complete covenant faithfulness even in the face of great trials. As such, He stands in the place of the promised Messiah Who would redeem Israel through His own righteousness and ultimately, through His sacrificial death.

1   Then Yeshua was led up by the Spirit into the wilderness to be tempted by the devil.

Mark's account of the Temptation (1:12–13) is extremely short:

> Immediately the Spirit impelled Him to go out into the wilderness. And He was in the wilderness forty days being tempted by Satan; and He was with the wild beasts, and the angels were ministering to Him.

We may presume that the story of Yeshua's Temptation was well-known by Mark's audience, and thus he needed only to allude to it in order to evoke the complete story in their minds.[2] Luke's account is even longer than Matthew's, and he reverses the order of the last two temptations, perhaps in order to show a progression from the desert, to the mountain, and finally to Jerusalem.

In this opening verse, Matthew writes that Yeshua[3] was "*led up* by the Spirit" (passive of ἀνάγω, *anago*, where the sense of "led *up*" has the topography in mind, going up from the river), while Luke has ἤγετο (*egeto*, passive from ἄγω, *ago*). Mark has the active ἐκβάλλω (*ekballo*), which the NASB translates "impelled by the Spirit," but the verb is probably more causative, emphasizing that Yeshua was "driven" by the Spirit into the desert (cf. Gen 3:24 Lxx where ἐκβάλλω is used where God "expels" Adam from the garden).

From Matthew's perspective, Yeshua was led into the wilderness for the purpose[4] of being tempted or tested (the Greek word πειράζω, *peirazo* can mean either "to test" or "to tempt"). This corresponds to Deut 8:2, which speaks of Israel's wanderings in the desert for the purpose of being tested. Matthew has the temptation begin after the 40 days of fasting. Both Mark and Luke put the temptation as occurring during the 40 days. It may be that Mark and Luke both consider the fasting to be itself a testing, which Satan attempted to exploit.

That the Spirit of God is credited with leading Yeshua into the desert in order to be tempted also accords with the regular connection of the Spirit in Israel's wanderings. Thus, Num 11:17, 25, 29 note the presence of the Spirit

---

[1] While the MT of Ps 11:5 could read "The LORD tests the righteous and the wicked, And the one who loves violence His soul hates," the Sages took the phrase (based upon the Masoretic accentuation) to read "The LORD tests the righteous, and the wicked and the one who loves violence His soul hates." The *vav* introducing the second clause is therefore taken as adversive rather than conjunctive. Cf. Mid. Rab. *Gen* 55.2; Mid. Rab. *Cant.* 2.46; Mid. Rab. *Num.* 15.12.

[1] So Carson, *Matthew,* p. 111.

[3] Matthew has the article (ὁ Ἰησοῦς) while Luke does not. Mark does not name Yeshua. The use of the article with proper names is the result of anaphora (reference to a previous mention) and thus occurs frequently in narrative (thus in the Gospels). It's less frequent use in the Epistles is therefore understandable.

[4] Note Matthew's use of the telic infinitive, πειρασθῆναι ὑπὸ τοῦ διαβόλου as opposed to Mark and Luke both of whom have πειραζόμενος.

upon the 70 elders chosen to assist Moses, and Neh 9:20 parallels the giving of the Spirit with that of the manna. The rebellion of the Israelites was a rebellion against the Spirit (Ps 106:33), which Isaiah describes by "they grieved His Holy Spirit" (cf. Is 63:10–14). The connection of the Spirit of God with Israel during her wilderness experience is also common in the rabbinic literature (cf. *Targum Yer.* to Ex 15.2; *Mechilta* on Ex 14:13, 15; b.*Sota* 30b; Mid. Rab. *Num.* on 11:17; Mid. Rab. *Exodus* on 15.1).

The "evil one" is referred to here as "the devil" (ὁ διάβολος, *diabolos*), but later as "the tempter" (ὁ πειράζων, *peirazon*) in v. 3, and "Satan" (σατάν, *satan*) in v. 10. Elsewhere, Matthew also uses the designation "evil one" (13:19, 38) and "the enemy" (13:39). *Diabolos* strictly means "slanderer" and is the normal word used by the Lxx to translate שָׂטָן, *satan*, which means "adversary" or "opponent." He is the "chief opposer of God, the archenemy who leads all the spiritual hosts of darkness."[1] The idea that the figure of Satan evolved or underwent a metamorphosis in the biblical literature, from merely one of the hosts of heaven to a demonic figure, fails to take into consideration the progressive revelation of the Bible. While surely the Apostolic Scriptures have far more to say about the evil one, his appearance in the Tanach is in concert with the expanded revelation of his essential evil character as portrayed in the Tanach.

Besides the fact that the Temptation afforded the perfect proof of Yeshua's fitness to be the Messiah, it also teaches us a very important lesson: the Spirit's leading is not always to bring a person to a place of shelter and comfort. Sometimes the Spirit leads into a realm of testing where one's faith and character may be proven. We may be assured, however, that such a testing would never be more than what can be endured, for the purpose of the testing is always to prove His faithfulness in sustaining those He has purposed to save.

> No temptation (or testing) has overtaken you but such as is common to man; and God is faithful, who will not allow you to be tempted (or tested) beyond what you are able, but with the temptation (or testing) will provide the way of escape also, so that you will be able to endure it. (1Cor. 10:13)

2 And after He had fasted forty days and forty nights, He then became hungry.

The fast for forty days and forty nights parallels not only Israel's 40 year wandering in the desert, but also the fast of Moses for the same period of time while upon Mt. Sinai (cf. Ex 34:28). The Exodus text specifically notes the Moses "did not eat bread or drink water," but Yeshua's fast was most likely from food alone, as Luke specifically states: "He ate nothing during those days" (Lk 4:2).

The notice that "He then became hungry" seems superfluous, for surely after fasting for forty days and forty nights, one would be hungry! But the NASB has reordered the words as found in the Greek. The original has this word order: "He fasted forty days and forty nights, afterward He was hungry." We should probably understand ἐπείνασεν (*epeinasen*, from πεινάω, *peinao*) to mean "famished." That is, the Gospel writers wish to convey that point that after such a long fast, our Master was physically without strength. Thus, the enemy's temptations came at a time when Yeshua would be re-

[1]Carson, *Matthew*, p. 112. Cf. Gen 3; 2Sam 19:23; Jn 8:37–40; 1Cor 11:10; 2Cor 11:3; 12:7; Rev 12:3–9; 20:1–4; 7–10. For examples of Satan in the Tanach, see 1Chron 21:1; Job 1:6–13; 2:1–7; Zech 3:1–2.

quired to rely entirely upon the strength provided by the Spirit. His humanity is thus fully in view. He faced the temptations of the evil one, not as a divine superhuman, but as a common man Who relied completely upon the Spirit for His victory. As such, He stands as the supreme example for all to follow.

We may still ask, however, how it was that the Son of God could be tempted to sin. Regardless of how we may construe the temptation, the obvious point is that the temptation consisted in Satan's invitation to act in a way that was contrary to the divine will. But if Yeshua was unable to sin since He was the divine Son of God, then how could the confrontation ever be construed as a *bone fide* temptation? While the answer to this conundrum once again puts us into the middle of the mystery of the incarnation itself, we may seek an answer by viewing temptation as a force and constructing an appropriate model. Consider this scenario: envision a locomotive moving at top speed down the railroad tracks. If someone were to stand on the tracks with hand outstretched, to stop the oncoming train, he would be bumped off the tracks without pause—the locomotive would not even register his presence. However, if the man were able to halt the train in its tracks, not only would the force of the locomotive be entirely stopped, but the man would also feel the full force or power of the oncoming train. In like manner, then, one who yields to temptation never feels the full force of it. Only the one who complete resists its power knows the full force of the temptation. In this way, Yeshua felt the full force of Satan's attack because He complete resisted the temptations.

3 And the tempter came and said to Him, "If You are the Son of God, command that these stones become bread."

The exact manner in which the three-phase temptation of our Master occurred is not certain, but it may have been more than merely carried out in the physical world. Standing atop a high mountain would not itself provide a glimpse of "all the kingdoms of the world," so some supernatural vision is presupposed. Did Yeshua walk from desert to Jerusalem and to the mountain, or was He transported in a supernatural way? Even Paul was not always certain whether the visions he received were "in the body or out of the body" (2Cor 12:2). Regardless, the temptations were real, and existed in the realm of human existence as evidenced by the fact that Yeshua was hungry (i.e., physically weakened).

The first temptation related to this very hunger. The manner in which the temptation is given does not question the divine nature of Yeshua—it rather presupposes it. The conditional clause, "If You are the Son of God" is grammatically a real condition, and should be understood to mean "Since you are the Son of God" or "Since you claim to be the Son of God." Satan is therefore not tempting Yeshua to prove His divine nature—that is a given as far as the temptation is concerned. Rather, in light of the fact that Yeshua was famished after His long period of fasting, the temptation Satan offered was to use His divine powers to fulfill His own needs. "Sonship of the living God, he [Satan] suggested, surely means Jesus has the power and right to satisfy his own needs."[1] But how could using His divine power to fulfill His own needs be construed as wrong? The answer lies in the fact that Yeshua had voluntarily given upon the use of some of His divine attributes in order to fulfill the mission given to Him by the Father, i.e., to come as a man to

[1] Carson, *Matthew*, p. 112.

redeem mankind. The temptation, then, was to use His sonship in a way inconsistent with His God-ordained mission. This is emphasized by Yeshua's response, which was to quote from Deut 8:3.

4 But He answered and said, "It is written, 'Man shall not live on bread alone, but on every word that proceeds out of the mouth of God.'"

Yeshua counters the tempting suggestion of Satan by quoting Scripture, introduced by "it is written." It is the inspired word of God that stands as the absolute rule upon which Yeshua's actions are based.

Deut 8:3

MT	Lxx	Matthew
לֹא עַל־הַלֶּחֶם לְבַדּוֹ יִחְיֶה הָאָדָם כִּי עַל־כָּל־מוֹצָא פִי־יְהוָה יִחְיֶה הָאָדָם	οὐκ ἐπ' ἄρτῳ μόνῳ ζήσεται ὁ ἄνθρωπος ἀλλ' ἐπὶ παντὶ ῥήματι τῷ ἐκπορευομένῳ διὰ στόματος θεοῦ ζήσεται ὁ ἄνθρωπος	οὐκ ἐπ' ἄρτῳ μόνῳ ζήσεται ὁ ἄνθρωπος, ἀλλ' ἐπὶ παντὶ ῥήματι ἐκπορευομένῳ διὰ στόματος θεοῦ.
Not upon bread alone does man live but upon all that comes forth from the mouth of Adonai does man live.	Not upon bread alone does man live but upon every word that goes forth through the mouth of God does man live.	Not upon bread alone does man live but upon every word that goes forth through the mouth of God.

Matthew quotes from the Lxx, leaving off the final clause since the former identical clause ("man shall live") is presumed by the strong contrast: "man does not live by X, meaning he does live by Y." The Lxx adds ῥῆμα (*rhema*, "word") as explanatory for the Hebrew כָּל־מוֹצָא פִי־יהוה, "all that goes forth of the mouth of Adonai," meaning all that God reveals and accomplishes through His divine proclamation.

The context of the quote is essential in understanding Yeshua's choice of this Scripture. Moses is reminding the Israelites that their physical existence was obviously dependent upon God, not upon their own abilities. The manna was clear proof of this, for God commanded that bread rain down from heaven in order to provide food for the people. Thus, their physical well-being was the direct result of God's miraculous provision. Indeed, the very reason that God brought the test of hunger upon the Israelites in the first place was so that they would know that their existence depended entirely upon the Almighty.

In this way, Yeshua is rebuffing Satan for the idea that He could use His divine powers in a self-serving way. "The Son of Man did not come to be served, but to serve, and to give His life a ransom for many" (Matt 20:28). His divinely ordained mission meant that the voluntary suspension of His divine attributes was necessary, and their use in a self-serving way would therefore annul the very reason for which He had come.

It is this same mind that we, as disciples of the Master, must also have. Our mission is not such that obedience to God's will is given in order to gain personally, but that in our obedience His Name might be sanctified upon the earth. Moreover, we must live with this reality in view: obedience to God is in itself a resignation to His promised provision, for it is when we rely fully upon Him that He is glorified, for when our needs are met, it is seen as the result of what the Almighty has done for us, not what we have been able to accomplish by our own strength.

Yeshua therefore demonstrates the reality of Hab 2:4, for while Israel demanded bread but died in the wilderness, Yeshua denied Himself bread, retaining His righteousness, and lived in faithful submission to God's word. "The righteous one will live on the basis of his faith."

5   Then the devil took Him into the holy city and had Him stand on the pinnacle of the temple,

The "holy city" is Jerusalem (cf. Neh 11:1; Is 48:2; Dan 9:24) where the Temple resided. Again, the manner of moving from one location to another is not given, but the scene is that of the Temple complex. The "pinnacle of the Temple" is literally "the wing of the Temple" (τὸ πτερύγιον τοῦ ἱεροῦ)[1], where "Temple" must stand for the entire complex, since Yeshua as a non-Levite would not have been allowed to enter the Temple proper. The Greek word πτερύγιον, "wing" is only found here in the Apostolic Scriptures. To what does this refer? We know that the rabbis considered the Temple to be at the center of Jerusalem (Josephus, *Contra Ap.* 1.196–8; b.*Yoma* 54a–b; *Tanchuma Qidd.* 10), and Jerusalem to be the earth's navel, and even the high point of the whole earth (b.*Qidd.* 69a). The highest corner of the Temple mount was the southeast corner, or else one might think of the high point of the southwest corner from which the shofar was played (cf. y.*Pesach* 35b). Regardless of the exact location, the picture the Gospel writers wish us to see is that Yeshua was standing at a place very high above the ground below.

6 and said to Him, "If You are the Son of God, throw Yourself down; for it is written, 'He will command His angels concerning You'; and 'On their hands they will bear You up, So that You will not strike Your foot against a stone.'"

The demands of Satan against our Master involved the prohibition regarding testing God. Testing God means presuming upon His grace and promises. God's people are to realize that God's mercies are always the direct outpouring of His gracious intentions, and not that which anyone can demand. Throwing oneself down from a high point would involve a presumption that God is required to act in miraculous ways to overcome one's own neglect or willful disregard for God's revealed will. Preserving life is a central theme in the Torah, and preserving one's own life is included in this. The sixth commandment which prohibits murder includes suicide as well.

Having been rebuffed in his first attempt by Yeshua's reliance upon the Scriptures, the evil one resorts to quoting Scripture as well, though he does so poorly, for though he quoted correctly, his application of the text itself was such as to turn that which was righteous into sin. This, of course, is always the way of the tempter, for he excels at turning righteousness into evil.

His quote, introduced by the common "for it is written," is from Ps 91:11–12. The context of the Psalm speaks of those who find their refuge in God, and abide in the shadow of the Almighty (v. 1). God is the One Who protects His own, and brings them through all manner of trouble (vv. 2–4). He offers safety from enemies as well as from natural calamity (vv. 5–8). But such protection is for those who have made God "their dwelling place," meaning those who have trusted in Him and have therefore chosen faithful-

[1] Lachs notes this rabbinic tradition regarding the Messiah: "When the King Messiah reveals himself he will come and stand on the roof of the Temple!" (*Pesikta Rabbati*, 36).

ness as their manner of life (v. 9). In other words, the context of the Psalm is that of those who live in faithful obedience to the God of the covenant, and who therefore are blessed by His protecting hand.

The quote, from Ps 91:11–12, is as follows:

MT	Lxx	Matthew
כִּי מַלְאָכָיו יְצַוֶּה־לָּךְ לִשְׁמָרְךָ בְּכָל־דְּרָכֶיךָ עַל־כַּפַּיִם יִשָּׂאוּנְךָ פֶּן־תִּגֹּף בָּאֶבֶן רַגְלֶךָ	ὅτι τοῖς ἀγγέλοις αὐτοῦ ἐντελεῖται περὶ σοῦ τοῦ διαφυλάξαι σε ἐν πάσαις ταῖς ὁδοῖς σου ἐπὶ χειρῶν ἀροῦσίν σε μήποτε προσκόψῃς πρὸς λίθον τὸν πόδα σου	τοῖς ἀγγέλοις αὐτοῦ ἐντελεῖται περὶ σοῦ καὶ ἐπὶ χειρῶν ἀροῦσίν σε, μήποτε προσκόψῃς πρὸς λίθον τὸν πόδα σου.
For He will give His angels charge concerning you, to guard you in all your ways. They will bear you up in their hands, that you do not strike your foot against a stone.	For he shall give his angels charge concerning you, to keep you in all your ways. They will bear you up on their hands, lest at any time you dash your foot against a stone.	He will command His angels concerning You; and On their hands they will bear you up, so that you will not strike your foot against a stone.

Matthew has given the quote by the evil one as directly from the Lxx, with the exception that "to keep you in all your ways" is left out. Moreover, the Lxx is essentially an accurate translation of the Hebrew. The fact that Satan leaves out the clause "to keep you in all your ways" does not warrant the charge that he misquoted Scripture, for such general quotations given in general formulations are in line with the manner in which the Tanach is quoted elsewhere. However, the deleted clause may point to the manner in which Satan was attempting to interpret and apply the Scripture wrongly. For in leaving out the clause, the general tenor of the Psalm, that those who find shelter in the shadow of the Almighty are the ones He protects, is de-emphasized.

What exactly was the force of the temptation as formulated by the tempter? It appears that he intends to entice Yeshua into using some significant miracle to prove His status as Messiah, much like the miracle of Elijah on Mt. Carmel, as proof of the superiority of Israel's God over the pagan god, Ba'al (cf. 1Ki 18). But the major miracle of attestation regarding the Messiah was His resurrection (Matt 12:39; 16:4). Other miracles that He performed were in line with what the prophets said the Messiah would do (cf. Matt 11:2–6; Lk 7:22), and were miracles involving compassion upon the sick and poor. Thus, the devil attempts to make faith subservient to miracles, when in fact, miracles are always understood only when preceded by faith (cf. Matt 13:58).

But more to the point, putting oneself in harm's way in order to force God to perform a miracle is strictly forbidden by the Torah, as Yeshua immediately makes known by quoting Deut 6:16 in order to refute the improper interpretation of Ps 91 by the enemy. This in itself ought to inform us regarding the Master's hermeneutic. Scripture, properly interpreted, coincides with other Scriptures. This presupposes the unity of the biblical text as the product of divine inspiration.

7 Yeshua said to him, "On the other hand, it is written, 'You shall not put the Lord your God to the test.'"

The counter quote is from Deut 6:16, and Yeshua introduces it by the common "it is written." He emphasizes, by the use of "on the other hand it is written" (literally, "again it is written," πάλιν γέγραπται), that one text may be properly understood and applied by the application of a second text. Yeshua does not quote this text, then, in order to refute the truth of Ps 91:11–12, but to show the manner in which it is to be properly interpreted and applied. Since the Torah expressly forbids putting God to the test, the protection promised in the Psalm cannot include those cases where God is disregarded and disobeyed. When one disregards the commands of God, one cannot count on God's blessing (cf. Gen 18:19).

Deut 6:16

MT	Lxx	Matthew
לֹא תְנַסּוּ אֶת־יְהוָה אֱלֹהֵיכֶם כַּאֲשֶׁר נִסִּיתֶם בַּמַּסָּה	οὐκ ἐκπειράσεις κύριον τὸν θεόν σου ὃν τρόπον ἐξεπειράσασθε ἐν τῷ Πειρασμῷ	οὐκ ἐκπειράσεις κύριον τὸν θεόν σου.
You shall not put the LORD your God to the test, as you tested Him at Massah.	You shall not tempt the Lord Your God, as you tempted Him in the temptation.	You shall not tempt the Lord your God.

The quote is directly from the Lxx, and essentially represents the Hebrew. The final clause is not quoted, since the major point is the prohibition regarding testing "the LORD your God."

What does it mean to "test God?" The incident at Massah (Ex 17) focused on the need for water. The people of Israel were quite sure that Moses had led them into the wilderness in order for them to perish: "Why, now, have you brought us up from Egypt, to kill us and our children and our livestock with thirst?" (Ex 17:3). The statement of the people was not so much a question of Moses' abilities, as it was a disregard for God's presence among them. He had promised to protect them and provide for them. Rather than arguing against Moses, and quarrelling among themselves, they should have sought God's help, for He had already promised to give it. Thus, Moses called the place Massah and Meribah (מַסָּה / מְרִיבָה) which mean "to test" (מסה) and "to dispute" (ריב). This means to "test God" is to act outside of the realm of faith—to fail to take God at His word, and even to act as though God is not to be trusted.

How then does Yeshua apply this to His current situation and the attack of the evil one who was prodding Him to demonstrate His divine Sonship through an extra-ordinary miracle? The point is that Yeshua did not need some extra-ordinary miracle to prove His Father's faithfulness. He had perfect faith, and thus He took His Father's word as proof enough. To require some additional miracle in order to prove God's faithfulness would at the same time prove His own faith to be deficient. To require a miraculous demonstration of God's faithfulness could only have preceded from a challenge of whether He was faithful in the first place. This would have been to test God.

The application of this principle to our own lives is clear. In a time when people are flocking after so-called "miracles" as a demonstration of God's presence and faithfulness, what the Scriptures call us to is a simple belief that what God has said, He will do. In many cases, the "signs and wonders" movement runs contrary to the direct command of Scripture, and the example of our Master, not to tempt God.

8 Again, the devil took Him to a very high mountain and showed Him all the kingdoms of the world and their glory;

As noted above, the precise manner in which one would be able to see "all the kingdoms of the world" from any elevation in Israel is not clear. It may involve some kind of spiritual vision, though if that were the case, the reason why Matthew would include a "very high mountain" is not clear (Luke has only "he led Him up" without including a "very high mountain," Lk 4:5). Perhaps Matthew is giving us a literary parallel to the end of his gospel, when Yeshua ascends the mountain and declares, "All authority has been given to me in heaven and earth" (Matt 28:16–18). What Satan deceitfully suggests he can give, the Son of Man acquires through His faithful life of sacrifice before the Father (cp. Phil 2:5–8).

It may be also that Matthew subtly wishes his readers to remember a similar situation when God took Moses up to Mt. Pisgah (Deut 3:27; 34:1–4) to show him all of the Land of Israel. Perhaps Matthew wants, once again, to emphasize that Yeshua is the fulfillment of which Moses was a foreshadow, in that ultimately the authority over the whole earth is granted to the risen and reigning Messiah.

The language of our verse is curious: "the devil took Him" (παραλαμβάνει αὐτὸν διάβολος). While παραλαμβάνω (*paralambano*) may mean "to gain control over someone," it may also merely mean "to take someone along," as on a journey. Yet here we see, once again, the mystery of the incarnation. Surely Yeshua could not be constrained against His will, so He willingly goes with the tempter to this final (Luke has it as the second) temptation. The point must be that the temptation of our Master was done in order to show us His own impeccable character as well as to instruct us in the manner in which we too may be victorious over the evil one's schemes.

The tempter "showed Him all the kingdoms of the world and their glory." Of course, the issue of the "glory" (δόξα, *doxa*) of the kingdoms of the world is relative. From the vantage point of the evil one, their glory resides in their self achievements. If these kingdoms possessed any glory in the eyes of the Messiah, it would be in their future acknowledgement of Him as God's rightful King. Indeed, He had come to "seek and to save those who were lost" (Lk 19:10), which ultimately would include those of the nations who were chosen to be saved. Thus, the only glory the nations really possess is dependent upon the completion of Yeshua's own salvific death, resurrection, ascension, and intercession.

9 and he said to Him, "All these things I will give You, if You fall down and worship me."

We know, of course, that Satan had no actual ability to give what he offered, since the sovereign of the universe is God: "The earth is the LORD's, and all it contains, the world, and those who dwell in it" (Psa. 24:1, cp. Ex 9:29; 1Cor 10:26). Yet the evil one is given, for a time, some authority within the inhabited world. Satan is known as the "god of this world" (2Cor 4:4) and the "ruler of this world" (Jn 12:31; 14:30; 16:11). In Eph 6:12 Satan is included in the "world rulers" (κοσμοκράτωρ, *kosmokrator*, cp. Mid. Rab. *Ex* 18.3). John also states (1Jn 5:19) that "whole world lies in the power of the evil one." The authority given to the evil one, in order to bring about the divine purposes, is nonetheless temporary. Indeed, the coming of the Messiah and His ultimate victory over death secured the end of Satan's reign, and his ultimate demise. Thus, what he holds out to Yeshua is nothing more than a dishonest salesman's ploy: the "goods" are not actually his to give.

But the temptation was that Yeshua could gain the ultimate authority without fulfilling His role as the suffering servant of the Lord. It was an offer to ascend the throne of Kingship while by-passing the cross, and more than that, a temptation to achieve power by worship of God's rival. This is always Satan's tactic, to offer power to those who would bow to his authority, a power that denies the very source of life and authority, that is, God Himself.

At first it seems that such a suggestion could hardly have been a temptation for our Master. Surely He would not have succumbed to idolatry as a means of gaining His rightful rule and reign. But we must again remember that Yeshua as the incarnate One, had accepted the character of mankind with many of its weaknesses. It is not a sin to be weak, and within the created soul of man there is an aversion to death. We hear this in our Master's garden prayer: "Father, if You are willing, remove this cup from Me" (Lk 22:42, cp. Mk 14:36). As our Master faced His own death, He did so as a man, and it was only natural that He should inwardly seek to overcome it. Thus, the offer of attaining glory without having to die as the Lamb of God contained some value from a strictly human perspective.

But we must also see that this third temptation was made known to us in order that we might understand the utter necessity of our Master's sacrifice. It was only through His full submission to the Father, rendering Himself as the guilt offering for those He would redeem, that His obedience would be perfect, and His mission complete. "Yet not My will but Yours be done" (Lk 22:42). There was no other way.

Satan specifically says "fall down and worship." This language is reminiscent of the Hebrew verb חָוָה (*chavah*, always in the *hishtafel* form) which generally means "to bow oneself" or even "to lay prone" before someone. For this reason, it is also very often used in the Tanach of worship (note these examples from the Psalms: 5:8; 22:28, 30; 29:2; 45:12; 66:4; 72:11; 81:10; 86:9; 95:6; 96:9). The verb used in our verse (προσκυνέω, *proskeuneo*) regularly is used by the Lxx to translate חָוָה. The Sages understood bowing as an indication of worship, and defined idolatry as bowing to anything or anyone other than God:

> [He who beguiles others is] one who says, "I am going to worship, "I shall go and worship," "Let's go and worship," "I shall make an offering," "I shall go and make an offering," "Let's go and make an offering," "I shall offer incense," ' 'I shall go and offer incense," "Let's go and offer incense," "I shall make a libation '" "I shall go and make a libation," "Let's go and make a libation," "I shall bow down," "I shall go and bow down," "Let's go and bow down" (m.*Sanhedrin* 7:10).

10 Then Yeshua said to him, "Go, Satan! For it is written, 'You shall worship the Lord your God, and serve Him only.'"

In this final temptation, Satan does not attempt to quote Scripture for obvious reasons! Nothing in the Tanach could be "twisted" to support the worship of anyone other than Israel's God. But once again, in our Master's response, He relies upon the Torah, quoting from Deut 6:13. But first He asserts His rightful authority and commands Satan to leave. He does not issue the command on the basis of His divine status as the Son of God, but on the basis of what is written in the Torah: "Go, Satan! *For* it is written...." This teaches us that we have the same authority to demand Satan's exit. The word of God stands as our weapon against the evil one as well: "And take the helmet of salvation, and the sword of the Spirit, which is the word of God" (Eph 6:17). Satan has no option but to yield to the powerful and authoritative word of God. This in itself is sufficient reason to be very familiar with God's word!

The direct and terse command that Satan was to leave comes up again when Peter suggests that Yeshua could attain His victory apart from the sacrificial death for which He had come:

> But He turned and said to Peter, "Get behind Me, Satan! You are a stumbling block to Me; for you are not setting your mind on God's interests, but man's" (Matt. 16:23)

The command in our text is ὕπαγε σατανᾶ (*hupage satana*). The verb ὑπάγω (*hupago*) may be used commonly to denote "going away," but it may also be used with a further nuance to mean "die." Thus Yeshua says, "The Son of Man is to go (ὑπάγω), just as it is written of Him" (Matt 26:24, cp. Mk 14:21), by which He means "the Son of Man is to *take the journey of death*." We may thus suggest that Yeshua's command to Satan is more on the order of "Die, Satan!" Indeed, the ultimate demise of the evil one will come through the death of the Messiah:

> Therefore, since the children share in flesh and blood, He Himself likewise also partook of the same, that through death He might render powerless him who had the power of death, that is, the devil, and might free those who through fear of death were subject to slavery all their lives. (Heb. 2:14–15)

Our Master quotes from Deut 6:13

MT	Lxx	Matthew
אֶת־יְהוָה אֱלֹהֶיךָ תִּירָא וְאֹתוֹ תַעֲבֹד	κύριον τὸν θεόν σου φοβηθήσῃ καὶ αὐτῷ λατρεύσεις	κύριον τὸν θεόν σου προσκυνήσεις καὶ αὐτῷ μόνῳ λατρεύσεις.
You shall fear only the LORD your God; and you shall worship Him ...	You shall fear the Lord your God, and him only shall you serve ...	You shall worship the Lord your God and him only shall you serve

In the Hebrew text, the sense of "only" is not found in the words themselves, but in the syntax of the sentence. אֶת־יהוה אֱלֹהֶיךָ is put first in the sentence,

[1]The Hebrew Matthews (with the exception of the Even Bohan) follow the Greek text in utilizing "worship" rather than "fear" as we find it in the MT. The DuTillet and Münster both have תשתחוה, while the Even Bohan has אתפלל, "I will pray to the Lord, and him only you will serve." This is obviously a misunderstanding of the Greek προσκευνέω, which apparently was read as προσχευ-'ομαι, giving yet another indication that the Even Bohan was a translation from the Greek, not an original Hebrew copy of Matthew.

[2]See Allison-Davies, 1.374.

[3]Allison-Davies, 1.374.

giving it the emphasis: "Adonai your God you shall fear." The same is true of the second clause, in which the object is thrown forward: וְאֹתוֹ תַעֲבֹד, "and *Him* you shall serve." Matthew quotes from the Lxx with the exception that he replaces "fear" (φοβέω, *phobeo*) with "worship" or "bowing" (προσκευνέω, *proskeuneo*).[1] We should also note that the Lxx at Deut 6:13 is identical with Deut 10:20, though the Hebrew text is not the same. But the opening lines of each verse is the same in the Hebrew, and this is the part that Yeshua quotes. The change from "fear" (יָרֵא / φοβέω) to "worship" (προσκυενέω) is interpretive but accurate. To "fear" God means to "obey" Him (cf. Deut 6:2, 24; 8:6; 13:4; Is 50:10; Ps 112:1; 128:1; Job 1:8; Prov 14:2), and thus to bow to His rule. Thus, Deut 6:13 (cp. 10:20), by commanding to "fear the Lord your God" means precisely what Yeshua says, "to worship" or "bow" before Him in the sense of recognizing His ultimate rule and sovereignty. It should also be noted that the parallelism is emphatic: those who fear/worship the Lord likewise serve Him. There is no Greek bifurcation of thought and deed in the Hebrew worldview.

11 Then the devil left Him; and behold, angels came and began to minister to Him.

The evil one has no choice but to obey the command of the Master, and so he leaves. Some have suggested[2] that since the verb "to leave" is actually in the present tense in the Greek, the meaning is "left *for a time*." But Matthew has used present tense verbs through the Temptation pericope, and so no special emphasis should be prescribed here. Luke has "When the devil had finished every temptation, he left Him until an opportune time" (4:13).

Mark notes the presence of angels who minister to Yeshua during the entire forty days (1:13) but Luke does not mention their presence. Matthew's use of "behold" (ἰδού, *idou*) is most likely a mark of solemnity, signalling not only the end of the trial but also the victory that Yeshua demonstrated over the enemy of our souls.

The text indicates that the angels "ministered" (διακονέω, *diakoneo*) to Yeshua, which can have the general sense of "serve" but also may mean "to give to eat," as in Matt 25:44,

> Then they themselves also will answer, 'Lord, when did we see You hungry, or thirsty, or a stranger, or naked, or sick, or in prison, and did not take care of You?'

We may also note the parallel to Elijah in 1Ki 19:5–8 who is fed by an angel *twice*, food which sustained him for forty days. But even more fitting is the story of the manna that sustained Israel in the desert.

> Jesus did not turn stones to bread. Nor did he force God to send angels. Instead he trusted the Father in heaven—and all his needs were met.[3]

We are therefore given the example of our Master: 1) we defeat the enemy by consistent application of the inspired word to our lives, and 2) we walk victoriously by faith in the One Who has promised to preserve us. Yeshua is the "author and completer of our faith" and we do well to fix our gaze upon Him (Heb 12:2).

12 Now when Yeshua heard that Yochanan had been taken into custody, He withdrew into Galilee;

Matthew is not always concerned with giving us precise chronological data. As the narrative stands, it might appear that the news regarding Yochanan's imprisonment, and Yeshua's return to the Galil, came immediately after the desert temptation. In fact, the Synoptics appear to imply that Yeshua's ministry began in the Galil. But John's Gospel indicates that Yeshua had an active ministry in Judea at the same time as Yochanan HaMatbil (Jn 1:19–2:12), before He returned north to the Galil via Samaria (Jn 3:22–4:42, cp. Lk 10:38). This being the case, we may question why the Synoptics are silent about Yeshua's earliest months of ministry. Carson gives the following suggestions:[1]

1. Since Yochanan had been removed from the scene through his imprisonment, Yeshua's ministry entered a new phase, which is the focal point of the Synoptic Gospels. They therefore begin the story of Yeshua's ministry at this point.
2. John, in his gospel may have been directing his story particularly to the disciples of John (cf. Acts 19:1–4), and thus he includes the time when the ministry of Yeshua and Yochanan overlapped.
3. For Matthew, the Galil holds particular significance as fulfillment of prophecy (4:14–16), and especially as the fulfillment of the gospel's extension to "all nations" (28:19). Thus he focuses upon Yeshua's ministry that began in the Galil.

We may therefore presume that some months had elapsed between the desert temptation and Yeshua's journey north to the Galil via Samaria, i.e., between verses 11 and 12 of our chapter.

Herod Antipas ruled over both Perea (where Yochanan was arrested) and the Galil, so Yeshua's withdrawal (ἀναχωρέω, *anachoreo*, "to return") was not for the sake of leaving Herod's domain of rule. Rather, it may have been that Yeshua recognized the immediate danger of being arrested Himself, and thus left the immediate area where He would have likewise been sought by Herod's police. The earlier threat against Yeshua as a newborn (cp. 2:22) appears to have been renewed, and it was therefore prudent for Him to withdraw in order to carry out His ministry. It is clear, however, that Yeshua's withdrawal to the Galil in no way curbed the enthusiasm of the people for Yochanan's message, for Yeshua Himself continues to proclaim "Repent, for the kingdom of heaven is at hand" (cf. 4:17).

It is not until chapter 14:3f that we are given the reason for Yochanan's imprisonment. The desert prophet had denounced the debauchery of Herod's marriage to Herodias, the wife of his brother Philip,[2] and as a result, was thrown into prison, and eventually executed.

13 and leaving Nazareth, He came and settled in Capernaum, which is by the sea, in the region of Zebulun and Naphtali.

According to Luke (4:16ff, cp. Matt 13:54–58, though this may be a separate incident), Yeshua's ministry in His hometown of Nazareth[3] was

[1]Carson, *Matthew,* p. 116.

[2]We will deal with the apparent "mix-up" of Herodias as Philip's wife and the notice of Josephus that Herodias was the wife another son of Herod, not Philip the Tetrarch, in comments on 14:3–4.

[3]The Greek texts of Matthew have Nazareth spelled differently three times (2:23; 4:13; 21:11). See comments above on p. 69. Ναζαρα is most likely the spelling that should be received.

initially received, but when He taught regarding God's mercies through the prophet Elijah to the widow of Zarephath, and through Elisha to Naaman, the obvious implication was that God intended to bless the Gentiles, and this was more than the Jewish population could tolerate. As a result, a mob intended to execute Yeshua on the spot (by throwing Him over a cliff), but He eluded their attempts and left Nazareth. Matthew gives us none of this information, most likely because his intention is to show the fulfillment of prophecy for Yeshua's ministry.

He came and settled in Capernaum – Capernaum (כְּפַר נַחוּם, *K^efar Nachum*, "village of Nahum?" or "village of consolation") is located on the northwest shore of the Kenneret (Sea of Galilee), and became the base for Yeshua's ministry. Mark (2:1) considers it Yeshua's "home," and Peter and Andrew were from Capernaum (Mk 1:29). It was a fishing village, and thus demanded the presence of a tax collector's booth (Matt 9:9). Mid. Rab. *Ecc.* 1.8 notes the presence of *minim* with Capernaum (though this is late, and may have been influenced by the Gospels). The ancient village is known in the Arabic as Tel Hum, where the ruins of a synagogue dating to the 2nd Century CE have been unearthed. Peter's house is traditionally located a mere stone's throw from the synagogue. The location of the village on the shores of the Kenneret link it to Matthew's use of the Isaiah prophecy that follows.

in the region of Zebulun and Naphtali – Nolland[1] notes that the phrase should most likely have Nazareth in mind as well, for Nazareth would have traditionally been located in territory of Zebulun and Capernaum in Naphtali. This, along with the seashore location of Capernaum, links the ministry of Yeshua to the prophecy of Isaiah.

14–16 This was to fulfill what was spoken through Isaiah the prophet: "The land of Zebulun and the land of Naphtali, by the way of the sea, beyond the Jordan, Galilee of the Gentiles— "The people who were sitting in darkness saw a great Light, and those who were sitting in the land and shadow of death, upon them a Light dawned."

The quote is from Isaiah 9:1–2 [Hebrew, 8:23–9:1], and is the fifth of ten quotes introduced by Matthew with the "fulfillment" formula, the first from Isaiah (cf. 8:17; 12:17; cf. 13:14; 15:7).

[1]Nolland, *Matthew* in the *NIGTC*, p. 171.

MT	Lxx	Matthew
כִּי לֹא מוּעָף לַאֲשֶׁר מוּצָק לָהּ כָּעֵת הָרִאשׁוֹן הֵקַל אַרְצָה זְבֻלוּן וְאַרְצָה נַפְתָּלִי וְהָאַחֲרוֹן הִכְבִּיד דֶּרֶךְ הַיָּם עֵבֶר הַיַּרְדֵּן גְּלִיל הַגּוֹיִם הָעָם הַהֹלְכִים בַּחֹשֶׁךְ רָאוּ אוֹר גָּדוֹל יֹשְׁבֵי בְּאֶרֶץ צַלְמָוֶת אוֹר נָגַהּ עֲלֵיהֶם	καὶ οὐκ ἀπορηθήσεται ὁ ἐν στενοχωρίᾳ ὢν ἕως καιροῦ τοῦτο πρῶτον ποίει ταχὺ ποίει χώρα Ζαβουλων ἡ γῆ Νεφθαλιμ ὁδὸν θαλάσσης καὶ οἱ λοιποὶ οἱ τὴν παραλίαν κατοικοῦντες καὶ πέραν τοῦ Ιορδάνου Γαλιλαία τῶν ἐθνῶν τὰ μέρη τῆς Ιουδαίας ὁ λαὸς ὁ πορευόμενος ἐν σκότει ἴδετε φῶς μέγα οἱ κατοικοῦντες ἐν χώρᾳ καὶ σκιᾷ θανάτου φῶς λάμψει ἐφ' ὑμᾶς	γῆ Ζαβουλὼν καὶ γῆ Νεφθαλίμ, ὁδὸν θαλάσσης, πέραν τοῦ Ἰορδάνου, Γαλιλαία τῶν ἐθνῶν, ὁ λαὸς ὁ καθήμενος ἐν σκότει φῶς εἶδεν μέγα, καὶ τοῖς καθημένοις ἐν χώρᾳ καὶ σκιᾷ θανάτου φῶς ἀνέτειλεν αὐτοῖς.
But there will be no more gloom for her who was in anguish; in earlier times He treated the land of Zebulun and the land of Naphtali with contempt, but later on He shall make it glorious, by the way of the sea, on the other side of Jordan, Galilee of the Gentiles. The people who walk in darkness will see a great light; Those who live in a dark land, the light will shine on them.	And he who is in anguish shall not be distressed but for a short time. Act, act quickly, O land of Zabulon, land of Nephthalim, and the rest inhabiting the sea-coast, and the land beyond Jordan, Galilee of the Gentiles. O people walking in darkness, behold a great light: you that dwell in the region and shadow of death, a light shall shine upon you.	The land of Zebulun and the land of Naphtali, by the way of the sea, beyond the Jordan, Galilee of the Gentiles—The people who were sitting in darkness saw a great Light, and those who were sitting in the land and shadow of death, upon them a Light dawned."

Matthew's quote does not exactly conform to either the MT or the Lxx, and it may be that it is Matthew's own midrashic translation (rather than reflecting a proto-Lxx text, or variants to the Hebrew text). He takes "by way of the sea" (דֶּרֶךְ הַיָּם) as a description of Zebulun and Naphtali. As far as Matthew is concerned, "Galilee of the Gentiles" is equivalent to Zebulun and Naphtali and the coastal regions they encompass. The MT uses the phrase in connection with the "path" of the glorious work of restoration by the Almighty, while the Lxx lists it as either a third region (in addition to Zebulun and Naphtali) or as a further qualification of the geographical description of Zebulun and Naphtali. "On the other side of the Jordan" connects to Yochanan's ministry in Perea. The fact that Matthew uses the Lxx spelling for Naphtali (Νεφθαλίμ, *Nefthalim*, with final μ) shows some dependence upon the Lxx. Other changes are obvious: MT/Lxx, "those who walk in darkness," Matthew, "those who *sit* in darkness; Lxx: "light shall shine upon *you*;" MT/Matt: "light will shine upon *them*." There are also other minor differences, such as the Lxx use of χώρα (*xora*, "land") where Matthew has γῆ (*ge*, "land"); Lxx: λάμψει (*lamspei*, from λάμπω, *lampo*, "to shine"), Matt: ἀνατέλλω (*anatello*, "to rise up, dawn"). There is little doubt that Matthew has given a midrashic rendering of the text in order to make his point, but his quote is not a misquote, but simply emphasizes the parts of the Isaiah text that are most germane to his story and purpose.

It may be that Matthew brings this quote into his Gospel in order to counter an already known argument by Yeshua's detractors, that "no prophet is to arise from Galilee" (Jn 7:52, cf. 1:46; 7:41–42). Here, in Isaiah's prophecy, those who dwell in the region of Zebulun and Naphtali, a region (from Isaiah's perspective) that would be dominated by Gentile populations, would see a great "light." In the rabbinic literature, "light" is sometimes a metaphor for the Messiah:

> He knoweth what is in the darkness (Dan. 2:22): this too refers to the deeds of the wicked, as it is written, And their works are in the darkness (Isa 29:15). And the light dwelleth with Him (Dan. 2:22) refers to the deeds of the righteous, as it is written, Light is sown for the righteous (Ps. 97:11). R. Abba of Serungayya (another name for Tiberias) said: 'And the light dwelleth with him" alludes to the royal Messiah. (Mid. Rab. *Gen.* 1.6)

> The tribal ancestors were engaged in selling Joseph, Jacob was taken up with his sackcloth and fasting, and Judah was busy taking a wife, while the Holy One, blessed be He, was creating the light of Messiah: thus, AND IT CAME TO PASS AT THAT TIME, etc. (the union of Judah and Tamar furthered the messianic line.) Before she travailed, she brought forth (Isa. 66:7). (Mid. Rab. *Gen.* 85.1)

Likewise, the rabbis recognized a messianic prophecy in the following text of Isaiah 9:6[5]:

> Another explanation: He said to him: 'I have yet to raise up the Messiah,' of whom it is written, For a child is born to us (Isa. 9:5). Until I come unto my Lord unto Seir (Gen. 38:14). R. Samuel b. Nahman said: We have searched all the Scriptures and we have nowhere found [it stated] that Jacob ever came together with Esau at Seir. What then is the meaning of, ' Unto Seir' ? Jacob [meant] to say to him: ' I have yet to raise up judges and saviours to exact punishment from you.' Whence this? For it is said, And saviours shall come up on mount Zion to judge the mount of Esau (Obad. I, 21). Israel asked God: 'Master of the Universe, how long shall we remain subjected to him? ' He replied: ' Until the day comes of which it is written, There shall step forth a star out of Jacob and a scepter shall rise out of Israel (Num. XXIV, 17); when a star shall step forth from Jacob and devour the stubble of Esau.' Whence this? For it is said, And the house of Jacob shall be a fire, and the house of Joseph a flame, and the house of Esau for stubble, and they shall kindle in them and devour them; and there shall not be any remaining of the house of Esau (Obad. 1:18). God said: 'At that time I will cause my kingdom to shine forth and I will reign over them,' as it is said, And saviours shall come up on Mount Zion, to judge the mount of Esau; and the kingdom shall be the Lord's (Obad. 1:21). (Mid. Rab. *Deut* 1.20).

Thus, an early understanding of the Isaiah 9 text indicates that it was viewed as a messianic prophecy, and it is beyond doubt that Matthew understood the "light" of Is 9:1–2 as referring to the Messiah. Moreover, the fact that Yeshua's ministry encompassed the regions of Zebulun and Naphtali gave a further link to the manner in which he saw Isaiah's prophecies fulfilled in Yeshua. It is also of interest that Zebulun and Naphtali were the first to be taken into exile (2Ki 15:29, where "Galilee" also specifically mentioned), and thus it was fitting that the Light of redemption should first be seen in these regions.

But it is the phrase "Galilee of the Gentiles" that is perhaps the most important to Matthew. While Galilee was, in ancient times, populated by a majority of non-Jews, and may still have had a large non-Jewish population in the time of Yeshua, there is plenty of evidence to show a strong Jewish population there. Moreover, while there were surely regional rivalries, and while Galilee may have remained under the pejorative connotation of being inferior in terms of community piety and *halachah* (cf. *y.Shabbat* 16.15d), we should resist the notion that regional communities were monolithic in their religious and *halachic* perspectives. The fact that following the destruction in 70 CE, many of the Pharisaic leaders retreated to the north, and were apparently warmly received, would indicate that a substantial and religious Jewish population existed there. But what we can see is that Matthew has the end of the story in mind as he writes the beginning. While Yeshua had declared that His mission was specifically to "the lost sheep of Israel," He nonetheless always envisioned the ingathering of the Gentiles as promised in the Abrahamic covenant. As such, throughout His ministry, He gives strong portends of the ultimate goal that all mankind should see and come to the light. For Matthew, this is a central theme, even if its reality does not occur until after the passion and ascension of the Messiah. The point is that Yeshua, as presented by Matthew as the promised Redeemer, is attentive not only to the manner in which He would draw Israel to Himself, but also how the Gentiles would be gathered into the people of Israel in accordance with the prophetic promises. Moreover, it is clear that Yeshua does not envision two separate groups (Jews and Gentiles) redeemed through two different divine actions, but that He intended, through His own redemptive work to gather both into the covenant made secure by the Almighty.

17 From that time Yeshua began to preach and say, "Repent, for the kingdom of heaven is at hand."

As noted above, Yeshua had already been speaking His message for some months in Judea, in concert with the forerunner ministry of Yochanan. Thus, the opening words of this verse, "From that time," should not be taken to mean that this is the beginning of the public teaching ministry of Yeshua. Rather, Matthew's point may well be that the light that would dawn upon the Galil had now begun in the words and message of Yeshua, and particularly in His presence there as the promised Redeemer.

"Preach and say" (κηρύσσειν καὶ λέγειν) should not be construed as describing different functions, but as a typical semitism, in which לֵאמֹר (*lemor,* "to say") introduces direct discourse.

The message of our Master was the same as that of Yochanan (on which, see comments on 3:2 above): a call for repentance (*teshuvah*) in light of the coming kingdom of Heaven. It should arrest our attention that quite often, in modern Christendom, the message of the "gospel" hardly matches that of our Master. In a time when the "gospel" is offered to the public as a means for fulfilling one's dreams, or overcoming life's burdens, nothing is of greater importance than to be reminded that at the heart of the gospel is the matter of repentance. Any gospel message that deletes this vital ingredient is woefully deficient.

18 Now as Yeshua was walking by the Sea of Galilee, He saw two brothers, Simon who was called Peter, and Andrew his brother, casting a net into the sea; for they were fishermen.

Beginning in this verse, and continuing through v. 22, we have the call of Yeshua to four of His talmidim. Many have seen the parallels to the call of Elisha by Elijah (1Ki 19:19–21): 1) Elijah is travelling, 2) he finds Elisha ploughing with oxen, 3) he puts his mantle upon Elisha as a sign of the prophetic call, 4) Elisha responds with a request to say farewell to his father and mother, and then he would "follow after him" (ἀκολουθήσω ὀπίσω σου), and 5) Elisha follows (becomes a disciple of) Elijah. While the parallels are obvious, there is one important difference: Elijah gives permission for Elisha to say his farewells, while Yeshua, in at least one instance (Matt 8:21–22, cp. Lk 9:59) tells one disciple to "Follow Me, and leave the dead to bury their own dead." While there are other explanations to Yeshua's words at this point, it seems warranted to say that Yeshua's demands for discipleship were heightened in light of the "kingdom of Heaven" that was quickly approaching. The urgency of the coming kingdom required equal urgency for undivided loyalty among Yeshua's disciples.

It is interesting that Yeshua chooses His disciples, in apparent distinction from the rabbinic dictum of *Avot* 1:6,

> Joshua b. Perahiah says, "Choose a teacher for yourself. And get yourself a fellow disciple. And give everybody the benefit of the doubt."

This difference highlights the sense of mission that Yeshua doubtlessly had. Not only would He choose talmidim, but He would also send them out to accomplish His mission.

The two brothers that Yeshua encounters as He walked along the shore of the Sea of Galilee[1] were Peter and Andrew. Matthew alerts us to the fact that Peter was called Simon, which would have been שִׁמְעוֹן in the Hebrew, given a popular etymology in Gen 29:33 of "the Lord has heard."[2] The name Peter (πετρός, *petros*) means "rock," and was the Greek equivalent of the Aramaic כֵּיפָא, *kefa'*. Matthew never includes the name *Kefa,* but always refers to the apostle as Peter or Simon.

Andrew (Ανδρέας, *Andreas*) is a good Greek name (but not found in the Lxx). He is mentioned only one other time by Matthew (10:2), and there also as the brother of Peter. He does not figure in significantly to the gospel narratives. According to John (1:35–49), Andrew was a former disciple of Yochanan HaMatbil.

Our text does not give us any insight into Yeshua's previous contact with Peter and Andrew. How, then, did He choose them to be His talmidim? It seems very probable that He did have a previous acquaintance with them and their family, but it is also possible that here we see Yeshua's ability to know about a person without having formerly met them.

When Yeshua encounters the brothers, they were "casting a net into the sea." The Greek word ἀμφίβληστρον (*amfiblestron,* used only here in the Apostolic Scriptures) denotes a circular net used for casting. To the edge of the net were attached small stones which made it sink quickly, engulfing the fish. When the net was drawn from a rope tied to the middle, the heavier stones would be gathered together and keep the fish entrapped.

Thus, Peter and Andrew made their living by fishing. The purpose for Matthew's specific note of their occupation is twofold. First, it sets up the manner of His calling them to be His talmidim, for He would send them out as "fishers of men." In this metaphor, their occupation does not change, just the objects netted. While they had made their living catching fish, now they would be engaged in gathering people. Secondly, the fact that Matthew specifies their occupation makes the parallel to the Elijah/Elisha pericope, as well as emphasizing that their becoming Yeshua's disciples would require a break with everyday affairs. It would be costly (in more ways than one) to

[1] The Greek θαλάσσα can mean either "sea" as we know it, or "lake." The same is true of the Hebrew יָם. The well known name, "Sea of Galilee" goes back to older English utilized in early English translations (Wycliff and Tyndale) when English "sea" could likewise have the meaning "lake."

[2] For a discussion of the etymology of שִׁמְעוֹן, see *KB, ad loc.* There does not appear to be a theophoric element in the name itself.

become a disciple of the Master.

19 And He said to them, "Follow Me, and I will make you fishers of men."

The first thing that arrests our attention is the fact that the Master is not giving the two brothers an invitation. His words are given as an unconditional command. In the Tanach, it is the Almighty Who issues such demands regarding a prophetic call (cf. 1Ki 11:31f; 19:15–21; 1Sa 16:1f). Here, Yeshua likewise functions as the sovereign Who has the right to issue demands to those He meets. We may presume that Peter and Andrew were well acquainted with Yeshua (certainly so on Andrew's part, since he was a disciple of Yochanan), for their response of obedience was positive and immediate.

The demand of the Master involved two aspects: 1) following Him, by which is meant to become His disciple and thus to emulate Him both in life and teaching, and 2) to be prepared for a mission of proclaiming the Gospel of the kingdom, by which they would gather in those who were called.

The order of the twofold aspect of discipleship is obviously important. They could not fulfill the mission of being "fishers of men" until they had sufficiently understood the message of Yeshua and were able to give it to others. And such an understanding could not be entirely gleaned simply by hearing the words of the Master. It was in the course of life, and in the manner in which Yeshua demonstrated the Gospel through His works and interaction with others, that the disciples would be able to see the Gospel unfettered by decades of traditions that had, in many cases, shielded its light from the eyes of Israel.

We should also note that the metaphor our Master uses, of being "fishers of men," is not something that was a well used metaphor. It is not found in the rabbinic literature. But it fit the situation of Peter and Andrew perfectly, for they were well aware of what fishing entailed. But it is important for us to recognize that the fishing they were doing was with a net, not with hook and bait! The giving of the good news of the kingdom was not a "snaring" of men into something they otherwise would have avoided. It was not "baiting the hook" to make the gospel appear appealing, when in reality it had a pointed barb at its core. Rather, in the metaphor of "fishing for men," the gospel itself was the "net" by which God would gather those He had chosen into His family. This is affirmed later by Paul when he wrote regarding the Gospel:

> For I am not ashamed of the gospel, for it is the power of God for salvation to everyone who believes, to the Jew first and also to the Greek. (Rom 1:16)

It is the work of the Spirit, in connection with the proclamation of the gospel, that brings about repentance toward God and faith in Yeshua the Messiah. The giving of the gospel, then, as pictured in the metaphor of fishing, is not one of enticement, but of the sovereign power of God whereby, through the gospel itself, those who are chosen are drawn to faith and rescued.

We should also note that Yeshua says that He would *make* them fishers of men. Their ability to net fish depended upon their learned expertise in that occupation. The task which Yeshua would commission them for, however, required His expertise—His power. Their success in fishing for men was something that would come from the training He would give them, as well as the power of the Spirit they would receive as the fruit of His labors.

20 Immediately they left their nets[1] and followed Him.

Once again, Matthew stresses the urgency of the matter by noting the immediacy of the men's actions (cf. Mk 1:16f). The kingdom was at hand, and there was no time to waste. But Luke appears to offer a fuller description of the events (5:1ff). According to his account, the call of Peter and Andrew to become disciples of the Master occurred after they had fished all night and caught nothing, so they had returned to the shore and were washing their nets. It was then that Yeshua used one of the boats as a floating podium, and addressed the crowd that had gathered on the shore. After teaching the people, He instructed Peter and the rest to go out again and cast their nets into the water. Even though Peter protested that doing so would be an exercise in futility, he and the rest complied, and ended up catching so many fish that it required the second boat to come to their aid. Having seen the miraculous powers of Yeshua, Peter mimics the words of Isaiah (6:5) and declares, "Go away from me Master, for I am a sinful man, O Lord!" But Yeshua assures him with the words often found in the Tanach, "Do not fear," and then He adds, "from now on you will be catching men." The miracle of the large catch of fish, at least from Luke's perspective, was a lesson in terms of the disciples' new occupation of "fishing for men." In the same way that they had been unsuccessful in their night-time endeavors at fishing, but had immediate success by the sovereign work of the Master, so their ability to "catch men" would be dependent upon the sovereign work of salvation, which only God Himself could affect.

So the sense of immediacy noted in Matthew and Mark should be understood in a general way: they did not hesitate in making the decision to leave their current occupation and follow the Master as He had commanded them to. The emphasis is upon an undivided heart to obey, even in view of personal sacrifice.

The pattern of discipleship given to us here by Matthew involves two aspects: 1) they left their nets, and 2) they followed Him. This emphasizes two general aspects which are true of all who would follow Yeshua, namely, that it involves personal sacrifice (giving up one's own life agenda) and conformity to the Master (following in His footsteps). Both of these suggest that a radical commitment of faith and obedience is the norm for disciples of Yeshua.

21 Going on from there He saw two other brothers, James the son of Zebedee, and John his brother, in the boat with Zebedee their father, mending their nets; and He called them.

Matthew makes it seem as though Yeshua continued to walk further along the beach. However, if Luke (5:1f) is describing a separate event which occurred in connection with Yeshua's initial approach to Peter and Andrew, then "Going on from there" might describe a different setting than that of Matthew and Mark. Regardless, two more brothers, Yaacov (Ἰακώβος) and Yochanan (Ἰωάννης) and their father, Zebedee (Ζεβεδαῖος) are mending nets as Yeshua approaches them.

The English translation of Yaacov by "James" is an early phenomenon, and not something peculiar to the KJV (as some have asserted). It is found

[1] A different Greek word is used for "net" in our verse than was used in the v. 18. Here, the word δίκτυον (*diktuon*) describes a net used for deep water fishing, as distinct from ἀμφίβληστρον, the circular net used for casting. It is possible that when Yeshua first approached them, they were fishing from the shore with the casting net, and that later they went out into the boats to fish the deep water with a different style of net. If this is the case, then Luke (5:1ff) is describing events after the fishermen had fished in the deep water during the night. Moreover, when Yeshua encounters James, John, and their father, Zebedee, they are mending the nets, something that does not figure into the story as Matthew and Mark portray it.

Yet, as Allison-Davies note (1.400), the similarities between the Synoptics seem far to great to suppose Luke's account to be entirely independent of Mark 1:16f and our text in Matthew.

in the Wycliffe translation, produced in 1380, which predates the KJV by 230 years. English "James" is an alteration of the Latin *Iacobus* which became *Iacomus,* and then *Iaomus,* and finally came into English as *James.* Similar linguistic transformations derive *John* from Latin *Iohannes.* These transformations are linguistically and not theologically driven.

Zebedee is from the Aramaic זַבְדַי (*zabday*) or Hebrew זְבַדְיָה (*zevadyah*), which are shortened forms of זְבַדְיָהוּ (*zevadyahu*), "gift of Yah."

This James is mentioned again by name in 10:2 and 17:1, but elsewhere referred to in the phrase "the sons of Zebedee" (20:20; 26:37; 27:56). James the son of Zebedee is never mentioned by name in John, though in 21:2 the "*sons* of Zebedee" are listed among the disciples. James the son of Zebedee was executed by Herod in about 43 CE according to Acts 12:1–3.

John is regularly known as "the brother of James" (Matt 10:2; 17:1; Mark 1:19; 3:17; 5:37; Luke 6:14) which would indicate that he was the younger of the two. He was also one of the Jerusalem "pillars" mentioned by Paul in Gal 2:9.

The fact that they were fishing together with their father means that they were likely not very old when Yeshua called them to follow Him. Matthew also introduces their mother in 20:20. The language of our verse makes it clear that fishing was the family occupation, and this re-emphasizes the fact that in leaving to follow Yeshua, they were leaving both family and livelihood.

The short "and He called them" hearkens back to v. 19 and thus Matthew feels no need to repeat it hear. Yeshua was calling them to follow Him and become "fishers of men." The use of the word "call" (καλέω, *kaleo*) finds its background in the Tanach. In the Wisdom literature, for instance, wisdom calls out to those who would follow her (e.g., Prov 1:24; 8:1, 4; 9:3, 15). But particularly in Isaiah, the idea of a divine "call" approaches the sense of "choosing." Note the following examples:

> Is 43:1 But now, thus says the LORD, your Creator, O Jacob, And He who formed you, O Israel, "Do not fear, for I have redeemed you; I have called you by name; you are Mine!"
> Is 43:7 "Everyone who is called by My name, And whom I have created for My glory, Whom I have formed, even whom I have made."
> Is 48:12 "Listen to Me, O Jacob, even Israel whom I called; I am He, I am the first, I am also the last." (Note also Is 45:3)

It is this sense of a divine call that is effectual, that is, which in the call itself secures a positive response, that the term gained its theological meaning in the epistles. Thus, those who are drawn to salvation by divine initiative are referred to as "the called ones" (Rom 1:1; 8:28; 1Cor 1:1; Gal 1:15). It is most likely that the word in our current text has already taken on this meaning. Yeshua's call to James and John is more than an invitation. By His calling them, He has also chosen them to be His disciples. Moreover, in the epistles God is the One doing the calling, and thus the results are secure. In our text, it is Yeshua, and the parallel (in terms of biblical theology) cannot be missed: Yeshua likewise exercises a divine prerogative in calling His disciples.

22 Immediately they left the boat and their father, and followed Him.

The words are clearly parallel to v. 20, but in this case James and John also leave their father. Mark adds that there were servants in the boat as well (Mk 1:20). The divine call produces instant obedience. The notice that "they followed Him" is not mere narrative—it has deeper theological significance. James and John left occupation and family in order to become disciples of the Master. Once again, the cost of discipleship is made clear, and illustrates the words of the Master in Lk 14:26,

> If anyone comes to Me, and does not hate his own father and mother and wife and children and brothers and sisters, yes, and even his own life, he cannot be My disciple.

Though the words should be allowed to retain their sharp, prophetic edge, the point of our Master is not that honoring father and mother has been suspended, but that becoming a disciple of Yeshua will require putting Him as the highest priority in life. Peter, Andrew, James, and John understood the radical nature of Yeshua's call, and their actions demonstrate and form the paradigm for those who would also be called as Yeshua's disciples.

23 Yeshua was going throughout all Galilee, teaching in their synagogues and proclaiming the gospel of the kingdom, and healing every kind of disease and every kind of sickness among the people.

This verse is the beginning of a new section (4:23–5:2) that offers a conclusion to chapters 3–4 and introduces the "Sermon on the Mount" in chapters 5–7. Thus, the chapter break in our English bibles between chapter four and five is not helpful.

This bridging section (4:23–5:2) is necessary to explain why a crowd had gathered to hear Yeshua's teaching. V. 23 describes His ministry in the Galil, v. 24 notes the widespread news of His activities, which brought even more people, so that (v. 25) crowds were following Him.

While the public ministry of Yeshua began in Nazareth and Capernaum, Matthew now alerts us to the fact that it was expanded to encompass the entire Galil. Once again, Matthew is showing the manner in which Yeshua's own ministry foreshadows the ultimate goal of proclaiming the gospel of the kingdom to all the nations. Having noted that the region was "Galilee of the nations" (v. 15), the fact that Yeshua's activity encompasses "all Galilee" is a portend of the final commission to make disciples of all the nations (28:19). In the same way, His healing of every disease and sickness answers to the "shadow of death" language in the quote from Is 9:1–2.

teaching in their synagogues and proclaiming the gospel of the kingdom
We should not try to make a large distinction between "teaching" (διδάσκω, *didasko*) and "proclaiming" (κηρύσσω, *kerusso*). The synagogue was a place of teaching and study, and there is no doubt that as Yeshua taught, He emphasized the manner in which the Scriptures (and particularly the Torah, which was the central synagogue text for study) called the people to a faithful submission to the rule of God as King over Israel. Thus, the teaching and proclamation of the kingdom were, for Yeshua, necessarily complimentary, as the subsequent Sermon on the Mount shows. Moreover, the gospel of the kingdom, which Yeshua proclaimed, found its basis in the Tanach. The gospel proclaimed by our Master was the gospel spoken of by Moses and the prophets.

Thus, Matthew summarizes the Galilean ministry of Yeshua with three participles: teaching, proclaiming, and healing. In so doing, he may be giving a general paradigmatic outline for the overall scope of Yeshua's ministry in that teaching and proclamation precede healing. That is, the revelatory value of His healing miracles could only be understood if one had previously be instructed (cf. 13:58).

We should not make too much of the fact that Matthew refers to the synagogues as "their synagogues" (cf. 9:35; 10:17; 12:9; 13:54) as though his own community viewed themselves as "other" than the synagogal community. Even though αὐτῶν ("their") has no immediate antecedent, the natural way to read this is that Matthew was referring to the Galilean population and thus the Galilean synagogues. Even if Matthew might be making a distinction between the traditional synagogues and the synagogues of The Way, he gives no substantiation for the claim that the followers of Yeshua had already abandoned the synagogue and began to forge a new entity called "the Church." By all biblical accounts, the early followers of Yeshua considered themselves as part of the larger synagogue community, and so did Rome.

In going to the synagogues, Yeshua's work differed from that of Yochanan HaMatbil, for he remained in the desert, and people therefore were required to go out to him in order to hear his message. Yeshua, however, went Himself to the people. This was likewise to set the pattern for His own disciples whom He would send, first to the lost sheep of Israel, and then to the nations.

healing every kind of disease and every kind of sickness among the people. (cp. 9:35) The healing work of our Master was bound together with His coming as Israel's redeemer. Sin and sickness are often linked in the Tanach (e.g., Deut 28:58–63; Is 53:5; Mic 6:13; Ps 103:3), so that when Matthew gives us the angelic announcement (1:21), "She will bear a Son; and you shall call His name Yeshua, for He will save His people from their sins," we are to understand that the Savior has come.

Matthew is emphatic in repeating the word "every" (πᾶσαν νόσον καὶ πᾶσαν μαλακίαν). In contrast to many modern day "faith healers," Yeshua healed all kinds of diseases: there were no "screeners" keeping the truly sick away from His public demonstration of God's power. Likewise, Yeshua's healing marked a distinction from that of Yochanan HaMatbil's ministry, for Yochanan healed no one. Moreover, the healing that Yeshua performed for those who were diseased and weakened with sickness was a clear demonstration of God's mercies.

> Before being confronted by the rigorous demands of the higher righteousness, Israel hears the good news of the gospel and receives the Messiah's healing, all this as a free gift.[1]

The gospel of the kingdom therefore entailed the whole person, soul and body. The sin and the woes it had brought through the agency of the tempter in the garden were now to be defeated by the Promised Seed of the woman.

24 The news about Him spread throughout all Syria; and they brought to Him all who were ill, those suffering with various diseases and pains, demoniacs, epileptics, paralytics; and He healed them.

The news about Yeshua's work and the manner in which it authenticated His message soon went beyond the confines of the Galil into the region

[1]Allison-Davies, *Matthew*, 1.415.

of Syria. The region of Syria is most likely not the Roman province, that is, the large region from the lands of the Euphrates to the Mediterranean and from the Syro-Arabian desert to Cilicia, but rather, as the rabbis reckon it,[1] the narrow territory to the north-northeast of Palestine, perhaps extending from Damascus to Antioch and on to the east (cf. Gal 1:21–23). Even though this region had a large Jewish population, we should probably understand Matthew's emphasis here to be the manner in which Yeshua was affecting the Gentiles. Though Yeshua does not leave the Land, His influence and message is felt beyond Israel's borders.

[1] m.*Dem* 6.11; m.*BavaKama* 7.7; m.*Rosh Hashaona* 1.4; m.*'Ed* 7.7; m.*AvodaZera* 1.8; m.*Shevuot* 6.2, 5, 6; m.*Ohol.* 18.7.

While Mark generally has Yeshua "teaching" and "casting out demons," Matthew centers attention upon the healing ministry of our Master. It may be that he does so in order to show the manner in which Yeshua fulfilled the words of the prophets. In 8:16–17 Matthew quotes Is 53:4 and in 11:4–6 he quotes or alludes to Is 26:19; 29:18–19; 35:5–6; 42:18, all of which have some connection to healing. On the other hand, to find texts from the Tanach that were fulfilled by casting out demons would have been far more difficult.

Here Matthew gives a representative list of the kinds of diseases that Yeshua healed, and he does so, no doubt, to emphasize that no disease could withstand His healing power. The general description is literally "all the severe ones, having multiple diseases and suffering severe torments." This is then further defined by the following phrase listing demoniacs, epileptics, and paralytics. The word "demoniacs" (δαιμονίζομαι, *daimonizomai*) is actually a participle and therefore literally "demonized." The word itself does not necessarily suggest "possession."[2] The word "epileptics" is literally "those moon-struck" (σεληνιάζομαι, *seleniazomai*), but is most likely describing what we know as epilepsy (cf. Matt 17:15). Apparently ancient man thought the condition was caused by the moon, and even our English "lunacy" is connected to the Latin *Luna*, "moon." Demonic activity and epilepsy is sometimes connected in the Gospels (cf. Matt 17:15) as well as in the rabbinic literature (b.*Gittin* 70a). Matthew's point is that Yeshua held sway both over the demons as well as the sickness brought into the world through Satan, the leader of demonic forces. He healed them, not by administering medicine to them, but through miraculous powers. The Redeemer was in their midst.

[2] The Greek verb διαμονίζομαι is found only in the Gospels: Matt 4:24; 8:16,28,33; 9:32; 12:22; 15:22; Mark 1:32; 5:15-16,18; Luke 8:36; John 10:21.

25 Large crowds followed Him from Galilee and the Decapolis and Jerusalem and Judea and from beyond the Jordan.

The notice that large crowds followed Him informs us that Yeshua was extremely popular with the masses, at least at the beginning of His public ministry. The various geographical designations also envelop the entire compass. Galilee is northwest, while the Decapolis ("ten cities") was the region northeast in the transjordan. Historians are not certain which cities comprised the Decapolis, but most agree on these nine: Abila, Canata, Dius, Gadara, Gerasa, Hippos, Pella, Philadelphia, and Scythopolis. Judea is southwest, and Trans-Jordan is southeast. Jerusalem is the center of the whole earth (cf. Ps 48:2), and so Matthew has essentially covered the compass. In doing so, he is emphasizing the manner in which Yeshua as the promised Messiah would bring about the promise to the Fathers, that all the nations would be blessed in Abraham's seed. His redemptive mission would begin in Israel, but it would eventually touch the whole world.

Chapter Five
Commentary

1–2 When Yeshua saw the crowds, He went up on the mountain; and after He sat down, His disciples came to Him. He opened His mouth and began to teach them, saying,

The opening verses of chapter five are closely tied to the previous context, while at the same time introduce Matthew's "Sermon on the Mount." Mark has no parallel to this pericope, but Luke does. Thus, this represents some reliance on common material used by Matthew and Luke but not by Mark. In Luke's account (Lk 6:17f), Yeshua has ascended a mountain and prayed through the night. In the morning, He called His disciples to Him, and chose twelve of them whom He designates as His "apostles" (שְׁלִיחִים, she-lichim), those sent out to accomplish His mission. After choosing the twelve, He comes down from the mountain with the twelve to a "level place" (and thus Luke's account is often referred to as the "Sermon on the Plain") where a large crowd of His disciples were gathered, as well as "a great throng of people from all Judea and Jerusalem and the coastal region of Tyre and Sidon" (6:17). They had come to hear Him teach, and to be healed from their diseases and set free from unclean spirits (6:18).

Matthew's story is a bit different. Yeshua has chosen only four of His disciples (Peter, Andrew, James, and John) when He delivers His "Sermon on the Mount." There is nothing said about His having chosen all twelve of His disciples after praying through the night, and Matthew has Yeshua ascending the mountain, while Luke has Him descending to a level place where the crowds awaited Him.

Early in the history of interpretation of Matthew's Gospel, Augustine suggested that Matthew and Luke were describing two different events in which Yeshua's discourses were similar but distinct. This view was almost universally held up to the Reformation period, when Calvin defended the view that the two accounts represent the same discourse, and the majority of teachers and commentators followed his lead.

The similarities between the accounts of Matthew and Luke are obvious: 1) both begin the sermon with beatitudes and end with the same simile, i.e., that current persecution of Yeshua's followers parallels the historical persecution of Israel's prophets, 2) almost everything in Luke's "Sermon the Plain" is contained in Matthew's account, 3) both accounts of the sermon are followed by similar events, i.e., entrance into Capernaum and healing the centurion's servant.

But there are differences as well. Luke's account is much shorter, and the material he does not include is scattered throughout the remainder of his Gospel. As noted above, Matthew speaks of a mountain while Luke's setting is that of plain. Moreover, Luke's discourse follows the choosing of the Twelve, which does not take place in Matthew until chapter 10.

It would seem that the material Matthew includes (which Luke leaves out or discusses elsewhere in his Gospel) may have been more germane to a Jewish audience, and thus its inclusion in Matthew's account. It is also very possible that Yeshua gave the same sermon more than once, as is often the case with itinerate preachers, and that Luke's account, while describing the same event, is more selective of the same themes and teaching points that may have been emphasized in other settings of the same sermon.

Likewise, Matthew's "mountain" language does not entirely exclude Luke's notice of a "plain" (see below). Yeshua could have come to a hilly or mountainous region, gone up to a higher point with His disciples, and then come down to a more level plateau where the crowds had gathered. The order of events (Matthew before the choosing of the Twelve; Luke afterward) is not conclusive in determining whether Matthew and Luke are describing the same event here, because strict chronology in Matthew's retelling of the story is not always something to which he adheres. Like the narrative of the Tanach, Matthew at times orders his material along thematic lines rather than in a strict narrative chronological sequence.

The Sermon on the Mount is the first of five discourses contained in the Gospel of Matthew. Some have suggested that Matthew chose these five discourses to parallel the five books of Moses (the Torah).

For further research on the setting of the Sermon on the Mount and its parallel in the Synoptics, see: W. D. Davies, *The Setting of the Sermon on the Mount* (Cambridge, 1963); D. A. Carson, *Matthew*, pp.122–28; John Nolland, *The Gospel of Matthew*, pp. 186–190 and the bibliography of sources he offers there; Donald Hagner, *Matthew 1–13*, pp. 84–85.

Discourse	Description
#1 – The Sermon on the Mount (5:1–7:29)	Character of the Kingdom of Heaven
#2 – Mission & Martyrdom (10:5–11:1)	Character of Discipleship
#3 – Parables of the Kingdom (13:1–53)	Success of the Kingdom of Heaven
#4 – Kingdom Authority (18:1–19:2)	Living Under God's Rule
#5 – Olivet Discourse (24:1–25:46)	The Victory of the Kingdom of Heaven

When Yeshua saw the crowds, He went up on the mountain; and after He sat down, His disciples came to Him.   These are the crowds of 4:25, and indicates that the Master's popularity had grown. The people were seeking Him for His teaching and His power to heal and overcome demonic powers (cf. Lk 6:18). The common posture of a teacher in the synagogual community was that of sitting,[1] and thus Yeshua assumes this position as the Teacher to whom the masses had come.

We need not necessarily understand the term "disciples" to be speaking particularly of the Twelve, since Matthew does not have the choosing of the Twelve until later. "Disciple" may at times denote those who simply were following Yeshua and accepting His teaching. In this case, "disciple" may be a sub-group of the larger "crowds." It may be that many were coming to hear His teaching and see His miraculous works, but some of them were genuinely His disciples. These are the ones who gather around Him as He sits to teach.

The notice that "He went up on the mountain" may be variously understood. The Greek τὸ ὄρος (*to oros*) "the mountain" may just as easily mean "the mountainous region" and not some well-known mountain or hillside. Most likely, Yeshua had retreated to the hill country west of the Kenneret. Moreover, the term Luke utilizes, i.e., "level place" (Lk 6:17, πεδίνος, *pedinos*), is only found here, and should not be understood as akin to the American prairie, but as a flat place among rough, rocky, or hilly terrain. The picture

[1]Lachs (*A Rabbinic Commentary on the New Testament*, p. 67–8) suggests that Matthew's notice of Yeshua sitting to teach betrays a 2nd Century redaction. But he confuses the posture of students (which was one of standing in the early decades, but changed to sitting after the death of Gamliel) with that of the Sage who sat to teach.

that emerges is one of Yeshua entering the hill country and then finding a level place that would accommodate the crowd that had gathered.

Many commentators have noted the parallel to Moses in the phrase "He went up on the mountain." Allison-Davies (*Matthew* 1.423-24) collate similar phrases in the Tanach, and note that the majority of these are found in the Torah, and with direct reference to Moses. Generally, those who emphasize the parallel to Moses do so in order to suggest that Matthew is presenting Yeshua as the "new Moses," Who comes with a "new Law" to replace the Mosaic legislation. Of course, this viewpoint is based upon a similar interpretation of the Sermon itself.

However, had Matthew intended for us to see a parallel between Yeshua's ascending the hill country and Moses' ascent to the top of Mt. Sinai, it seems that he would have made more explicit allusions to the Sinai pericope. In fact, there are none. Rather, if there is a parallel to Moses, it is that Yeshua intends to bring the people to a correct understanding of the Torah and its proper application in light of the Kingdom of Heaven, not to replace it with something new.

and He opened His mouth and began to teach them saying   To "open one's mouth" is a Hebraic way of noting a solemn discourse, or a proclamation particularly germane to the events at hand (cf. Job 33:2; Ps 51:15; 78:2; Prov 31:9; Ezek 3:27; 29:21). Only Matthew retains this semitic expression.

The opening of the Sermon has become known as the "beatitudes," based upon the repeated word "blessed" (μακάριος, *makarios*), which reflects the Hebrew אַשְׁרֵי (*ashrei*). This mode of speech is repeatedly found in the Psalms and Proverbs,[1] and is common in the rabbinic literature as well.[2]

It is instructive to note how Matthew has structured his Gospel up to this point. Before Yeshua ever teaches or gives His commands, He is known to the reader as the One Who fulfilled prophecy, as the Son of David and the Son of God, and (through the words of Yochanan HaMatbil), as the promised Messiah Who would "baptize with the Holy Spirit and fire." He is presented as the Son of God, and lauded as the One in Whom the Father is pleased. It is only after we are well aware of the status of Yeshua of Natzeret that we then hear His own words. This accords with the rabbinic teaching that one must acknowledge the sovereignty of God before one is able to submit to His commandments:

> Said R. Joshua b. Qorha, "Why does [the passage of] Shema precede [the reciting of Deut 11:13ff which begins "And it will come to pass if you hearken...?"] "So that one may first accept upon himself the yoke of the kingdom of heaven and afterwards may accept the yoke of the commandments. (m.*Berachot* 2.2)

Thus, Matthew follows this same pattern. Before Yeshua utters a word, or begins His teaching, we have come to understand Who He is, and having accepted Him as the Messiah, are enabled to hear and submit to His words.

Many have sought to find a literary structure for the Beatitudes, but there is no consensus. As Matthew records them, they consist of nine sayings, all linked by the opening word "Blessed." The first eight are all cast in the third person ("they"), while the final beatitude is put in the second person ("you").[3] If we seek a chiastic structure, the following pattern emerges.

[1] Ps 1:1; 2:12; 32:1-2; 33:12; 34:8; 40:4; 41:1; 65:4; 84:4-5,12; 89:15; 94:12; 106:3; 112:1; 119:1-2; 127:5; 128:1; 137:8-9; 144:15; 146:5; Prov 3:13; 8:34; 28:14.
[2] Eg., t.*Chaggigah* 2.1; b.*Chaggigah* 14b; b.*Berechot* 3a.

[3] We are not surprised at all by the sudden switch to the 2nd person from the previous string of 3rd person sayings. This not only occurs frequently in Biblical passages, but it is prevalent in rabbinic literature as well, including the liturgy of the Siddur. Moreover, the fact that the final beatitude is much longer than the previous eight is also not uncommon. For example, note the ברוך שאמר of the Shacharit Service. See also the remarks of David Daube, *The New Testament and Rabbinic Judaism* (Hendrickson, 1998), pp. 196–201.

Those poor in spirit —> kingdom of heaven
> Those who mourn —> comforted
>> Those who are gentle —> inherit the earth
>>> Those who hunger & thirst after righteousness —> satisfied
>>>> **Those who show mercy —> shown mercy**
>>> Those pure in heart —> see God
>> Those who are peacemakers —> called sons of God
> Those persecuted for the sake of righteousness —> kingdom of heaven

Those persecuted as disciples of Yeshua —> great reward in heaven

If this chiastic arrangement has warrant, then the major emphasis is placed upon "showing mercy," and the structure itself may help define the categories:

1) poor in spirit = those persecuted as disciples of Yeshua
2) mourn = persecuted for righteousness
3) gentle = peacemakers
4) hunger & thirst after righteousness = pure in heart

Again, from the structure we may suggest that all of these categories flow from the fountain of showing mercy (the central point of the chiasm), and this accords with the overall emphasis of our Master's teaching and example, in which the showing of mercy takes a preeminent position.

3 Blessed are the poor in spirit, for theirs is the kingdom of heaven.

The use of μακάριος, *makarios*, "blessed," requires our attention. The two terms used in the Tanach for blessing are אַשְׁרֵי (*'ashrei*) and בָּרוּךְ (*baruch*). In the Tanach, μακάριος is always used to translate אַשְׁרֵי and no other term. On the other hand, בָּרוּךְ is never translated by μακάριος, but most often by εὐλογητός (*eulogetos*) or εὐλογέω (*eulogeo*), and sometimes by the alliterated βαρουχ (*baroux*). This being the case, it is clear that the use of μακάριος by the Gospel writers answers to אַשְׁרֵי and not בָּרוּךְ. Moreover, אַשְׁרֵי is never used of God, but always of the blessing that comes upon a person who lives righteously. Thus, the major component of this "blessing" as found in our text is that it encompasses the divine action toward one who has obeyed God and acted in accordance with His prescribed commandments.

The vast majority of English translations have "blessed," but some have opted for the word "happy" (TEV, Youngs). While "blessed" certainly contains the idea of "happy," it is much more than that, for as the Beatitudes themselves show, one may be "blessed" even in a state of mourning. Thus, "blessing" captures the idea of a conscience at peace before the Almighty— the sense that one exists under the protection of divine favor regardless of the current circumstances. Furthermore, the perspective of some commentators that the blessing promised in the Beatitudes is eschatological misses the fact that in the coming of Messiah, the eschaton has invaded the present. While in some sense the ultimate and final blessing awaits the age of peace and the world to come, those who walk in righteousness participate in a genuine foretaste of the eschatological blessings in the here and now.

The Greek word translated "poor" is πτωχός (*ptoxos*), which has a basic meaning of "being economically disadvantaged" but also carries an extended metaphoric sense of one being "thrust on divine resources." Luke simply

One may also note the parallels between the Beatitudes and the language of Isaiah 61:2–11. See the remarks of Allison-Davies, *Matthew*, 1.437.

says "poor" without adding "in spirit," and some have therefore suggested that the opening Beatitude deals primarily with those who are impoverished of material things. But this is too simplistic. Poverty can be self-imposed, as the parable of the Prodigal demonstrates. Here, the sense of "poor in spirit" is of those who have recognized their own spiritual bankruptcy and have therefore cast themselves entirely upon God's mercies. Further, if the chiastic structure noted above has merit, then the "poor in spirit" may be those who have undergone persecution because they have been willing to follow Yeshua and accept Him as the Messiah. Such persecution upon oneself or upon family and community members could surely bring despair.[1] As such, they are powerless ("impoverished") in and of themselves to change the circumstances, and must rely entirely upon God's help.

It is in this full reliance upon God that those who are "poor in spirit" obtain the kingdom of heaven. They do not achieve entrance therein through their own strength or prowess, nor by their material wealth, nor even from the lack thereof. They receive the present benefits of God's reign (the shalom of a conscience right before the Almighty and the comfort this brings) and await the future, eschatological reign of God in which the troubles of this fallen world will be vanquished.

Here, then, in the opening Beatitude, the emphasis is laid upon reliance upon God for entrance into the kingdom. Far from teaching a salvation through one's own righteous deeds, the Master begins by reinforcing that membership in the kingdom of heaven is a gift from God to those who have admitted their own spiritual poverty.

4 Blessed are those who mourn, for they shall be comforted.

The second Beatitude references those who mourn (πενθέω, *pentheo*). But what is the cause of this mourning? Contrary to the majority of Church Fathers who understood this to be a "mourning over one's sin," the context and parallel to Is 61 further the idea of persecution begun in the first Beatitude. In Is 61:2–3 the same motif of comforting those who mourn is found:

> To proclaim the favorable year of the LORD and the day of vengeance of our God; To comfort all who mourn, to grant those who mourn in Zion, giving them a garland instead of ashes, the oil of gladness instead of mourning, the mantle of praise instead of a spirit of fainting.

In this passage, Israel is oppressed by her enemies, her evil captors.

> Her cities are in ruin (v.4) and her people know shame and dishonor (v. 7). In sum God's own are on the bottom, the wicked on the top. So mourning is heard because the righteous suffer, because the wicked prosper, and because God has not yet acted to reverse the situation.[2]

The same is true for those who accept and will accept Yeshua as the promised Messiah. Though walking in righteousness, they will nonetheless be persecuted, even unto death, and thus where one would expect jubilation, mourning comes instead. But the promise of our Master is that in the midst of mourning, comfort will come.

> "Comfort, O comfort My people," says your God. "Speak kindly to Jerusalem; and call out to her, that her warfare has ended, that her

---

The phrase "poor in spirit" (עֲנֵי רוּחַ) is not found in the Tanach nor in the rabbinic literature. It is found several times in the DSS: 1QM 11:9; 14:6–7; 1QS 4:3; 1QH 5:22. It is interesting that this phrase should appear in the DSS, for the sect imposed a vow of poverty upon all of its members.

[1] This may also be strengthened by the parallel to Is 61:1–2: "The Spirit of the Lord GOD is upon me, because the LORD has anointed me to bring good news to the afflicted (πτωχός). He has sent me to bind up the brokenhearted, to proclaim liberty to captives and freedom to prisoners;"

[2] Allison-Davies, *Matthew*, 1.448.

> iniquity has been removed, that she has received of the LORD's hand double for all her sins." (Is 40:1–2)

These words of the Master are not, then, an encouragement to mourn in order to receive the blessing. The mourning comes as a result of evil perpetrated upon God's people. The blessing comes from God whose sovereign design will inevitably validate the righteous and punish the wicked. The persecution of God's people will give way to comfort in the Kingdom.

It is interesting that following the destruction of the Temple, some of the Sages called for a life of mourning, though they recognized this could not be sustained by the masses. There were those who refrained from eating meat or drinking wine as a sign of mourning (t.*Sota* 15.11). Likewise, the Sages taught that those who mourn in Zion will be privileged to rejoice in her future glory: "Whoever mourns for Zion will be privileged to behold her joy, as it says, Rejoice you with Jerusalem...(Is 66:1)" (b.*BavaBatra* 60b). Though the destruction of the Temple awaited the time following our Master's earthly ministry, the Temple service had been besmirched by the self-serving desires of the priesthood. It may be, therefore, that the mourning envisioned in our text is not only in regard to the persecution that Yeshua's followers would endure, but also in regard to the spiritual decline of the nation.

The blessing promised upon those who mourn is that they would be "comforted" (παρακαλέω, *parakaleo*). The agent of the passive verb is obviously God Himself, Who, through His Messiah, would bring about the promised comfort for Israel (Is 40:1f; cp. 2Cor 1:5). Indeed, the Bavli may contain an earlier reference to the name of Messiah being "the comforter":

> Rab said: The world was created only on David's account. Samuel said: On Moses account; R. Johanan said: For the sake of the Messiah. What is his [the Messiah's] name? — The School of R. Shila said: His name is Shiloh, for it is written, until Shiloh come (Gen 49:10). The School of R. Yannai said: His name is Yinnon, for it is written, His name shall endure for ever: e'er the sun was, his name is Yinnon (Ps 72:17). The School of R. Haninah maintained: His name is Haninah, as it is written, Where I will not give you Haninah (Jer 16:13). Others say: His name is Menahem the son of Hezekiah, for it is written, Because Menahem ['the comforter'], that would relieve my soul, is far (Lam 1:16). The Rabbis said: His name is 'the leper scholar,' as it is written, "Surely he hath borne our griefs, and carried our sorrows: yet we did esteem him a leper, smitten of God, and afflicted (Is 53:4). (b.*Sanhedrin* 98a)

The word of our Master, then, is given to encourage all those who mourn, who experience the pain of this fallen world, but who likewise have given themselves over to the merciful hand of God. It is His promise that for those who entrust themselves to Him, He will bring comfort where mourning once existed. And such comfort is assured in that the King has come, and the victory is therefore certain.

> Your sun will no longer set, nor will your moon wane; for you will have the LORD for an everlasting light, and the days of your mourning will be over. (Is 60:20)

5 Blessed are the gentle, for they shall inherit the[1] earth.

In some of the early manuscripts (D, 33, latin, sy^{rc}, bo^{ms}), verse 5 is found after v. 3. Lachs[2] thinks this represents a more original order, since the "poor in spirit" of v. 3 would be more naturally followed by "gentle" or "meek." While it is true that the two verses (3 and 5) seem naturally to go together, this also gives a reason why scribes might have rearranged the order. Thus, it is better to stay with the traditional verse order, which also has the greater weight of manuscript evidence (א, B, C, *f*^{1}, *f*^{13}, etc.).

The English word "gentle" (NASB, WEB) here translates the Greek πραΰς (praus), which has a basic meaning of "not being overly impressed by a sense of one's importance." Thus, most other English translations use the English word "meek" (KJV, RSV, NRSV, ESV, CJB, NIV). We find Matthew using the same Greek word in 11:29, "Take My yoke upon you and learn from Me, for I am <u>gentle</u> and humble in heart …" as well as in the Lxx quote from Zech 9:9 in 21:5, "Say to the daughter of Zion, 'Behold your King is coming to you, <u>gentle</u>, and mounted on a donkey…." Peter also uses the term in his first epistle (1Pet 3:4). Admonishing women not only to adorn themselves with outward beauty, he writes, "but let it be the hidden person of the heart, with the imperishable quality of a <u>gentle</u> and quiet spirit, which is precious in the sight of God." We see, then, that the word generally has the sense of "humble," "meek," "gentle," and even "submissive." These positive qualities do not envision weakness of any sort, but rather stress a response of faith in the power of God Who controls the events of life. It may also be the case that our word in this context has some sense of "the powerless," those who have been marginalized by the ruling authorities and who are unable, in and of themselves, to affect any change in their situation. When such people commit themselves to the protection and power of the Almighty, they evidence a "meek" spirit in the midst of being persecuted. And as noted above, the other two times that our word is used, it is descriptive of Yeshua Himself. Thus, our Master stands as the model for us of meekness.

If the chiastic arrangement of the Beatitudes suggested above has warrant, then the "gentle/meek" are parallel to "peacemakers." This would give the picture that those who are gentle do not have it in their hearts to overpower those who stand in opposition to them, but who, in putting their trust in God, seek to make peace. Once again, this does not mean that the gentle shy away from speaking the truth, and even speaking the truth with vigor, as modelled by our Master (e.g., Matt 23). But it would mean that the character of the gentle is such that peace is their goal, that is, the winning of those who oppose them over to the truth rather than subjugation.

for they shall inherit the earth   We should understand the Greek γῆ (ge), here translated "earth" as "the Land"— "the shall inherit the Land."[3] The promise of possessing the Land is regularly tied to obeying the *mitzvot*. We find this in the second part of the *Shema* (Deut 11:13–21), which concludes "so that your days and the days of your sons may be multiplied on the land which the LORD swore to your fathers to give them, as long as the heavens remain above the earth." This is based upon the promise made to the Fathers, as noted in the prayer of Moses (Ex 32:11ff) –

Remember Abraham, Isaac, and Israel, Your servants to whom You swore by Yourself, and said to them, 'I will multiply your descendants as the stars of the heavens, and all this land of which I have spoken I

---

[1]Neither the Lxx of Ps 37:11, which appears to be quoted here, nor the Hebrew, has the article: וַעֲנָוִים יִירְשׁוּ־אָרֶץ. However the Targum to Ps 37:11 does contain the article, and it may be the Matthew was influenced by the Targum. Also note Is 61:7, κληρονομήσουσιν τὴν γῆν.

[2]Tobias Lachs, *A Rabbinic Commentary on the New Testament*, p. 74.

[3]Allison-Davies (1.450) argue for a cosmic sense of γῆ here, but while this surely could be the case, the many parallels offered from the Tanach would opt for the more usual "Land" as the translation.

will give to your descendants, and they shall inherit it forever.'
This promise that obedient Israel would "inherit the Land" became a regular motif in the prophets (Is 49:8; 57:13; Zech 8:12), and particularly in the Psalms. In fact, it seems clear that Yeshua had Ps 37 in mind as He taught this Beatitude. Note the following verses from this Psalm:

> 9 For evildoers will be cut off, But those who wait for the LORD, they will inherit the land.
> 11 But the humble will inherit the land and will delight themselves in abundant prosperity.
> 22 For those blessed by Him will inherit the land, but those cursed by Him will be cut off.
> 29 The righteous will inherit the land and dwell in it forever.
> 34 Wait for the LORD and keep His way, and He will exalt you to inherit the land; when the wicked are cut off, you will see it.

This same motif is found in extra-biblical literature as well. In Jub 32:19 we read, "And after that they shall get possession of the whole earth and inherit it forever." In Enoch 5:7 the same language is employed: "The elect shall possess light, joy, peace, and they shall inherit the land." Likewise Didache 3, after exhorting the people to flee from "every kind of evil," quotes our verse:[1] "Instead, be humble, for 'the humble shall inherit the earth (Land)'" (Did 3:7).

This language, of inheriting the land forever, is equivalent to having a place in "the world to come." Note Is 60:21,

> Then all your people will be righteous; they will possess the land forever, the branch of My planting, the work of My hands, that I may be glorified.

This verse formed the basis for the rabbinic dictum that "all Israel have a place in the world to come" (m.*Sanhedrin* 10.1). While the rabbis of the Mishnah and Bavli (cf. b.*Sanhedrin* 100a) considered one's Jewish status as the basis for a place in the world to come, Yeshua here considers one's righteous character as the proof of covenant membership. The meek are the ones who inherit the Land, not simply those who could trace their lineage to Jacob.

6   Blessed are those who hunger and thirst for righteousness, for they shall be satisfied.

Luke's parallel has "Blessed are you who hunger now, for you shall be satisfied." Matthew alerts us to the fact that the "hunger" and "thirst" is to be understood metaphorically of one's soul-longing for righteousness. This does not necessarily negate physical hunger and thirsting, but focuses attention upon how one's desire for righteousness encompasses one's entire life. As Proverbs teaches:

> Keep deception and lies far from me, give me neither poverty nor riches; Feed me with the food that is my portion, that I not be full and deny You and say, "Who is the LORD?" Or that I not be in want and steal, and profane the name of my God.

As Allison-Davies note:

[1] An increasing number of scholars question whether Didache quotes Matthew, or simply has possession of the same source (Q^mt) that Matthew utilized. The fact that Didache 3:7 includes the article (τὴν γῆν) would favor the idea that it quotes Matthew, or at least used the same source as Matthew. In balance, it still seems to me that the overall message of Didache fits the late 1st Century better than mid-1st Century.

[1] Allison-Davies, *Matthew,* 1.451-2, quoting L. Goppelt, *TWNT* 6, p. 18.

> It [righteousness] clarifies the object of 'hunger,' which in Q remained unspecified. It does not, however, simply spiritualize a physical need. Even in Luke = Q 'the hungry are men who both outwardly and inwardly are painfully deficient in the things essential to life as God meant it to be, and who, since they cannot help themselves, turn to God on the basis of his promise.[1]

Later, our Master will teach that His true disciples seek above all else "the kingdom and His righteousness" (6:33), which is parallel to "hunger and thirst after righteousness." Thus, in the same manner that we naturally work to sustain our physical lives through food and drink, so we are to earnestly and habitually seek after righteousness. We are to follow God's ways in every aspect of our life.

This inner hunger and thirst is not something passive, but active. Indeed, the more we strive to fulfill our inner longing for God's righteousness, the more our hunger increases. Thus, while the physical analogy is clear, the reality is much different. When we eat food, our hunger subsides. But when we feed upon the word of God, and set our hearts to meditate upon His ways, our spiritual hunger increases.

This metaphoric use of "hunger" and "thirst" to denote a spiritual striving is not something new in the teaching of our Master. The Psalmist writes, "My soul thirsts for God, for the living God; when shall I come and appear before God?" (Ps 42:2), and consider the words of Amos,

> "Behold, days are coming," declares the Lord GOD, "When I will send a famine on the land, not a famine for bread or a thirst for water, but rather for hearing the words of the LORD." (Amos 8:11)

Moreover, a similar metaphor is found among the Sages. Note *Mekilta* on Ex 15:22–26 (2.87 in Lauterbach):

> *They went three days in the wilderness and found no water* (Ex 15:22) … What is the meaning of "And found no water?" … the allegorists say: They did not find words of Torah which are likened to water. And whence do we know that the words are likened to water? It is said: "Ho, every one that thirsts, come you for water," etc. (Is 55:1).

[2] Allison-Davies, *Matthew,* p. 453.

> R. Tanchum b. R. Chanilai said: Whosoever starves himself for the sake of the words of Torah in this world, the Holy One, blessed be He, satisfies him in the world to come, as it is written, *they feast on the abundance of Your house, and You give them drink from the rivers of Your delight* (Ps 36:9). (b.*Sanhedrin* 100a)

Some have suggested that the word "righteousness" (δικαιοσύνη, *dikaiosune*) means "justification," i.e., the gift of God given on the basis of faith. Others think it speaks of "eschatological vindication of the elect." But it seems clear from the other uses of righteousness in the Sermon on the Mount (cf. 5:10, 20; 6:1, 33), that the word here should have the same meaning, namely, "right conduct which God requires." Most telling in this regard is 5:10, ""Blessed are those who have been persecuted for the sake of righteousness, for theirs is the kingdom of heaven." Here, righteousness cannot mean "justification by God," nor eschatological vindication. It means that Yeshua's disciples are persecuted because of the righteousness which they have, and which others see. "It is recognizable behavior of some sort."[2] Moreover, if we follow the pattern of the Beatitudes, we see that righteousness in this case is not something given *per se,* but something possessed. The poor are not given poverty, the meek are not given meekness, the pure in heart are not given purity, and the peacemakers are not given peace. Likewise, the emphasis is not that those who hunger and thirst after righteousness are given righteousness, but that each of these qualities are the evident character of those who are true followers after God.

The metaphor of hungering and thirsting is worthy of further consideration, especially as it pertains to righteousness. The righteous are not here congratulated, as though they had obtained something in its fulness. Being hungry and thirsty for righteousness means that one is well aware of one's need for more. Righteousness must ever be sought—it is the goal that lies ahead. As Paul remarks (Phil. 3:12) –

> Not that I have already obtained it or have already become perfect, but I press on so that I may lay hold of that for which also I was laid hold of by Messiah Yeshua.

And again he writes (v. 14), "I press on toward the goal for the prize of the upward call of God in Messiah Yeshua." While it is certainly clear that those who have put their faith in Yeshua have been declared righteous, and have been forever absolved of the guilt and penalty of sin, this reality causes an unquenchable thirst in the soul for conformity to Messiah. We may never consider that our race is finished, that somehow we are allowed to sit idle as though the crown has already been awarded. Rather, the inner working of the Ruach so moves and motivates us that we strive to become what we have already been declared to be, i.e., righteous in Messiah. We should remember the message of our Master regarding the Pharisee and the tax collector (Lk 18:9–14), in which the Pharisee who considered himself righteous is, in fact, not, and the one who knows his own shortcomings "went down to his house justified (righteous)." Thus, "those who hunger and thirst after righteousness are blessed, not those who think they have attained it."[1]

for they shall be satisfied   The verb is future passive, and once again, God is the divine agent, the One Who brings the satisfaction. While the future tense may indeed emphasize the eschatological reversal, in which the hungry and thirsty in this life are fully satisfied in the world to come, it does not negate the fact that the future has invaded the present in the coming of Messiah and the work of the Ruach in establishing His reign among His people. It may be, as well, that the "messianic banquet" is envisioned, at which the the elect from all nations will dine at table with Abraham, Isaac, and Jacob (Matt 8:11).

But the point here is that hungering and thirsting after righteousness brings a real satisfaction to the soul, because God sees to it that the soul is satisfied, and He alone is able to do this work. Nothing is more clear when we consider the human plight, that mankind in general is constantly striving for some measure of significance; of being satisfied at the end of the day, that one's life and efforts had some genuine meaning. Yet, in our own fallen minds, we fail to realize that true satisfaction begins with knowing God and pleasing Him. We spend ourselves in finding ways to be satisfied, but find our souls constantly longing for what seems always just beyond our grasp. Here, the words of our Master direct us to the foundational aspect of being

[1]Allison-Davies, *Matthew,* 1.453.

truely satisfied. It is when we "drink for the streams of His delight" that we discover our true significance, and it is in this that we are enabled to fulfill the very purpose for our existence. The soul that longs for Him is satisfied, even if this longing continues to increase. It is in this striving that we are at once fulfilled and ever becoming.

7 "Blessed are the merciful, for they shall receive mercy.

"Merciful" translates the Greek ἐλέμονες (*elemones,* the adjectival form of ἔλεος, *eleos,* "mercy"). In the Lxx, our word regularly translates חַנּוּן (*chanun*), "merciful," "kind," "gracious." Luke's parallel (6:36) is: "Be merciful, just as your Father is merciful," where the word is οἰκτίρμων (*oiktirmon,* the adjectival form of οἰκτρίω, *oiktrio,* "to be compassionate"). In the Lxx, *oiktirmon* most often translates רָחוּם (*rachum*) or רָחַם (*racham*), "to love, have mercy on someone, show compassion."

The point of our Master's words are apparent: one who shows others mercy will themselves be shown mercy. This is also a theme in the rabbinic literature.

> Whoever has pity on people will obtain pity from heaven (b.*Shabbat* 151b)
> As long as you are merciful, the Merciful One is merciful to you (t.*Bava Qama* 9.30)

Matthew is very much taken with the concept of mercy, and it forms a central theme in his Gospel (cf. 9:13; 12:7; 23:23). Yeshua regularly teaches on the need to show mercy (5:43–8; 18:21–35; 25:31–46) and demonstrates mercy in His own actions (9:27–31; 15:21–8; 17:14–18; 20:29–34). Yet the concept of mercy is in need of redefining in our own times. Being merciful does not mean turning a blind eye to that which needs correction, or to the base desires of some. Parents who give into their children just because "everyone is doing it" are not demonstrating mercy. Mercy evidences itself to those in genuine need, not in giving in to those who are manipulative for their own gains. This is because mercy is tied to righteousness and justice. When the Almighty punishes the wicked, His mercy is not diminished, nor could it be. Likewise, hand-feeding the wild animals may appear on the surface as "merciful," but in reality it is detrimental to their continuing existence. Giving handouts to the vagrant may seem an act of mercy, but it may actually be enabling him to remain in his sorry state. So mercy is forestalled unless it is combined with wisdom.

What our Master enjoins upon us here is the willingness to show mercy to those in genuine need—to those who are, for whatever reason, in great need of forbearance and understanding. They may be suffering under the consequences of their own sinful choices, but if they are seeking to change and to overcome their troubles, they need to be shown mercy—they need a helping hand extended without concomitant judgment.

Our Master's words here may, however, envision more than the practical reality of consequences, i.e., that people who show mercy to others are far more likely to be shown mercy themselves. While this is true, the picture of the eschaton may likewise be in view. Those who show mercy do so because they have themselves experienced the mercy of the Almighty: "be merciful even as your Father in heaven is merciful" (Lk 6:36). "He who is forgiven much loves much" (cf. Lk 7:47). In this regard then, our Master's words are not limited to showing mercy only to one's close associates. At times, it appears that the emphasis placed by the Sages upon the distinction between Israel and the nations translated into a boundary for showing mercy:

> R. Eleazar also said: Whosoever lacks knowledge, one may have no mercy upon him, as it is written, For it is a people of no understanding: therefore he that made them will not have mercy upon them, and he that formed them will show them no favour. [Is 27:11] (b.*Sanhedrin* 92a, cp. b.*Berachot* 33a)

Yet Yeshua's teachings emphasize that one is to show mercy to all without distinction. Where there is a genuine need, showing mercy is appropriate, regardless of whether the person meets one's personal standards or not.

> "It is 'the meek' who are also 'the merciful.' For to be meek is to acknowledge to others that *we* are sinners; to be merciful is to have compassion on others, for they are sinners too."[1]

[1]Carson, *Matthew*, p.134, quoting John Stott, *Christian Counter-culture*, (IVP, 1978), p. 48, emphasis his.

Likewise, the use of "mercy" in Hos 6:6 may bear upon Yeshua's words here and throughout Matthew's Gospel, as they pertain to the whole matter of "mercy." Hosea 6:6, in which "mercy" (חֶסֶד, *chesed*) denotes "loyalty in relationship," is cited in Matt 9:13 and 12:7.

> For I delight in loyalty (חֶסֶד, ἔλεος, "mercy") rather than sacrifice, and in the knowledge of God rather than burnt offerings.

Both times our Master quotes this text, He is rebuking the Pharisees, apparently because in their zeal to maintain a rigid Torah observance, they had failed to see that showing mercy was actually the very thing God desires. In Matt 23:23, the weightier matters of the Torah, which some of the Pharisees had neglected, are "justice, mercy, and faithfulness." In striving to be faithful, the Pharisees had neglected the demonstration of mercy conjoined with justice. From Yeshua's perspective, showing mercy is the concrete expression of loyalty to God. "What God demands is not so much activity directed Godward ('I desire…not sacrifice') but lovingkindness benefiting other people ('I desire mercy')."[2]

[2]Allison-Davies, *Matthew*, p. 455.

It is fitting for us who have come to love and follow after God's Torah, that we take to heart these words of our Master. It is easy in our zeal to be jealous for God's ways, and all the more since we have come to recognize that much of His "instructions in righteousness" (=the Torah) have been either neglected or abolished in the theology of Christianity. Yet many who have been ill-taught regarding the enduring value and practical advantage of obey the Torah are not, in and of themselves, intending to disobey God. They have believed a message based upon an developed theology that is, in many ways, deficient and even errant. Nonetheless, they have a desire to please the Almighty. We will do well to show mercy, and to encourage our brothers and sisters in the faith to reconsider the enduring words of Scripture, to take them to heart, and to act upon them. It will be in our showing mercy that the words of our Master will ring true, and have their due effect.

8 Blessed are the pure in heart, for they shall see God.

This sixth beatitude has no parallel in Luke. Matthew, however, seems to be intent upon preserving the overall structure of our Master's sayings. If the chiastic structure suggested above has merit, then those who are "pure in heart" is parallel to those who "hunger and thirst after righteousness" (v. 6). This would help to define the meaning of "pure" (καθαροὶ, *katharoi*) by the term "righteousness." Inner purity is the fountain from which righteous deeds flow. The Greek term for purity (καθαρός, *katharos*) is the regular term utilized by the Lxx to translate the Hebrew טְהוֹרָה (*t'horah*), which is most often used to denote ritual or ceremonial purity. It would seem most likely that our Master used this word in His teaching here, and by doing so, combined both the sense of inner purity (cf. Ps 51:12) and the outward obedience to God's instructions (Torah).

The parallel of "pure in heart" to Ps 24:3–6 is obvious:

> Who may ascend into the hill of the LORD? And who may stand in His holy place? He who has clean hands and a pure heart (καθαρὸς τῇ καρδίᾳ), who has not lifted up his soul[1] to falsehood and has not sworn deceitfully. He shall receive a blessing from Adonai and righteousness from the God of his salvation. This is the generation of those who seek Him, who seek Your face—even Jacob.

In this context, purity of heart is manifest in proper oath taking, where to lift one's soul to falsehood is further defined in the parallelism by swearing deceitfully. Moreover, that fact that the reward for the pure of heart is that they will receive *righteousness* strengthens the suggestion that this beatitude is parallel to "those who hunger and thirst after righteousness" of v. 6.

In a Hebrew perspective, the heart (לֵב, לֵבָב, *leiv, leivav*) is the seat of the intellect and volition (Gen 6:5; Ex 4:21; Jer 3:16; 2Sam 24:10; 1Ki 11:3; Neh 3:38, etc.) as well as the place where the divine presence is encountered (Ps 10:17; 17:3; 27:8; cf. Eph 3:17). The idea of purity in heart thus involves both an inward conformity to God's ways as well as the concomitant actions that inevitably proceed from one's inner self. The two can never be divided, as though one could be pure in actions without first being pure in heart. Thus, singleness of heart is another way of describing an utter lack of hypocrisy. Those who are "double-minded" (סֵעֵף, *sei'eif*) are contrasted to those who love the Torah (Ps 119:113). James, who doubtlessly has Ps 24:3–4 in mind, admonishes, "Draw near to God and He will draw near to you. Cleanse your hands, you sinners; and purify your hearts, you double-minded" (Jms 4:8).

Matthew emphasizes this theme in other places of his Gospel as well. In the Sermon itself (5:27–30), our Master teaches us that the sin of adultery begins in the heart, and the hypocrisy of the Pharisaic leaders is pictured as a cup that is clean outwardly, but inside is full of impurities. In other words, what matters is what goes on in the heart, because the heart governs all of one's actions.

The blessing promised to those who are pure in heart is that "they will see God" (αὐτοὶ ὄψονται τὸν θεὸν). These words strike us as strange, for the Scriptures teach us that God is a spirit, and therefore invisible to the human eye (John 1:18; 4:24; Col 1:15; 1Tim 1:17). Moreover, God instructed Moses that "You cannot see My face, for no man can see Me and live!" (Ex 33:20). Yet we read similar language in Ex 24:9-10, "Then Moses went up with

---

[1] The Hebrew of Ps 24:4 has נַפְשִׁי, "my soul" rather than נַפְשׁוֹ, "his soul." Some Hebrew manuscripts read נַפְשׁוֹ but both L and Aleppo have נַפְשִׁי. If נַפְשִׁי is the correct reading (and the strength of manuscript evidence does support this), then the meaning would be: "who has not sworn in vain by My soul," meaning "who has not evoked the divine Name in a false oath."

The Lxx has ψυχὴν αὐτοῦ, "his soul," as do other versions.

Aaron, Nadab and Abihu, and seventy of the elders of Israel, and they saw the God of Israel…." The Lxx translators were not comfortable with such straightforward language, and so translated the verse: "And they saw the place where the God of Israel stood…." But this translation betrays a theological position—the Hebrew text is very clear: they saw the God of Israel.

The rabbis had similar difficulty with the Ex 24 text.[1] Targum Onkelos reads "And they saw the Glory of the God of Israel," meaning they saw the *Shekinah*. Likewise, the phrase "As for me, I will behold Your face in righteousness" (Ps 17:15)[2] is interpreted to mean one is worthy to behold the *Shekinah*:

> If a man gives but a farthing to a beggar, he is deemed worthy to receive the Divine Presence, as It is written, I shall behold Your face in righteousness [*zedakah*], I shall be satisfied when I awake with Your likeness" (b.*Bava Batra* 10a)

The angels are said to see the face of God:

> See that you do not despise one of these little ones, for I say to you that their angels in heaven continually see the face of My Father who is in heaven. (Matt 18:10)

Moreover, the idea that God will be seen is found in connection to the eschatological redemption and renewal:

> There will no longer be any curse; and the throne of God and of the Lamb will be in it, and His bond-servants will serve Him; they will see His face, and His name will be on their foreheads. (Rev 22:3–4)

In this text, the One Who is seen is the One Whose Name is written on their foreheads, and this surely alludes to the divine Name written on the crown of the High Priest: קוֹדֶשׁ לַיהוה, Holy to Adonai. Indeed, this sense of seeing God in the eschaton is referenced in the Talmud in connection to the interpretation of Ex 24:10 —

> A favorite saying of Rab was: [The future world is not like this world.] In the future world there is no eating nor drinking nor propagation nor business nor jealousy nor hatred nor competition, but the righteous sit with their crowns on their heads feasting on the brightness of the divine presence, as it says, And they beheld God, and did eat and drink. (b. *Berachot* 17a)

It is surely true that the verb "to see" may also mean "to know" (cf. Is 6:9; Ex 16:6; Lev 5:1; Is 29:15; Ecc 6:5, etc.), and some have suggested that this the meaning of our beatitude: "Blessed are the pure in heart, for they shall know God." And this is, of course, true. But the language that utilizes the verb "to see" intends that we understand this knowledge of God as that which comes through close association. For the Gospel writers, this knowledge of God has come to its fulfillment in the person of the Messiah: "He who has seen Me has seen the Father" (Jn 14:9). Ultimately, then, the blessing attached to those who are pure in heart is that they will come to know God (to see Him) as He truly is—as perfectly and completely revealed in His Son, Yeshua. And this revelation of the Father is not inferior to knowing the

Father directly. Yeshua is "the radiance of His glory and the exact representation of His nature" (Heb 1:3).

9 Blessed are the peacemakers, for they shall be called sons of God.

Peacemakers (εἰρηνοποιός, *eirenopoios*) are those who work for reconciliation; who seek to bring about peace where it is lacking. The word (used only here in the Apostolic Scriptures) is not found in the Lxx. It is a compound word made up of the word for peace (εἰρήνη, *eirene*) and the verb "to do or make" (ποιέω, *poieo*). It does not connote a "pacifist" or simply the sense of "peace." Peacemakers are those who "love their enemies" and seek to reconcile their differences (Matt 5:44; Lk 6:27, 35). Even where such reconciliation is illusive, peacemakers refuse to heighten the discord. They do not throw fuel on the fire. As James writes: "And the seed whose fruit is righteousness is sown in peace by those who make peace" (3:18).

Since Adonai is the source of peace (Job 25:2), and since He is the One Who ultimately brings peace to His people (Ps 29:11; Is 26:12), those who likewise are peacemakers are known as His sons, for they follow in the footsteps of their Father.

But this does not imply "peace at any cost." Yeshua Himself said "Do not think that I came to bring peace on the earth; I did not come to bring peace, but a sword" (Matt 10:34). Ultimately, He is the "prince of peace" (Is 9:6[5]), and it is through His power to reign as King over all the earth that He will bring about a final and lasting peace. But peace is the fruit of righteousness, not that which results from a miscarriage of justice. As the prophet Zechariah teaches us:

> These are the things which you should do: speak the truth to one another; judge with truth and judgment for peace in your gates. (Zech 8:16)

In our world it is common to hear of "peace" as an entity unto itself. But true peace is always the result of justice and righteousness. "There is no peace for the wicked, says Adonai" (Is 48:22, cp. 57:21).

The parallel to our beatitude in the chiastic scheme we have proposed is that of the gentle or meek (v. 5). Peacemakers are those who are willing to humble themselves under the mighty hand of God and await His verdict. Instead of seeking retaliation against their opponents, they rather seek avenues of reconciliation and peace. As the Psalmist admonishes: "Depart from evil and do good; Seek peace and pursue it" (Ps 34:14). Hillel was known for teaching this same message:

> Hillel said: "Be of the disciples of Aaron, loving peace, and pursuing peace, loving your fellow creatures and bringing them near to the Torah." (*Avot* 1.12)

10 Blessed are those who have been persecuted for the sake of righteousness, for theirs is the kingdom of heaven.

Once again, this beatitude finds no parallel in Luke. Some have suggested that it was added by Matthew for structural purposes.[1] Perhaps this is so, but it does not mean that Matthew added this beatitude to the word our

[1] Allison-Davies (1.459) suggest that Matthew structures much of his material around the number three. Thus, the beatitudes are three groups of three (nine total).

Master taught. Rather, if structural concerns are at work here, it is because Matthew saw in our Master's teaching a pattern he wished to emphasize. In the chiastic arrangement we have suggested, the central beatitude is that of mercy, which parallels a significant theme throughout the Gospel. And thus this beatitude, which focuses on those who have been persecuted for righteousness, is parallel to those who mourn.

Persecution (διώκω, *dioko*) refers to physical as well as verbal abuse. And in our verse, the verb is in the perfect tense, which would suggest both past persecution and that which is on-going in the present. (Note that the *ESV* has the present: "Blessed are those who are persecuted for righteousness' sake"). Thus, the persecution here envisioned is not confined to the current time of Yeshua's teaching, but is broadened to include any form of persecution that came as a result of doing righteousness.

The cause of the persecution is specific: "for the sake of righteousness" (ἕνεκεν δικαιοσύνης). Some have suggested that ἕνεκεν be understood as simply identifying those who are persecuted, thus: "Blessed are the persecuted righteous." But the more natural way to understand the Greek is that righteousness is the cause for the persecution. Moreover, this accords with the close parallel in 1Pet 3:14 – "But even if you should suffer for the sake of righteousness, you are blessed" (ἀλλ᾽ εἰ πάσχοιτε διὰ δικαιοσύνην μακάριοι), where the Greek is unambiguous: the persecution is "on account of" righteousness. Did Peter have access to the Matthew beatitudes? Or to the source that Matthew himself used? It is impossible to know, but the parallel, even if not verbally identical, is remarkably close. And in the context of Peter's epistle, the persecution is specifically upon those who are followers of Yeshua, for the next verses (15–16) read:

> but sanctify Messiah as Lord in your hearts, always being ready to make a defense to everyone who asks you to give an account for the hope that is in you, yet with gentleness and reverence; and keep a good conscience so that in the thing in which you are slandered, those who revile your good behavior in Messiah will be put to shame.

We may presume, then, that our Master's primary focus is likewise upon those of His followers who were presently being slandered and who would endure the increased persecution that would come upon them at the hands of His enemies.

We should not confuse the calamity that comes upon us as a result of our own failings with the persecution that results from righteous living. When we suffer various hardships, it is easy to reason that we are being persecuted and that our suffering is no fault of our own. But often, if we reflect more sincerely, many of the hardships we endure are, in some measure, either the result of our own bad choices, or the inevitable consequences of living in a fallen world. It is not uncommon to find the "victim mentality" alive and well among those who are "religious."

for theirs is the kingdom of heaven – The promised blessing upon those who are persecuted for the sake of righteousness is the same as in the first beatitude (v. 3), and thus it forms an *inclusio*, framing the first eight. The final beatitude (vv. 11–12) has a far different structure and therefore most likely acts a bridge between the beatitudes and the remainder of our Master's teaching in this pericope. It still figures into the overall structure of the beatitudes, but does double duty as a bridge to the next section. As such, the promise of the "kingdom of heaven" frames the eight beatitudes that are cast in the third person. The final beatitude switches to second person ("blessed are you..."). The force of this *inclusio* is to teach that all of the beatitudes essentially promise the same blessing (the kingdom of heaven) simply described in various ways. Possession of the kingdom of heaven is citizenship under the reign of God and all of the attended blessings that come as a result. Such blessings await their full realization in the eschatological reign of the Messiah, but they are nonetheless enjoyed in part now, for the King has come, and the future has invaded the present.

11–12 Blessed are you when people insult you and persecute you, and falsely say all kinds of evil against you because of Me. Rejoice and be glad, for your reward in heaven is great; for in the same way they persecuted the prophets who were before you.

Luke's parallel (6:22–23) includes four aspects of persecution:

> Blessed are you when men hate you, and ostracize you, and insult you, and scorn your name as evil, for the sake of the Son of Man.

Matthew has only three: 1) insult, 2) persecute, and 3) slander. If we understand Matthew's "persecute" to mean "drive away," then it may be parallel to Luke's "ostracize you." Further, Luke's opening item, "men hate you" may be a general heading which is then explained by the following three terms. In essence, the two are essentially saying the same things.

The change to the second person ("blessed are you") from the third person ("blessed are they," i.e., poor in spirit, etc.) is curious and numbers of explanations have been offered. But it seems very probable to me that the previous beatitudes were directed to the general public who had gathered to hear our Master's teaching, while this final beatitude is directed specifically to His disciples. All of the previous beatitudes apply to them as well, but this final one has the persecution they would inevitably endure in view. This also makes sense with the analogy to the persecution of the prophets. In the same way that the prophets of old came to Israel with the words of the Almighty, and were often rebuffed by the people, so the disciples who would carry the message of Yeshua would meet with a similarly hostile reception. Moreover, it was the prophet's faithfulness to the message they had received that resulted in their persecution, and the same would be experienced by the Apostles of our Master.

This parallel to the prophets is all the more interesting when it is understood that the opening line lacks a specified subject. The NASB, NIV and NRSV supply "people," ESV has "others," while the KJV and RSV have "men" (parallel to Luke's account which actually has the word "men" [ἄνθρωποι, *anthropoi*] as the subject). But the Greek leaves the subject unspecified, and in the subsequent context of Matthew's Sermon, it seems clear that those who oppose the message and example of Yeshua are clearly in view, i.e., the synagogue officials who would eventually exclude the followers of Yeshua (so Luke's "ostracize you"). Who else would have made the accusation that Yeshua was intent upon destroying the Torah and the Prophets (5:17)? So while the persecution here described could be envisioned in a general sense, it most likely has the already growing animosity against Yeshua as its primary reference.

The hostility against Yeshua's disciples is noted to consist of "insults," "persecutions," and "slander." Insults would include the stinging jokes and innuendoes, and even public humiliation, (something strictly forbidden by the Sages). "Persecution" might include power of the court which would find them guilty of blasphemy or improper associations (especially with Gentiles), and this might dovetail with "say all manner of evil against you falsely." This final clause might well envision the false witnesses that were marshalled into courts to condemn the disciples on false charges. Interestingly, if our understanding of this final beatitude is on track, the persecution at the hands of Paul before his coming to faith in Yeshua may be seen as a partial fulfilment of Yeshua's words.

This final beatitude contains the only imperatives: "rejoice and be glad." Both of these imperatives are present tense, which could be understood to mean "keep on rejoicing and being glad." Moreover, the rejoicing and gladness is not in spite of the persecution, but because of it. The persecution that comes upon Yeshua's disciples links them with the prophets of old who also were persecuted in the same way (οὕτως, *houtos*). Thus, the prophets of old were persecuted because they were the genuine spokesmen for God. In the same way, Yeshua's disciples are the authoritative witnesses of the Messiah, and their persecution at the hands of His enemies is proof of this.

Some have suggested that the concept of rejoicing in suffering is a purely Christian teaching, without parallel in the rabbis. But note this Baraita:

> Our Rabbis taught: Those who are insulted but do not insult, hear themselves reviled without answering, act through love and rejoice in suffering, of them the Scriptures say, But they who love Him are as the sun when he goes forth in his might (Jud 5:31). (b.*Shabbat* 88b)

Neither the words of the rabbis, nor those of our Master, extol suffering in and of itself. Yeshua Himself taught His disciples to pray "deliver us from evil." But the rejoicing in suffering comes from recognizing that when we suffer for the righteous Name of our Master, we may count on His blessing, not because we have suffered, but because we have stood steadfast in the truth and acted faithfully with it.

The blessing that is promised is that "your reward in heaven is great." Many have understood this to be an eschatological blessing, that is, something that awaits the final redemption. Surely there is a sense that our hope is cast upon the final redemption and the shalom of the world to come. But "our reward in heaven" may just as well emphasize that God Himself is fully aware of our suffering and its cause, and He has set Himself to reward us as we are faithful. This, in itself, brings consolation in the midst of suffering. Moreover, the whole blessing is cast in the mode of God's providence. Thus, when the disciples of Yeshua suffer because they carry His message and live in accordance with His words and example, they may be assured that their suffering is "neither new, nor accidental, nor absurd."[1] Persecution against the disciples is like the persecution of the prophets of old; Yeshua foretold it, so it is not accidental; and it was (and is) used by the Almighty to expand His kingdom and to bring about His desired purposes, so it is not absurd (i.e., without meaning).

[1]Quoted from Carson, *Matthew*, p. 137.

13 You are the salt of the earth; but if the salt has become tasteless, how can it be made salty again? It is no longer good for anything, except to be thrown out and trampled under foot by men.

We may presume that in this verse and the ones which follow (vv. 13–16), Yeshua continues His instructions specifically to the Twelve, the particular audience of the final beatitude. This is seen in that the second person pronoun ("you," always in the plural in these verses, and put first both in v. 13 and 14 for emphasis), is utilized as it was in the final beatitude. Thus, the talmidim are compared to salt and light, each of which have a profound influence on everything with which they come in contact.

But Yeshua has moved from the perspective of blessing (the beatitudes) to that of the responsibility to live righteously for those who would be His disciples. In the beatitudes, the essential character or disposition of the righteous is highlighted, as well as the gifts or blessings that the Almighty gives to those who are righteous. Here, our Master urges His disciples to take up the task of righteous living, and thus vv. 13–16 form a kind of heading or bridge to the following section (5:17–7:12) which will describe in greater detail those who live as the Sermon on the Mount demands.

There are synoptic parallels, but with various and expanded themes. Mark contains a saying of Yeshua regarding salt (9:49–50), but it is found in a different setting and with additional import:

> For everyone will be salted with fire. Salt is good; but if the salt becomes unsalty, with what will you make it salty again? Have salt in yourselves, and be at peace with one another."

Here, salt is a metaphor of the final judgment as well as that of personal assessment and judgment in living righteously. Luke's parallel (14:34–35) is closer to Matthew:

> Therefore, salt is good; but if even salt has become tasteless, with what will it be seasoned? It is useless either for the soil or for the manure pile; it is thrown out. He who has ears to hear, let him hear.

Of course, the metaphor of the salt in Matthew also contains a general sense of judgment, for those who are the talmidim of Yeshua function as salt, but all others are "thrown out and trampled under foot by men," which envisions the final judgment in which the unrighteous are condemned. Here, Yeshua is not considering Israel to be the salt of the earth, but His true disciples. Moreover, the fact that His disciples are the salt of the *earth* (γῆς, *ges*) may envision a wider influence than simply the confines of Israel. Though Yeshua's initial mission is the "lost sheep of Israel," He continues to indicate that His message and its affect would have a much wider audience. As the salt of the earth, the Gentiles are once again brought into the picture.

You are the salt of the earth   The paradox with the former beatitudes is given in stark contrast. "The world is saved precisely by those it persecutes."[1] But it is not clear how our Master uses the metaphor of salt in this saying. Salt (ἅλας, *halas*[2]) is used in the rabbinic literature as that which is essential for life: "The world cannot exist without salt" (m.*Soferim* 15.8). The use of salt in the Scriptures and rabbinic literature provides a number of options for its understanding in our text:

[1] Allison-Davies, *Matthew*, 1.472.

[2] The Greek ἅλας is the common word for "salt" in the Lxx and Apostolic Scriptures. Classical Greek usually has ἅλος.

[1]Julian Preuss (*Biblical and Talmudic Medicine* [Aronson, 1993], p. 402) gives this explanation of salting a newborn: "The 'salting' was an indispensable part of the treatment of the newborn. Galen states it is for *symmetrois aloin peripattomenon;* so that the skin will become thicker and harder than the inner parts of the body. Soran has a separate chapter entitled *peri alismou* ["concerning salting"].... Moschion writes that the ancients used to wash the baby with saltwater and wine. We specialists (!) carefully apply finely powered salt and sodium carbonate on the baby. This procedure is supposed to simultaneously cleanse and act as an astringent, so that the skin becomes hard and able to withstand rashes or *exanthemata....* The procedure is absolutely not a religious ceremony."

1. Salt was used as preservative for foods, particularly for meat and vegetables. As a result, salt is used metaphorically in the sense of "preserving something from decay or demise." In b.*Ketuvot* 66b, "the salt of money is diminution (others read 'benevolence')," which is spoken in regard to Nakdimon ben Gorion, means that the *preservation* of money is giving of charity. We may also note m.*Sota* 9.15, which speaks of the "wisdom of the Sages" becoming "putrefied," i.e., spoiled as opposed to preserved (note Col 4:5 and the comments below, #3).

2. In connection with salt as a preservative, Lev 2:13 commands that salt be added to all of the grain offerings offered on the altar (cp. Ezek 43:24). This was to be symbolic of the enduring nature of God's covenant with Israel.

3. Thus, the Tanach speaks of the "covenant of salt" (Lev 2:13; Num 18:19; 2Chr 13:5). The Davidic covenant is described as a covenant of salt as is the Mosaic covenant of the Torah. In this same connection, to "eat salt" with someone may describe mutual covenant membership. Thus, in Ezra 4:14, those who eat the salt of the palace cannot be witnesses against the king.

4. Salt was used for purification. In 2Ki 2:19–23, Elisha performs a miracle in that he uses salt to purify bad drinking water. In a similar fashion, salt mixed with incense (Ex 30:35) renders the mixture "pure and holy." We may understand Mk 9:50 in this light: "Have salt in yourselves and be at peace with one another" may mean "have your hearts pure and so be at peace with one another." Similarly, Paul admonishes (Col 4:5), "Let your speech always be gracious, seasoned with salt…," by which he may mean that one's speech should be purified (holy), and thus not with an admixture of senseless talk or course jesting (cp. Eph 5:4).

5. Salt may have been used for medicinal purposes. We read in Ezek 16:4 (cp. b.*Shabbat* 129b) that newborns were rubbed with salt.[1]

6. Salt was, of course, used as a condiment for food (cf. Job 6:6).

It is impossible to determine precisely if one or another of these uses of salt are to applied to our text. And we should most likely presume that our Master intended to let His metaphor of salt be multifaceted. The fact that "you are the salt of the earth" is paralleled in the next verse to "you are the light of the world" shows that salt is to be taken in very broad sense, i.e., that which affects all substances to which it comes in contact. The message and person of Messiah is essential to spiritual life, even as salt is to one's physical existence. This is the primary point of the metaphor. That the witness of Messiah borne by the disciples would preserve, purify, heal, and bring to fruition the new covenant are all aspects of the salt metaphor.

but if the salt has become tasteless, how can it become salty again?   Much discussion has ensued over whether salt can, in fact, lose its savor. We know that sodium chloride is a stable compound and is not transformed through dilution. But as many have noted, salt in ancient Israel was generally obtained through evaporation pools at the edge of the Dead Sea (cf. Ezek 47:9–11; Zeph 2:9), meaning that the salt which was gathered could be mixed with impurities, and the more impurities, the less the salt was usable as salt. Carson[1] notes that the salt would be more soluble than the other impurities, and therefore if allowed to become wet, would lose its salty properties and leave the useless impurities. This makes perfect sense with our Master's teaching. The righteous life and message of the talmidim was that which would affect the expansion of the kingdom of Heaven. If, however, they allowed impurities to be mixed in, their effective witness for the Master would be lost.

Our English translation has "if the salt has become tasteless." The Greek word translated "tasteless" is μωραίνω (*moraino*) which usually means "to make foolish" or "to be foolish." Luke has the same term (Lk 14:34) but Mark has ἄναλος (*analos*), "to lose saltiness." Some have suggested that the difference between Matthew/Luke and Mark can be traced back to a Hebrew or Aramaic original of Matthew, in which the Hebrew verb תָּפַל (*taphal*) was used, and which can mean either "unsavory" or "foolish."[2] Thus, the different words found in Matthew/Luke and Mark may express the play on the word תפל itself, which could be understood both as "foolish" and as "that which is insipid" or "that which loses its saltiness." Black further proposes that there was a play on the word תבל (*tabbel*) meaning "to season:"

> A further confirmation that the word [תפל] was original is that it gives a word-play with the Aramaic for "salted," "seasoned," *tabbel*.[2]

Whatever the case, the point is simply that in some manner, salt could lose its primary function as a substance to affect other things, and thus the analogy to the disciples is clear. Only in their faithfulness to Yeshua and His message of righteousness would they be enabled to fulfill their mission as His disciples.

how can it be made salty again? This question on the lips of our Master is rhetorical. Once salt has become so diluted through the admixture of impurities, there was no effective way to reclaim it, particularly if such dilution happened because the salt supply became wet. This sense, that once salt has lost its saltiness it is worthless, may also parallel Yeshua's use of other metaphors that teach the need for a new beginning (the old wineskin/new wineskin; new patch on old cloth). If the current generation of Israel was to be the "salt of the earth," but had become diluted through false teachers and even idolatry, then there was need for a new generation to return to its effectiveness as the bearers of God's truth.

Of course, the supersessionists of the emerging Christian Church took this and other teachings of our Master to indicate the replacement of Israel by the Church. Israel was the salt that had lost its savour, and the Church, established by the Apostles, was the new salt. It may be that the rabbinic literature contains a response to the Church's use of Yeshua's words about salt:

> 'When salt becomes unsavory, wherewith is it salted'? He replied: 'With the after-birth of a mule'. 'And is there an after-birth of a mule'? 'And can salt become unsavory'? (b.*Bekarot* 8b)

[1]Carson, *Matthew*, p. 138.

[2]See Matthew Black, *An Aramaic Approach to the Gospels and Acts* (Hendrickson, 1998), p. 166.

The Hebrew Matthews show an interesting array of readings in Matt 5:13. The Münster has: אַתֶּם הֵם מֶלַח הָאָרֶץ וְאִם הַמֶּלַח יִתָּפֵל בְּמֶה יִמְלָח. The DuTillet has: אתם הם מלח בארץ ואם המלח יתנפל במה ימלח. Where the DuTillet text seems clearly to have יתנפל, in Herbst's transcription he has התנבל. The Even Bohan, however, has: מלח אתם בעולם אם המלח יבטל טעמו במה יומלח where בטל (transposition of תבל?) has the sense of "to annul, suspend, make void."

If the saying of our Master was being used in the Christian Church as teaching the demise of Israel because she had lost her effectiveness (=saltiness), and if the rabbinic saying was given in response to such a belief, then the point of the saying is that it is impossible for Israel to lose her saltiness (a mule is sterile and therefore has no after-birth, meaning that the question "When salt becomes unsavory, wherewith is it salted?" speaks of something that never could occur). Yeshua's point is that it has occurred and could do so again, but neither of these means the final end and replacement of Israel.

It is no longer good for anything, except to be thrown out and trampled under foot by men. Luke has: "It is useless either for the soil or for the manure pile; it is thrown out. He who has ears to hear, let him hear" (Lk 14:35). Minerals harvested from evaporation pools along the Dead Sea, if the salt content was low, could be plowed into the fields to give the soil nutrients, and could be added to the manure pile and then used as fertilizer. But if the salt supply had entirely lost its saltiness, it was worthless. It was thrown into the street to be trodden under the feet of travelers.

[1] Quoted from Carson, *Matthew*, p. 139, who quotes Tasker.

> The point is that, if Jesus' disciples are to act as a preservative in the world by conforming to kingdom norms, if they are "called to be moral disinfectant in a world where moral standards are low, constantly changing, or non-existent…. they can discharge this function only if they themselves retain their virtue.[1]

The language of being "thrown out and trampled under foot" may well have judgment in mind (cf. 8:12; 22:13; 25:30). For Yeshua, there is no middle ground. Those who walk in righteousness are His disciples, and accomplish the task to which they are commissioned. All others are judged.

14–15 You are the light of the world. A city set on a hill cannot be hidden; nor does anyone light a lamp and put it under a basket, but on the lampstand, and it gives light to all who are in the house.

This second metaphor strengthens the idea that the salt metaphor was intended to evoke Israel's chosen mission as God's witness upon the earth. For the prophets regularly speak of Israel as a "light:"

> Is 42:6 "I am the LORD, I have called you in righteousness, I will also hold you by the hand and watch over you, And I will appoint you as a covenant to the people, As a light to the nations,
> Is 49:6 He says, "It is too small a thing that You should be My Servant To raise up the tribes of Jacob and to restore the preserved ones of Israel; I will also make You a light of the nations So that My salvation may reach to the end of the earth."
> Is 60:3 "Nations will come to your light, And kings to the brightness of your rising.
> Dan. 12:3 "Those who have insight will shine brightly like the brightness of the expanse of heaven, and those who lead the many to righteousness, like the stars forever and ever.

The rabbinic literature also uses the metaphor of "light" for teachers of the truth as well as for Israel as a worshipping nation:

> When R. Abbahu arrived at the Emperor's Court from College,

the ladies of the court went out to receive him and sang to him: Great man of thy people, leader of thy nation, lantern of light, thy coming be blessed with peace. (b.*Sanhedrin* 14a)

In his last hours Rabban Johanan ben Zakkai kept weeping out loud. "O Master," his disciples exclaimed, "O tall pillar, light of the world, mighty hammer, why are you weeping?" (ARN, 25)

Herod then said: I am Herod. Had I known that the Rabbis were so circumspect, l should not have killed them. Now tell me what amends I can make. He replied: As you have extinguished the light of the world, [for so the Rabbis are called] as it is written, For the commandment is a light and the Torah a lamp, go now and attend to the light of the world [which is the Temple, of which] it is written, And all the nations become enlightened by it. (b.*Bava Batra* 4a)

Jerusalem is the light of the world, as it says, And nations shall walk at your light (Is 60:3); and who is the light of Jerusalem? God, as it is written, But the Lord shall be to you an everlasting light (Is 60:19). (Mid. Rab. *Gen* 59.5)

With the words of the prophets as background, it becomes clear that in claiming His talmidim to be the "light of the world (κόσμος, *kosmos*)," Yeshua is making an emphatic statement: Israel as a nation had strayed from the truth and had lost her way. Only in returning to the message of the prophets and thus to the teachings of the Messiah they foretold, would Israel once again be able to carry the light of the truth to the nations. In calling His disciples the "light of the world," Yeshua is not displacing Israel from her ordained role as God's chosen people, but calling Israel back to covenant faithfulness. Indeed, His disciples, each of them "sons of Israel," were the beginning of the eschatological renewal promised by the prophets, for the light had come into the world in the arrival of Messiah (Jn 1:4ff; 8:12; 12:46), and the talmidim were to be witnesses of that light (v. 16).

A city set on a hill cannot be hidden;   Some have suggested that these words of our Master refer to the New Jerusalem, and there is plenty of data to show that the restored Jerusalem in the eschaton was thought of as a city raised to great heights from which its light would spread to the whole world (Is 2:2–4; 60:1–22; Mic 4:1–3; Rev 21:10–11). *Pesiqta de Rab Kahana* 20.7 reads, "Jerusalem is destined to be a beacon for the nations of the earth, and they will walk in its light." However, the Greek lacks the article with "city," and the metaphor works with any city. Rather, the metaphor is used to emphasize a main point: those who are true disciples of the Master will be His witnesses—they can do nothing less. Even as a city situated upon a hill cannot be hidden, so the lives and message of the true disciples of Yeshua will inevitably shine forth. No one can be a secret disciple of the Master, for an essential aspect of being His disciple is to give witness to Who He is and what He has taught.

nor does anyone light a lamp, and put it under a basket[1]   This aspect of discipleship is made explicit as well in the lamp metaphor. The small terra cotta oil lamp that was so commonly used in the time of Yeshua is surely what is envisioned here. The point of lighting it was to offer light to those in the house. No one would think of lighting the lamp and putting it under a basket or in some way obscuring its light. In the same way, discipleship has as its primary goal the dissemination of the Master's teachings, both in word

[1] "basket" translates Greek μόδιος (*modios*), not found in the Lxx, and found only two other times in the Apostolic Scriptures (Mk 4:21; Lk 11:33). It is actually a loanword from Latin (*modius*) and refers to a "peck-measure," that is, a basket holding sixteen sextarii, or about 36 liters.

and deed. It is entirely incongruous, then, for anyone to claim to be His disciple but refuse or fail to give witness of Him, and to lead others to become His disciples as well. As we shall see, praying in one's "closet" is appropriate (6:6), but being a "closet disciple" is impossible. Yeshua will teach this as well in the parable of the talents. Talents are to produce talents, they are not to be hidden away (25:14ff). Obviously, Yeshua is training His talmidim for their final mission, to make disciples of all the nations (28:19-20).

16 Let your light shine before men in such a way that they may see your good works, and glorify your Father who is in heaven.

Now Yeshua drives His teaching home to the talmidim. The light they have received is to be shown forth to others with the result that they too will glorify the Father. In the Greek, our verse begins with οὕτως (*houtos*), which gives the sense "in the same way."[1] In the same way that a city on a hill is evident, and a lamp is lit for the purpose of giving light, so the talmidim of Yeshua are to walk and talk in such a manner that the attention of others will be arrested and drawn to the truth of the "Father who is in heaven."

We may note several important aspects of this concluding verse. First, the light is that of the disciples: "Let *your* light shine before men." The message and life to which we are to give witness is our life and message—it belongs to us because we have been given new life through faith in the Messiah. Granted, the light we have is given to us, not something we have produced. But we give witness of a life transformed through God's gracious and miraculous work. We are witnesses of what we personally know to be true.

Secondly, our light is to shine before *men* (ἄνθρωποι, *anthropoi*). This could just a well be understood as "mankind," and includes people of every category, Jew and non-Jew alike. While Yeshua's initial instructions to His talmidim was to go only to the lost sheep of Israel, His teaching here envisions the final commission in which discipleship among the nations is enjoined. God is the sovereign Who has chosen those who will be saved. We, however, are to give witness of the Master to all without discrimination. For we are privileged to be His workers by whom those from "every tribe and tongue and people and nation" will be redeemed (cf. Rev 5:9).

Thirdly, the light that Yeshua's disciples shine forth consists of good works (τὰ καλὰ ἔργα): "that they may see your *good works*." It is through living the *mitzvot* that Yeshua's disciples give witness to the glory of the Father. Yeshua's perspective on "evangelism" is therefore *mitzvot* driven. Only in a Western perspective could anyone conclude that "witnessing" means "handing out tracts." Not that there is anything necessarily wrong with disseminating the truth in written form, but to think that this is the primary mode of witness is to disregard our Master's words. He demands "life-style evangelism," a life-style that demonstrates to a watching world the His *mitzvot* bespeak His glory, honor, and wisdom. This is the very message of the Torah itself (Deut 4:6–8):

> So keep and do them, for that is your wisdom and your understanding in the sight of the peoples who will hear all these statutes and say, 'Surely this great nation is a wise and understanding people.' For what great nation is there that has a god so near to it as is the LORD our God whenever we call on Him? Or what great nation is there that

[1] The placing of "in such a way" in the middle of the clause as the NASB does, fails to emphasize the connection to the previous verses. Thus, the NIV is better: "In the same way, let your light shine before men…." ESV/NRSV have nearly the same translation as the NIV: "In the same way, let your light shine before others…." KJV, "Let your light so shine before men…." is ambiguous as to whether "so" relates to the previous context or what follows.

has statutes and judgments as righteous as this whole Torah which I am setting before you today?

Fourthly, the result of people seeing the *mitzvot* is that they "glorify your Father who is in heaven." This is precisely what Moses taught Israel. If Israel would keep the Torah and live it out in faithfulness before the nations, then the nations would surely admit that Israel's God is both unique and greater than all other gods. This is the ultimate goal, that God's Name should be sanctified (set apart) upon the earth, that He should receive the glory that He deserves as the Creator and benevolent King of the universe. Likewise, in the Disciples' Prayer (6:9–13), the opening request is that God's Name should be hallowed (seen as holy). Note also that the Father is referred to as "*your* Father who is in heaven." The *mitzvot* which characterize the lives of Yeshua's talmidim are done in the context of a covenant/family relationship with the Almighty. They are not carried out begrudgingly as the unreasonable demands of a distant potentate, but are the willing and joyful response of children to their Father Who has called them into covenant relationship with Himself and each other. Thus, Yeshua teaches "My Father is glorified by this, that you bear much fruit, and so prove to be My disciples" (Jn 15:8). And Peter writes: "Keep your behavior excellent among the Gentiles, so that in the thing in which they slander you as evildoers, they may because of your good deeds, as they observe them, glorify God in the day of visitation" (1Pet 2:12).

Fifthly, the result of this life-style evangelism as envisioned and commanded by our Master is that others will "glorify your Father who is in heaven." How does one glorify God? The answer is that they begin to live out the "good works" (the *mitzvot*) as well. This in no way suggests "salvation by works." Rather, it means that people are so struck by the validity and truth of the life they see in Yeshua's disciples, that they desire the same for themselves. They recognize that apart from a relationship with God by which they could invoke Him as Father, they have missed the very purpose for which they have been created. They desire the same relationship with the Almighty that they see lived out by Yeshua's talmidim. They are drawn to a life of righteousness, not to a creed or to an association within some religious organization.

Surely, this single teaching of our Master does not tell the whole story of evangelism, nor does it fully develop the whole scope of rebirth through the work of the Spirit in connection with the Good News. But it does give the general picture, and it does describe the ultimate goal, that of glorifying God as the very purpose of life itself.

This brief description by our Master of effective evangelism stands in remarkable contrast to the vast majority of what is usually labelled "evangelism" in our day. Developed after the sales model of our modern world, many approach "evangelism" as a means to "making the sale," which means getting people to agree to a set of religious axioms. "Evangelism" classes teach "openings" and "closes" just like any good sales school does. Success is reached when the person being "evangelized" prays the "sinner's prayer." But this is a far cry from what we hear from Yeshua as the mandate for His talmidim. The light that they shine forth is first and foremost a light that emanates from their doing the *mitzvot,* and which bespeaks an enduring covenant relationship with their Father in heaven. It therefore emphasizes the need to make disciples, not merely to bring someone to "say yes" to a minimal number of religious truths.

We may also note how this emphasis upon "doing good works" (the *mitzvot*) moves logically to the next paragraph, in which Yeshua outlines His perspective toward the Torah itself. Since the light that He demands of His disciples is that which comes forth from their doing good works, the accusation that He was teaching the abolition of the Torah must be corrected. Far from abolishing the Torah and the Prophets, Yeshua came to make the *mitzvot* shine forth from His disciples. For our Master, effective evangelism and living in obedience to the Torah go hand in hand.

As salt and light, the talmidim of Yeshua have been given both the ability and the responsibility to take up the challenge given to Israel of old, to be a light to the nations. Matthew's universalism is once again emphasized, for though the initial mission is to the lost sheep of Israel, the ultimate goal is that all of the nations of the earth should come to the light, and acknowledge Israel's God to be the One, true, and only God. This is what the Messiah intends to accomplish, and He has commissioned His disciples to be His servants by which the ancient promise to Abraham would come to fruition.

17   Do not think that I came to abolish the Torah or the Prophets; I did not come to abolish but to fulfill.

Verses 17–20 form a natural heading to the larger section (5:21–48) in which Yeshua contrasts His own interpretation and teaching from the Torah with well-known teachings generally received by the Jewish community He addresses. These verses also carry forward the previous teaching of our Master that His talmidim are to shine forth the light of truth through the doing of the *mitzvot*.[2]

The overall structure of vv. 17–20 is important for understanding their meaning:

Statement/Heading:
   Negative: Do not think that I came to abolish the Torah or the Prophets
   Positive: I did not come to abolish but to fulfill
   Proof: God's word is eternal
   Negative: Until heaven and earth pass not the smallest aspect of God's word will pass away
   Positive: all will be accomplished
Application/Halachah for Yeshua's Talmidim:
   Negative: whoever annuls even the least commandment & so teaches others to annul the commandments will be least in the kingdom of Heaven
   Positive: whoever does the commandments & teaches others to do them will be called great in the kingdom of Heaven
   Conclusion:
   Positive: one's righteousness must exceed that of the scribes and Pharisees
   Negative: else one will not even enter the kingdom of Heaven

This structure helps us see several important points:
   1. the concept of "abolish" is further defined by the structure as "annulling" and teaching others to "annul" the commandments

---

[1]Since Matthew 5:17–20 for a *crux interpretum* for the issue of Yeshua and the Torah, the amount of work done on these verses by Christian scholars is enormous. For bibliographies, consult the following:

Allison-Davies, *Matthew*, 3 vols. (in the *ICC* commentary), 1.502-3.
Donald Hagner, *Matthew* 2 vols. (in *The Word Bible Commentary*), 1.102.
John Nolland, *The Gospel of Matthew* (in the *NIGTC*), p. 216.

[2]See Samuel Byrskog, "Matthew 5:17–18 in the Argumentation of the Context," *Revue Biblique,* 104(4) (1997), 557–571.

2. "fulfilling" is further defined by the structure as "doing" the commandments and teaching others to do them
3. those who enjoy membership in the kingdom of Heaven are known for their righteousness
   a. the standard of righteousness is the eternal word of God: the Torah and Prophets
   b. the practical benchmark is the righteousness for which the scribes and Pharisees are known

The opening verse of this section therefore makes it clear that Yeshua did not consider His teaching to be at variance with Moses, and He did not ever want His talmidim to think that it did. To interpret the ensuing context (the so-called "antitheses") as though Yeshua was replacing the words of Torah with His own teaching is completely wrongheaded. As Allison-Davies remark:

> As the introduction or preamble to 5:21–48… it is intended to prevent the readers of the First Gospel from making two errors. First, it plainly states that the six subsequent paragraphs are not to be interpreted—as they have been so often by so many—as 'antitheses', 'antitheses' that, in at least two or three instances, set aside the Torah. Instead, Jesus upholds the law, so that between him and Moses there can be no real conflict. Then, secondly, and despite the concord declared by 5:17–19, 5:20 tells us that what Jesus requires of his followers surpasses what has traditionally been regarded (by the scribes and Pharisees) as the requirements of the Torah.[1]

[1]Allison-Davies, *Matthew,* 1.481-2.

Do not think that I came to abolish the Torah and the Prophets   The opening negative imperative (Μὴ νομίσητε from νομίζω, *nomizo*) is not rhetorical, as though it means "I surely hope no one thinks." These opening words of our Master rebuts a real misunderstanding. Apparently there were those who thought Yeshua was speaking against the Torah. But how could this have been the case? On what grounds would Yeshua have been so misunderstood as to require a clear and direct rebuttal to the misunderstanding?

Some have suggested that this opening phrase was redacted by Matthew in the post-destruction era, when the emerging Christian Church was moving toward an antinomian misunderstanding of the Master's words. They would point to any lack of the synoptic parallel to strengthen this approach. But we have similar language in Matt 10:34 ("Do not think that I came to bring peace on the earth; I did not come to bring peace, but a sword") which does have a synoptic parallel (Lk 12:51) and could therefore not be construed as entirely redactional by Matthew. It is far better, then, to see in these words the clear statement of our Master Who was rebutting some misunderstanding that had arisen over His teaching.

It is better to posit such a misunderstanding as springing from the fact that Yeshua was at variance with the standard or familiar interpretation of key Torah texts. In disagreeing with the authorities of His day over exactly how the Torah was to be interpreted and applied, He may have been accused of dismantling the rabbinic opinions and as such, would have been judged as abolishing the Torah. For the ruling interpretations of the Sages were considered necessary for the proper application of Torah. We read in *Perkei Avot* 3.11 a list of those who have no place in the world to come:

R. Eleazar the Modite says, "(1) He who treats Holy Things as secular, and (2) he who defiles the appointed times, (3) he who humiliates his fellow in public, (4) he who removes the signs of the covenant of Abraham, our father, (may he rest in peace), and (5) he who gives interpretations of Torah which are not according to oral halachah, even though he has in hand learning in Torah and good deeds, will have no share in the world to come.

It is this last item that interests us here: "he who gives interpretations of Torah which are not according to oral halachah" (הַמְגַלֶּה פָנִים בַּתּוֹרָה שֶׁלֹּא כַהֲלָכָה אַף עַל פִּי).[1] Here, changing the interpretation of a Torah text, and thus offering a radically different *halachah* based upon the reinterpretation, is considered an egregious error, equivalent with other crimes that cause a forfeiture of a place in the world to come. It is therefore understandable how Yeshua, giving as He does a different interpretation of Torah texts than did some of His contemporaries, might be accused of "abolishing" the Torah. Interestingly, later on Paul would also be accused of teaching against the Torah of Moses (Acts 21:21ff).

We may also compare the note included by Luke in his history of the Apostles (Acts 6:14):

> for we have heard him say that this Nazarene, Yeshua, will destroy this place and alter the customs which Moses handed down to us."

I came The "I have come/I came" sayings found in the Gospels speak to Yeshua's self understanding of His mission. We may note the following:

> Matt. 10:34 "Do not think that I came to bring peace on the earth; I did not come to bring peace, but a sword. (cf. Lk 12:51)
> Mark 1:38 He said to them, "Let us go somewhere else to the towns nearby, so that I may preach there also; for that is what I came for."
> Luke 12:49 "I have come to cast fire upon the earth; and how I wish it were already kindled!
> John 9:39 And Yeshua said, "For judgment I came into this world, so that those who do not see may see, and that those who see may become blind."
> John 10:10 "The thief comes only to steal and kill and destroy; I came that they may have life, and have it abundantly.
> John 12:27 "Now My soul has become troubled; and what shall I say, 'Father, save Me from this hour'? But for this purpose I came to this hour.
> John 12:46 "I have come as Light into the world, so that everyone who believes in Me will not remain in darkness.
> John 18:37 Therefore Pilate said to Him, "So You are a king?" Yeshua answered, "You say correctly that I am a king. For this I have been born, and for this I have come into the world, to testify to the truth. Everyone who is of the truth hears My voice."

In summary, Yeshua came:

1. To fulfill the Torah and the Prophets
2. To preach the goodnews of the kingdom
3. To bring judgment upon the earth

[1] The Kaufman manuscript has different wording here: וְהַמַּאֲדִים אֶת פְּנֵי חֲבֵירוֹ אפעל פִי, "and he who humiliates the face of his companion publicly," but this same idea is given earlier in the paragraph as well and is most likely a textual problem in the Kaufman manuscript. Note b.*Sanhedrin* 99a, המגלה פנים בתורה, "he who misinterprets the Torah."

4. To give abundant life to His sheep
5. To offer Himself as a sin offering
6. To bring light to those in darkness
7. To testify of the truth

In our immediate text, Yeshua's mission is to "fulfill the Torah and the Prophets." It may well be that this phrase is a broad description of all that His mission entailed.

to abolish   The Greek word is καταλύω (*kataluo*) which is used most often used to describe the destruction of physical things, such as buildings (Matt 24:2; Mk 13:2; Lk 21:6). The same verb is used to describe the words of Yeshua when He said, "Destroy this temple and in three days I will raise it up" (John 2:19; cp. Matt 26:61; 27:40; Mk 14:58; 15:29). The word is also used in the sense of "nullify" or "render ineffective," especially in reference to laws or decrees (cf. 2Macc 2.22; 4.11; 4Macc 5.33).

Some have suggested that by "abolish" Yeshua means "to wrongly interpret." Young is representative of this view:

> The word "abolish" means "to interpret incorrectly." In the Greek the word *kataluo* means "abolish," and its dynamic Hebrew equivalent *batel* is often used in contexts that deal with interpreting Scripture. One cancels Torah when it is misunderstood.[1]

While it may be true that misinterpretation was viewed by the Sages as equivalent to abolishing the Torah, it is not clear that the Hebrew word בַּטֵּל (*batel*) is the dynamic equivalent of Greek καταλύω. In the 40 times καταλύω is found in the Lxx, it never translates בַּטֵּל. In the seven times בַּטֵּל is found in the Tanach, most often it is translated by καταργέω (*katargeo*, "to nullify," "to become ineffective," cf. Ezra 4:21, 23-24; 5:5; 6:8) and once by ἀργέω (*argeo*, "to linger, stop," cf. Qoh 12:3). Granted, the use of בַּטֵּל in the Hebrew of the 1st Century may not be reflected by Lxx usage, and it is clear that the verb is found in rabbinic contexts discussing the undoing of rabbinic dictum (e.g., m.*Gittin* 4.1; b.*Avodah Zarah* 32b). Ultimately, the meaning in the sense of "abolish" is best learned from its opposite, "to fulfill." He did not come to render the Torah and the Prophets as useless for His talmidim, but to make the words of the inspired texts all the more applicable and real in their lives.

> This does not mean that Jesus was unaware of the fact that his arguments would seem unusual to some of the conformists of his day — but even in these cases he would by no means be described as an innovator. In order to prevent such an impression, he opened his exposition with a preamble (Mt. 5:17–20). His interpretation of the texts that follow this preamble may have appeared quite daring or unconventional to a number of his hearers. Nevertheless he begins by emphasizing that he did not come to undermine the meaning of the Torah by his exegesis, on the contrary he came to establish the true significance of the Torah and place it on firmer ground.[2]

the Torah and the Prophets   Here, the Greek noun νόμος (*nomos*) most certainly means "Torah," being used together with "Prophets" to denote the Tanach. Some of stressed that the lack of "Writings" (כְּתוּבוֹת, *ketuvot*) in the description of the Tanach indicates that Matthew was writing at a time before the canonization of the final section. Note that in Lk 24:44 all three are

[1] Brad Young, *Jesus the Jewish Theologian* (Hendrickson, 1995), p. 265. Note also Blizzard & Bivin, *Understanding the Difficult Words of Jesus* (Destiny Image, 1994), pp. 114-15 who take the same view.
See also the comments of David Flusser, *Judaism and the Origins of Christianity* Magnes Press, 1988), p. 504, n. 40.

[2] Flusser, Ibid., p. 495.

mentioned: "… that all things which are written about Me in the Torah of Moses and the Prophets and the Psalms must be fulfilled" (where "Moses" stands for the Torah and "Psalms" for the *Ketuvot* or Writings). But earlier in the chapter (24:27) we read: Then beginning with Moses and with all the prophets, He explained to them the things concerning Himself in all the Scriptures." Here, as elsewhere (cf. Matt 11:13; 22:40; Lk 16:16, 29, 31; John 1:45), the common phrase "Torah and Prophets" stands for the entire Tanach.

But why does Yeshua include the word "Prophets" here? In the next verse, He speaks only of the Torah without mentioning the Prophets. It is possible that the word "Torah" is used broadly in v. 18 to include all of Scripture. More probable, however, is the idea that by including "Prophets" in the opening verse of the section, Yeshua intended to emphasize the "fulfillment" aspect of His ministry. Allison-Davies suggest this as the reason why the word "Prophets" is included:

> But there here must, we fancy, be an important motive. And it is probably this: for Matthew, who has seen in the coming of Jesus Messiah the fulfilment of the OT prophecies, not only is the prophetic portion of the Scriptures no less important than the five books of Moses, but 'the law and the prophets' together constitute in his eyes a united prophetic witness: 'the prophets and the law prophesied until John' (11:13). So Matthew cannot simply let it be said the Jesus fulfilled the law or that Jesus fulfilled the prophets: he must tell us that he fufilled both.[1]

but to fulfill   As everyone recognizes, the meaning given to the verb "to fulfill" (πληρόω, *pleroo*) in our verse is key to understanding the entire section. For if Yeshua clearly did not come to abolish the Torah and the Prophets, but to "fulfill" them, in understanding what He means by "fulfill" we discover a central emphasis of His mission and work.[2]

It has been a fairly standard Christian understanding to interpret the meaning of "fulfill" here as "to finish, to complete." The interpretation of the verse is then that Yeshua fulfilled the Torah in every way and as a result, it not longer is a functioning component of God's will in the lives of Christians. While its precepts and wisdom are still valuable, the Torah has ceased to have direct application to the life of faith for followers of Yeshua. If our verse stood in isolation of any larger context, such an interpretation of the word "fulfill" would be within the realm of possibilities. But such a meaning cannot stand here, for the obvious reason that the following verses (which are explanatory of the opening verse), Yeshua clearly admonishes His talmidim to "do" and to "teach" the Torah. Moreover, the appeal to the enduring creative order ("until heaven and earth pass away") makes no sense if in this opening verse Yeshua has declared the Torah and Prophets to be finished. Furthermore, the fact that "fulfill" must append not only to the Torah but also to the Prophets renders this interpretation impossible. No one would claim that the words of the Prophets have been "finished" in the sense of no longer having an active and direct application to the lives of believers.

Others note that most often in the Apostolic Scriptures, the verb *pleroo* is used in the fulfillment formula introducing prophecy: "that the words of the prophet X might be fulfilled" (or similar verbiage), and that it should be so interpreted here. Carson is representative:

> The best interpretation of these difficult verses says that Jesus fulfills

[1] Allison-Davies, *Matthew*, 1.484.

[2] For a fuller discussion on the meaning of "fulfill" in Matt 5:17, see my paper "What Does Πληρόω Mean in Matthew 5:17" available at www.torahresource.com.

the Law and the Prophets in that they point to him, and he is their fulfillment. The antithesis is not between "abolish" and "keep" but between "abolish" and "fulfill." 'For Matthew, then, it is not the question of Jesus' relation to the Law that is in doubt but rather its relation to him!'... Therefore we give *pleroo* ("fulfill") exactly the same meaning as in the formula quotations, which in the prologue (Matt 1–2) have already laid great stress on the prophetic nature of the OT and the way it points to Jesus.[1]

[1]Carson, *Matthew*, pp. 143-44.

There is a significant problem, however, with this interpretation, and that is simply that in the quotation formula, the verb "fulfill" is always in the passive mood: "that the words of prophet X *might be fulfilled.*" Yeshua, however, does not say that the Torah and Prophets are "fufilled" (passive) in Him, but rather that He came "to fulfill" (active) them.

Of course, there is surely the sense that all of God's purposes find their fulfillment in Yeshua: "For as many as are the promises of God, in Him [Yeshua] they are yes; therefore also through Him is our Amen to the glory of God through us" (2Cor 1:20). But to understand "fulfill" in our verse as entirely enveloped in the work of Yeshua Himself does not fit with the following context. For there He admonishes His talmidim both "to do" and "to teach" the Torah, meaning that His having come to "fulfill" the Torah is seen in the way the Torah would be active in their lives and the lives of those they would teach.

A number of commentators[2] have pointed to the fact that the Hebrew term that most likely stands behind the Greek *pleroo* is the hifil of קוּם, i.e., הָקִים (*qum, haqiym*). The verb *qum* has the meaning "to arise, get up, stand up" and in the hifil "to erect, establish, confirm." We find this form of *qum* used regularly in covenant contexts of the Tanach. For example, God promises to "establish" a covenant with Noah (Gen 6:18; 9:9, 11, 17), with Abraham (Gen 17:7, 9), with Isaac (Gen 17:21; 26:3), and with Israel (Ex 6:4). In each of these examples, the hifil form of *qum* is used. This regular use of the verb *qum* to mean "establish, confirm" is thus believed to be the background for Yeshua's use of *pleroo* in our verse, thus to give the meaning, "I came to establish or confirm the Torah and the Prophets." However, a significant problem with this view is that in the Lxx, *pleroo* never is used to translate the verb *qum*. Moreover, *pleroo* is most often used to translate the Hebrew verb מָלֵא (*mala'*), "to be full, to fill up, to complete something."[3] Further, (so it is argued), the verb *mala'* is not used in the sense of "establish" or "confirm."

[2]Note Brad Young, *Jesus the Jewish Theologian*, p. 265.

[3]The DuTillet has מלא in 5:17 as does the Münster. The Even Bohan has: אל חחשבו שבאתי להפר תורה אלא להשלים, using the hifil of שָׁלַם, "to complete."

If we do place weight upon the Lxx use of *pleroo* as the normal translation for *mala'*, "to be full, fill up, complete," and thus postulate that our Master used this Hebrew word when He proclaimed His purpose to "fulfill" the Torah and the Prophets, there remains the question whether *mala'* can have the sense of "establish or confirm," a meaning that would best fit the overall context of our passage. And in fact, there are several instances where *mala'* does have this meaning.

Note Jer 44:25:

'As for you and your wives, you have spoken with your mouths and fulfilled it (מלא) with your hands, saying, "We will certainly perform our vows that we have vowed, to burn sacrifices to the queen of heaven and pour out drink offerings to her." Go ahead and confirm (קום) your vows, and certainly perform (עשה) your vows!'

What is striking in this text is the combined use of מָלֵא and עָשָׂה ("to do"), which exactly parallel πληρόω (*pleroo*) and ποιέω (*poieo*, "to do") in Matthew 5:17-20. In the Jeremiah passage it is clear that to "fulfill" with one's hands what has been spoken by the mouth is to "perform" the vow and thus to "confirm" (הֵקִים) it.

Another text also uses the verb *mala'* in the sense of "establish" or "confirm" — 1Ki 1:13–14. Here, Adonijah has declared himself king at the prospect of David's soon demise. The prophet Nathan goes to Bathsheba and alerts her of the situation, and then gives his counsel:

> "Go at once to King David and say to him, 'Have you not, my lord, O king, sworn to your maidservant, saying, "Surely Solomon your son shall be king after me, and he shall sit on my throne"? Why then has Adonijah become king?' "Behold, while you are still there speaking with the king, I will come in after you and confirm (מלא) your words."

Once again, the use of *mala'* in connection with one's words takes on the sense of "confirm" or "make more certain."

In both of these instances (Jer 44:25, 1Ki 1:14), the Lxx translates the Hebrew *mala'* with *pleroo*, the same verb used in our Matthew text. It seems entirely warranted, then, to understand *pleroo*, "to fulfill" in our text to mean "establish, confirm." Not only is there good lexical warrant for interpreting *pleroo* in this manner, but it also fits well with the following context. Yeshua's purpose in terms of the Torah was to bring it back to its original intention, and thus to "establish or confirm" it in the lives of His talmidim. For through the many rabbinic fences that had been added to the written Torah, it had become so encumbered as often to be a burden. What is more, having adopted the theology that Jewish status was the basis for righteousness before God, the rabbis had shifted the Torah from its original purpose to that of establishing their Jewish identity. Yeshua's purpose was to unravel the Torah from the web of man-made laws, and bring it back to its original purpose—to aid, protect, and guide the people of God, and to constantly bring them to a greater reliance upon and faith in Him.

We may thus understand our verse in this way:

> "Do not think that I have come to render the Torah and Prophets in any manner as ineffectual. On the contrary, I have not come to render them ineffectual, but to confirm their words and establish them in your lives."

18 For truly I say to you, until heaven and earth pass away, not the smallest letter or stroke shall pass from the Torah until all is accomplished.

The opening "For" (γάρ, *gar*) connects this verse to the former as giving further support for the claim that Yeshua did not come to subvert the Torah. Luke (16:17) has: "But it is easier for heaven and earth to pass away than for one stroke of a letter of the Torah to fail (πίπτω, *pipto,* "to fall")."

In seeking the general meaning of our verse, it becomes clear that there are some obvious parallels with the previous statement of our Master.

v. 17	v. 18
to abolish (καταλύω)	to pass away (παρέχομαι)
Torah and Prophets	Torah
all is fulfilled (πληρόω)	all is accomplished (γίνομαι)

In this way, v. 18 helps to clarify, amplify, and emphasize the statement of v. 17. "To abolish" is explained as "to pass away." The earlier "Torah and Prophets" is now narrowed to "Torah," showing that the Torah is, in fact, the foundation upon which the Prophets exist. "Fulfill" is further explained as "accomplished" or "performed."

The opening words of our verse introduce us to a repeated phrase used by our Master, i.e., the use of "amen" (translated "truly" by most English versions) with "I say" as introducing an emphatic statement: ἀμὴν γὰρ λέγω ὑμῖν, literally, "For amen I say to you." In Matthew, the use of ἀμήν (*amen*) as an introductory emphatic term (always with "I say to you") is found 30 additional times (5:26; 6:2, 5, 16; 8:10; 10:15, 23, 42; 11:11; 13:17; 16:28; 17:20; 18:3, 13, 18-19; 19:23, 28; 21:21, 31; 23:36; 24:2, 34, 47; 25:12, 40, 45; 26:13, 21, 34). Mark has the phrase 14 times (1 is disputed textually), and Luke 6 times. John always uses the double "amen, amen" ("truly, truly"), 25 times. The Greek ἀμήν is a loanword from Hebrew אָמֵן (*'amein*) which is most often used as a response in an oath ceremony or as a liturgical response. The double "amen and amen" is found at the end of each of the first three books of the Psalter (Ps 41:13; 72:19; 89:52). The primary meaning of the Hebrew term is linked to the verb אָמַן (*aman*) meaning "to be firm, trustworthy, or safe." The hifil stem of אָמַן connotes "faithfulness," "to trust," and "to be trustworthy" while the nifil connotes "to be permanent," "to endure." Thus, the noun אָמֵן (*'amein*) generally means "surely!" as a solemn affirmation validating an oath, especially in covenant contexts.

The use of "amen" as an affirmation of one's own teaching, however, finds scant parallels outside of its use by Yeshua in the Gospels. Some have suggested that Yeshua utilized "amen" in order to avoid using an oath, but this finds little support in any parallel literature.[1] Moreover, in rabbinic literature, responding with "yes" (= "amen") is equivalent to an oath, and using the double "yes, yes" (cf. Matt 5:37 and the constant use of "amen, amen" in the Gospel of John) also constitutes an oath.[2]

Chilton[3] has suggested that the Greek *amen* in the "I say" formula of Yeshua derives from an original Aramaic בְּקוּשְׁטָא (*beiqusheita*) meaning "in truth," which was translated into the Greek as *amen.* However, the Peshitta has *amein* in this place, as does the DuTillet. The Even Bohan does have באמת אני אומר לכם ("In truth I say to you") while the Münster has the double *amen,*

[1]"That Jesus' command not to swear played any part in its use is nowhere indicated." (Schlier, "אמן" in *TDNT,* 1.337); "That 'amen' has anything to do with Jesus' avoidance of oaths seems unlikely." (Allison-Davies, *Matthew,* 1.490).

[2]cf. b.*Shevuot* 36a. Also note the work of David Daube, *The New Testament and Rabbinic Judaism,* pp. 388ff.

[3]Bruce Chilton, "'Amen'—an Approach through Syriac Gospels," *ZNW* 69 (1978), pp. 203–11.

[1]Scheiler, Op. cit., 1.338.

אמן אמן אני אמר לכם. While Chilton's suggestion is interesting, it finds little support in the extant manuscripts.

More than likely, our Master's use of the phrase "amen I say to you" derives from an increased use of "amen" in liturgical settings of the Hellenistic period, and is used for emphasis. But not merely a literary emphasis, but more akin to an equivalent "Thus says Adonai" found so often in the Tanach. When Yeshua says "amen I say to you," He is not only claiming to be God's prophetic spokesman, but He is affirming His own authority as the Messiah of God, Who speaks with divine authority. Consider Matt 24:35: "Heaven and earth will pass away, but My words will not pass away."

> Thus in the ἀμήν (amen) preceding the λέγω ὑμῖν ("I say to you") of Jesus we have the whole Christology *in nuce* ("in a nutshell"). The one who accepts His word as true and certain is also the one who acknowledges and affirms it in his own life and thus causes it, as fulfilled by him, to become a demand to others.[1]

The argument of our Master in the current verse, then, is that His coming could not be to invalidate the Torah since the Torah itself is inviolable: "not the smallest letter or stroke will fall from the Torah." As the incarnate One, Yeshua came in submission to the Torah, not as standing above it (cf. Gal 4:4). Both in word and deed He affirms what the Psalmist declares: "Forever, O LORD, Your word is settled in heaven" (Ps 119:89).

We may consider the parallel use of the created universe as a standard of permanency in the Tanach. Thus, the language employed to demonstrate that the Davidic covenant is eternal utilizes the created order:

> His [David's] descendants shall endure forever and his throne as the sun before Me. It shall be established forever like the moon, and the witness in the sky is faithful." Selah. (Ps 89:36–37)

> "Thus says the LORD, 'If you can break My covenant for the day and My covenant for the night, so that day and night will not be at their appointed time, then My covenant may also be broken with David My servant so that he will not have a son to reign on his throne, and with the Levitical priests, My ministers. (Jer. 33:20–21)

Consider as well Psalm 148:3–6

> Praise Him, sun and moon; Praise Him, all stars of light! Praise Him, highest heavens, and the waters that are above the heavens! Let them praise the name of the LORD, for He commanded and they were created. He has also established them forever and ever; He has made a decree which will not pass away.

Likewise, the inviolability of the covenant made with Israel is described in terms of the created world by Jeremiah:

> Thus says the LORD, Who gives the sun for light by day and the fixed order of the moon and the stars for light by night, Who stirs up the sea so that its waves roar; the LORD of hosts is His name: "If this fixed order departs from before Me," declares the LORD, "Then the offspring of Israel also will cease from being a nation before Me forever." (Jer 31:35–36)

It is often remarked that though the Tanach uses the created universe as a standard for eternal viability, Yeshua is well aware that the present heavens and earth will be destroyed, as noted above in His words that "Heaven and earth will pass away, but My words will not pass away" (Matt 24:35). Peter also reiterates what must have been an accepted teaching of his day:

> But the day of the Lord will come like a thief, in which the heavens will pass away with a roar and the elements will be destroyed with intense heat, and the earth and its works will be burned up. (2Pet 3:10)

On the basis of Matt 24:35, Allison-Davies conclude:

> Mt 5:18b, like 24:35 par., envisions the end of the heaven and earth (without stating the manner of their passing)… The law—in contrast to Jesus' words…therefore only endures until the heavens and earth are gone. It is not eternal.[1]

Hagner, who takes a similar view, though he rightly emphasizes the enduring viability of the Torah for the current age:

> The words of the first clause… "until heaven and earth pass away," are not simply a popular way of saying "never"…. They refer instead to the end of time as we know it and the beginning of eschatology proper, that is, the time of the regeneration of the created order…. In other words, the law, as interpreted by Jesus, will remain valid until the close of the age.[2]

However, the idea that Yeshua knew of the eventual passing of the heavens and the earth (Matt 24:35) does not mean that in the verse under investigation He intends to teach that the Torah has a limited span of viability. The context, along with the parallels given above from the Tanach, would emphasize that the point of our Master's words is the eternal inviolability of the Torah. Montefiore makes this point well:

> …some commentators do not seem to understand what the divineness of the Law means. It is all very well for a modern critic with his comfortable distinctions between letter and spirit, human element and divine element, and so on. These were quite unknown in Jewish society in the age of Christ. If you believed that the Law was divine, you believed that it was all divine, and not only a few sentences here and there; you took the Law at its own valuation. The Law does not claim to be divine here and human there, permanent in one place and transitory in another. It is *all* divine and *all* permanent. God ordered the Jews not to eat rabbits every bit as much as He ordered them not to murder or to commit adultery. He ordered them not to wear a garment of linen and woollen every bit as much as He ordered them to show justice and pity to the orphan and the widow. If Jesus showed any hesitation in admitting this, or rather if his teaching was even inconsistent with it, the Rabbis, with their acute logic, could easily have exposed him. But I fancy that Jesus would hardly have agreed with some of the things which are said about him.[3]

The fact that the rabbis also seem to be inconsistent regarding the eternal nature of the Torah, and that some even appear to teach that the Torah

[1] Allison-Davies, *Matthew*, 1.490.

[2] Hagner, *Matthew*, p. 107.

[3] C. G. Montefiore, *The Synoptic Gospels* 2 vols. (Macmillan, 1909), 2.490.

(or parts of it) would be abolished in the Messianic Age, is often noted by commentators on our text. Note the following:

> The Tanna debe Eliyyahu teaches: The world is to exist six thousand years. In the first two thousand there was desolation; two thousand years the Torah flourished; and the next two thousand years is the Messianic era, but through our many iniquities all these years have been lost. (b.*Sanhedrin* 97b).

In this text, however, the ages are divided as 2000 years from creation to the time when Abraham was 52 years old and began to convert pagans to the worship of the true God, 2000 years from Abraham's 52nd year to 172 years after the destruction of the Temple, and the final 2000 years is the period in which the Messiah would appear. But this rabbinic saying does not imply that the Torah ceases, only that the giving of the Torah to Abraham was a distinguishing factor in identifying the subsequent era.

> Our Rabbis taught: A garment in which kil'ayim (mixture) was lost (could not be extracted) may not be sold to an idolater, nor may one make of it a packsaddle for an ass, but it may be made into a shroud for a corpse. R. Joseph observed: This implies that the commandments will be abolished in the Hereafter. Said Abaye (or as some say R. Dimi) to him: But did not R. Manni in the name of R. Jannai state, 'This was learnt only in regard to the time of the lamentations but for burial this is forbidden'? — The other replied: But was it not stated in connection with it, 'R. Johanan ruled: Even for burial'? And thereby R. Johanan followed his previously expressed view, for R. Johanan stated: 'What is the purport of the Scriptural text, Free among the dead? (Ps 88:6) As soon as a man dies he is free from the commandments'. (b. *Niddah* 61b)

The discussion relates to a forbidden garment containing wool and flax. Since it is ruled as usable for a shroud in which to bury the dead, the conclusion is that "the commandments will be abolished in the Hereafter" (לְעָתִיד לָבָא). But the context seems to imply that the "Hereafter" does not refer necessarily to the Messianic Age,[1] but to the period between a person's death and his resurrection. The conclusion is that a dead person is free from the commandments (cp. Rom 7:1).

On the other hand, there are clear statements of the rabbis regarding the eternality of the Torah:

> AND THE HEAVEN AND THE EARTH WERE FINISHED-WAYYEKULLU (II, 1). I have seen an end to every purpose (*tiklah*), but Your commandment is exceeding broad (Ps 119:96): everything has a measure, heaven and earth have a measure, except one thing which has no measure: and what is it? The Torah, [of which it is written,] The measure thereof is longer than the earth, etc. (Job 11:9). (Mid. Rabbah *Genesis*10.1)[2]

The point of all this discussion, as it relates to the words of Yeshua in our text, is that He taught the unchanging nature of the Torah. The fact that He uses the created order as a standard for the inviolability of the Torah, and later (Matt 24:35) speaks of His own words existing even when the heavens and earth pass away, should not be so tightly drawn together, as though He

[1]See W. D. Davies, *Torah in the Messianic Age and/or the Age to Come* (SBL, 1952), p. 80 for further discussion on this text. The whole work is an in depth discussion of the rabbinic view of the permanence of the Torah.

[2]Note also Mid. Rab. *Exodus* 6.1, "...no letter shall ever be abolished from the Torah...."

is saying that when the heavens and earth pass away, the Torah will likewise pass away. In our current text, the emphasis is upon the eternal nature of the Torah as the indestructible word of God.

not the smallest letter or stroke (ἰῶτα ἓν ἢ μία κεραία)   The "smallest letter" translates Greek ἰῶτα (*iota*), which represented the Hebrew *yod* to a Greek speaking audience. The *yod* is the smallest letter in the Hebrew Aleph-beit when written in the square, Aramaic script, which has been shown to have been well established in the 1st Century.[1]

An interesting rabbinic tale regarding the *yod* is found in the midrash:

> When God gave the Torah to Israel, He inserted therein positive and negative commands and gave some commandments for a king, as it says: Only he shall not multiply horses to himself... Neither shall he multiply (יִרְבֶּה) wives to himself, that his heart turn not away; neither silver and gold (Deut. 17:16-17). But Solomon arose and studied the reason of God's decree, saying: 'Why did God command, "He shall not multiply wives to himself?" Is it not "That his heart turn not away"? Well, I will multiply and still my heart will not turn away. Our Sages said: At that time, the *yod* of the word *yarbeh* went up on high and prostrated itself before God and said: 'Master of the Universe! Have You not said that no letter shall ever be abolished from the Torah? Behold, Solomon has now arisen and abolished one. Who knows? Today he has abolished one letter, tomorrow he will abolish another until the whole Torah will be nullified?' God replied: 'Solomon and a thousand like him will pass away, but the smallest tittle (קוֹצָה) will not be erased from you.' (Mid. Rab. *Exodus* 6.1)[2]

The Greek word translated "stroke" is κεραία (*keraia*), which has been various interpreted. A popular understanding is that it refers to the crown or *keter* that was placed on various letters. These did not affect the meaning of the words, and thus it is taught that even the scribal embellishments to the text would be preserved. However, it is quite certain that this is a later scribal phenomenon, something that was not extant in the 1st Century.[3] More likely, the combination of *iota* and *keraia* should be understood as an hendiadys meaning "the smallest stroke of the smallest letter."[4] Not only is our Master affirming the eternal nature of the written Torah, He is doing so in the strongest of ways. The rabbis affirm this same perspective:

> It is written [Lev. 22:32] לֹא תְחַלְּלוּ אֶת-שֵׁם קָדְשִׁי Ye shall not profane my holy name: whosoever shall change ח into ה, destroys the world [for then לֹא תְהַלְּלוּ written with ה, makes this sense, Ye shall not 'praise' my holy name.] It is written [Ps. 150:6] כֹּל הַנְּשָׁמָה תְּהַלֵּל יָהּ Let every spirit praise the Lord: whosoever changeth ה into ח destroys the world. [It would read "Let every spirit profane the Lord."] It is written [Jer. 5:12], כִּחֲשׁוּ בַּיהוה They lied against the Lord: whosoever changeth ב into כ destroys the world. [It would read "Like the Lord they lied."] It is written [Deut. 6:4], יהוה אֱלֹהֵינוּ יהוה אֶחָד , The Lord our God is one Lord: he that changeth ד into ר, destroys the world. [It would read "The Lord our God is another Lord."] (Midrash Tanchuma B'reishit 1)

until all is accomplished   The way this is translated it sounds as though when "all" (πᾶς, *pas*) is accomplished, then matters of the Torah would pass away. But this is not necessarily the force of the conjunction ἕως (*heos*,

[1]The Nash papyri, dated to the early 1st Century, is written in the square letters.

[2]Rashi understands the קוֹצָה to describe the small prick on the top of the *yod*, (comments to b.*Menachot* 29a, see Jastrow, *Lexicon*, p. 1340).

[3]See Tobias Lachs, *Rabbinic Commentary*, p. 88.

[4]This is Lach's suggestion which I find convincing.

"until"). The Lxx regularly translates עַד, *'ad*, "as far as, unto, until" with the word ἕως, and sometimes the Hebrew עַד can have the sense of "with a view toward" or "resulting in" (e.g., Ps 110:1). While the first "until" ("until heaven and earth pass away") may well have its normal temporal sense, the same word in the final clause ("until all is accomplished") may bear the sense of "resulting in." Thus, "with the result that all is accomplished."

The almost identical phrase is found in Matt 24:34, "Truly I say to you, this generation will not pass away until all these things take place" (ἕως ἄν πάντα ταῦτα γένηται). The emphasis here is not to describe when the generation will pass away, but upon the fact that those things spoken of will be accomplished within that generation. In similar fashion, Yeshua describes the eternal nature of the Torah which results in the accomplishment of all that God wills to be done through it.

all is accomplished   γένηται (from γίνομαι, *ginomai*, "to be, exist, happen") is parallel to the previous "fulfilled" of v. 17. God has a purpose in the Torah, and it is linked by our Master to the prophets, for He speaks initially of "the Torah and the Prophets." Nothing will stand in the way of God's purpose in regard to the Torah, for the Torah embodies the eternal covenant made with His chosen people, and the Prophets have spoken the word of Adonai through which He accomplishes all of His holy will.

19 Whoever then annuls one of the least of these commandments, and teaches others to do the same, shall be called least in the kingdom of heaven; but whoever keeps and teaches them, he shall be called great in the kingdom of heaven.

The English has the word "then" — "Whoever then annuls." The Greek term is οὖν, *oun*, "therefore," and once again links this verse to the previous context.

> Within the present context of Matthew, 5:19 follows well upon 5:18: if the law remains valid even down to its jots and tittles, then it must be practised and taught in its entirety. A liberal attitude towards the law is not in order; all antinomian tendencies are excluded.[1]

Once again, we see a close parallel to the previous verses:

v. 17	v. 18	v. 19
to abolish	pass away	annul/teach
Torah and Prophets	Torah	commandments
fulfill	accomplished	do/teach

These parallels continue to aid us in understanding our Master's words. The idea of abolishing the Torah is to act as though it has passed away (cease to exist), and thus to annul the effect of the commandments. Conversely, to fulfill is to live in the context of God's purpose to accomplish His will through the Torah, and thus to obey it ("do") and teach others to do likewise.

[1]Allison-Davies, *Matthew*, p. 496.

The logic of our Master continues straight forward: since the Torah and the Prophets are the eternal word of God, nothing of them can fail or be overturned. Moreover, since the Torah and Prophets constitute the unchanging word of the unchanging God, each part is important—nothing is superfluous. Every word, indeed, every letter is one with the whole, meaning that as God revealed His truth through the written word, all of it stands equally important (cf. James 2:10). From this, then, the only logical conclusion one may reach is that for anyone to speak of the Torah and Prophets otherwise, that is, as unimportant or irrelevant, is to contradict God Himself.[1]

Moreover, the present verse proves beyond doubt that the phrase "until all is accomplished" of the previous verse could not have been envisioned by Yeshua as having already occurred, for if such were the case, there would have been no reason to enjoin obedience to the Torah upon His disciples.

The parallelism of our verse is quite apparent, for Yeshua presents the two halves of our verse in terms of a clear contrast. We may represent this parallel graphically as follows:

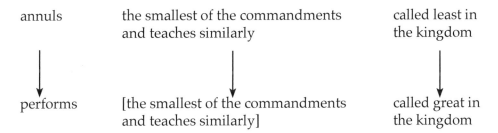

annuls   the smallest of the commandments   called least in
and teaches similarly   the kingdom

performs   [the smallest of the commandments   called great in
and teaches similarly]   the kingdom

For our Master, the opposite of "annul" (λύω, *luo*, which hearkens back to καταλύω, *kataluo* of v. 17) is "to do" (ποιέω, *poieo*), even as the opposite of "least in the kingdom of heaven" is "great in the kingdom of heaven." This parallelism, then, helps us understand what is meant by "annul." Those who annul a commandment do so by failing to observe or obey it, and by teaching others to likewise disregard it. The verb λύω (*luo*) means "to loose," "to unbind," and by extension "to destroy." In terms of a commandment or law, "to loose" it is to take away its binding character—to render it irrelevant or incapable of exacting a penalty—to wipe it from the law books. Some may argue that this is exactly what Yeshua did in His sacrificial death, that He removed the ability of the Torah to condemn sinners, to mete out a penalty for disobeying it. Surely it is true that the substitutionary death of our Messiah rendered those who are "in Him" free from the condemnation of the Torah, but He did so, not by annulling the Torah, but by taking upon Himself the full penalty prescribed by the Torah for transgressors. Indeed, if it would have been possible for God to simply annul the Torah, then there would have been no reason for Yeshua to have died. Instead of bearing the penalty of the Torah for His people, it could have simply been annulled, rendered ineffective, and done away with, meaning there would have been no need for satisfying its righteous demands. In fact, it is the eternal viability of the Torah (based as it is upon the unchanging nature of God Himself) that requires payment for sin, and thus the death of Yeshua as our sin offering substantiates the eternal nature of the Torah rather than annuls it, for it is the Torah itself that requires death as the wages for sin (e.g., Gen 2:17; Ezek 18:3, 20; cf. Rom 6:23).

But since Yeshua has already taught that the Torah is eternal and unchangeable, His statement here is not suggesting that one can actual annul

[1]Some commentators wonder at the use of the demonstrative "these" (τούτων) in the phrase "the least of these commandments, and question the to which commandments Yeshua refers. Some have concluded that He refers to His own commandments, as demonstrated by the following context (the so-called "antitheses"). But the demonstrative ("these") in Matthew never looks forward, but always references that to which mention has already been made. Moreover, the context, and the connectives (ὀυν) make it clear that "these commandments" refers to those enumerated by even the smallest stroke and letter of the Torah.

any commandment, but that in living as though it were annulled, and teaching others accordingly, that person would be rendered least in the kingdom of heaven. In other words, despite the efforts of some to diminish the relevance of the Torah both for themselves and for others, it remains forever the revelation of God's righteous standards.

[1]Quoted from Allison-Davies, *Matthew*, 1.497.

To "be called" least in the kingdom of heaven is not merely a matter of designation, but a statement of reality. When God "calls" someone least or greatest, He is stating what is true, what is actually the case, and so "called" is the functional equivalent of "to be." In this way, the double use of "least" ("least commandment / least in the kingdom") is a play on terms. As Bengel notes, "As we treat the word of God, so does God treat us."[1]

It is possible that by "annul" Yeshua may well be referring to the manner in which some of the Sages rendered aspects of the Torah irrelevant or beyond the reach of the common man by their layers of tradition. In Mark 7 we hear our Master saying:

> "Neglecting (ἀφίημι) the commandment of God, you hold to the tradition of men." … He was also saying to them, "You are experts at setting aside (ἀθετέω) the commandment of God in order to keep your tradition" (Mk 7:8–9, cf. Matt 15:6).

And further on in this same narrative we read Yeshua's assessment of the Pharisaic teachers:

> thus invalidating (ἀκουρόω) the word of God by your tradition which you have handed down; and you do many things such as that (Mk 7:13)

Thus, annulling a commandment may occur not only by those who entirely disregard it, but also by those who would misinterpret it, or even replace it with other religious or man-made laws.

A difficulty arises in trying to understand the contrastive "least/great in the kingdom of heaven" in our Master's teaching. Is Yeshua saying that even those who annul commandments will be received into the kingdom, though occupying a lower rank than those who do the commandments? It seems difficult to reckon such an understanding with v. 20, in which one's righteousness must exceed that of the scribes and Pharisees in order to enter the kingdom. Yet we should consider the fact that the scribes and Pharisees represented two conflicting realities. On the one hand, they were clearly known for their zealous attention to the Torah and to its most minute details. That is the commendable aspect to which Yeshua refers. On the other hand, in seeking to make the Torah manageable, they instituted means by which one could be credited with keeping the Torah while in fact, disregarding it. That is, through the rulings of their traditions they set aside some of the commandments. Moreover, in doing so, they betrayed a motivation for obedience that was less than sterling, a motivation more concerned with appearance before men than before the Almighty (cf. Matt 23:5). But this is a general fault of fallen mankind in general. It was just that the scribes and Pharisees were a very ready example for out Master to use in His teaching.

We should not, however, miss the primary point of our Master's teaching here, which is to emphasize the call to wholehearted obedience to the whole Torah, motivated from a heart of love to God. He is not offering various "seating assignments" in the kingdom, as though some will be in "box seats" and others in the "bleachers." Those who truly desire to honor Him will strive to be great in the kingdom by doing all in their power to obey even the least of the commandments. No true child of the King would set it as his goal to be least in the kingdom. True "sons of the kingdom" (cf. Matt 8:12; 13:38) love God with all the heart, soul, and might (Deut 6:4ff). That to which Yeshua is therefore calling His disciples is a radical obedience that flows from a heart of love to God and then to one's neighbor. He is making it clear that to be His disciple is an all or nothing proposition.

But are there various ranks in the kingdom of heaven? Or to say it differently, will some be rewarded more than others? The answer seems to be "yes," though it is by no means certain that varying rewards create a difference in rank for eternity. Several passages in Matthew may be noted:

> He who receives a prophet in the name of a prophet shall receive a prophet's reward; and he who receives a righteous man in the name of a righteous man shall receive a righteous man's reward. And whoever in the name of a disciple gives to one of these little ones even a cup of cold water to drink, truly I say to you, he shall not lose his reward. (Matt 10:41–42)

> He said to them, "My cup you shall drink; but to sit on My right and on My left, this is not Mine to give, but it is for those for whom it has been prepared by My Father. (Matt 20:23)

We may also note the mention of rewards in John's second epistle and the apocalypse:

> Watch yourselves, that you do not lose what we have accomplished, but that you may receive a full reward. (2John 8)

> Behold, I am coming quickly, and My reward is with Me, to render to every man according to what he has done. (Rev 22:12)

The idea of varying rewards in the world to come is well attested in the rabbinic literature as well.

> He said to him: 'You saw a well regulated world.' [He asked further]: 'In what condition did you see us [students]?' He replied: 'As our esteem is here, so it is there. I also [he continued] heard them saying, Happy he who comes here in full possession of his learning. I also heard them saying, No creature can attain to the place [in heaven] assigned to the martyrs of the [Roman] Government.' Who are these? Shall I say R. Akiba and his comrades? Had they no other merit but this? Obviously even without this [they would have attained this rank]. What is meant therefore must be the martyrs of Lud. (b.*Bava Batra* 10b)

> R. Jeremiah questioned R. Zera: What is meant by, The small and great are there [in the next world]; and the servant is free from his master? (Job 3:19) Do we then not know that 'the small and great are there'? — But [it means that] he who humbles himself for the sake of the Torah in this world is magnified in the next; and he who makes himself a servant to the [study of the] Torah in this world becomes free in the next. (b.*Bava Metzia* 85b)

Thus, it seems most probable that Yeshua, while teaching His disciples to strive to be great in the kingdom of heaven through living out the commandments and teaching others to do the same, recognized that there would be those who were "least" in the kingdom, who, though living in obedience to the weightier matters of the Torah, fail to take account of the "least" of the commandments as well. But by acknowledging that there would be some who, though called the least, were nonetheless *bona fide* members of the kingdom of Heaven, Yeshua does not diminish His requirement that His disciples should strive to be great in the kingdom by being careful to obey even the least of the commandments.

The fact that Yeshua can speak of the "least of these commandments" (τῶν ἐντολῶν τούτων τῶν ἐλαχίστων) reminds us that there was an ongoing rabbinic exercise in the categorizing of the commandments in the 1st Century and perhaps earlier. Indeed, the evaluation of the commandments was a significant topic in early Judaisms, if the subsequent literature (Mishnah, *midrashim*, Talmuds) is any indication. As Urbach shows, there were various viewpoints among the Sages.

> The question of the relative value of the commandments found expression in many varied forms in the teaching of the Sages. On the one hand we find dicta that proclaim the absolute equality of all the precepts, and on the other we encounter clear distinctions drawn between more important and less important commandments, and methods of classifying precepts and transgressions according to various criteria.[1]

Various Sages and schools gave different criteria of evaluation for the commandments. For instance, Rav Judah (3rd Century Amora), commenting on m.*Shevuot* 1.6, says:

> This is the meaning ... the light (transgressions) are those involving positive or negative commandments; and the grave (transgressions) are those punished by "extinction" or death by sentence of the court.[2]

Thus, he based the criteria for valuation of the *mitzvot* on the severity of the penalty that the transgressions entail.

R. ben 'Azzai (2nd Century Tanna) saw it differently. On the verse "Only be steadfast in not eating the blood ... " (1Sam 14:34) he remarked:

> Now there are three hundred[3] similar positive precepts in the Torah! It comes to teach us, therefore, that if in regard to blood, than which there is no lighter precept among all the commandments, Scripture admonished you thus, how much more so in the case of the other precepts.[4]

Urbach explains:

> The eating of the blood is something repulsive; consequently it is easy to abstain from it. Lightness and stringency are not measured by the extent of the reward or punishment involved in doing the precept or transgression, but according to the effort required to fulfill the commandments or to refrain from the transgressions. So, too, a precept not entailing expenditure of money, or involving danger to life, is called "a light commandment".[5]

[1] Ephraim E. Urbach, *The Sages* (Harvard, 1975), p. 345.

[2] cf. b.*Shevuot* 12b.

[3] This number contradicts the standard rabbinic teaching that there are 365 negative precepts in the Torah. The number 300 here may be a scribal error.

[4] *Sifre* Deuteronomy §76.

[5] Urbach, Op. cit., 346.

Along these same lines R. Simeon b. Yochai (2nd Century Tanna) explained the stringency of the commandment to honor one's parents. The effort required to keep this commandment elevates it to a high position.

> For it is taught, R. Simeon b. Yochai said: Great is (the precept of) honoring father and mother, for the Holy One, blessed be He, put it above the honor due to Him. It is stated, "Honor your father and your mother," and it is said "Honor the Lord with your substance" (Prov 3:9). With what should you honor Him? With the substance that He graciously bestows upon you—setting aside the gleanings, the forgotten sheaf, the corners of the field; separating the heave-offering, the first tithe, the second tithe, the poor man's tithe, and the dough-offering; preparing a booth, a palm-branch, a ram's horn, tefillin, and fringes; feeding the poor and the hungry, giving drink to the thirsty. If you have, you are obligated to do any of these things; but if you have not, you are not obligated to do any of these things. But when we come to the commandment of honoring parents, whether you have substance or not, you must "honor your father and your mother," even if you have to go begging.[1]

We know that Yeshua had also come to a conclusion on laws which were light[2] and those which were heavy, and that He agreed with those who made a law such as honoring father and mother an extremely stringent or heavy one, for it is on this very basis that He rebukes the Pharisees, and admonishes them not to neglect the "weightier" matters of the Torah by becoming entangled in the "lighter" precepts (Matt 23:23)—"but these are the things you should have done without neglecting the others." Thus, Yeshua was fully aware of, and participant in, the debate over the valuation of commandments. In the end, however, the majority opinion appears to coincided with Yeshua's own position, as we read in *Avot*:

> And be heedful of a light precept as of a weighty one, for you know not the reward given for the precepts.[3]

With this brief look into the rabbinic material, we can see that Yeshua's strong emphasis upon doing the "least of these commandments" was in concert with the general teaching of the Sages. The difficulty, however, was that often a disparity existed between what the Sages taught and what they actually practised. Yeshua demands "doing and teaching" others, in that order. Likewise, His criteria for evaluating the commandments were the precepts of love and mercy. Those *mitzvot* that required the greatest expenditure of one's own life in the service of God and others were, for Yeshua, the "weightier" matters of the Torah. Yet it was in giving attention to even the least ("lightest") of the *mitzvot* that one's love for God was demonstrated and strengthened, which in turn prepared a person to fulfill the weightier matters of the Torah. Far from negating even the least commandment, Yeshua teaches His disciples that the Torah is a unified expression of God's will and must therefore be received and obeyed as a whole. Moreover, as the following context (the so-called "antitheses") makes clear, Yeshua's perspective was not to replace the Torah with His teaching, but to uncover its true import from the misinterpretations and traditions of the Sages that had negated its proper application in day to day living.

[1] y.*Peah* i, 1 (15d).

[2] The common rabbinic language is "light" and "heavy," and this doubtlessly corresponds to Yeshua's use of "least" in our text, and "weightier" in Matt 23.

[3] m.*Avot* 2.1.

20 For I say to you that unless your righteousness surpasses that of the scribes and Pharisees, you will not enter the kingdom of heaven.

The connective "For" (γάρ, *gar*) along with the opening "I say to you" signals the conclusion of the matter in an emphatic way. Not only must all aspects of the Torah be taken to heart by the disciple of Yeshua, there must also be due attention to living out its precepts and commands.

This is now the fourth appearance of the word "righteousness" (δικαιο-σύνη, *dikaiosune*) in our Gospel (cf. 3:15; 5:6, 10). As noted earlier, the term in Matthew always means "moral conduct in accord with God's will." While in the Pauline epistles, the word "righteousness" encompasses both a forensic as well as a moral component, in Matthew the word always denotes correct action in one's daily life. Thus, when Yeshua demands that one's "righteousness surpasses that of the scribes and Pharisees," He is talking about the manner in which obedience to the Torah is manifest by one's actions. This is plain by the fact that the scribes and Pharisees also possess righteousness, though of a sort insufficient to enable them to enter the kingdom of heaven.

This is the first mention of the associative "scribes and Pharisees" in Matthew.[1] Previously he has mentioned "chief priests and scribes" (2:4) and "Pharisees and Sadducees" (3:7). The scribes (γραμματεύς, *grammateus* = סוֹפְרִים, *sopherim*) were later known as "Sages" or חֲכָמִים, *chakhmim* ("wise ones") and were the teachers of the Torah (Lk 5:17; Acts 5:34, cp. Ezra 7:6, 11; Neh 8:1), those who were the "lawyers" in the sense of interpreting the legal principles of the Torah and administered justice in the courts. These were functions that previously belonged to the priests. They were the intellectual leaders of the Jewish community and its most prominent citizens (cf. Matt 23:6–7; Mk 12:38–9; Lk 20:46). It is common to describe the scribes as a professional class rather than a party or sect. Thus, some of the Pharisees were scribes but not all scribes were Pharisees, though it may have been that in the majority of cases, scribes and Pharisees were synonymously linked.[2] Thus, the common use of "scribes and Pharisees" in Matthew may well mean "scribes who are Pharisees." Regardless of the exact identification, for Yeshua they represented the Jewish leadership of His day, those who bore the responsibility of teaching and leading the people in truth and righteousness.

At first it appears that Yeshua's use of the scribes and Pharisees as the benchmark for righteousness contradicts His view that they act hypocritically (cf. Matt 23). However, it is not the teaching of the scribes and Pharisees with which Yeshua takes exception, but their unwillingness to live out what they teach: they don't practice what they preach. What Yeshua commends of the scribes and Pharisees in our present verse is their attention to even the most minute detail of the Torah. But the manner in which the fall short is their unwillingness to allow love and mercy to be the deciding factor in matters of conflicting *halachot*. Furthermore, the Oral Torah, which was in its final stages of development in the 1st Century, had in some cases eclipsed the clear and direct commands of the Torah itself, providing legal "fine print" that essentially negated the commands of Scripture. Perhaps Hillel's *Prosbol* ruling is one of the most obvious examples:

> [A loan against which] a prosbol [has been written] is not cancelled [by the Sabbatical year]. This is one of the things which Hillel the Elder ordained. When he saw that people refrained from lending

[1] The couplet is found 10 more times in Matthew: 12:38; 15:1; 23:2, 13-15, 23, 25, 27, 29.

[2] See E. Rivkin, "Scribes, Pharisees, Lawyers, Hypocrites: A Study in Synonymity," *HUCA* 49 (1978), pp. 135–42.

one another money [on the eve of the Sabbatical year] and [thereby] transgressed that which is written in the Torah, Beware lest you harbor the base thought [. . and so you are mean to your kinsman and give him nothing (Deut 15:9)], Hillel ordained the prosbol [whereby the court, on behalf of the creditor, may collect unpaid debts otherwise cancelled by the Sabbatical year]. (m.*Shevi'it* 10:3)

Yet we read in Deut 15:2,

> This is the manner of remission: every creditor shall release what he has loaned to his neighbor; he shall not exact it of his neighbor and his brother, because the LORD's remission has been proclaimed.

Thus, it was in these two ways that the righteousness of the scribes and Pharisees was insufficient: they failed (in some cases) to practice what they preached, and they usurped some of the commands of the Torah in favor of their own rulings or reinterpretations. It will be Yeshua's purpose in the following context to teach clear examples of how the Torah had been overshadowed by the rulings of men, and how it should actually be understood and obeyed by His disciples.

How then is our righteousness (our lives of obedience to God) to surpass that of the scribes and Pharisees? First, it is clear that we must respect the level of righteousness which the scribes and Pharisees did possess, that is, their sincere desire and efforts to know the Torah down to its smallest details. Clearly we cannot obey the Torah if we do not know it. Thus, the words of our Master here are a strong incentive to know what the Scriptures teach. But the fact that Yeshua taught the need for the righteousness of His disciples to surpass that of the scribes and Pharisees clearly means that what they possessed was not sufficient for entering the kingdom. With all of their learning and study, they had neglected the heart of the Torah itself, that is, Yeshua. For Yeshua is the goal of the Torah as pertains to righteousness (Rom 10:4). Secondly, then, we will be enabled to surpass the righteousness of the scribes and Pharisees only when we understand the Torah from the perspective of Yeshua.

And what is that perspective? It is first that the Torah as given by God stands supreme over the teachings of men. To the extent that man's teaching and laws agree with God's revelation, well and good. But whenever there is a variance, the word of God remains the undisputed authority. Secondly, it is inevitable that in the fallen world, our ability as the redeemed people of God to keep the commandments of God will sometimes be hampered and even thwarted. This is the case when two commandments seem to conflict. When we are confronted with such either-or situations, the true nature of our hearts is revealed. Is there really a conflict, or are we trying to rationalize our way around obeying one of God's commandments? The heart of faith and love to God will attempt to find a way to do both of the commandments that appear to conflict. But even in our best efforts, there will be times when obeying both commandments is impossible. Then we have to decide which of the two we will perform. And this is where the example of our Master is so important. For Yeshua, the deciding factor in such cases was that of love and mercy. This is precisely why we see Him healing on the Shabbat, for in doing so, He was demonstrating the manner in which mercy became the deciding factor. For the scribes and Pharisees, performance of the commandment was paramount, and the needs of others took second place. Not so with our Master. By His own actions He has taught us that love for our neighbor tips the scales when deciding between two conflicting commandments. Thus, our righteousness will surpass that of the scribes and Pharisees when mercy and love are the governing factor in *halachic* decisions.

This in no way means that we may willy-nilly disregard the commandments of God. More often than not, we will be able to find a way to obey commandments that, at first, appear to conflict. And our love for God will be demonstrated when we do our best to find that way. But when a genuine conflict arises, in which we can only obey one of two commandments, then we must follow the one that best extols love and mercy. The story of the good Samaritan demonstrates this principle. The two conflicting commandments that confronted the Levite were 1) that he could not fulfill his priestly duties while in an unclean state, and the possibility existed that if he stopped to help the injured man, he could contract ritual impurities; 2) the commandment to love one's neighbor as oneself. Now in our minds, the answer seems obvious: the life of the injured man should take precedence over the laws of ritual purity. And this is the point: love and mercy should clearly govern one's decision in the matter. In Yeshua's parable, however, what seems apparent to us was not so apparent to the Levite.

It is this principle of love and mercy as the governing factor in Torah obedience that is expounded in the following context, in which the prevailing interpretations and *halachah* of the Sages ("you have heard it said") is scrutinized by Yeshua's own understanding of the Torah ("but I say to you"). The matter of loving one's neighbor (vv. 21–26) begins in the heart and is seen in a willingness to forgive and to be forgiven. Love for one's neighbor governs the tongue and guards against *lashon hara* (evil speech). Sexual purity (vv. 27–30) begins in the heart as well, and is an extension of loving one's neighbor. Fornication is always the fruit of selfishness. Marital fidelity (vv. 31-32) is the highest example of keeping one's vows, and even though the ruling authorities may offer all kinds "valid" reasons for divorce, remaining faithful to one's vow takes precedence. Moreover, one's wife is one's closest "neighbor," and "loving one's neighbor as oneself" begins first at home. Having emphasized the high importance of keeping one's marriage vow, Yeshua goes on to speak of vows in general (vv. 33–37). While many "loopholes" had been created by the Sages to allow one to forego the consequences of one's vow, Yeshua returns to the Torah's perspective, that one should make a vow with full intention of keeping it. Again, keeping one's vow is clearly to love one's neighbor, for in breaking a vow, others are always hurt. In vv. 38–42, the misuse of the legal system (*lex talionis*) is addressed, and the rule of love for one's neighbor is affirmed as the primary criterion in community relationships. And finally, in vv. 43–48 Yeshua addresses the manner in which this central command, "to love one's neighbor as oneself," had been reinterpreted to include "hate your enemy," and thus stripped of its original importance and value.

It is clear, then, that the manner in which the righteousness of Yeshua's disciples will surpass that of the scribes and Pharisees is a tenacious adherence to the Torah, governed by a heart of love to God and to one's neighbor. Such is only possible when the Torah is written on the heart (Jer 31:31–34).

We come now to the section of Yeshua's teaching often called "the Antitheses" (5:21–48). The six topics are nicely divided into two sets of three, which is signaled by the use of "again" in v. 33 which introduces the second set, as well as by the fact that the first and fourth both have the full introductory formula, "you have heard that the ancients were told."

The first set of Yeshua's antitheses involve (1) murder/hate, (2) adultery/lust, and (3) divorce/remarriage. The second set includes (4) vows, (5) taking revenge, and (6) loving one's neighbor.

It is not uncommon to find in popular teaching of the Church an interpretation of these six antitheses as somehow isolated from 5:17–20 and even in apparent disregard of them. For some would have us believe either that Yeshua is here contrasting His teaching with that of Moses, or else adding His teaching to that of Moses in order to add a spiritual dimension which it otherwise lacked.

> Jesus' demands in these antitheses go beyond the Mosaic Law and are different in kind. For example, His proscription of divorce (vv. 31-32) is not mere exposition of Moses, looking for its spiritual heart. Where Deuteronomy allowed divorce, Jesus prohibited it. He charges ones who initiate divorce (except in the case of *porneia*) with causing adultery. Again, where the Law allowed and regulated oaths, Jesus prohibited them (vv. 33-37). His command is different in kind from the Old Testament command which He quotes. The truthful character of the members of His kingdom makes oaths unnecessary and wrong. As a final example, while His command to love one's enemies (vv. 43-47) does not specifically abrogate any command of the Law, neither can it be construed as an exposition of the Law. Jesus gives a command of quite a different order from those in the Law.[1]

[1]Gerry Breshears, "The Place of the Law in the Life of the Believer in Christ," Western Conservative Baptist Seminary, n.d., p. 3.

Yet in the former verses it is clear that Yeshua affirms the Torah as the eternal will of God, and that to which all should listen and obey. The notion that in our text He "gives a command of quite a different order from those in the Law" is effectively to say that He changed or overturned it. Nor, as we have shown above, can one appeal to some sense of "fulfill" in 5:17 as, for all practical purposes, being equivalent to "abolish." As noted, when Yeshua stated that He had come to "fulfill" the Torah, His intended meaning (as the context clearly shows) involved "doing" the commandments and teaching others to "do them," not "finishing them" in the sense that they are no longer necessary or relevant.

Nor will it work to understand the antitheses as commending an inner, spiritual component of the Torah which it otherwise lacked. Everywhere in the Torah and the Prophets, the matter of one's heart (thoughts, intentions, moral decisions) is addressed. What else could be meant by circumcision of the heart (Deut 10:16; 30:6)? And the very core idea of loving God with all of one's heart (Deut 6:5; 10:12; 11:13; 13:3) surely addresses the inward reality of faith and obedience (faithfulness).

How then should we understand the six antitheses present in our text? First, it is clear that Yeshua is not contrasting His teaching with that of the Torah of Moses. Secondly, then, it seems clear that He is contrasting, by way of emphasis, a prevailing or widely accepted understanding of the Torah which, though presented as the proper interpretation of Moses' words, had in some way missed the mark. Numbers of suggestions have been offered as to what this might entail.

A number of commentators have understood the antitheses as a further explanation of the final statement of 5:20, "unless your righteousness surpasses that of the scribes and Pharisees, you will not enter the kingdom of heaven." The antitheses expound what our Master meant by one's righteousness exceeding that of the Scribes and Pharisees.

> The six antitheses are prepared for in 5:17–20 by the report both of Jesus' insistence that he came not to abolish the Law but to see it fulfilled more effectively, and of his stern words on the need for an abundant righteousness.[1]

But the question is whether exceeding the righteousness of the Scribes and Pharisees means to do something new, or something otherwise unknown by them, or if it means to obey the Torah of Moses as God intended all along, but which had been obscured or negated by a wrong understanding of the Torah itself. Allison-Davies, in introducing 5:21–48, hold that Yeshua does introduce something new, something that "surpasses" the Torah:

> Its primary function is, quite simply, two-fold: to show, through six concrete examples (i) what sort of attitude and behavior Jesus requires and (ii) how his demands surpass those of the Torah without contradicting the Torah.[2]

A more common understanding is that Yeshua here is contrasting His own exposition of the Torah with that of the rabbis:

> By means of six bold antitheses representing the teaching of Jesus, Matthew now contrasts Jesus' exposition of the true and ultimate meaning of the Torah with the more common, rabbinic understandings of the commandments. In this way the incomparable ethical demands of the kingdom are set forth, and in this way examples are provided showing how the righteousness of the Pharisees is to be exceeded.[3]

This, in my opinion, is closer to the mark, and as we shall see, the language employed by Yeshua corroborates the fact that He does have prevailing and common teachings of the Sages in mind which He intends to correct in line with His own teaching. But it seems to me that there are several other factors that should be mentioned here. First is the *halachic* principle of love which forms a watershed for Yeshua's teaching. What I mean by this is that for our Master, when conflicting *halachot* are encountered, the deciding factor is love for one's neighbor (Lev 19:18). In the later rabbinic literature (which might well express prevailing views of the earlier centuries), conflicting *halachot* are resolved either by following the majority (e.g., y.*Berachot* 8b) or by giving preference to a positive commandment over a negative one (e.g., b.*Shabbat* 132b). For Yeshua the decision rests upon which commandment better expresses love for one's neighbor (e.g., healing on the Shabbat as an act of kindness to one's neighbor, Lk 13:10f). Making love for one's neighbor a deciding factor in *halachic* decisions is not, however, something novel with Yeshua. The very context of Lev 19:18 shows that loving one's neighbor is a primary factor in how one is to obey the Torah. When Lev. 19:17 states with regard to one's neighbor, "you shall not incur sin because of him," it is em-

[1]Nolland, *Matthew* in *NIGTC*, p. 228.

[2]Davies-Allison, *Matthew*, 1.508.

[3]Hagner, *Matthew* in The Word Commentary, 1.111.

phasizing that even in reproof one must be careful to do so without anger or malice. Note the exposition of this text in 1QS 5:25–6:1:

> [to reprove] his fellow in truth, humility and lovingkindness. (vacat) He should not speak to him in anger, with grumbling, with a [stiff] neck or with a wickedly [zealous] spirit. He must not hate him because of his own [uncircumcised] heart. Most assuredly he is to rebuke him on the day of the infraction so that he does not bear punishment because of him.

Here, obedience to the command to "reprove one's neighbor" (Lev 19:17) is understood to be properly followed only when one's heart is governed by love.

Secondly, while the theme of "Spirit" and "word" is more fully developed in the Pauline literature (cf. Rom 2:29; 7:6; 2Cor 3:3, 6), it is not without mention in the teachings of our Master. In His words to Nicodemus (Jn 3:1–7), the idea of being "born by water and Spirit" (v. 5) captures the metaphoric language of Ezek 36:25-26 in which the "sprinkling of water" accompanies the giving of a "new heart" and putting "My Spirit" within them. For Yeshua, "being born again" was not a theological category but a vital reality in terms of the work of the Spirit of God "circumcising" the heart and by so doing, empowering the individual to obey God out of a sincere motivation of love. And this is not relegated to some post-Pentecost phenomenon, but is taught by our Master to Nicodemus as the normal work of God upon those who are His, something of which a "teacher of Israel" should have been fully cognisant. The fact that Nicodemus was apparently ignorant of the spiritual dimension emphasized by Yeshua highlights the very contrasts He is making in our text. For Yeshua, the ability to live a life of righteousness that surpassed the piety of the Scribes and Pharisees was not something achieved by sheer determination or self-discipline alone. Such ability is the fruit of a heart made new by a new birth brought about by the Spirit of God. Thus, in the antitheses of our text, Yeshua is exposing those who lived as though the Torah was primarily legislation for determining *halachah* rather than the living and abiding word of God to which the heart, moved and controlled by the Spirit Himself, willingly submits on the principles of love for God and for one's neighbor.

It is not, then, the words of the Torah to which Yeshua makes exception, nor even the general teaching of the Sages (though in some cases the rabbinic traditions did run contrary to the Torah itself, cf. Mk 7:8, 9, 13). It was the fact that in emphasizing obedience to the Torah (which is in itself a noble thing), the Sages had neglected (in some measure) to stress the necessity of the spiritual dimensions as the very fountain from which proper obedience flows. And in legislating the manner in which the Torah was properly to be followed, they had elevated performance over the principle of love. Yeshua's antitheses, then, are given as a clear corrective to this situation, as a means of re-planting Torah obedience back into the spiritual soil of love for God and for one's neighbor.

Thirdly, while it seems clear that Yeshua was not giving new teaching, nor expressing something that had not already been well expressed in the Torah (as rightly understood), we should not overlook the obvious fact that Yeshua, in the words He uses, expressing His own, unique authority. Each of the six antitheses are introduced by a similar formula: "you have heard…

but I say to you." Some have suggested that the use of "heard" points to a non-written (i.e., oral) teaching, but this is not the case. Rather, the rabbinic literature, in using this same expression, shows that the "heard...say" formula was a common way to express a well known teaching or even a surface reading of the text ("heard"), followed by a variant or more informed interpretation ("say").

Note, for instance, the midrash on Ex 19:20 in *Mekhilta*. Here, in reference to the commandment "honor your father and thy mother," the writer says: "I might understand, 'honor them with words only'." The phrase "I might understand" is אֲנִי שׁוֹמֵעַ, "I hear," or "I might hear." The midrash goes on to refute this proposition and to show that the commandment refers not only to respectful speech but also to the duty of maintaining your parents. Daube shows that the rabbinical technical terms for "literal meaning" were שָׁמוּעַ and מִשְׁמַע, "that which is heard."[1]

> Furthermore, הַשׁוֹמֵעַ, "he who hears," is used in the sense of "he who sticks to the superficial, literal meaning of Scripture" in the hermeneutical rule according to which "a general summary (like the notice concerning man's creation in the first chapter of Genesis) may be followed by detailed facts (the story of man's creation in the second chapter) which are merely a repetition giving more particulars; he who hears—i.e., he who takes Scripture literally—will form the erroneous belief that the second account refers to different facts, but in reality it is merely a repetition with more particulars.[2]

Note in this regard another example from R. Yudah HaNasi in his comments on the phrase "And the Lord came down upon mount Sinai:

> I might hear this as it is heard, I might understand this according to its literal meaning (שׁוֹמֵעַ אֲנִי כִּשְׁמוּעַ). But thou must say (אָמַרְתָּ): If the sun, one of the many servants of God, may remain in its place and nevertheless be effective beyond it, how much more He by whose word the world came into being.[3]

This, then, gives a setting for Yeshua's exposition. It is academic life, dialectic exegesis, in which the text is considered from comparative texts and ideologies rather than from a narrow, "surface" reading. Yeshua follows the Rabbinic pattern of "hear" and "say," to introduce a known teaching or what might appear to be an obvious interpretation and then to contrast it with His own teaching.

But once we have seen that the formula "you have heard...but I say" has its roots in rabbinic dialog and midrash, we should also notice a significant difference. Never (as far as I can find) in the rabbinic literature does a given rabbi or Sage follow the opening "you have heard" or "it is heard" with the first person singular contrastive "but I say," something that occurs in each of the six antitheses of our Matthew text. The rabbinic pattern is to reference another authority or to state another received interpretation. When Yeshua, therefore, introduces His teaching with the formula "but I say," He is expressing His own authority, based not upon the teachings of others, but upon His own position as the chosen Messiah. Thus, His interpretation and application of the Torah is not one among many, but is the final word. As the one Who brings the kingdom of God, He is also the Priest Who authoritatively and accurately interprets and teaches the Torah of God.

[1] David Daube, *The New Testament and Rabbinic Judaism,* (School of Oriental and African Studies, 1956), p. 56; Lachs (*A Rabbinic Commentary on the New Testament*, p. 91) disagrees with Daube's assessment on the basis that the Pharisees received their interpretations via Oral Torah, and this was not restricted to the literal meaning of the text.

[2] Daube, Ibid. This is from the 32 principles of interpretation of Eliezer ben Yose HaGelili. These are listed and expounded in R. Adin Steinsaltz, *The Talmud: A Reference Guide* (Random House, 1989), pp. 147-154. The principle alluded to here is number 13.

[3] *Mekhilta* on Ex. 19:20.

The evaluation of the commandments was a significant topic in early Judaisms, if the subsequent literature is any indication. As Urbach shows, there were various viewpoints among the Sages.

> The question of the relative value of the commandments found expression in many varied forms in the teaching of the Sages. On the one hand we find dicta that proclaim the absolute equality of all the precepts, and on the other we encounter clear distinctions drawn between more important and less important commandments, and methods of classifying precepts and transgressions according to various criteria.[1]

Various Sages and schools gave a different criteria of evaluation for the commandments. For instance, in the Amora Rav Judah's comments on m.*Shavuot* 1.6 (b.*Shavuot* 12b) he says:

> This is the meaning . . . the light (transgressions) are those involving positive or negative commandments; and the grave (transgressions) are those punished by "extinction" or death by sentence of the court.[2]

Thus, he based the criteria for valuation of the mitzvot on the severity of the penalty that the transgressions entail.

R. ben 'Azzai saw it differently. On the verse "Only be steadfast in not eating the blood . . . " he remarked:

> Now there are three hundred similar positive precepts in the Torah! It comes to teach us, therefore, that if in regard to blood, than which there is no lighter precept among all the commandments, Scripture admonished you thus, how much more so in the case of the other precepts.[3]

Urbach explains:

> The eating of the blood is something repulsive; consequently it is easy to abstain from it. Lightness and stringency are not measured by the extent of the reward or punishment involved in doing the precept or transgression, but according to the effort required to fulfill the commandments or to refrain from the transgressions. So, too, a precept not entailing expenditure of money, or involving danger to life, is called "a light commandment." [4]

Along these same lines R. Simeon b. Yochai explained the stringency of the commandment to honor one's parents. The effort required to keep this commandment elevates it to a high position.

> For it is taught, R. Simeon b. Yochai said: Great is (the precept of) honoring father and mother, for the Holy One, blessed be He, put it above the honor due to Him. It is stated, "Honor thy father and thy mother," and it is said "Honor the Lord with thy substance" (Prov 3:9). With what should you honor Him? With the substance that He graciously bestows upon you—setting aside the gleanings, the forgotten sheaf, the corners of the field; separating the heave-offering, the first tithe, the second tithe, the poor man's tithe, and the dough-offering; preparing a booth, a palm-branch, a ram's horn,

[1]Ephraim E. Urbach, *The Sages* (Harvard, 1979), p. 345.

[2]b.*Shavuot* 12b.

[3]*Sifre* Deuteronomy §76.

[4]Urbach, Op. cit., p. 346.

[1]y.*Pe'ah* i, 1, p. 15d. Quoted from Urbach, Op. cit., p. 346.

[2]The Greek text of Mt 5 speaks of the "least" commandment, but the common Hebrew terms are a "light commandment" (מצוה קלה) and a "weighty commandment" (מצוה חמורה).

[3]m.*Avot* 2.1.

[4]From the Shacharit Service , *The Complete Metsudah Siddur*, (Metsudah Publications, 1990), p. 14-15.

[5]*DJD* V., p. 43.

phylacteries, and fringes; feeding the poor and the hungry, giving drink to the thirsty. If you have, you are obligated to do any of these things; but if you have not, you are not obligated to do any of these things. But when we come to the commandment of honoring parents, whether you have substance or not, you must "honor thy father and thy mother," even if you have to go begging.[1]

We know that Yeshua had also come to a conclusion on laws which were light[2] and those which were heavy, and that He agreed with those who made a law such as honoring father and mother an extremely stringent or heavy one, for it is on this very basis that He rebukes the Pharisees, and admonishes them not to neglect the "weightier" matters of the Law by becoming entangled in the "lighter" precepts (Matt. 23:23)—"but these are the things you should have done without neglecting the others." Thus, Yeshua was fully aware of, and participant in, the debate over the valuation of commandments. In the end, however, the majority opinion coincided with Yeshua's own position, as we read in Avot:

> And be heedful of a light precept as of a weighty one, for you know not the reward given for the precepts.[3]

The righteous or pious will obey from the heart, which means they will desire to keep all the precepts of God regardless of whether they are light or weighty. One's rewards come from pleasing God, and this means doing what He commands.

This same idea is reflected in the Prayer Book. For instance:

> These are the precepts, the fruit of which man enjoys in this world [while] the principle [reward] is preserved for him in the World-to-Come. They are: honoring father and mother, [performing] deeds of kindness, early attendance in the House of Study morning and evening, providing hospitality to guests, visiting the sick, participating in making a wedding, accompanying the dead [to the grave], concentrating on the meaning of prayers, making peace between fellow men—and the study of Torah is equal to them all.[4]

Each of these would not have been classed as "weighty" by the Pharisees Yeshua rebukes, yet in the end the stance of the Sages is that "the study of Torah is equal to them all," meaning that the end of true Torah learning is the performing of these deeds. Thus, these deeds, which might have at one time been considered "light," have gained a high or weighty status. And in the majority they may be grouped under the heading of "love" or showing of "mercy."

It was not only Yeshua who saw in the main-stream Pharisaism something in need of rebuke. The Qumran society had also taken a stand against them in regard to the valuation of commandments. In 4QPsa 1:27 it is stated that the Pharisees "have chosen the light matters" (כיא בחרו בקלות).[5] By this we might understand that they had chosen those commandments which required the least sacrifice on their part—those which could be performed without a humbling of the soul.

With this before us, then, it is possible to interpret Yeshua's teaching as addressing the issue of commandment evaluation. The Pharisees had chosen to do the "light" commandments, those which required the least amount of effort to fulfill, while they were constantly neglecting (and thus breaking) the weightier ones, those which required a greater sacrifice to fulfill. In stating at the opening that each and every commandment (regardless of its valuation) was important to live righteously, Yeshua sets the stage for His antitheses. But He does it in a most intriguing way. He states a law which all would agree was valued as weighty (introduced by "you have heard it said"), and then shows that the inward, heart attitude is just as weighty a commandment (introduced by "but I say to you").

21 "You have heard that the ancients were told, 'You shall not commit murder' and 'Whoever commits murder shall be liable to the court.'

The first of the antitheses relates to murder. The "ancients" (ἀρχαίοι, *arxaioi*), since it is in the plural, most likely refers to the generation in the wilderness that first received the Torah. The Sixth Word, which prohibits murder, is quoted directly from the Lxx (Ex 20:13; Deut 5:17).

To the quote of the Sixth Word is added the phrase "whoever commits murder shall be liable to the court." The actual Greek has "he shall be liable to the judgment (κρίσει, *krisei*)," but the term may well stand for the court that administers the judgment. This whole last phrase finds no direct parallel in either the Tanach or rabbinic literature, but surely summarizes the obvious point of texts like Ex 21:12, Lev 24:17, Num 35:12 or Deut 17:8–13. The point is that a murderer deserves the full penalty prescribed in the Torah, but such penalty cannot be administered until recognized judges have heard the necessary witnesses and determined that a murder has actually taken place. Here is something with which no one in Yeshua's audience would disagree.

22 "But I say to you that everyone who is angry with his brother[1] shall be guilty before the court; and whoever says to his brother, 'You good-for-nothing,' shall be guilty before the supreme court; and whoever says, 'You fool,' shall be guilty enough to go into the fiery hell.

Yeshua now makes His point by comparing murder, considered a "heavy" commandment by some (since it bore the death penalty) with anger, something that could not even be punished by the earthly tribunal. He uses "brother" as another way of saying "neighbor," a semitic idiom. It thus is not gender-specific, but includes anyone in the community, male or female.

It seems obvious[2] that Yeshua's words are construed in a three-tiered progression. Anger, when unchecked, proceeds to insult ("you good-for-nothing") and unrestrained insult proceeds to slander ("you fool"). Likewise the severity of the offence matches the increasingly powerful courts. The first is merely the court, literally "the judgment" (κρίσει, *krisei*) as in the previous verse. Next is the "supreme court," literally "sanhedrin" (συνέδριον, *sunedrion*),[3] and finally "hell fire," literally, "the fire of Gehenna." Yeshua is showing the progression of anger, which begins inwardly but if allowed to remain and grow, evidences outward, destructive behavior. Indeed, this is why it is linked with murder. In Gen 4:5 we learn that Cain became "very angry," which eventually led to the crime of murder against his brother. Thus, what might be considered a light commandment, "You shall not hate

[1]Some Greek manuscripts add εἰκῇ, "in vain, randomly" here, giving the sense of "…angry with his brother *without a cause.*" While the manuscript evidence would be sufficient to warrant this reading, it is more likely that this was added as a way to soften the stark comparison of anger with murder than that it was omitted by scribal error. For that reason it is considered a secondary reading.

[2]Nolland disagrees, *Matthew* in *NIGTC*, p. 230.

[3]While the Greek *sunedrion* could also be used of local courts (cf. Matt 10:17; Mk 13:19; m.*Makkot* 1.10; m.*Sanhedrin* 1.6; t.*Sanhedrin* 7.1), since it has the article here ("the sanhedrin"), it most likely means the high court that convened in Jerusalem.

your fellow man (literally "your brother") in your heart" (Lev 19:17) must be rather understood as a weighty one, because left to grow, the possibility is ripe that it will proceed to a whole garden of sins, including murder.

How is it that Yeshua considers being angry against one's neighbor, or even casting verbal insults, a punishable transgression before the earthly court? Anger is a sin of the heart, and until it bears outward actions of a punishable nature, no earthly court has the jurisdiction or ability to assess any penalties. Some suggest that Yeshua is simply using this language in a metaphoric sense, meaning that even though sins of the heart are not punishable in their early stages, they should be feared as though they were punishable by the court because allowed to remain, the possibility exists that overt punishable actions will result. Thus, Yeshua emphasizes that all sin begins in the inner thoughts of a person, and it is here where the work of sanctification must be most carefully and diligently employed (cf. Matt 15:19; James 1:13–16). We find a similar emphasis in the rabbinic materials.

> R. Eliezer said: "He who hates his brother belongs to the shedders of blood!" (*Derek Eretz Rabba* XI [quoted from Lachs, *Rabbinic Commentary on the NT*, p. 91)

> If a person has violated a minor religious requirement, in the end such a person will violate a major religious requirement. (*Sifre* 186–187, commenting on Deut 19:11–13)

> A tanna recited before R. Nachman b. Isaac: "He who publicly shames his neighbor is as though he shed blood." (b.*Bava Metzia* 58b)

> All who descend into Gehinom [subsequently reascend] except who do not reascend, viz., he who commits adultery, publicly shames his neighbor, fastens an evil epithet [nickname upon his neighbor]. (b.*Bava Metzia* 58b, quoted from Lachs, Ibid.)

This last quote is reminiscent of Yeshua's words in our text, that one who says to his neighbor, "you fool," is guilty of "hell fire" (literally "the Gehenna of fire, τὴν γέενναν τοῦ πυρός).[1]

The evidence of inner anger is displayed by the calling of names. The first is *Raka* (ῥακά), a Greek transliteration of Aramaic רֵיקָא (*reiqa*), meaning "empty-headed," "good for nothing," or "fool." This word is not uncommon in the rabbinic literature,[2] though it is found only this one time in the Apostolic Scriptures. Interestingly, in the rabbinic literature the word is most often found in the context of a teacher or Sage berating someone of inferior status. One example also shows the manner in which the offender is brought to judgment in the "court" of public appeal.

> Once R. Eleazar son of R. Simeon was coming from Migdal Gedor, from the house of his teacher, and he was riding leisurely on his ass by the riverside and was feeling happy and elated because he had studied much Torah. There chanced to meet him an exceedingly ugly man who greeted him, 'Peace be upon you, Sir'. He, however, did not return his salutation but instead said to him, 'Raca, how ugly you are. Are all your fellow citizens as ugly as you are?' The man replied: 'I do not know, but go and tell the craftsman who made me, "How Ugly is the vessel which you have made".' When R. Eleazar

[1]"Gehenna" (γέεννα) is the Greek rendering of Hebrew גֵּיהִנּוֹם, *Ge Hinnom*, which literally is "valley of [the son(s) of] Hinnom," and referred originally to the valley that runs north-south on the west side of Jerusalem and east-west on the south side. Jeremiah (19:6–7) prophesied that this valley, called Ben-hinnom (גֵּיא בֶן־הִנֹּם), would become known as the "valley of Slaughter" (גֵּיא הַהֲרֵגָה), that is, the valley of God's judgment. This designation eventually took on a general, metaphoric or typical meaning for God's final judgment, and the picture of fire was added (cf. *3Enoch* 33.5; 44.3; *Sib. Or.* 1.100). The reference to "Gehenna" is found seven times in Matthew (5:22, 29-30; 10:28; 18:9; 23:15, 33), three times in Mark (9:43-47), once in Luke (12:5), and once in James (3:6).

In 2Ki 23:10 and Jer 7:31, we see that the valley of Hinnom was used for human sacrifice in idolatrous worship. In later times, this same location was used for burning Jerusalem's trash, and thus the constant fires gave a suitable metaphor for a place of God's judgment.

[2]b.*Ta'anit* 20b; b.*Berachot* 20a; b.*Gittin* 58a; b.*Bava Batra* 75a

realized that he had done wrong he dismounted from the ass and prostrated himself before the man and said to him, 'I submit myself to you, forgive me'. The man replied: 'I will not forgive you until you go to the craftsman who made me and say to him, "How ugly is the vessel which you have made".' He [R. Eleazar] walked behind him until he reached his native city. When his fellow citizens came out to meet him greeting him with the words, 'Peace be upon you O Teacher, O Master,' the man asked them, 'Whom are you addressing thus'? They replied, 'The man who is walking behind you.' Thereupon he exclaimed: 'If this man is a teacher, may there not be any more like him in Israel'! The people then asked him: 'Why'? He replied: 'Such and such a thing has he done to me.' They said to him: 'Nevertheless, forgive him, for he is a man greatly learned in the Torah.' The man replied: 'For your sakes I will forgive him, but only on the condition that he does not act in the same manner in the future.' Soon after this R. Eleazar son of R. Simeon entered [the Beit Hamidrash] and expounded thus, 'A man should always be gentle as the reed and let him never be unyielding as the cedar. And for this reason the reed merited that of it should be made a pen for the writing of the Torah, Teffilin and Mezuzot. (b.*Ta'anit* 20a-b)

From anger to verbalizing that someone is a "good for nothing," Yeshua capstones His triad of v. 22 with "whoever says 'You fool' shall be guilty enough to go into the fire of Gehenna." Here, the phrase "You fool" is one word in the Greek, μωρέ (*moré*). Some take this as an adjectival form of Greek μωρός (*moros*) which means "foolish" or "stupid." Our English "moron" is derived from this Greek word. If so, this could be interpreted as a Greek explanation of the previously transliterated Aramaic *raka.* But such an explanation disregards what seems to be a triadic, progressive structure, in which calling someone *moré* is a more serious offence than the previous *raka.* Others have considered *moré*, like *raka*, to be a transliteration of the Hebrew word מוֹרֶה (*moreh*), from the root מָרַה, *marah*, "to be recalcitrant, rebellious" (cf. Deut 21:18, 20). It is also possible that the Greek word had become a common loan word among the Jewish communities.[1] We may have too little data to be certain which option best fits our context.

Regardless, the over all meaning of our Master's words is clear: anger, and the fruit of it, which is insult and slander, must not be allowed to remain in the hearts or mouths of those who seek righteousness. If one is honestly concerned about the "weighty" commandment prohibiting murder, then one will be diligent to make sure the root from which murder springs, i.e., growing anger, never is allowed to grow in one's heart. Moreover, since slander damages the reputation of another (and sometimes permanently), it is spoken of in the Tanach as a kind of murder (cf. Ps 31:13f; 51:1–4; Is 59:3).

The question still remains, however, how Yeshua could construe anger or its fruit of insulting words as a punishable crime in an earthly court. Some commentators simply consider His words to be hyperbole, arguing that by using the same phrase, "liable to the court/Sanhedrin/fire of Gehenna," He is metaphorically saying that the sins of the heart and lips are equally grave ("weighty") as the sin of murder. Others seek to emend the text or find redactional layers which brought about the difficulty.[2] Lachs,[3] noting the difficulty, gives the following explanation:

> Anger, however, is not an offense at law; one who is overcome with anger toward another may be morally culpable but he cannot be

[1] Jastrow (*Dictionary of the Talmud*, p. 749) notes that מורה is found in the rabbinic literture as a transliterated form of the Greek μωρέ. Cf. *Sifre*, Deut. §218; *Mid. Ps.* 9 (46b).

[2] Allison-Davies (1.515-16) suggest that the first two clauses ("angry with his brother"/"says to his brother 'raka'") where original and essentially equivalent. Matthew added the third phrase ("says 'you fool'") with the ultimate punishment ("fire of Geheena") for emphasis, and in doing so, made the whole saying appear as containing an ascending order of punishment, thus creating the difficulty. However, this approach still fails to explain who one could be "liable before the court" for these offenses which find no legal status of a civil crime in either the biblical or rabbinic legislations.

[3] Lachs, *Rabbinic Commentary on the NT,* p. 91.

tried because of it by a human tribunal. He is answerable before a heavenly court and is judged by the "laws of Heaven," a rabbinic term for moral culpability for acts not covered by the laws of man, and this appears to be the meaning of "liable to judgment" in v. 22.

The difficulty with this explanation is that the very same phrase, "liable to judgment (or the court)" is used in v. 21 of the murderer, and here it clearly means an earthly, not heavenly, court. Yet it is possible that Yeshua used the phrase in v. 21 of earthly judges, and the same phrase in v. 22 of the heavenly court, for surely the final clause, which casts the punishment into the sphere of divine judgment ("fire of Gehenna"), envisions a heavenly court. Moreover, on the basis of Ex 21 and the use of אֱלֹהִים (*Elohim*) to refer to earthly judges (since they speak with the authority of God Himself), the move from "earthly court" to "heavenly court" is not so far fetched. If one were to reverence the local courts and the high court of the Sanhedrin, how much more should one reverence the highest court of all, the court of Heaven. This theme is found in the rabbinic literature as well:

> Antigonos of Sokho received [the Torah] from Simeon the Righteous. He would say, "Do not be like servants who serve the master on condition of receiving a reward, but [be] like servants who serve the master not on condition of receiving a reward. And let the fear of Heaven be upon you." (m.*Avot* 1.3)

> When Rabban Johanan ben Zakkai fell ill, his disciples went in to visit him. When he saw them he began to weep. His disciples said to him: Lamp of Israel, pillar of the right hand, mighty hammer! Wherefore weepest thou? He replied: If I were being taken today before a human king who is here today and tomorrow in the grave, whose anger if he is angry with me does not last for ever, who if he imprisons me does not imprison me for ever and who if he puts me to death does not put me to everlasting death, and whom I can persuade with words and bribe with money, even so I would weep. Now that I am being taken before the supreme King of Kings, the Holy One, blessed be He, who lives and endures for ever and ever, whose anger, if He is angry with me, is an everlasting anger, who if He imprisons me imprisons me for ever, who if He puts me to death puts me to death for ever, and whom I cannot persuade with words or bribe with money — nay more, when there are two ways before me, one leading to Paradise and the other to Gehinnom, and I do not know by which I shall be taken, shall I not weep? They said to him: Master, bless us. He said to them,: May it be [God's] will that the fear of heaven shall be upon you like the fear of flesh and blood. His disciples said to him: Is that all? He said to them: If only [you can attain this]! (b.*Berachot* 28b)

> Within and without shalt thou overlay it [speaking of the Ark of the Covenant, Ex 25:10]. Raba said: Any scholar whose inside is not like his outside, is no scholar. Abaye, or, as some say, Rabbah b. 'Ulla said: He is called abominable, as it is said: How much less one that is abominable and impure, man who drinketh iniquity like water (Jb 15:16). R. Samuel b. Nahmani, in the name of R. Jonathan: What is the meaning of the scriptural statement: Wherefore is there a price in the hand of a fool, to buy wisdom, seeing he hath no understanding (Prov 17:16) i.e., woe unto the enemies of the scholars, who occupy themselves with the Torah, but have no fear of Heaven! R. Jannai proclaimed: Woe unto him who has no court, but makes a gateway

for his court! Raba said to the Sages: I beseech you, do not inherit a double Gehinnom! (b.*Yoma* 72b)

In this last quote from Yoma, to "have no court" means "to disregard the court of Heaven," while "makes a gateway for his court" means "to establish one's own earthly court." Here the sense of "court" is used to encompass both earthly and heavenly and the saying moves easily between the two. We may postulate that Yeshua does the same thing in our text. Thus, while a murderer has a clear liability within the earthly court, the heart given over to anger has an equally clear liability before the heavenly court, which should be regarded with even a greater fear and reverence.

23–24 Therefore if you are presenting your offering at the altar, and there remember that your brother has something against you, leave your offering there before the altar and go; first be reconciled to your brother, and then come and present your offering.

This teaching of Yeshua is connected to and based upon the conclusion stated in the previous verse, namely, that one should govern his life with a full recognition that it is before the court of Heaven that one ultimate lives. Yet it takes the conclusion one step further. In v. 22, the words are addressed to the person who is angry with his brother. Here, the tables are turned, and the one addressed is the person who knows that a brother has a valid claim ("something against you") that needs to be resolved. In the previous verse, the anger has already been kindled (note the use of the singular verbs in v. 21, but the switch to the plural "you" in vv. 23–24). In these verses, the worshipper realizes that a situation exists that could make one's brother angry. Such a situation needs to be resolved in order to remove what might otherwise become a point of contention, and thus breed anger. Once again, the ruling principle is love for one's brother.

The scenario envisioned presumes the existence of the Temple and the sacrificial system. The phrase "presenting your offering at the altar" does not envision a common person approaching the altar, which is strictly prohibited by the Torah (Num 18:7), but presenting one's offering to the priest who in turn takes it to the altar.

and there remember that your brother has something against you – The giving of a sacrifice presupposes a repentant and submissive heart to God. It is incongruous, then, to know that something has been neglected in regard to one's brother, something that could well cause him to become angry, and to disregard it as unimportant. Such disregard bespeaks a false piety that considers outward acts of worship (presenting an offering) as detached from heart obedience to God's commandments. Once again, the court of Heaven is to be reckoned with, for though the priest officiating at the altar could never know of such a conflict with one's brother, God knows.

What does it mean to "have something against" another person (ἔχω + κατά, *echo* + *kata*, the verb "to have" + the preposition "against")? The only real parallel of this construction in the Lxx is Job 31:35:

> Oh that I had a hearer, and if I had not feared the hand of the Lord; and as to the written charge which I had against any one, (σιγγραφὴν δέ ἥν εἶχον κατά τινος)

Here, "to have something against" is in the form of a written document, something within the realm of a legal claim. In the Apostolic Scriptures, the closest parallel to the language of our Matthew text is found in the repeated charge of Yeshua against the congregations in Rev 2:4–20:

> 4 But I have this against you (ἔχω κατὰ σοῦ), that you have left your first love.
> 14 But I have a few things against you (ἔχω κατὰ σοῦ), because you have there some who hold the teaching of Balaam...
> 20 But I have this against you (ἔχω κατὰ σοῦ), that you tolerate the woman Jezebel...

In each of these examples, the "something against you" is a clear, evident sin. For Job, the language incorporates a legal document, while in the charges against the congregations by Yeshua, the issues involve spiritual unfaithfulness manifest in overt actions.

We should presume that the same applies in our text. The person presenting his offering (δῶρον, *doron*, "gift") remembers that his brother has a legal claim against him, or that in some tangible way he has sinned against his brother. By example this could be that the worshipper has promised to repay a debt, and has not yet done so. Or has something in his possession that he could have rightfully returned to its owner, but has retained it for himself. The fact that the meaning of "has something against you" deals with legal, verifiable issues may also be strengthened by the fact that the ensuing verses deal with settling matters with one's opponent on the way to court.

The point is that Yeshua's command to leave one's offering and first be reconciled to one's brother involves a valid claim, not a mere difference of opinion, or a wrongful claim. Surely there were those who opposed Yeshua and His disciples on theological and *halachic* grounds! Such differences would not have prohibited them from engaging in acts of worship at the Temple.

first be reconciled to your brother, and then come and present your offering – This is the only time in the Apostolic Scriptures that the Greek verb διαλλάσσομαι (*diallassomai*), "to reconcile" is found. The verb (διαλλάσσω, *diallasso*) is found 10 times in the Lxx with various meanings: "to reconcile" (e.g., Judges 19:3; 1Sam 29:4); "to change" (e.g., Wis 19:18); "to die, depart from life" (2Macc 6:27). In view of the fact that the claim is a legal one, that is, one which is valid, to "reconcile" with one's brother means to fulfill one's legal obligations to him. In the examples given, this would mean to pay the overdue debt, or to return an item that belongs to him.

Only after one has discharged his rightful obligations to his brother is he free to return and offer his gift at the altar. The point is clear, and expands upon the teaching in v. 22: the court of Heaven knows the heart and is fully aware of what otherwise might be hidden to others. The valid claim against the worshipper by his brother must therefore be satisfied in accordance with the law as established by the earthly court before one's worship will be accepted by the court of Heaven.

There is ample application of these principles to our own lives in spite of the fact that the Temple and sacrifices are no longer available. The overriding emphasis seems clear: one cannot expect that one's worship will be acceptable to God while one is unwilling to discharge his legal and brotherly obligations to those who are members of his community and thus his fellow worshippers. This highlights the fact, well attested in the rabbinic literature as well, that one's heart intentions form an integral part of valid worship. We may note as an example m.*Pesachim* 3.7:

> He who goes to slaughter his Passover lamb, to circumcise his son, or to eat the betrothal meal at his father-in-law's house, and remembers that he has left some leaven in his house, if he can go back and remove it and go on to do his religious duty, let him go back and remove it. But if not, let him nullify it in his heart. [If he was going] to help against an invasion or to save someone from drowning in a river, from thugs, from a fire, or from a suddenly collapsed house, let him nullify it in his heart. [If he was going] to enjoy the festival rest on a pleasure jaunt, let him go back immediately [and remove the leaven].

> For transgressions done between man and the Omnipresent, the Day of Atonement atones. For transgressions between man and man, the Day of Atonement atones, only if the man will regain the good will of his friend. (m.*Yoma* 8.9)

25–26 Make friends quickly with your opponent at law while you are with him on the way, so that your opponent may not hand you over to the judge, and the judge to the officer, and you be thrown into prison. Truly I say to you, you will not come out of there until you have paid up the last cent.

The scenario drawn here seems to posit a similar yet different case. In the former verses, one who recognizes that his brother (meaning "covenant member") has a valid claim against him (such as an unpaid debt), goes and pays the debt, and the situation is resolved. Here, however, there exists a dispute which can only be resolved in court. However, the description is that of a Roman-Greco court, not that of a Jewish court. First, there is a single judge, but as far as we can tell, a valid *bet din* (court) among the Jewish communities of the 1st Century consisted of a minimum of three judges (m.*Sanhedrin* 1.1ff). Secondly, the court proceedings as pictured have the judge handing the offender to the "officer" (ὑπερέτης, *huperetes*) but in Luke's account (12:58) the word is πράκτωρ (*praktor*) which means "bailiff" or "constable," or even "one who is in charge of a debtor's prison" (so *BDAG*, ad. loc.). Thirdly, punishment by imprisonment was foreign to the Jewish courts of the 1st Century and surely was not the penalty for debt.[1] It was, however, common in the Roman-Greco legal system. We should surmise, then, that the scenario here presented has to do with a legal claim by an outsider upon someone within the Jewish community. Indeed, the word translated "opponent" (ἀντίδικος, *antidikos*) can mean not only an "opponent at law" but also an "enemy."

Moreover, the verb translated "make friends" is εὐνοέω, *eunoeo*, and is used only here in the Apostolic Scriptures. Lachs[2] suggests that an original Hebrew term, לְשַׁלֵּם (*l'shalem*) might have been misunderstood by a Greek translator, for the word can mean "to make peace" but also has a legal sense of "pay in full" (cf. b.*Sanhedrin* 95a). Regardless, the meaning is the same: if an outsider has a valid claim against you, pay the debt before you get to court because the judge may rule for additional damages including prison time. And if such is the case, the debt, to the last cent, will have to be paid

[1]See Lachs, *Rabbinic Commentary*, p. 94; Allison-Davies, *Matthew*, 1.520.

before being released from debtor's prison.

Here again, the point is that earthly courts have power to administer justice, and in some cases, to mete out punishments for criminal behavior. If this is so, how much more sovereignty and power does the court of Heaven have! Therefore, as disciples of our Master Yeshua, we must live with the realization that we answer to the court of Heaven and if we live in this way, we will need never fear the earthly courts.

> R. Yose says, "Let your fellow's money be as precious to you as your own. And get yourself ready to learn Torah, for it does not come as an inheritance to you. And may everything you do be for the sake of Heaven. (m.*Avot* 2.12)

27–28 You have heard that it was said, 'You shall not commit adultery'; but I say to you that everyone who looks at a woman with lust for her has already committed adultery with her in his heart.

From the sin of anger which is the fountain from which murder flows, Yeshua now moves to the inward sin of lust which has the potential of growing into the sin of adultery.

He begins with a shortened form "you have heard it said" which was fully given in v. 21, "you have heard that the ancients were told." As before, this opening introduces a well known teaching, the seventh of the Ten Words: לֹא תִּנְאָף, *lo' tin'af*, "you shall not commit adultery." The idea that Yeshua introduces something here otherwise not taught in the Torah is wrong. In the Ten Words themselves, the final commandment, "you shall not covet" includes "your neighbor's wife" as well as "your neighbor's maid servant" (Ex 20:17). Coveting the wife or maid servant of another man, which surely includes lust, is therefore prohibited by the commandment.

Nor is Yeshua the first to equate the lust of the heart with the actual act of immorality. In the *Testament of Issachar* 7:1–2 (dated to the 1st Century BCE or earlier), we read:

> I am a hundred and twenty-two years old, and I am not aware of having committed a sin unto death. I have not had intercourse with any woman other than my wife, nor was I promiscuous by lustful look.

The rabbinic literature contains very similar teaching, and though later than Yeshua's day, may give evidence of an early teaching of at least some of the Sages.

> Unchaste imagination is more injurious than the sin itself... (b.*Yoma* 29a)

> *Shall commit* [Num 5:6] – The future indicates that they have only intended to commit a sin, but have not yet done so. This is to teach you that the moment a man contemplates sin, it is as though he has committed a trespass against the Omnipresent One. (Mid. Rab. *Num* §8.5)

How, then, are we to understand the apparent antithesis given by Yeshua if, in fact, there is every indication that His emphasis upon the sin of lust was a well known teaching in His day? The answer may be found in an exegetical debate between Shammai and Hillel referenced in the Talmud. In b.*Qiddushin* 43a the debate is over an exegetical question: if two verses teach the same thing, can a general *halachic* rule be made from them? Hillel said "no," and Shammai, "yes." Hillel then points to the use of the demonstrative "that" (הַהוּא, *hahu'*) in Lev 17:4, "…bloodguiltiness is to be reckoned to <u>that</u> man. He has shed blood and <u>that</u> man shall be cut off from among his people." Hillel goes on to reason that if someone had sent his agent into the field to slaughter a sacrifice (which Lev 17:4 prohibits), the agent, not the sender, is liable, since the text says "that man." Shammai, of course, interprets the verse to mean "whoever slaughters a sacrifice outside of the Tabernacle is liable," and appeals to the sin of David in having Uriah killed as proof.

> Now, when it was taught: If he says to his agent, 'Go forth and slay a soul,' the latter is liable, and his sender is exempt. Shammai the Elder said on the authority of Haggai the prophet: His sender is liable, for it is said, you (David) have slain him with the sword of the children of Ammon (2Sam 12:9). What is Shammai the Elder's reason? — He holds that two verses with the same purpose throw light [on others], and he rejects the exegesis of *ha-hu* [as opposed to] *hu*. Alternatively, he accepts that exegesis; and what is meant by liable? He is liable by the laws of Heaven. Hence it follows that the first Tanna holds him exempt even by the law of Heaven! — But they differ in respect to a greater or a lesser penalty. (b.*Qiddushin* 43a)

The point that Shammai is making is that David was liable for Uriah's death, even though Uriah was killed by the swords of Ammon, and he does so on the basis of the prophet Nathan's own words who charged David with murder (2Sam 12:9). Thus, for Shammai, *intention* to kill incurs liability even if someone else does the killing, but it does so by the "laws of Heaven," since intentionality cannot very often be proven in an earthly court. But then the question is asked how Hillel could have answered such an argument, since to oppose Shammai would mean that even the court of Heaven does not hold intentionality liable. The answer is that Hillel considered the "sender" liable but to a lesser penalty.

It may be possible, then, since the debates of Hillel and Shammai are early (late 1st Century BCE), that a similar legal argument was extant in Yeshua's day. Perhaps the prevailing legal standard was that only the person himself who actually committed the crime was liable, even if he did so at the urging or request of another. In other words, *intentionality* was not considered of any significant importance in the courts of Yeshua's day.

Yeshua is clearly opposed to such an idea, for the courts of Heaven are fully aware of one's intentions, and such intentions inevitably lead to sinful actions. It may be, if our assessment of the Shammai/Hillel debate is on track, that here is another instance in which Yeshua sides with Shammai against Hillel, as He appears to do later in the divorce pericope.

everyone who looks at a woman with lust for her – the word for lust here is ἐπιθυμέω (*epithumeo*) which is the same Greek word used in the Lxx of Ex 19:17 to mean "covet," and as noted earlier, this combines the seventh and tenth commandments, even as Yeshua does here. The Greek construction (preposition πρός + infinitive) "represents result and implies that the sin lies not in the entrance of a thought but in letting it incite passion" (Allison-Davies, *Matthew*, 1.523). It is the intention to allow the initial thought to grow into lustful passion that involves the sin. Temptation alone is not a transgression, but if temptation is not immediately rejected, it quickly becomes lust.

We may note in passing that the words of our Master appear to address males in particular: "everyone who looks at a woman with lust for her," where πᾶς (*pas*, "everyone") as well as the participle ὁ βλέπων (*ho blepon*) are masculine in the Greek. In a wider sense, however, the principles of our Master's teaching apply to all. Sexual lust, wherever it may reside, is a sin that should be reckoned for what it truly is—a transgression against one's neighbor and against Heaven.

29–30 If your right eye makes you stumble, tear it out and throw it from you; for it is better for you to lose one of the parts of your body, than for your whole body to be thrown into hell. If your right hand makes you stumble, cut it off and throw it from you; for it is better for you to lose one of the parts of your body, than for your whole body to go into hell.

These verses demonstrate with hyperbolic ferocity the seriousness of Yeshua's call to holiness (cf. also Matt 18:9). He speaks in prophetic tones that shock our senses and that is His intention. Obviously He is not teaching self-mutilation! Destroying a part of the body does not save one from hell. He is rather teaching us that purity of heart is to be considered of greater importance than even physical life. If one is intent upon saving one's flesh from injury and disease, how much more should he be diligent to guard his soul from the ravages of sin. The believer "amputates the passions of the soul without touching the body" (Origen, *Comm. on Matt.* 15.4, quoted from Allison-Davies, *Matthew*, 1.524).

The right eye may have been understood as having higher importance than the left (so Lachs, *Rabbinic Commentary*, p. 97), or else it is so designated to suggest a "glance" or "perception" rather than a close, intimate gaze with both eyes. The eye is listed first since the previous verses emphasize that lust is the function of eyes. In the Mark parallel (9:42–47), hand, foot, and eye are listed (in that order).

With the idea of the lust of the eye, Yeshua adds the actions of the right hand. In Semitic idiom, the right hand is the hand of strength and authority (e.g., Ex 15:6,12; Ps 16:8; 20:6; Is 48:13). Some have suggested that the "right hand" continues the sense of sexual sins (cf. Song of Solomon 2:6; 8:3) but this is doubtful. Rather, the point is that one's physical strength must be coupled with one's spiritual strength. Once again, the point is that one's spiritual ability to withstand temptation and sin is even more important than one's physical strength. For if one has only wholeness of body but is weak spiritually, the whole body will perish. But spiritual purity, the sanctification that proceeds from genuine faith, preserves both body and soul.

It seems quite possible that Paul is aware of this teaching of Yeshua, for he too speaks of "putting to death the members of your earthly body" in Col 3:5–6.

> Therefore consider the members of your earthly body as dead to immorality, impurity, passion, evil desire, and greed, which amounts to idolatry. It is because of these things that the wrath of God will come upon the sons of disobedience,

For Yeshua, hell (γέεννα, *geenna*, "Gehenna") is a reality, the place of God's final judgment against sinners. Kingdom righteousness (that which surpasses that of the scribes and Pharisees, v. 20), involves the divinely supplied gift of spiritual strength, the ability to pursue righteousness and shun the sinful desires of the flesh and the world. Once again, Yeshua is not teaching a "works-rightouesness" here. He is not saying that by living morally one secures for himself a favored position before the Almighty. What He is saying is that those who are His true disciples, those who have been "born again," who have been born "of water and Spirit" (Jn 3:3, 5) will strive to overcome the sinful nature and will ultimately be victorious in this struggle.

But His call to holiness is a radical one. For His followers, holiness is priority one, and all other things, even those that are good, if they stand in the way of sanctification, must be removed. This demonstrates the place where the *Shema* is worked out in every day living. To love the LORD with all of one's heart, soul, and might means to be wholly set apart to Him.

31–32 It was said, 'WHOEVER SENDS HIS WIFE AWAY, LET HIM GIVE HER A CERTIFICATE OF DIVORCE'; but I say to you that everyone who divorces his wife, except for the reason of unchastity, makes her commit adultery; and whoever marries a divorced woman commits adultery.

The previous discussion of sexual sins, which begin in the heart when lustful thoughts are entertained and allowed to grow into sinful desire, forms the obvious background for this teaching on divorce. Divorce, which causes adultery, is the end result of sin fostered first in the heart. Divorce does not "just happen." It is the result of a process that begins with the sins of selfishness, lust, hatred and bitterness. In 19:1–12 (cp also Mk 10:11–12; Lk 16:18), the subject of divorce and remarriage is more fully developed by our Master Who is confronted with the issue by some Pharisees who want to "test" His *halachah* on divorce. There, as here, the Torah provision for divorce (Deut 24:1–4) is brought forward as the basis for formulating the current *halachah*. In 19:1–12, however, Yeshua appeals to Gen 2:24 as the more foundational text regulating the marriage covenant, and He views Deut 24:1–4 as a necessary concession because of the sinful heart of men. Though Yeshua does not appeal in this case to Gen 2:24, the general idea of marriage as an enduring covenant is clearly at work, and this definitely undergirds Yeshua's teaching at this point.

We may first compare the quote from Deut 24:1—

For studies on the biblical teaching of divorce and remarriage, see Gordon P. Hugenberger, *Marriage as a Covenant* (Baker, 1994); David Instone-Brewer, *Divorce and Remarriage in the Bible* (Eerdmans, 2002); John Murray, *Divorce* (Preb & Reformed Pub., 1980).

MT	Lxx	Matthew
וְכָתַב לָהּ סֵפֶר כְּרִיתֻת וְנָתַן בְּיָדָהּ וְשִׁלְּחָהּ מִבֵּיתוֹ	γράψει αὐτῇ βιβλίον ἀποστασίου καὶ δώσει εἰς τὰς χεῖρας αὐτῆς καὶ ἐξαποστελεῖ αὐτὴν ἐκ τῆς οἰκίας αὐτοῦ	ὃς ἂν ἀπολύσῃ τὴν γυναῖκα αὐτοῦ δότω αὐτῇ ἀποστάσιον
he writes for her a certificate of divorce and puts it in her hand and sends her from his house	he writes for her a certificate of divorce and puts into her hand and sends her out of his house	whoever sends away his wife, let him give her a certificate of divorce

First, it is apparent that the "quote" is actually not a quote at all, but a legal prescription based upon Deut 24:1. Matthew uses two key terms from the Lxx translation: (1) both use ἀποστάσιον (*apostasion,* "bill of divorcement"), (2) both use the verb δίδωμι (*didomi,* "to give") when speaking of delivering the bill of divorcement to the wife. Except for these two terms, it is clear that Yeshua is simply stating a *halachic* axiom based upon Deut 24:1 and not quoting the text directly. This fact informs the text as a whole, for in simply stating the *halachic* rule, i.e., that a "valid divorce" occurs only when a proper *get* (גֵּט or גִּיט, *geit/giyt*) is written and actually delivered to the woman, Yeshua is showing how the emphasis in His day was on "proper paper work" without due attention to the heart of the matter, i.e., whether a divorce was valid in the first place. Indeed, the overall conclusion of these verses is that "proper paper work" for an invalid divorce is nothing less that a form of publicly sanctioned adultery. Once again, the antithesis brought by Yeshua is His contrast between a well accepted practice or belief and what the Torah actually teaches by stressing one's heart submission to God.

The rabbinic *halachah* regarding divorce is contained in the Mishnah Tractate *Gittin* ("Bills of Divorcement"). The entire Tractate is taken up with the proper way to write and deliver a bill of divorcement, and what constitutes a valid *get* and thus a valid divorcement. This is what one would expect in light of the fact that the Mishnah is essentially a body of casuistic law and not a treatise on ethics or theological beliefs. But in spite of this, the emphasis of the Mishnah makes Yeshua's point that much stronger. When the issue of divorce arose among the Jewish communities of His day, recourse to the legal rulings of the Sages as to how one goes about satisfying the legal requirements was the primary focus. Yeshua intends to take the matter back to a more fundamental question, namely, whether divorce was valid in the first place.

Clearly the Torah (Deut 24:1–4) speaks to the issue of divorce, and gives legal procedures for enacting a divorce. But the overall emphasis of the Deut text focuses on the issue of a woman remarrying her first husband after having been divorced, marrying another man, and then divorced from him. While the scenario presented in the Torah text presupposes divorce, its point is to limit the "shuffling" of women back and forth between different men. Such a practice undermines the core element of marital sanctity and is therefore prohibited. Therefore, though the Deut passage presupposes divorce, it hardly sanctions it as God's intended program.

Yet Deut 24:1 does indicate that a recognized divorce existed in ancient Israel, and that the Torah itself, while not encouraging divorce, does make a provision for it. The major issue of interpretation for Deut 24:1, however, is what Moses means by the words "some indecency:"

> When a man takes a wife and marries her, and it happens that she finds no favor in his eyes because he has found some indecency in her, and he writes her a certificate of divorce and puts it in her hand and sends her out from his house…

The Hebrew for "some indecency" is עֶרְוַת דָּבָר (*'ervat davar*), literally "an indecent matter." Thus, the first thing to recognize in this text is that it limits divorce to the case where "an indecent matter" is discovered in the wife.

A great deal of discussion, both ancient and modern, has surrounded the meaning of *'ervat davar* in Deut 24:1, and no clear consensus has been reached. If the issue were one of sexual infidelity through an act of adultery, then the death penalty would be enacted (Lev 20:10). If the husband suspected his wife of adultery, but there was insufficient evidence to prove it, he would be required either to forego any further action in the matter, or require his wife to undergo the test of the bitter water (Num 5:11ff). We should presume, then, that *'ervat davar* describes something other than adultery or suspected adultery. The Hebrew word עֶרְוָה, *'ervah* often means "naked" (e.g., it is used regularly in describing sexual relations in Lev 18), and sometimes is used euphemistically for the genitals. It is also used metaphorically of unguarded regions of a land (e.g., Gen 42:9, 12). But the word also came to mean something indecent or inappropriate, as in the requirement that excrement not be in the camp, for such would be "indecent" (Deut 23:15).

The rabbis were divided on how to interpret the "indecent matter" of Deut 24:1. The most famous and well known debate existed between Hillel and Shammai, as found in m.*Gittin* 9:10 –

> The House of Shammai say, "A man should divorce his wife only because he has found grounds for it in unchastity, "since it is said, Because he has found in her indecency in anything (Dt. 24:1)." And the House of Hillel say, "Even if she spoiled his dish, "since it is said, Because he has found in her indecency in anything." R. Aqiba says, "Even if he found someone else prettier than she, "since it is said, And it shall be if she find no favor in his eyes (Dt. 24:1)." (m.*Gittin* 9:10)[1]

[1]A fuller account of this Mishnah and the debate between Hillel and Shammai is found in *Sifre* Deut §269.

The two interpretations as well as Akiva's extended interpretation all depend upon the Hebrew עֶרְוַת דָּבָר, *'ervat davar*. Some of the difficulty results from the fact that this is not normally how we would expect the Hebrew to be written. עֶרְוַת דָּבָר has the "indecency" as a construct of "matter," thus literally, "an indecency of a matter," where we would rather expect דְּבַר עֶרְוָה, "a matter of indecency." This led the Sages to question why the Hebrew was written in such a peculiar fashion. Hillel reasoned that the word דָּבָר, "matter" seemed to be superfluous. The phrase could just as well have been written without it: "he finds in her an indecency." He therefore reasoned that the additional word דָּבָר was to be interpreted as adding something additional to the meaning of עֶרְוַת. Since עֶרְוַת expressed "indecency," the addition of דָּבָר meant "any other matter," therefore, "even if she spoiled his dish." In contrast, Shammai considered the two words to express a single idea, that is, unchastity or indecency, and limited valid divorce to the case where a wife had acted inappropriately with another man, albeit short of actual adultery. Akiva was a Hillelite, and took the import of Deut 24:1 even further. Since the verse includes "she finds no favor in his eyes," he understood this to be a third category beside the two noted by Hillel, namely that a man could divorce his wife because he found someone else more pleasing.

Generally, the rulings of Hillel were followed by the majority, and we may presume that his "no-fault" divorce policies were considered normative for the majority of the Jewish communities. The fact that the debate is between Hillel and Shammai, both early Sages, would warrant us presuming that such liberal views of divorce were extant in the time of Yeshua. This sets the background for Yeshua's antithesis. In a time when divorce was granted for any reason, Yeshua calls for a reassessment of the sanctity of marriage itself.

It seems very possible, in light of the rabbinic debate just mentioned, that Yeshua's exception clause ("except for the reason of unchastity") is His understanding of *'ervat davar* in Deut 24:1, and if so, He clearly aligns Himself with the minority ruling (Shammai), i.e., that the only valid grounds for divorce is that of some form of sexual sin. The Greek word translated "unchastity" is πορνέια (*porneia*) which has a wide range of meanings, but is always tied to some form of sexual deviancy. It regularly translates זְנוּת (*z'nut*) in the Tanach, a word derived from the verb זָנָה, *zanah*, "to commit fornication," and regularly used of prostitution (e.g., Gen 38:24; Lev 19:29). The Hebrew word for "harlot" is זֹנָה (*zonah*). Thus, its use in this context, especially as Yeshua's equivalent for *'ervat davar* of Deut 24:1, would indicate that it has some sexual overtones.

Instone-Brewer has also pointed to another factor that suggests Yeshua's "except for *porneia*" was His understanding of *'ervat davar* along the lines of Shammai. In the Mishnah quoted above (m.*Gittin* 9:10), the Hebrew text has an interesting clue. As I noted earlier, the Hebrew phrase in Deut 24:1 is awkward, and one would expect *davar* to come first, followed by *'ervah*, yielding "an indecent matter." Shammai, understanding the phrase to mean precisely this, changes the order of the words in the Mishnah:

> The school of Shammai says: A man should not divorce his wife except he found in her a matter of indecency (דבר ערוה), as it is said: *For he finds in her an indecent matter* (ערות דבר). (m.*Gittin* 9:10).

Significantly, the order of the words in our Matthew text follow Shammai: παρεκτὸς λόγου πορνείας, "except for a matter of *porneia*."

The primary question, however, still remains: what does *porneia* encompass? The reason that this is an important question is that for Yeshua it is *porneia* that offers the grounds for a valid divorce and thus the right to remarry without committing adultery. Some have interpreted *porneia* in a very narrow sense, making it mean adultery,[1] while others understand it to mean incest in the sense of marriage within the forbidden degrees of Lev 18.[2] One hardly thinks that *porneia* would mean adultery here, because Deut 24:1 does not deal with clear cases of adultery since these would have been dealt with as a capital offence. Nor does *porneia* suggest marriages within the forbidden degrees, since such marriages were ruled invalid from the beginning, and did not require a divorce but rather were annulled.[3] The best we can say is that *porneia* involves some sin of a sexual nature which falls short of witnessed adultery but has nonetheless severed the marital bond between the husband and wife.

makes her commit adultery – A man who divorces his wife for invalid reasons causes her to commit adultery. How so? This must be understood against the backdrop of the Ancient Near East in which a woman, sent forth from her husband's house, had little recourse but to remarry in order to sustain her own life. From Yeshua's point of view, since in the case of an invalid divorce she was still considered to be the man's wife, marrying another man constituted adultery. But the culpability of such a thing is laid at the feet of the husband who wrongfully divorced her.

What of a woman who has committed *porneia* and is therefore given a valid divorce by her husband? Is she free to remarry? Yeshua actually does not approach this question, though Deut 24:1–4 would indicate that such did

[1]Allison-Davies, *Matthew* 1.530f

[2]See the explanation of Hagner, *Matthew*, 1.124.

[3]David Novak, "Annulment in Lieu of Divorce in Jewish Law" in Jackson, ed., *The Jewish Law Annual*, vol. 4 (Brill, 1984).

occur in ancient Israel and apparently without being considered as an act of adultery. Legally, a woman given a valid divorce is free to remarry, for this was the purpose of divorce in the first place. The Mishnah gives the shortest valid wording of the *get*: "Lo, you are permitted to any man" (m.*Gittin* 9.11). The idea, then, that Yeshua permitted divorce but prohibited remarriage is invalid. In the 1st Century CE, divorce and the right to remarry were bond together. In fact, this is Yeshua's point: an invalid divorce gives no right to remarry in God's eyes. A valid divorce does. However, in the case of the unfaithful wife who is given a valid divorce, her status as one who has engaged in *porneia* is made clear, and one would have to wonder what kind of man would be willing to marry her under these circumstances.

and whoever marries a divorced woman commits adultery – This final clause of our text must be read in light of the context in which Yeshua is apparently speaking to the "no fault" divorces that abounded in His day. Whereas the legal authorities considered a divorce valid as long as the "paper work" was properly filed, Yeshua rather returns to the words of the Torah (Deut 24:1) in order to bring its divine message to bear upon the events of His day. "No fault" divorce was, as far as Yeshua was concerned, no divorce at all. Women who were dismissed from their husband's home by such invalid "bills of dismissal" were, in God's eyes, still rightfully married. As such, they were not "free to marry" another man, even though the *get* they held in their hand said they were. Therefore, any man who married such a woman was taking to himself the wife of another man, and this constituted adultery.

33–37 **"Again, you have heard that the ancients were told, 'You shall not make false vows, but shall fulfill your vows to the Lord.' But I say to you, make no oath at all, either by heaven, for it is the throne of God, or by the earth, for it is the footstool of His feet, or by Jerusalem, for it is the city of the great King. Nor shall you make an oath by your head, for you cannot make one hair white or black. But let your statement be, 'Yes, yes' or 'No, no'; anything beyond these is of evil.**

This fourth antithesis relates to the issue of vows and oaths. Normally a vow (נֶדֶר, *neider;* נָדַר, *nadar,* "to vow" / ὄρκος, *orkos,* "vow") is offered to God, while an oath (שְׁבֻעָה, *sh'vu'ah;* שָׁבַע, *shava'* "to swear" / ὀμνύω, *omnuo,* "to swear") is made with one's fellow man. However, the terms were often used interchangeably so we should not make a major point of their appearance together in this text.[1]

The opening phrase "you have heard that the ancients were told" matches the opening line of v. 21 and is probably used structurally to group the sayings into two groups of three. Thus, this antithesis marks the beginning of the second set.

The well known axiom prohibiting false oaths and the command to fulfill one's vows to the Lord is based upon texts like Lev 19:12, "You shall not swear falsely by My name, so as to profane the name of your God; I am the LORD" and Num 30:2 "If a man makes a vow to the LORD, or takes an oath to bind himself with a binding obligation, he shall not violate his word; he shall do according to all that proceeds out of his mouth." The opening statement, then, is not a direct quote from the Torah but a general paraphrase combining several Torah texts. Nor does the Greek of Matthew match that of the Lxx in either of these two texts.[2] It may be that Ps 50:14 (Lxx 49:14) is in mind: "Offer to God a sacrifice of thanksgiving and pay your vows to the

[1] See the comments of Lachs, *Rabbinic Commentary,* pp. 100-101.

[2] The DuTillet of v. 33 offers no substantial help. The Hebrew is essentially a translation of the Greek. The Münster has the same reading as the DuTillet with the exception that it has the plural "vows" where the DuTillet has the singular. The Even Bohan has a different text from either the DuTillet or the Münster. It reads: לא תשבעו בשמי לשקר ותשיב לה" שבועתך, "Do not swear in My name falsely and return to Adonai your vow."

Most High."

Obviously Yeshua is not contradicting the clear statement of the Torah which commands that a person is to make honest vows which he intends to fulfill. At first reading, the Master's words seem to prohibit oaths or vows altogether, but if we put His words into the context of early Judaisms as we know them, a different emphasis is recognized.

As far as we can tell, the taking of oaths and vows had become a common thing in Yeshua's time, so common that it had become customary to utter thoughtless, even outrageous vows. In b.*Shabbat 116a*; b.*Bava Metzia 85a*; b.*Makkot* 5b we read of vows such as "may I lose my sons if…," "may I not see the comfort of the Messianic Age if…" and similar vain words. Such thoughtless uttering of oaths prompted the Sages to find ways to limit the taking of oaths. Their words directly parallel those of Yeshua in regard to oaths. After a typical Talmudic story of a person who swears and suffers, the Sages conclude, "Be you guilty or innocent, do not swear."[1] In like manner we read,

> Be careful with vows, and not hasty with them, for he who is hasty with vows will end by false swearing (מועל בשבועית), and he who swears falsely, denies me, and will never be forgiven.[2]

> The Holy One, blessed be He, said to Israel, 'Do not imagine that you are permitted to swear by My name even in truth…[3]

In Philo we read:

> To swear not at all is the best course and most profitable to life, well suited to a rational nature which has been taught to speak the truth so well on each occasion that its words are regarded as oaths; to swear truly is only, as people say, a second-best voyage, for the mere fact of his swearing casts suspicion on the trustworthiness of the man. Let him, then, lag and linger in the hope that by repeated postponement he may avoid the oath altogether.[4]

Josephus indicates that the Essenes avoided taking oaths,[5] and the Qumran sect appears to share a similar reluctance regarding vows (though there is some ambiguity, cf. 11QTemple 53-54; CD 7.8; 9.9–12; 15–16; 1QS 5.8; 6.27).

Yeshua continues by prohibiting oaths by "heaven," "earth," Jerusalem," or by one's own "head." We find similar references in the Mishnah among the debates of what constituted a valid or binding oath, and what did not:

> "I impose an oath on you," "I command you," "I bind you,"—lo, these are liable. "By heaven and earth," lo, these are exempt. "By [the name of] Alef-dalet [Adonai]" or "Yud-he [Yahweh]," "By the Almighty," "By Hosts," "By him who is merciful and gracious," "By him who is long-suffering and abundant in mercy," or by any other euphemism—lo, these are liable. "He who curses making use of any one of these is liable," the words of R. Meir. And sages exempt. "He who curses his father or his mother with any one of them is liable," the words of R. Meir. And sages exempt. He who curses himself and his friend with any one of them transgresses a negative commandment. [If he said,] "May God smite you," "So may God smite you," this is [language for] an adjuration which is written in the Torah (Lev.

[1] y.*Shavu'ot* §6 37a.

[2] b.*Mattot* 79a.

[3] Mid. Rab. *Num* 22.1.

[4] Philo, *On the Decalogue* 17.

[5] *Bell.* 2.135.

5:1). "May he not smite you," "may he bless you," "may he do good
to you"— R. Meir declares liable [for a false oath taken with such a
formula]. And sages exempt. (m.*Shevu'ot* 4.13)

He who says, "Not-unconsecrated produce shall I not eat with you,"
"Not-valid [food]," and, "Not pure," "[Not] clean [for the altar]," or
"Unclean," or "Remnant," or "Refuse"— is bound. [If he said, "May
it be to me] like the lamb [of the daily whole offering]," "Like the
[temple] sheds," "Like the wood," "Like the fire," "Like the altar,"
"Like the sanctuary," "Like Jerusalem"— [if] he vowed by the name
of one of any of the utensils used for the altar, even though he has not
used the word *qorban*—lo, this one has vowed [in a binding way as if
he had vowed] by *qorban*. R. Judah says, "He who says, 'Jerusalem,'
has said nothing." (m.*Nedarim* 1.3)

[If] he said to him, "If one litigant said to the other, 'I accept my father
as reliable,' 'I accept your father as reliable,' 'I accept as reliable three
herdsmen [to serve as judges]'"— R. Meir says, "He has the power
to retract." And sages say, "He has not got the power to retract." [If]
one owed an oath to this fellow, and his fellow said, "[Instead of an
oath], take a vow to me by the life of your head," R. Meir says, "He
has the power to retract." And sages say, "He has not got the power
to retract." (m.*Sanhedrin* 3.2)

If these rabbinic discussions give evidence of the early debates over
what did and did not constitute a binding oath, then it becomes clear that
the problem addressed by Yeshua was one of legal ambiguity in the matter
of oaths and vows. The tangle of legal rulings surrounding the whole matter
of oaths and vows had made them practically ineffective. As such, the integrity of a person's words had lost their value to the "red tape" of the legal
system. Yeshua therefore teaches that one's word should be enough without
needing to rely upon legal constructs that could be manipulated to one's
advantage later on.

Moreover, it becomes clear that Yeshua is not prohibiting oaths or vows
altogether, but is teaching that one's oath should be simple and honest, and
made with the full recognition that God is witness to one's oath. For this reason, to swear by "heaven" or "earth" is the same as to swear by God's name,
for heaven and earth belong to Him. Is 66:1 says, "Thus says the LORD,
"Heaven is My throne and the earth is My footstool." Likewise, Jerusalem is
His dwelling place, and to swear by the Holy City is the same as evoking the
witness of God: "Beautiful in elevation, the joy of the whole earth, is Mount
Zion in the far north, the city of the great King" (Ps 48:2). "To swear by one's
head" is equivalent to the Hebrew חַיֵּי רֹאשְׁךָ, "by the life of your head," meaning by oneself (as we noted in the above quote from m.*Sanhedrin* 3.2). Once
again, such an addition to one's oath is superfluous, since one should recognize that God alone is the One who maintains life. Black hair may represent
youth, and white hair the aged. In other words, we cannot halt time and
keep from growing old. Our times are in His hands, for it is "in Him we live,
and move, and exist" (Acts 17:28).

*But let your statement be, 'Yes, yes' or 'No, no'; anything beyond these is of
evil.* Thus, our Master's conclusion is not that oaths or vows are prohibited,
for saying "yes" or "no" was considered an oath:

R. Elazar said, "Yea is an oath, and nay is an oath": Raba said, "But only then if yea and nay are said twice." (b.*Shavu'ot* 36a)

Likewise, the Sages taught the same thing regarding simply saying "yes" and "no" as a valid oath:

"Let your nay and yea be both *zedek*." (b.*Bava Metzia* 49a)

R. Huna said, "The yea of the righteous is a yea; their no is a no." (Mid Rab *Ruth* vii. §6, on 3.18)

According to *Mechilta*, the Israelites answered "Yea, yea and nay, nay to the commands at Sinai" (*Mechilta* on Exodus, 20:1, 2).

Thus, while not prohibiting vows or oaths altogether, Yeshua does bring us back to the very import and message of the Torah, namely, that our words should be fully spoken in truth and with integrity. James reiterates the essence of our Master's teaching:

But above all, my brethren, do not swear, either by heaven or by earth or with any other oath; but your yes is to be yes, and your no, no, so that you may not fall under judgment. (James 5:12)

It seems apparent that Yeshua's words here were understood by His Apostles as we have construed them, that is, not as prohibiting oaths altogether, but requiring that His disciples make simple vows with full intention of fulfilling them. Thus, Paul himself took a Nazirite vow (Acts 18:18), and he helped four men complete their vow in Jerusalem (Acts 21:23) which would have required the taking of a vow. Likewise, Paul uses oath formulae in Rom 1:9; 2Cor 1:23; Gal 1:20; Phil 1:8, and the angel of John's Apocalypse swears "by the God of heaven" (Rev 10:6). Once again, the antithesis that Yeshua gives us is between a superficial adherence to Torah commandments for the sake of men, and obedience from the heart that longs to please the Almighty Himself.

38–39 You have heard that it was said, 'An eye for an eye, and a tooth for a tooth.' But I say to you, do not resist an evil person; but whoever slaps you on your right cheek, turn the other to him also.

The law of *lex talionis* (law of retaliation) is found in Ex 21:25; Lev 24:19ff, and Deut 19:21. The Sages have always understood the application of the *lex talionis* of the Torah to be in the sense of equivalence, that is, equivalent payment equal to the evaluation of the loss. The idea of physical mutilation as a means of lawful punishment has no example in the Scriptures, except for the penalty for a woman who injures a man's private parts—her hand is to be cut off (Deut 25:11–12). However, the Sages interpret this as they do *lex talionis*, and understand the penalty to be the equivalent value of a hand. The only example we find is during warfare, when the soldiers of Israel defeated Adoni-Bezek, and cut off his thumbs and big-toes (Judges 1:6). But this is not a penalty of justice *per se* but a humbling of a defeated enemy in war.

In our context, however, Yeshua quotes a representative line from the *lex talionis* but places it in the context, not of physical injury but of public humiliation. For a slap on the cheek is not an injury to the body but to one's soul and sense of personal dignity. Some have suggested that the idea of the "right cheek" would mean that a right handed person doing the striking would do so with the back of the hand, giving an even greater sense of public humiliation. As we shall see, the Mishnah considers a back-handed slap of even greater consequences.

The Mishnah gives five areas where damages may be lawfully sought:

> He who injures his fellow is liable to [compensate] him on five counts: (1) injury, (2) pain, (3) medical costs, (4) loss of income [lit.: loss of time], and (5) indignity. (m.*BavaQama* 8.1)

It is to the fifth category that Yeshua makes reference, and the Mishnah uses His same analogy:

> He who boxes the ear of his fellow pays him a *sela*. R. Judah says in the name of R. Yose the Galilean, "A *maneh*." [If] he smacked him, he pays him two hundred *zuz*. [If] it is with the back of his hand, he pays him four hundred *zuz*. (m.*BavaQama* 8.6)

A *maneh* was equivalent to 25 *selas* and 100 *zuz*. To give an idea of these evaluations, a pair of oxen for plowing could cost 200 *zuz* (m.*BavaBatra* 5.1). It can be seen, then, that public humiliation, if pressed, could be quite expensive, for a back-handed slap could cost one the equivalent of two pair of oxen.

It may well be in the context of these legal penalties for public insult that Yeshua gives His teaching. It is not as though He diminishes the grave results of public insult, but His method of dealing with it is not to seek monetary payment, but rather to combat such insult with humility. One is not to "resist an evil person," which in this context must mean "one is not to retaliate with equivalent insults." Moreover, to "turn the other cheek" means to allow additional insults to go unchallenged. It is not through hauling the insulter into court and demanding payment, but through a humble and gracious spirit that the one insulted will be seen as righteous. Nothing illustrates this more than the example of Yeshua Himself:

> For you have been called for this purpose, since Messiah also suffered for you, leaving you an example for you to follow in His steps, who committed no sin, nor was any deceit found in His mouth; and while being reviled, He did not revile in return; while suffering, He uttered no threats, but kept entrusting Himself to Him who judges righteously. (1Pet 2:21–23)

Understood in this way, the teaching of our Master is not in reference to bodily injury, or to someone attacking another person to inflict bodily harm. He is dealing rather with the wounds of public defamation and teaches us that humility, not returning insult for insult, and allowing the Almighty to deal with the one who has tried to inflict public insult, is the way of righteousness.

Some of the Sages taught the same thing:

> Has it not been taught: Concerning those who are insulted but do not insult others [in revenge], who hear themselves reproached without replying, who [perform good] work out of love of the Lord and re-

> joice in their sufferings, Scripture says: But they that love Him will be as the sun when he goes forth in his might? (Judges 5:31) — [That means,] indeed, that he keeps it in his heart [though without taking action]. But Raba said: He who passes over his retaliations has all his transgressions passed over. — [That speaks of the case] that an endeavour was made to obtain his reconciliation, and his consent is obtained. (b.*Yoma* 23a)

> If you are struck you must forgive the offender even though he does not ask for your forgiveness. (t.*BavaQama* 9.29)

Likewise, in the Daily Prayers we recite:

> My God, guard my tongue from evil and my lips from speaking deceitfully. To those who curse me, may my soul be unresponsive; and let my soul be like dust to all. (*The Complete Metsuda Siddur*, p. 140)

40–42 If anyone wants to sue you and take your shirt, let him have your coat also. Whoever forces you to go one mile, go with him two. Give to him who asks of you, and do not turn away from him who wants to borrow from you.

> In the Luke parallel (6:29–30), the wording is somewhat different:

> Whoever hits you on the cheek, offer him the other also; and whoever takes away your coat, do not withhold your shirt from him either. Give to everyone who asks of you, and whoever takes away what is yours, do not demand it back.

Some have understood the idea of "take away" to mean "rob" or "steal" but the verb (αἴρω, *airo*) does not generally have this sense. So Luke is not suggesting that someone robs a person of something, he is obligated to offer him other things as well. Luke's "takes away" is probably equivalent to Matthew's picture of taking one's shirt as legal compensation in a lawsuit.

We should recognize that these verses continue in the same context already established, that is, Yeshua's call for humility and forbearance on the part of His disciples. Someone who takes a person to court must be presumed to have a valid claim. In the illustration given by our Master, the plaintiff sues for compensation, and the defendant is portrayed as very poor, since the clothes on his back are his only valuable possessions. Rather than seeking some legal loopholes, or counter-suit, the one who knows that a claimant has a valid case against him should fully comply and seek to make full restitution, even if it means giving up what might be rightfully retained. For the inner garment (the "shirt") was not protected under Torah law, but the outer tunic may have been (Ex 22:26–27, though in this case, the tunic is taken as security, not debt recovery). Thus, in a willingness to make full restitution where a debt is owed, the poor person will be seen as righteous and in such willing compliance, may receive mercy.

The second illustration is that of forced travel. In 1st Century Roman society, a Roman soldier had the authority to require any common person to assist him in his travels, especially to carry his equipment. Apparently such a requirement could only be extended for a mile (the Greek μίλον, *milon* was about 20% shorter than our modern mile). Yeshua, however, requires that

His disciples give double the request.

> It is natural to suppose that Matt 1:41 is concerned with the situation
> which would arise if a Jewish civilian is impressed as baggage-carrier
> by a Roman soldier of the army of occupation. If the victim is a fol-
> lower of Jesus, he will give double what is demanded. The first mile
> renders to Caesar the things that are Caesar's, the second mile, by
> meeting oppression with kindness, renders to God the things that are
> God's. (Manson, *Sayings*, p. 160, quoted from Lachs, *Rabbinic Com-
> mentary*, p. 105)

Our Lord's instructions on this topic are concluded with His requirement that His disciples be gracious and giving. His words are in the form
of a parallelism, so that He is not talking about two things, i.e., being gracious and willing to loan to someone who asks to borrow. Rather, the two are
speaking of the same thing, that is, a generous spirit that considers God to be
the supplier of all one's needs. Interestingly, a discussion on "revenge" and
"bearing a grudge" in the rabbinic materials also incorporates the idea of
loaning to someone who asks:

> What is revenge and what is bearing a grudge? If one said to his
> fellow: 'Lend me your sickle', and he replied 'No', and to-morrow
> the second comes [to the first] and says: 'Lend me your axe'! and he
> replies: 'I will not lend it to you, just as you would not lend me your
> sickle' — that is revenge. And what is bearing a grudge? If one says
> to his fellow: 'Lend me your axe , he replies 'No', and on the morrow
> the second asks: 'Lend me your garment', and he answers: 'Here it is.
> I am not like you who would not lend me [what I asked for]' — that
> is bearing a grudge. (b.*Yoma* 23a)

In the same way, Yeshua teaches us that a humble heart is also a heart willing to give to others who are in need.

Surely His teaching does not stand against the rightful establishment
of just laws, nor do His words set aside the rights of personal ownership.
But His teaching is predicated upon the belief that the Father is the One Who
supplies our needs, and we therefore retain a "loose grasp" upon our material possessions in the sense that it is not difficult for us to let others use what
we have when we see them in need.

**43 You have heard that it was said, 'You shall love your neighbor and
hate your enemy.'**

Once again, Yeshua is teaching the manner in which His disciples were
to exceed the righteousness of the scribes and Pharisees (v. 20) by applying
to their lives the Torah as understood within the context of its original intent
and spiritual import. This verse and the following are structured in a way to
emphasize how the prevailing interpretation of a key Torah text (Lev 19:18)
was to be corrected in line with the spirit of the Torah as God's instructions
in righteousness, not as a means of cultural and ethnic identity. The Torah
does not set up boundaries between people groups, but between what is
righteous and what is unrighteous.

The structure of this final antithesis may be outlined as follows:

1. *Prevailing teaching*: love your neighbor and hate your enemy
2. *Yeshua's teaching*: love your enemy and pray for those who persecute you
3. *Reason*: do this so that you will be known as sons of your Father Who is in heaven because
   He shows His benevolence to both the evil and good by giving them sun and rain
4. *Discussion*: If you love only those who love you, you are like the tax collectors and the Gentiles (and thus your righteousness has certainly not exceeded that of the scribes and Pharisees)
5. *Conclusion*: Be perfect as your Father in heaven is perfect

In stating what was the prevailing teaching by the now common "You have heard" introduction, Yeshua takes a line from Lev 19:18, "love your neighbor" (וְאָהַבְתָּ לְרֵעֲךָ). It is not necessary for Him to quote the whole line or even the whole verse, because the reference to just these words is sufficient to cause the entire context to arise in the minds of His audience. It is typical in rabbinic citations to give just a few important words of a context to reference it as a whole. Clearly Yeshua is not disputing the Torah commandment (note in Luke's parallel [6:27–28, 32–36] the positive commandment to love one's neighbor is not even mentioned) but is seeking to rescue it from the limiting interpretation put upon it by the teachers of His day. So the primary issue at stake is the identification of "neighbor" and "enemy." Yeshua clearly expands the commandment of Lev 19:18 to a much wider circle of people than that of the current teaching of those to whom He speaks.

The Greek terms used in "love your neighbor and hate your enemy" reflect the wider range of meanings both for "love" and "hate" in the corresponding Hebrew terms. The verb אָהַב ('ahav) "to love" has a wider range of meaning than is usually attached to our English word "love." Generally, in English "love" is put as a higher commitment in terms of relationship than words such as "like," "show favor," or "respect." Yet both the Hebrew word *'ahav* (and its corresponding noun, *'ahavah*) and the Greek word (ἀγαπάω, *agapao* and its corresponding noun, ἀγάπη, *agape*) are wide enough to include all of these shades of meaning, from close intimacy in friendship to showing respect or being favorably disposed toward a person. The same may be said for the concept of "hate." The Hebrew word most often translated by our English "hate" is שָׂנֵא (*sanei'*) and it is most often translated in the Lxx with the Greek word μισέω (*miseo*), the same word used in our text. Once again, our English word "hate" usually speaks of an extreme dislike, but that is not the case with either the Hebrew or Greek term. Just as *'ahav* or *'ahavah* may denote a wide range of favorable responses in relationship, so *sanei'* and *miseo* can denote "dislike," "disfavor," "disregard" as well as the more severe feelings of "detest," "despise," and "hate." Moreover, our English words "love" and "hate" generally take on an active meaning, so that to "love" someone can hardly be envisioned without the sense of showing one's affections in one way or another. Likewise, our English word "hate" pictures overt actions of aggression and malice. While the Hebrew and Greek terms can include such heightened meanings, they also include more passive responses such as "appreciate," "regard," "show respect" on the one hand, and "disregard," "withhold praise," and "avoid" on the other. This being the case, there is every possibility that Yeshua's words should be understood to encompass a wider range of interpersonal relationships than merely the extremes of "love" and "hate" as our English would have it.

We encounter the same difficulties with our English words "neighbor" and "enemy." The Greek word πλησίον (*plesion*) means in its first sense "close, near, nearby." By extension, the meaning of "neighbor" as one who is (in one sense or another) near or close by. But the word itself cannot identify the various levels of human relationship which it encompasses. A *plesion* could be someone as close as a family member, or a member of one's closest circle of friends, or it could denote anyone who might be at any given moment within one's immediate presence and surroundings. The same is true of the Greek word ἐχθρός (*exthros*) translated "enemy" which corresponds to the Hebrew אוֹיֵב (*'oyeiv*). While these terms can denote someone who is seeking to do physical harm, as an enemy in warfare or a murderer, they can also describe someone who is an adversary in the arena of social, political or religious mores.

Given the wide range of meanings in the Hebrew and Greek words (meanings that do not so easily attach to our English words "love" and "hate"), we ought to be careful about interpreting our Master's words within the narrow range of the English terms chosen by our translators. In the context, it seems clear that Yeshua, though widening the application of these terms beyond that of the prevailing teaching, still limits them in some measure. He expects that one is able to pray for one's "enemies," meaning that they are people with whom one is acquainted. Moreover, those who are identified as "enemies" by Yeshua are those who may be "greeted," for He teaches that if one greets only one's "brothers," he has not fulfilled the commandment to "love." Thus, by extension, one is also to "greet" one's enemies. This means that they are within a community setting where such a greeting could be done. The point is that Yeshua's teaching in this whole matter of loving one's neighbor as well as one's enemies is cast within the context of one's own community (however widely that might be defined). To give an extreme example of what I mean, Yeshua is not teaching His disciples that they should show favor, respect, consideration and loyalty to a Roman general whose purpose was to slaughter the Jews and destroy the Holy City as Titus was to do in 70 CE. To extend His words to such a scenario is to wrest them from their obvious context and meaning. But what He was teaching is that within 1st Century Judaisms, where various sects identified themselves as over against other sects, and treated "outsiders" with hatred and malice, there needed to be a change of perspective. Even to those with whom one disagreed, and perhaps strongly disagreed, one needed to extend one's respect, favor, and appreciation just as one would do with those who formed their immediate circle of friends.

We know the source of Yeshua's statement to "love your neighbor" (Lev 19:18). But where does He derive the current teaching "hate your enemy?" Some have suggested that this was a well-known tradition among the Jewish communities, but substantiation from the extant rabbinic materials is not so easily found. In *Avot de Rabbi Natan* we read the following comments on m.*Avot* 2.11 "R. Joshua says, "Envy, desire of bad things, and hatred for people push a person out of the world." :

AND HATRED OF MANKIND: What is that? This teaches that no man should think of saying, "Love the Sages but hate the disciples;" or "Love the disciples but hate the *'am ha-'aretz.*" On the contrary, love all these. But hate the sectarians, apostates, and informers; and so said David: *Do I not hate them, O Lord, that hate Thee? And do I not strive with those that rise up against Thee? I hate them with utmost hatred; I count them mine enemies* (Ps 139:21f).

But does it not say, *But thou shalt love they neighbor as thyself: I am the Lord* (Lev 19:18): and why is that? Because I [the Lord] have created him.

Indeed, if he acts as thy people do, thou shalt love him; but if not, thou shalt not love him. (*ARN* 1.16)

In the Qumran literature we have another example:

He is to teach them both to love all the Children of Light-each commensurate with his rightful place in the council of God-and to hate all the Children of Darkness, each commensurate with his guilt and the vengeance due him from God. (1QS 1.9-11)

We may speculate, then, that though we find little in the rabbinic and early Jewish literature to warrant a well-known teaching to the effect of "hate your enemy," practically speaking the various sects of Judaism in the 1st Century CE were known for harsh treatment of each other, and their attempts to strengthen the boundary markers that separated them. It seems most possible to me that it was in the context of such sectarian battles over Torah interpretation and *halachah* that Yeshua gives His teaching. For His followers were already being marginalized among the main sects and were soon to be expelled from the community of some synagogues (cf. Matt 10:17; 23:34; Jn 9:22; 16:2). As such, they could easily have adopted the prevailing teaching that allowed them to consider those outside of the sect of The Way as their enemies, as those they were no longer required to love. But Yeshua's perspective is different. Even those who might persecute His disciples were still to be treated with kindness and respect. To put it simply, the followers of Yeshua were not to engage in the sectarian wars that had created divisions between Pharisees, Sadducees, Zealots, Essenes, and others.

44–45 But I say to you, love your enemies and pray for those who persecute you, so that you may be sons of your Father who is in heaven; for He causes His sun to rise on the evil and the good, and sends rain on the righteous and the unrighteous.

The teaching of Yeshua, that one is to love one's enemies (here the word is plural while in the previous verse it is singular) is not something innovative or new. Indeed, Yeshua is simply teaching Torah here.

If you meet your enemy's ox or his donkey wandering away, you shall surely return it to him. If you see the donkey of one who hates you lying helpless under its load, you shall refrain from leaving it to him, you shall surely release it with him. (Ex. 23:4–5)

If your enemy is hungry, give him food to eat; and if he is thirsty, give him water to drink; (Prov. 25:21)

We find similar teaching from the Sages:

> "If you see your fellow's ass or ox fallen on the road, do not ignore it; you must surely help him raise it" (Deut 22:4). The present formulation serves to state the religious requirements in a negative way. Elsewhere it says, "When you see" (Ex 23:5), which serves to state the religious requirement in a positive way. "…your fellow's ox": I know only that I deal with the one belonging to your fellow. What about the one belonging to your enemy? "Your enemy's ox" (Ex 23:4). Then why does it say "your fellow"? This teaches that the Torah takes full account of the impulse to do evil. (*Sifre* Deut §225)

An interesting story is related in Talmud that may illustrate the command of Yeshua that His disciples pray for those who persecute them:

> There were once some lawless men in the neighborhood of R. Meir who caused him a great deal of trouble. R. Meir accordingly prayed that they should die. His wife Beruria said to him, "How do you justify that such a prayer be permitted? Because it is written, 'let *chatta'im* (sins) cease?' Is it written *chot'im* (sinners)? It is written *chatta'im* (sins). Further, look at the end of the verse *and let the wicked be no more*. Since sins will cease there will be no more wicked men. Rather pray for them that they should repent, and these will be no more wicked." He did pray for them and they repented. (b.*Berchot* 10a)

We may note Luke's additions in regard to praying for those who persecute:

> But I say to you who hear, love your enemies, do good to those who hate you, bless those who curse you, pray for those who mistreat you. (Lk 6:27–28)

The point is that one's response to one's enemies should flow from a genuine desire that they find God's favor, not His wrath. To love one's enemies is entirely incongruous to the hope that they would perish or undergo severe punishment. If they are acting in evil ways, the heart of love and mercy prays that they might forsake such evil, not that they would be trapped in it. As Bengel notes, "obtain by your prayer blessings for those who wrest blessings from you" (quoted from Allison-Davies, *Matthew*, 1.553).

This general perspective of benevolence should be the goal of Yeshua's disciples on the basis of Lev 19:2, "You shall be holy, for I the LORD your God am holy." In other words, those who follow Yeshua ought to have as their highest goal to be holy even as God is holy, to show themselves to be "sons of your Father who is in heaven." That being the case, the benevolent actions of God form the paradigm for how one is to treat their enemies: He allows the evil and good ones to see another day (He sustains their lives), and He provides sustenance for them (He sends rain to the righteous and the unrighteous). If this is how the Holy One treats those who are rightly His "enemies," how much more should we show benevolence toward our enemies, and all the more since we desire to follow in the ways of HaShem!

Paul seems to have this teaching of our Master in mind when he writes about the command to love as an imitation of God's benevolence:

> Therefore be imitators of God, as beloved children; and walk in love,

just as Messiah also loved you and gave Himself up for us, an offering and a sacrifice to God as a fragrant aroma. (Eph. 5:1–2)

46–47 For if you love those who love you, what reward do you have? Do not even the tax collectors do the same? If you greet only your brothers, what more are you doing than others? Do not even the Gentiles do the same?

The teaching of Yeshua in these verses involves a stinging comparison. In v. 20, the high watermark for righteousness, that which He expects His disciples to exceed, is that of the scribes and Pharisees. Here He points to those within the society of the 1st Century Judaisms who comprised the lowest degree, that of toll collectors and Gentiles. We may note the similar usage of this social grouping in Matt 18:17, where a member of the community who has sinned and failed to repent of his sin even after being duly admonished, is to be regarded as "Gentile and a tax collector." So the rebuke that Yeshua gives is by saying that one who does not love his "enemy" has put himself on par with those in the society who were known for having no regard for righteousness whatsoever.

The Greek word translated "tax collectors" is τελώνης (*telones*) and

> does not refer to the state officials who collected poll and land taxes (*publicani*) but rather denotes Hellenistic tax farmers or the despised Jewish tax farmers and their agents who, having purchased the toll collecting concessions, collected indirect taxes for the Romans. The latter are infamous for their abuses of the system and were generally denied Jewish civil rights (m.*Sanhedrin* 3.3; b.*BavaQama* 94b; b.*Sanhedrin* 25b).[1]

[1] Allison-Davies, *Matthew*, 1.558.

In spite of their underhanded methods, and even their placing of extreme burdens on the people, these Jewish toll collectors were to be loved as part of the larger Jewish community even if they were in cahoots with Rome. This does not mean that justice was swept away, or that one's lawful rights were to be entirely abandoned. But it means that those who were, in one sense, rightfully despised by the Jewish society at large were not to be abandoned by those who were Yeshua's disciples. Even tax collectors could have a change of heart and actions, as the story of Zaccheus shows (Lk 19:1–8).

The obvious overarching instruction given to us by Yeshua here is that one cannot simply extend love to those who reciprocate. While surely it is easiest to love those who love in return, the way of our Master is to extend love even to those who give no love in return, or even return evil. Once again, this mimics the very actions of God Himself, Who, while we were still His enemies, loved us with an everlasting love as demonstrated in the giving of His Son (Rom 5:10). Moreover, love that is only demonstrated in the sphere of love may not be love at all. For in simply loving those whom one knows will return that love, one's motives could be questioned. Perhaps the benevolence shown was motivated out of what one hoped they would receive back. But to extend love without thought of receiving something in return is to love after the pattern of God's love, Who is in need of nothing, and therefore loves entirely for the good of the one loved.

The Greek word translated "Gentile" is ἐθνικός (*ethnikos*) rather than the common term employed by Matthew, which is ἔθνος (*ethnos*). *Ethnikos* is found only four times in the Apostolic Scriptures: Matt 5:47; 6:7; 18:17; 3Jn 7.

In our text as well as Matt 18:17, *ethnikos* is grouped with "tax collectors." In Matt 6:7, the *ethnikos* use "meaningless repetitions" in their prayers, which Yeshua warns against. In 3Jn 7, John notes that there were workers sent forth from the community who received nothing from the *ethnikos,* and he therefore appeals for them to be supported in their work. In this case, *ethnikos* seems to be those who are not believers, or at least not part of the collective group to which John writes.

Since Matthew usually uses *ethnos* to denote "non-Jews" (i.e., Gentiles), Lachs suggests that the *ethnikos* has a different meaning.

> We suggest that the term *ethnikos* refers to the *am ha-aretz*, lit., "the people of the land." Originally it meant only the farming population. Subsequently it came to connote those who were lax in the taking of the tithe from the produce of the field, thus causing the unsuspecting purchaser to eat untithed food and thereby to violate a biblical law. Finally, *am ha-aretz* became a term for the ignoramus, the unlettered, and the boor. (Tobias Lachs, *Rabbinic Commentary on the NT*, p.110)

It may be then, if Lachs is correct, that the pairing of "Gentiles and tax collectors" was a convenient way to describe a class of people who were unconcerned with the righteous requirements of the Torah.

48 Therefore you are to be perfect, as your heavenly Father is perfect.

These word of Yeshua seem clearly to be patterned after Lev 19:2, "You shall be holy, for I the LORD your God am holy." However, Deut 18:13 has "You shall be blameless before the LORD your God," and the Lxx translates "blameless" (תָּמִים, *tamim*) with τέλειος (*teleios*), the same word used by Matthew. In a very real sense, Yeshua has combined the two thoughts, for to be holy as God is holy means to act in such a way as to be blameless. In Mid. Rab. *Gen* 46 we read: "just as He is, so should you [strive] to be."

This concluding statement of Yeshua is more than just the conclusion to this final antithesis. It forms a fitting conclusion to the entire section, for the goal of the disciple of the Master, while striving to exceed the righteousness of the scribes and the Pharisees, was nonetheless to have as an ultimate goal and motivation to be "holy even as God is holy."

When we consider the six antitheses as a whole, it becomes apparent that, contrary to popular teaching of some within Christian circles, Yeshua is not pitting His own teaching against that of the inspired books of Moses, nor is He suggesting that His teaching is superior to that of Moses. Rather, He is showing how a misunderstanding of the Torah in His day had bound it to the traditions of men in such a way as to divest it of its spiritual vigor and divine intent. In an effort to "manage" the Torah so that one could say "all these things I have kept" (Matt 19:20), the traditions had, in some cases, transformed the living word of God into cultural and ethnic traditions that defined the various Jewish sects rather than describing the Almighty Who had revealed the Torah in the first place.

In the manner in which Yeshua gives us His teaching in these antitheses, it is clear that what He demands on the basis of the Torah itself is far from manageable. As He interprets the Torah, it requires a constant guarding of one's heart and thoughts, a shunning of hatred as though it was the first step toward murder; a careful keeping of oneself from the lusts of the flesh that, if allowed to be fostered, bring forth the sin of adultery and ruin the sanctity of marriage. Based upon the clear teaching of the Torah, Yeshua calls His disciples back to a recognition of how one's words ought always to be as sound and true as the most solemn of oaths, and how one's natural inclination is to take revenge and to guard one's rights at the expense of others. He calls for us to love those who are unlovely, and even those who present themselves as our antagonists and enemies. His words, like those of the Torah, are "unmanageable" in the sense that when we grasp them, we admit that we are unable of our own strength to live up to the high standard of the Torah as He has taught it to us.

And this is the very point: being holy as God is holy requires first to recognize that apart from God's imparting to us both the willingness to pursue holiness and the strength to accomplish it, we are without hope. But in giving us this view of God's holy requirements—how we are to live righteously in an unrighteous world, He has likewise reminded us that God provides the means to accomplish such a goal. Yeshua bids us to "take My yoke upon you and learn from Me" (Matt 11:29). He does not expect that we would be able to live as we ought on our own strength. He rather promises to be with us (Matt 28:20) in such a way as to encourage and strengthen us in the pursuit of holiness, and by His grace to bring us to that desired goal.

Moreover, in the following chapters we will see the wisdom of His teaching and the manner in which He fills our hearts with understanding as we seek to walk in His footsteps. The bar of righteousness is not set too high by our Master, because He intends to lift us up to meet its standards.

Chapter Six
Commentary

Chapter six Yeshua gives to His disciples, and to us, instructions regarding the very practical ways of righteousness in three important areas of piety: giving to the poor, praying, and fasting. That these three aspects of a pious life were paramount in the minds of the early Sages is seen by the repeated reference of them in their writings. "R. Chiyya said, He who turns his eyes away from almsgiving is as if he worshipped idols" (b.*Ketuvot* 68a). "Almsgiving weighs as much as all the other commandments" (b.*Bava Batra* 9a). "R. Eleazar said, Three things annul the severe decree and these are they: prayer, charity, and repentance" (Mid. Rab. *Qohelet* 5.6). Many more examples could be offered, but these are sufficient to show that in the perspective of the Sages, the three areas of piety mentioned by Yeshua in our text were of prime importance.

The structure of the first 18 verses of our chapter may be seen as follows:

> Introduction: righteous deeds must proceed from a proper motivation, v. 1
> 1. Almsgiving, vv. 2–6
> 2. Prayer, vv. 7–8
>   Pattern for prayer (the Disciples' Prayer), vv. 9–15
> 3. Fasting, vv. 16–18

Each of the three sections has a similar and thus parallel structure:

> 1. Warning not to act as the hypocrites who make their pious acts public for the sake of self-honor
> 2. Statement: "they will receive their reward"
> 3. Proper way to exercise piety: do it privately
> 4. Promise: the Father Who sees in secret will reward in secret

[1] So Allison-Davies, *Matthew*, 1.573–74; Nolland, *Matthew*, p. 273;

There are no synoptic parallels to the three sections, but only to the "Lord's Prayer" section of vv. 9–15 (cf. Mk 11:25–26; Lk 11:2–4).

This clear structural similarity has caused some commentators to suggest that vv. 9–15 are out of place, or were inserted by later redactors.[1] But it is just as likely that Yeshua did include His pattern for prayer following His exhortation not to pray as the hypocrites. We should remember that our Master's teaching here continues His exhortation of 5:20, that the righteousness of His disciples must exceed that of the scribes and Pharisees.

Introduction: Deeds of Righteous

1 Beware of practicing your righteousness before men to be noticed by them; otherwise you have no reward with your Father who is in heaven.

Yeshua's primary teaching in regard to doing the *mitzvot* is that they should be done for the sake of God's approval, not the approval of men.

[1]Each of the extant witnesses of a Hebrew Matthew (Even Bohan, DuTillet, Münster) have צְדָקָה in 6:1. The Peshitta has the same (זדקה).

[2]Carson, *Matthew*, p. 164.

[3]Alfred Edersheim, *The Temple: Its Ministry and Services* (Religious Tract Society, n.d.), p. 26

[4]Lachs, *Rabbinic Commentary the New Testament*, p. 112.

[5]Carson, *Matthew*, p. 164.

[6]See Allison-Davies, *Matthew*, 1.579.

There is a textual variant on the word "righteousness" (δικαιοσύνη, *dikaiosune*). Some later manuscripts have ἐλεημοσύνη (*eleemosune*), "almsgiving." This reflects the later rabbinic use of צְדָקָה, *tzedakah* to mean "charity, giving to the poor." It may also suggest that an original semitic text was translated into the Greek, one translation retaining the exact meaning of *tzedakah* and others translating with an equivalent meaning current within rabbinic Judaism.[1] It may be that "righteousness" here pertains particularly to the giving of charity to the poor, the meaning attached to *tzedakah* in the teaching of the Sages.

The warning Yeshua gives is straightforward: if the motivation for doing righteous deeds is so that men will see and render praise to the one doing them, such selfish motivation negates the righteous deed itself, and no reward will be forthcoming from the Father. Here we are reminded that doing the *mitzvot* from a heart of love for God and one's neighbor is, in fact, rewarded by the Almighty, whether in this life or in the world to come. God does reward obedience, not always as we might expect, but He does bless those who obey Him.

2 So when you give to the poor, do not sound a trumpet before you, as the hypocrites do in the synagogues and in the streets, so that they may be honored by men. Truly I say to you, they have their reward in full.

There are several interpretations of what "sounding trumpets" means. Some older commentators suggest that there was the practice of sounding a shofar at the time of collecting alms in the Temple for the relief of some who might be in particular need. But there is nothing in the rabbinic literature to indicate that anything like this ever occurred in the Second Temple, and this interpretation appears to stem from early Christian expositors who assumed its correctness.[2] Others, like Calvin, thought that almsgivers themselves blew a shofar to announce the giving of gifts, especially significantly large gifts, but once again, there are no historical data to support such a claim. Edersheim[3] and Lachs[4] mention that in the Temple there were 13 "trumpets" in the Temple (see m.*Sheqalim* 5.1) which were containers shaped in the form of a trumpet and were containers for *tzedakah*. Apparently they were so shaped to prevent unscrupulous people from taking out instead of putting in a donation. Lachs also suggests that the verb "to sound" a trumpet (σαλπίζω, *salpizo*) is a translation of עָבַר, *'avar,* "to pass through," used in connection with sounding a trumpet, as in Lev 25:9–

> You shall then sound a ram's horn abroad [literally, "cause the trumpet sound to pass through"] on the tenth day of the seventh month; on the day of atonement you shall sound a horn all through [עבר] your land.

Lachs suggests that the Greek translator misunderstood להעביר, "to cause to pass through" as meaning "blow a trumpet," when it really meant "to cause to pass." Thus, "to cause to pass a trumpet" meant "to pass the collection plate" for *tzedakah*. While this sounds plausible, there is little data to suggest that this actually happened. Others suggest that the "sounding of a trumpet" referred to noise that coined money would make in the brass collection "trumpets" of the Temple.[6]

Carson notes the work of A. Büchler[5] who suggested that the reference to blowing trumpets refers to the proclamation of public fast days. At such times prayers for rain were recited in the streets, and it was thought that the giving of alms insured the efficacy of the fasts and prayers. Such occasions afforded ample opportunity for public giving of alms for ostentatious purposes.

When Yeshua says that "they have their reward in full," He is saying that those who give alms for the praise of men do, in fact, receive such praise. But that is all they receive. Their reward is from men and thus it is temporal and fleeting. The praise of men is fickle; the praise of God remains forever.

3–4 But when you give to the poor, do not let your left hand know what your right hand is doing, so that your giving will be in secret; and your Father who sees what is done in secret will reward you.

Yeshua makes it clear that giving to the poor is no option for His disciples. He does not say *"if* you give to the poor" but *"when* you give to the poor,"[1] implying that giving charity to those in need is an expected activity of those who call Him "Master."

Not allowing the left hand to know what the right hand is doing may have its origins in the Semitic idiom for immature naïvety. In Jonah 4:11, for instance, the young children are described as those "who do not know their right hand from the left." Thus, to give alms in such a way that one does not know the left from the right hand may mean to give them out of a sincere, unencumbered heart, even as a child would do. Regardless of the exact meaning, the purpose of the phrase is clear: there should not be an accounting of one's giving of alms in order to receive the acclaim of men. Giving of alms should be done in secret.

The Sages were in full agreement with the need to give alms in secret, and judging by the number of times they teach this, it would seem that the public display of giving alms was a constant problem.

> R. Eleazar said: A man who gives charity in secret is greater than Moses our teacher. (b.*Bava Batra* 9a)

> *God will bring every work into judgment, with every secret thing whether it be good or whether it be evil.* What is the meaning of *whether it be good or evil?* R. Yannai said: "It is he who gives money to the poor publically!" For R. Yannai once saw a man give money to a poor man publically. He said: "It had been better that you gave him nothing than you should have given him and put him to shame. (Mid. Rab. *Qoh* 12.14)

> A name made great is a name destroyed. (m.*Abot* 1.13)

According to m.*Sheqalim* 5.6, there were two chambers in the Temple, one called the "Chamber of Secrets" and the other the "Chamber of Utensils." People would put alms into the chamber of secrets, and from these funds, the needs of the poor would be met by the priests. Donations put in the chamber of utensils would be used for the maintenance of the Temple utensils. Like the teaching of our Master, the giving of alms in the Temple was to be done in secret. Thus, Yeshua's teaching is, once again, very much in line with many of His contemporary teachers.

The reward for giving in secret comes directly from God Who sees

[1] The Greek construction utilizes a present participle (ποιοῦντος) which indicates the action is customary or regular. Thus, the translation of the NASB, utilizing the temporal word "when," seeks to capture the nuance of the participle.

all that is done, whether publicly or privately. There is no indication of the nature or place of the reward,[1] but we may presume that there is a reward in this world as well as in the world to come. For obeying God from the heart is its own reward, both now and in eternity.

5 When you pray, you are not to be like the hypocrites; for they love to stand and pray in the synagogues and on the street corners so that they may be seen by men. Truly I say to you, they have their reward in full.

We now come to the second section of our chapter in which Yeshua gives instructions about prayer. Here He focuses not upon the time or words of prayer (in contrast to the mishnaic and talmudic tractates of *Berachot*) but upon the heart motivation that leads one to pray in the first place. This is not to say that the Sages were unconcerned about one's heart motivation in the whole enterprise of prayers. But clearly the rabbinic *halachah* related to the liturgical prayer services is heavily weighted upon the proper time for praying the various prayers, the subject matter of the prayers (and in some cases, the precise wording of the prayers), and the manner in which one was to conduct himself during prayers.

As in the previous teaching on almsgiving, it is the applause of men that apparently motivated some in their prayers, and that which is the focus of Yeshua's warning. To pray so that others might see and think that one was especially pious was to pray as a hypocrite, for prayer is not for eyes of others, but for the ears of the Almighty.

Once again, Yeshua presumes that prayer is a normal and regular activity of His disciples ("*when* you pray," not "*if* you pray"). But in the normal and regular activity of prayer, the disciples of the Master must be certain that their purpose for praying is right and not like that of the hypocrites.

Who are the "hypocrites?" While this term later became a favorite for describing those who were "outsiders" (i.e., Christians of Jews and *visa versa*, e.g., *Didache* 8.1–2), here it is used in its normal sense of those who say one thing and do another, or who seek to mask their true motivations by outward actions. Yeshua is talking to His own community here, so the charge of hypocrisy is in the context of an intramural dialog and not "Church" vs. "Synagogue" as it has been so often read.

Prayer was common in the synagogues, but it was not uncommon outside of the synagogue as well. If we take the notices of the Mishnah as reflecting the reality of the 1st Century, then the set times for prayer would have caused some to pray wherever they found themselves at the appointed hour. Furthermore, there were occasions when prayers were specifically outside. For instance, in m.*Taanit* 2.1-2, prayers on fast days were conducted in the public squares, and the Greek word translated "street corners" (πλατεîα, *plateia*) could just as well mean "public square." It may have been that such occasions offered some the public venue they desired in order to be seen by others as they prayed. This does not mean that everyone who prayed in public, whether in the synagogue or in the out-of-doors, did so selfishly. But such public meetings always offered an opportunity for those who prayed for the wrong reasons.

As in His teaching on almsgiving, so here Yeshua teaches that praying for the recognition of others does have its own reward, one that is of no true value. When a person only desires the accolades of men, they receive their reward in full, meaning that no reward is forthcoming from God.

6 But you, when you pray, go into your inner room, close your door and pray to your Father who is in secret, and your Father who sees what is done in secret will reward you.

If Yeshua were here teaching against all manner of public prayer, then certainly the Apostles as well as the early believers who congregated in the assemblies of The Way missed the point, for there are plenty examples of public prayer among the early followers of Yeshua (e.g., Matt 18:19–20; Acts 1:24; 3:1; 4:24–30). Rather, what Yeshua is stating here (in almost a hyperbolic fashion) is the need to test one's motives. If one is unable to pray in a private room (ταμεῖον, *tameion* can be a storeroom without windows, a bedroom, or an inner room of a house), then one ought to recognize that their motivation for prayer is wrong-headed in the first place. As in the previous chapter where Yeshua offers a radical approach to curbing hypocrisy (such as dismembering a hand that offends, or plucking out a wondering eye), so here He teaches that one who has become motivated for prayer by what others will see should rather pray in private until prayer becomes what it is intended to be, a conversion between the person and God Himself. As Carson writes, "Not piety but a reputation for piety is his concern."[1]

[1]Carson, *Matthew*, p. 164.

Once again, the Father, Who knows all things, and therefore knows the prayer offered in secret, will reward the one who communes with Him out of proper motives. Thus we learn that true prayer has a reward. And what is this reward? Once again, Yeshua does not give us the answer directly, but we may bring the fuller scope of Scripture to bear upon the question. For the reward of genuine prayer is first and foremost communion with God Himself. It is in the times of prayer where we, without concern for what others may see or perceive, pour out our hearts to God and find in these times of praise and request a settled shalom, resting upon a strengthened faith that God is both able and willing to accomplish His purposes in us. What a reward it is to have our faith strengthened, our focus for life made clear, and even in the midst of a fallen world to experience the shalom of God's presence and the assurance of His all encompassing providence. And beyond this, the reward that we receive from prayer offered to God alone is that He promises to hear our requests, to take heed to our needs, and to answer according to His kind and gracious will. "The effective prayer of a righteous man can accomplish much" (James 5:16).

7–8 And when you are praying, do not use meaningless repetition as the Gentiles do, for they suppose that they will be heard for their many words. So do not be like them; for your Father knows what you need before you ask Him.

Here Yeshua continues to give instructions about the proper motivation for prayer, and how such a motivation may affect not only the *place* where one prays but also the *way* one prays. He instructs His disciples not use "meaningless repetition" (βατταλογέω, *battalogeo*), a word that is rare (only here in the Apostolic Scriptures) and outside of the Apostolic Scriptures is found only in reference to this verse. It may be related to the Aramaic word בַּטַל, *battal,* "idle, useless," or it may be onomatopoetic, like our own word "babble." The NIV has "do not keep on babbling like pagans." Such "babbling" is defined further in the next clause in the sense of "many words." So we might envision here a the repeated mantras of pagan worship in which

[1]Lachs, *A Rabbinic Commentary on the NT,* p. 166.

the ill-directed idolator believer that a constant repetition of the same words over and over again will gain the attention of the god.

Lachs, on the other hand, suggests that the word translated "Gentile" or "pagan" (ἐθνικός, *ethnikos*) was used of the unlearned among the Jewish population, the *am ha-aretz* (people of the land) who were untrained in *halachah* and who therefore would simply repeat the same lines over and over again.[1] Regardless of the exact meaning of the term, the point Yeshua is making is clear: God does not weigh the value of prayer by the number of words the prayer contains. He does not need to be informed by long and repetitious prayers—He already knows what we need before we ask. Indeed, the idea that longer prayers, or prayers utilizing repetitions of certain words, would gain God's attention more than a simply request or utterance of praise is, in itself, a form of idolatry. For the heart of idolatry is the notion that one is able to control God. But proper prayer does not have as its focus the idea that one can control or even persuade God through one's prayer. Rather, true prayer seeks to know the heart and will of God and to be strengthened in one's faith to rely upon His sovereignty for the outcome of His will in one's life.

This does not mean the extended times of prayer are wrong. Yeshua Himself prayed at length (Lk 6:12), repeated Himself in prayer (Matt 26:44) and taught His disciples that they should always be in prayer and not give up (Lk 18:1). What it does mean is that we should assess and reassess our motivations in prayer, and that we not think that somehow by certain carefully crafted prayers, or by praying the same prayer over and over again, we will have greater success before the Almighty.

We find a similar emphasis among the teachings of the Sages and in early Jewish literature.

> Be not rash with your mouth, nor let your heart be hasty to utter a word before God, for God is in heaven, and you upon the earth; therefore let you words be few. (Ecclesiasticus 5.2; Sirach 7.14)

> A man's words should always be few toward God. (b.*Berachot* 61a)

> The righteous has only to say one word and it is accepted by God, and therefore it was not necessary for him [Moses] to pray long. (*Sifre* Num, §105)

> God said to Moses, "My children are in distress and you are making long prayers!" (*Mechilta* on Ex 15:25)

The point our Master is making is that prayer does not have as one of its primary functions the need to inform God about our situations or our needs. He already knows these! The God Who sees in secret is the God Who knows all things. Therefore, our prayers should be focused upon communion with Him to discern His will, to know His ways, and to be strengthened in a life of doing the *mitzvot* (righteousness).

Prayer, by its very nature, is then a confession of God's greatness and His sovereignty. For in praying we submit to His will, and in seeking His help we confess that He is able to give that help, to change the course of events, and to bring about in our lives what otherwise could never happen. Prayer, in the final analysis, is a demonstration of our faith and reliance upon God, not a vehicle to coerce Him into action.

The Disciples' Prayer – [The Lord's Prayer]

We come now to the well-known model prayer given to the disciples by their Master. The prayer gained an early liturgical use, and the various manuscripts of the Greek text evidence this use by the variants that have entered in. Luke's text (11:2–4) is shorter and most commentators conclude that Luke preserves the original text of the prayer, and that Matthew's version is expansive by way of liturgical additions. Likewise, as one would expect, the later Greek manuscripts show evidence of attempts to harmonize the two versions, as is noted, for instance, in the KJV. Mark (11:25–26) mentions only the need to forgive those who have sinned against oneself and that the manner in which one forgives others is the way God will also forgive.

Matthew 6:9–13	Luke 11:2–4
9 Οὕτως οὖν προσεύχεσθε ὑμεῖς· Πάτερ ἡμῶν ὁ ἐν τοῖς οὐρανοῖς· ἁγιασθήτω τὸ ὄνομά σου· 10 ἐλθέτω ἡ βασιλεία σου· γενηθήτω τὸ θέλημά σου, ὡς ἐν οὐρανῷ καὶ ἐπὶ γῆς· 11 τὸν ἄρτον ἡμῶν τὸν ἐπιούσιον δὸς ἡμῖν σήμερον· 12 καὶ ἄφες ἡμῖν τὰ ὀφειλήματα ἡμῶν, ὡς καὶ ἡμεῖς ἀφήκαμεν τοῖς ὀφειλέταις ἡμῶν· 13 καὶ μὴ εἰσενέγκῃς ἡμᾶς εἰς πειρασμόν, ἀλλὰ ῥῦσαι ἡμᾶς ἀπὸ τοῦ πονηροῦ. [ὅτι σοῦ ἐστιν ἡ βασιλεία καὶ ἡ δύναμις καὶ ἡ δόξα εἰς τοὺς αἰῶνας. ἀμήν.]	2 εἶπεν δὲ αὐτοῖς· ὅταν προσεύχησθε λέγετε· Πάτερ, ἁγιασθήτω τὸ ὄνομά σου· ἐλθέτω ἡ βασιλεία σου· 3 τὸν ἄρτον ἡμῶν τὸν ἐπιούσιον δίδου ἡμῖν τὸ καθ᾽ ἡμέραν· 4 καὶ ἄφες ἡμῖν τὰς ἁμαρτίας ἡμῶν, καὶ γὰρ αὐτοὶ ἀφίομεν παντὶ ὀφείλοντι ἡμῖν· καὶ μὴ εἰσενέγκῃς ἡμᾶς εἰς πειρασμόν.
9 Pray, then, in this way: Our Father who is in heaven, Hallowed be Your name. 10 Your kingdom come. Your will be done, On earth as it is in heaven. 11 Give us this day our daily bread. 12 And forgive us our debts, as we also have forgiven our debtors. 13 And do not lead us into temptation, but deliver us from evil. [For Yours is the kingdom and the power and the glory forever. Amen.]	2 And He said to them, When you pray, say: Father, hallowed be Your name. Your kingdom come. 3 Give us each day our daily bread. 4 And forgive us our sins, For we ourselves also forgive everyone who is indebted to us. And lead us not into temptation.

The textual difficulties in this text are several, owing no doubt to the familiarity of the prayer within the Christian Church, and the manner in which its liturgical use influenced scribes. Most are minor. For instance, in v. 10 some manuscripts (D*, bo^mss) omit ὡς (*hos*, "as") yielding "May Your will be done in heaven and on earth." Likewise, the word ἐπιούσιον (*epiousion*) usually translated "daily" or "this day" is difficult, and various versions offer different readings by way of explanation.[1]

The more significant variants deal with the ending of the prayer in Matthew.[2] The NASB puts the final sentence in brackets to indicate that it is found only in later manuscripts, while most other modern translations

[1]See Bruce Metzger, *A Textual Commentary on the New Testament* (UBS, 1971), pp. 15–16 for notes on the textual variants.

[1]See Donald A. Hagner, *Matthew* in *The Word Bible Commentary*, vol. 33A (Word, 2001), pp. 144-45 for a listing of the various endings of the prayer found in the manuscripts.

leave the sentence out of the text entirely, noting its presence only in marginal notes (NIV, ESV, NET, etc.). The additional phrase, "For Yours is the kingdom and the power and the glory forever. Amen," is not found in ℵ B D Z 0170 *f*1 pc lat mae Or and is therefore most likely a later addition, based upon 1Chron 29:11, "Yours, O LORD, is the greatness and the power and the glory and the victory and the majesty, indeed everything that is in the heavens and the earth; Yours is the dominion, O LORD, and You exalt Yourself as head over all." The fact that the phrase is found in the later manuscripts and is included in the Textus Receptus (on which the KJV was based) has made it a common part of the Prayer since the early printings of the English Bible. The Douay Version, which became the standard Bible for the Roman Catholic Church, however, did not include the longer ending, and as a result the liturgical practice of the Catholic Church differed from that of the Protestant Church in the reciting of the Prayer. Interestingly, the Wycliffe translation did not include the longer ending thought the Geneva Bible did. Thus, even among various Protestant denominations, the reciting of the Prayer in liturgy differs.

9 Pray, then, in this way: 'Our Father who is in heaven, Hallowed be Your name.

Yeshua instructs His disciples to "pray in this way," indicating that what follows is not a set prayer but a model for what constitutes valid prayer. Many have suggested that the Prayer Yeshua gives is actually a kind of "table of contents" relating the primary aspects that constitute genuine prayer. In this regard, the Prayer begins with (1) an affirmation of praise for the holiness of God's Name and a recognition of His universal rule, and ends with (2) various petitions relating to one's physical and spiritual needs.

Many have noted the parallels to liturgical prayers in the synagogue of Yeshua's day, particularly those found in the *Kaddish* and *Shomeneh Esreh* (Eighteen Benedictions). The difficulty with making such parallels, however, is that one cannot be certain how early these prayers arrived at the final form and whether therefore they were sufficiently extant in the time of Yeshua to form the template for His own model prayer.

With regard to the *Shomeneh Esreh,* the Bavli mentions that Samuel Hapiqquli "arranged the *Shomeneh Esreh* in order before Rabban Gamliel at Yavneh" (b.*Berachot* 28b). This does not mean that he composed the prayers at this time, but what exactly is meant is not certain. It could be that he gave the fixed order of the prayers, or that he argued for the proper wording of the prayers. Since Yavneh is generally dated to around 90 CE, this might indicate that the *Shomeneh Esreh* prayers were still in the process of being fixed as late as the end of the 1st Century. If indeed the general structure of the *Shomeneh Esreh* benedictions was fixed in the early 1st Century, then structurally there is a parallel to Yeshua's Prayer, for the *Shomeneh Esreh* begin with three prayers of praise, followed by 12 (13) benedictions of petition, and end with three prayers of thanksgiving. In the longer version of Matthew's text, the final prayer ("For Yours is the kingdom…) could be construed as thanksgiving, and thus the same structure obtains. Yet, as many have noted, the very brevity of Yeshua's Prayer stands in contrast to the much longer *Shomeneh Esreh,* and it touches only on a few of the themes extant in the Eighteen. The following table shows the parallels.

Matthew	Shomeneh Esreh
Our Father who is in heaven, Hallowed be Your name.	#1 - God of Abraham, God of Isaac, God of Jacob, the great and mighty God, … for His own Name sake in love.
Your kingdom come. Your will be done, on earth as it is in heaven.	#3 - We will sanctify Your Name in the world just as they sanctify it in the highest heavens…Adonai will reign forever.
Give us this day our daily bread.	#9 - Bless for us, Adonai our God, this year and all the varieties of its produce…
And forgive us our debts, as we also have forgiven our debtors.	#6 - Pardon us, our Father, for we have sinned… (cf. Palestinian recention)[1]
And do not lead us into temptation, but deliver us from evil.	#7 - Look, please, upon our affliction, and defend our cause: and redeem us speedily for the sake of Your Name…

[1] The Palestinian recension has: "Forgive us, our Father, for we have sinned against You. Blot out our transgression from before Your eyes. Blessed are You, O Lord, Who forgives much."

The parallels are evident in terms of general theme but do not necessarily share common terms in each case.

We may also note close parallels to the *Kaddish* prayer of the synagogue. The earliest mention of the *Kaddish* is attributed to R. Yose b. Chalafta (ca. 150 CE) in *Sifre* Deut, §306 (cf. also b.*Berachot* 3a). Its primary function was to conclude the service following sermons on Aggadah, since it was determined that all such services should end with words of consolation, i.e., references to the Messianic age. Once again, whether the *Kaddish* as we know it today was extant in the time of Yeshua cannot be substantiated.

Matthew	Kaddish
Our Father who is in heaven, Hallowed be Your name.	Exalted and sanctified be His great Name in the world which He created…
Your kingdom come. Your will be done, on earth as it is in heaven.	May He rule His kingdom in your lifetime and in your days
Give us this day our daily bread.	(?) May there be much peace from heaven and good life upon us and upon all Israel
And forgive us our debts, as we also have forgiven our debtors.	
And do not lead us into temptation, but deliver us from evil.	

As can be seen, while there are clear parallels to the sanctification and exaltation of the Name and the rule of God's kingdom upon the earth, the petitions for food, for forgiveness of debts (sins), and protection from testing and evil find no parallels in the *Kaddish.*

Owing to the possible late formulation of the *Shomeneh Esreh* and the *Kaddish,* along with the fact that the parallels that do exist are more thematic in nature than verbal, some commentators have suggested that neither were instrumental in forming a model for Yeshua's Prayer. Lachs is representative of this viewpoint:

[1]Tobias Lachs, *A Rabbinic Commentary on the New Testament* (KTAV, 1987), p. 118.

The *Shemoneh Esreh,* however, emerges as the prayer par excellence only at the *end* of the first Christian century during the patriarchate of Rabban Gamaliel II. Furthermore, the Lord's Prayer is so scant, that to see in it a mini-*Shemoneh Esreh* is imaginative. Finally, the observation of the tripartite division fails, since in the best MSS of the NT the last line, i.e., a liturgical ending of the Lord's Prayer, is lacking.

The *Kaddish,* too, fails as a model for the Lord's Prayer, for the similarities of a few phrases is hardly enough to warrant this hypothesis.[1]

Lachs suggests that *tephillah qetzarah,* a "short prayer" is the model after which Yeshua fashions His Prayer. In m.*Berachot* 4.4 we read:

> R. Eliezer says, "One who makes his prayers a fixed task—his prayers are not [valid] supplications [of God]." R. Joshua says, "One who walks in a place of danger prays a short prayer (תְּפִילָה קְצָרָה). "He says, 'God save your nation, Israel. In all critical times let their needs be before you. Blessed are you, O God, who hearkens to prayer.'"

Likewise, in the Tosefta we read:

> If one is traveling in a place of danger or of robbers, he should pray a short prayer (תְּפִילָה קְצָרָה). What is a short prayer? Rabbi Eleazar says: "Perform Your will in heaven and bestow satisfaction on earth upon those who revere You, and do that which is good in Your sight. Blessed are You who hears prayer" (t.*Berachot* 3.2)

We also note mention of an abbreviated *Shomeneh Esreh* in b.*Berachot* 28b:

> R. Gamaliel says, "Each day one should recite the Prayer consisting of eighteen [benedictions]." R. Joshua says, "[Each day one says] an abbreviation of the eighteen benedictions." R. Aqiba says, "If one's prayer is fluent he says the eighteen benedictions." "And if not, [one says] an abbreviation of them."

What we discover from these notices is the clear possibility that short prayers were composed on the spot in times of danger or special need, as well as the fact that abbreviated forms of the *Shomeneh Esreh* were permissible (and apparently common) at the time of R. Akiva (late 1st Century). Given this scenario, it seems very possible that Yeshua's Prayer is formulated in line with the practice of short prayers or even as an abbreviated form of longer, liturgical prayers already extant in the synagogue. Moreover, even though prayers such as the *Shemoneh Esreh* arrived at their final form much later than the time of Yeshua, it seems very warranted to see their basic structure occurring much earlier. Thus, Yeshua's use of common themes in His model Prayer were almost surely based upon extant forms of prayer in the synagogues of His day, emphasizing those kinds of things (such as forgiving others) which were particularly central to His own teachings.[2]

[2]In recent times, a number of commentators (e.g., Donald A. Hagner, *Matthew* in *The Word Bible Commentary,* vol. 33A [Word, 2001]) have suggested that the entire Prayer is eschatological in its focus and is a prayer for the consummation of the salvation purchased by Messiah for His people. Thus, Hagner is forced to understand the petition "give us our daily bread" as " Give us today the eschatological bread that will be ours in the future." For discussion of this perspective, see Allison-Davies, *Matthew,* 1.593-94.

We may conclude with regard to the general purpose of the Prayer that Yeshua gave it as a model for short prayers which would be composed by the individual or as an abbreviated form of longer prayers already extant in the synagogue. What we can see is that in general ways, the components of the Prayer are in clear harmony with, and even show some remarkable parallels to, the standard synagogue prayers as we now have them, and as they existed (in one form or another) in the early 1st Century.

We should also note the section in the *Didache* 8.1–3 that parallels Matthew's text of the Prayer.

> But do not let your fasts coincide with those of the hypocrites. They fast on Monday and Thursday, so you must fast on Wednesday and Friday. Nor should you pray like the hypocrites. Instead, "pray like this," just as the Lord commanded in his Gospel: "Our Father in heaven, hallowed be your name, your kingdom come, your will be done on earth as it is in heaven. Give us today our daily bread, and forgive us our debt, as we also forgive our debtors; and do not lead us into temptation, but deliver us from the evil one; for yours is the power and the glory forever." Pray like this three times a day.

The text of the *Didache* is remarkably close that of Matthew, differing in only minor details. For instance, in the phrase "Our Father in <u>heaven</u>," "heaven" is singular while in Matthew it is plural (though most English translations do not reflect the plural). Likewise, "debt" is singular in the *Didache* but plural in Matthew. But such differences are negligible. What is striking is that the *Didache* as we now have it in the manuscripts available include the long ending. Also of considerable interest is the instruction to "pray like this three times a day." In the Mishnah (m.*Berachot* 4.1), the *Shemoneh Esreh* are likewise to be prayed three times each day.

Whether the *Didache* actually knew of Matthew's Gospel or whether both the author of the *Didache* and Matthew utilized common sources, one cannot be certain. But it seems very likely that the text of Matthew's Gospel (note the *Didache's* reference to what the "Lord commanded in His Gospel") was known by the author of the *Didache*. Whether the long ending to the Prayer was added later, we cannot be certain, due to the paucity of *Didache* manuscripts. But if the long ending was original to the *Didache*, it would give strong weight to an early attestation for the long ending.[1]

Our Father Who is in heaven[2] – Yeshua instructs His disciples to address God as their Father. The plural "our" suggests a corporate setting but does not rule out individual prayer, since it is not uncommon that synagogue prayers easily switch between the singular and plural.

The address "Father Who is in heaven" is a favorite of Matthew, used 13 times. Elsewhere it is only found in Mk 11:25–26 (though v. 26 is disputed in the manuscripts). It is curious that a title so often used by Matthew entirely disappears (with the exception of Mark's one use) in the rest of the Apostolic Scriptures. Addressing God as "Father" is found often, however, and Paul makes it clear that calling out to God as Abba is the special privilege of those who have come to Him through faith in the Messiah (Rom 8:15; Gal 4:6). Luke's more simple "When you pray, say, "Father…" may reflect an original "Abba," and if so, Matthew's "Our Father" emphasizes the close, familial relationship that exists as the basis of prayer in the first place. If we seek an answer as to why Matthew's common use of "our Father" is not repeated in the remainder of the Apostolic Scriptures, we would most likely find the answer to be that Matthew is greatly influenced by the synagogue liturgy. In m.*Sota* 9:15 we read, "Upon whom shall we depend? Upon our Father in heaven." And in the *Shemoneh Esreh*, petitions 5 & 6: "Cause us to return, our Father, to Your Torah…"; "Pardon us, our Father, for we have

[1]For further comments on the *Didache's* relationship to Matthew, see Aaron Milavec, *The Didache* (Newman Press, 2003), pp. 308ff; Kurt Niederwimmer, *The Didache* in *Hermeneia* (Fortress, 1998), p. 134–36; Peter J. Tomson, "The Halakhic Evidence of Didache 8 and Matthew 6 and the Didache Community's Relationship to Judaism" in Huub Van de Sandt, ed., *Matthew and the Didache* (Fortress, 2005), pp. 131–41.

[2]An interesting textual variant occurs in the Even Bohan Matthew, which has only אבינו, not אבינו שבשמים as do the Du-Tillet and Münster. Manuscript A of the Even Bohan does include שבשמים (see George Howard, *Hebrew Gospel of Matthew* [Mercer, 1995], p. 24). Apparently the Even Bohan is following the Lukan text (Lk 11:2) which some believe retains the original reading of Q. But the addition in Even Bohan of "our" conforms to only one manuscript, L, Codex Regius, 8th Century.

sinned…." Interestingly, the use of "our Father in heaven" in Yeshua's Prayer may have influenced a scribal change in m.*Berachot* 5.1:

> One may stand to pray only in a solemn frame of mind. The early pious ones used to tarry one hour [before they would] pray, so that they could direct their hearts to the Omnipresent (הַמָּקוֹם).

However, other manuscripts of the Mishnah have לַאֲבִיהֶם שֶׁבַּשָּׁמַיִם, "to their Father Who is in heaven." It seems quite possible that "our Father Who is in Heaven" became some well known as a "Christian" prayer that such language, used earlier in rabbinic prayers, was changed.

Vermes, commenting on the use of Abba in prayers, points to the interesting story found in b.*Ta'anit* 23b, where famous rabbis known to be "rainmakers" such as Hanan and his first cousin Hilkiah were petitioned to make prayers for rain:

> Hanan the Retiring was the son of the daughter of Honi the Circle-Drawer. When the world needed rain, rabbis would send to him kindergarten children, and they would take hold of the hem of his garment and say to him, "Abba, Abba, give us rain!" He would say before the Holy One, blessed be he, "Do it for the sake of these, who don't know the difference between the Abba who gives rain and the Abba who does not give rain."

From the very beginning of the Prayer, then, we are reminded of two very important truths. First, that we relate to God as a son to a father. Prayer presumes a kind of natural approach, and openness to bring our true praise and petitions to God without fear of being rebuffed, and with every expectation of being heard. We come to God in prayer because we know that He is our Father, and we are His children. We do not come to Him as to a stranger, but to One Who has brought us into His family and Who acts toward us as a father.

But secondly, the fact that we address Him as "our Father Who is *in heaven*" reminds us that we are addressing the One Who dwells in unapproachable glory. While we address God as "Abba," with all that such a close relationship entails, we also must remember that He is heaven, and we are upon the earth.

> Do not be like servants who serve the master on condition of receiving a reward, but [be] like servants who serve the master not on condition of receiving a reward. And let the fear of Heaven be upon you. (m.*Avot* 1.3)

In our prayers, then, we remember both that God is our Father, and that He longs to have us draw close to Him, while at the same time confessing His greatness and seeking to draw close to Him in ways that befit our King. Further, however, the fact that we address Him as "our Father Who is in heaven" strengthens our resolve to petition Him for what is impossible for us to accomplish on our own strength. The Father Who is in heaven is the One Who can do all of His holy will.

> Judah b. Tema says, "Be strong as a leopard, fast as an eagle, fleet as a gazelle, and brave as a lion, to carry out the will of your Father who is in heaven. (m.*Avot* 5.20)

Hallowed be Your name. – The word translated "hallowed" is ἁγιασθήτω (*hagiastheto*) which is a 3rd person aorist imperative. The imperative is often encountered (usually in the aorist tense) in prayer petitions.[1] It carries with it the sense of "may you do this" or "please grant this." The familiarity of the *Paternoster* in the translation of KJV has persuaded most modern English translations to retain "hallowed" as a translation, even though this is archaic English (NIV, ESV, NRSV). The NET Bible has "may your name be honored" which is really not quite accurate. The Greek verb ἁγιάζω (*hagiazo*) corresponds to the Hebrew קָדַשׁ (*qadash*) as confirmed by the fact that the Lxx regularly uses ἁγιάζω to translate קָדַשׁ, which has as its primary focus in the Tanach the separation of something or someone from that which is unholy in order to be used or appear in the *sanctum* of the Tabernacle or Temple. Thus, this opening petition is both a recognition of the holiness of God's Name and a petition that His Name should made holy in the lives and affairs of men.

But the translation of the 3rd person imperative is difficult in English since we only have 2nd person imperatives (the subject being "you"). The petition that God's Name should be made holy indicates that the pray-er wants God to act in sanctifying His Name. This could be better understood in the sense "set apart Your holy Name," that is, "vindicate Yourself," which refers to an actual establishment of His revealed promises and will. This is the theme of the *Kaddish* as we have seen. The tension which always exists in prayer is that caused by what one knows to be true on the basis of faith in what God has said (His word) and the actual events that occur in the fallen world. If God has made promises, then why do we not see the fulfillment of these promises? If God is a just God, then why do we experience injustice? If God is all glorious and holy, then why do people so often regard Him as unholy, or even as non-existent? If God is sovereign, why do bad things happen to good people? In short, the tension of prayer is the problem of evil, and this opening petition seeks to address this problem by asking God to make actual the holiness of His Name in the world, to reveal Himself in the widest possible ways.

Here, once again, we see the Hebraic perspective of the Name. The Name of God is one and the same with all that God is. The Name of God is indistinguishable from God Himself. We see this repeatedly in the Tanach:

> A son honors his father, and a servant his master. 'Then if I am a father, where is My honor? And if I am a master, where is My respect?' says the LORD of hosts to you, O priests who despise My name. But you say, 'How have we despised Your name?' (Mal 1:6)

> But when he sees his children, the work of My hands, in his midst, They will sanctify My name; Indeed, they will sanctify the Holy One of Jacob and will stand in awe of the God of Israel. (Is 29:23)

> "I will vindicate the holiness of My great name which has been profaned among the nations, which you have profaned in their midst. Then the nations will know that I am the LORD," declares the Lord GOD, "when I prove Myself holy among you in their sight." (Ezek 36:23)

Thus, when the request is given that God should vindicate His Name, it has nothing to do with a correct pronunciation of His Name, but rather that His

[1] cf. Blass-DeBrunner, *Greek Grammar*, §337.4; Daniel Wallace, *Greek Grammar Beyond the Basics* (Zondervan, 1996), p. 488.

very Person, His works and His will, would be known for what they truly are, that is, that He should be known as the One and only God Who, in complete holiness reigns in all of the universe.

Further, the manner in which God has chosen to vindicate His Name is through the life of obedience lived out by His people. Thus, God's Name is "profaned among the nations" because through Israel's disobedience, God was required to punish her by dispersing her from the Land, making it appear as though He was unable to sustain her there (Ezek 36:19–21). Conversely, when Israel lives in obedience to the Torah, the nations marvel at the greatness of her God (Deut 4:5–8). With this in mind, the one who offers this opening petition is at the same time committing themselves to obeying God as a means by which His Name will be seen as holy. Ultimately, since "only when the kingdom comes in its fullness will God be wholly honored and glorified as is His due,"[1] this first request of the Prayer is also eschatological in scope, which leads to the second petition.

We should also note that the Name of the Father is sanctified by the acceptance of His Son. Thus Yeshua taught:

> For not even the Father judges anyone, but He has given all judgment to the Son, so that all will honor the Son even as they honor the Father. He who does not honor the Son does not honor the Father who sent Him. (John 5:22–23)

The true sanctification of the Name of God is impossible if one rejects the Messiah of God. In this respect, when we pray that God's Name should be sanctified, we are at the same time affirming that such will occur only as we honor Yeshua as the Son He has sent.

10 Your kingdom come.[2] Your will be done, on earth as it is in heaven.

The Bavli, in a statement attributed to R. Yochanan, states (in regard to fulfilling one's obligation for reciting the *Birkat HaMazon* [blessing after the meal]): "Any blessing which does not make mention of *malkut* [kingdom] is not regarded as a blessing." This talmudic statement may be confined to a proper fulfillment of the *Birkat HaMazon*, but it may be understood as true for benedictions in general. Thus, the inclusion of "Your kingdom come" at the beginning of the Prayer may reflect this rabbinic dictum.

On the "kingdom" in general, see the comments on 3:2 (pp. 82f) and the Excursus on "The Kingdom of Heaven" (pp. 84–93). For Matthew, the kingdom of Heaven has already arrived in the person of Messiah but is not yet completely established. The longing of every true disciple of the Master is that His full and complete rule upon the earth would be established.

We should not see in this petition a redefining of the "kingdom" in Christian terms (=the Church as God's ruling agent) since to do so would be anachronistic. Rather, the kingdom to which our Master refers is the rule of God anticipated and spoken of by the prophets, a theme that permeates the pre-Christian Jewish as well as the rabbinic literature.[3] In this sense, "kingdom" is personified as "coming" and thus stands as a convenient term for the whole idea of God's kingly reign. Thus the Tanach speaks of God coming, which is here expressed as the kingdom coming. Note the following as examples:

[1] Allison-Davies, *Matthew*, 1.603.

[2] DuTillet & Münster: תבוא מלכותך; Even Bohan: ויתברך מלכותך, "may Your kingdom be blessed." This reading corresponds to no known Greek variant. It may be that the Even Bohan was not comfortable with the concept of the "kingdom coming" since this is not the language of the Tanach.

In Luke, a variant is found in a few manuscripts and quotations from the Church Fathers for the phrase "Your kingdom come" – "may Your Holy Spirit come upon us and cleanse us." Tertullian (*Adv. Marc.* 4.26) conflates both readings: "may Your Holy Spirit be upon us and cleanse us; may Your kingdom come." These variations were most likely introduced into the Lukan text through their inclusion in baptismal liturgies.

[3] cf. *As. Mos.* 10.1; *Sib. Or.* 3.46–48, 767; *Ps. Sol.* 17.3; 1QSb 4.25–26; 1QM 6.6; 12.7; *Tg. Zech* 14.9; *Tg Obad* 21 (as noted in Allison-Davies, 1.604).

Say to those with anxious heart, "Take courage, fear not. Behold, your God will come with vengeance; The recompense of God will come, but He will save you. (Is 35:4)

Get yourself up on a high mountain, O Zion, bearer of good news, Lift up your voice mightily, O Jerusalem, bearer of good news; Lift it up, do not fear. Say to the cities of Judah, "Here is your God!" Behold, the Lord God will come with might, with His arm ruling for Him. Behold, His reward is with Him and His recompense before Him. (Is. 40:9–10)

This request that God's kingdom should come in its fulness highlights the tension of prayer itself. Has not God determined the flow of history and thus the exact moment when the kingdom will be realized in its complete form? How then are we to understand a petition that seeks to gain the ear of the Almighty in order that He should hasten the redemption in the coming of the kingdom? Are we to understand that our prayers could somehow move God to bring the kingdom sooner than He otherwise would? An interesting rabbinic story takes up this subject:

> Elijah would frequent the session of Rabbi. One day, which was the New Moon, he waited for him, but he did not come. [Rabbi] said [to Elijah, when he saw him next], "What is the reason that the master delayed?" He said to him, "I was waiting until I awoke Abraham from his sleep and washed his hands and he said his prayer, then I put him to rest again, and I did the same with Isaac and Jacob." "Then why not wake them up all at once?" "I thought that their prayer for mercy would then be too strong and they would bring the messiah not at the time appointed for his coming." (b.*BavaMetzia* 85b)

This same enigma may be noted in Matt 24:14 "This gospel of the kingdom shall be preached in the whole world as a testimony to all the nations, and then the end will come." This appears to teach that hastening the spread of the Gospel would also hasten the return of the Lord. Likewise 2Pet 3:11–12 seems to indicate that through "holy conduct and godliness" we are able to "hasten" the day of the Lord.

Here, then, we are faced with a kind of dilemma that can only be accepted but not explained. The petition that God's kingdom would come in the Prayer cannot be viewed as different than the other petitions that surround it, which are constructed as genuine requests that one offers in hope that God would incline His ear and grant them. As Allison-Davies write:

> So does not the instruction to pray, 'thy kingdom come,' presuppose that the coming of God's kingdom is, like bread, forgiveness, and deliverance, a proper object of petition?…In short, does not Mt 6.10 imply that the supplication of the saints can reach God and help induce him to act?[1]

We can only conclude that this opening petition for the coming of the kingdom both expresses one's own heart desire for the complete and full reign of God upon the earth as well as offering a petition that one expects God to grant according to His all wise and sovereign will. We pray that God's kingdom would come now because that is our greatest desire. But at the same time, we pray in full recognition that God will act in accordance

[1] Allison-Davies, *Matthew*, 1.604.

with His predestined plan.

Your will be done on earth as it is in heaven – In reality, the first three petitions of the Prayer, (1) that God's Name would be sanctified, (2) that God's kingdom should come, and (3) that God's will would be done on earth as it is in heaven, all are one request spoken from varying vantage points. For God's Name will be fully sanctified in the establishment of the kingdom for all things will be accomplished in accordance with His will.

"Your will be done" is common in the rabbinic literature.

> Annul your will in the face of His will. (m.*Avot* 2.4)

> R. Eliezar says, "May your will be done in the heavens above, and grant ease to those who fear you, and do what is good in your own eyes. (t.*Berachot* 3.7)

> May it be your will, O Lord our God, to establish peace in the upper family and in the lower family. (b.*Berachot* 17a)

> Do your will in heaven and give rest of spirit to them that fear you beneath. (b.*Berachot* 29b)

Should we understand the construction of the Greek (utilizing ὡς, *hos,* "as, like") to be saying that the rule of God is already realized in heaven, and that the meaning is "on earth as it is in heaven" or does the phrase mean "both in heaven and on earth"? Given the fact that in Matthew, "heaven" is constantly viewed as a holy place, untarnished by rebellion against God's rule, the former option (the one that is most traditional as well) is to be favored. Even so, the point of the phrase is simply that God's will would be accomplished throughout the universe.

In one sense, the will of God is demonstrated whenever any individual obeys and honors Him. In b.*Sota* 36b the story is retold of Potiphar's wife's attempt to seduce Joseph. In rebuffing her advances, the Talmud makes the assertion that Joseph "sanctified the Holy Name in private." Even the deaths of Nadav and Avihu, Aaron's sons, are viewed as a sanctification of the Holy Name (b.*Zevachim* 115a). Likewise, Peter admonishes us to "sanctify Messiah as Lord in your hearts" by being ready witnesses of the hope that we have in Him.

But in an ultimate sense, the phrase under study has an eschatological aspect as well. To pray that God's will would be done "on earth as it is in heaven" looks forward to the time when the whole "earth will be full of the knowledge of Adonai as the waters cover the sea" (Is 11:9). In that day, no one will need to teach his neighbor to be faithful to God, "for they will all know Me, from the least of them to the greatest of them" (Jer 31:34). We should not, however, think of this as an either-or but a both-and.[1] Our prayer that God's will would be done on earth as it is in heaven involves our current submission to Him and obedience to His Torah as well as our hope for the coming of His eschatological kingdom. As members of His kingdom now, we live in the reality of the fullness of the kingdom that will be ushered in at the return of our Messiah.

11 Give us this day our daily bread.

The initial petitions, which sought to render due praise to God and His

[1] In this regard, Hagner's translation, "Bring your eschatological kingdom. Cause your will to be fulfilled on earth as it is in heaven" is too exclusively end times oriented (Donald Hagner, *Matthew* 1–13 in *WBC* (Word, 1993), p. 144

universal sovereignty, now give way to "we" petitions, that is, requests that encompass the needs of the one praying. The first is for food, and in itself is a recognition that God is the supplier of all bodily nourishment (cf. Ps 107:9; 146:7; Prov 30:8–9). The rabbinically formulated blessings said before eating consistently focus on the reality that the food to be eaten has been given by God. Likewise, the Torah commandment to bless God after one has eaten and is satisfied (Deut 8:10) is specifically given in order to overcome the human tendency to think that one has produced their own food through their own efforts (cf. Deut 8:13–14).

The Greek word ἐπιούσιος (*epiousios*, translated "this day" = "today" in KJV, NASB, NIV, NRSV, NET, etc.) is notoriously difficult owing to the fact that it has not been found outside of the Gospels (except in literature influence by them).[1] *BDAG* gives the following four possibilities, all of which have found their way into the manuscripts by variants and expansions: (1) necessary or needful for existence; (2) for the current day, today; (3) for the coming day, i.e., the day the follows early morning, but it could mean tomorrow; (4) that which belongs to it, thus "each day."

[1] Allison-Davies, *Matthew*, 1.607. The reference to the use of ἐπιούσιος in the side margins of the Lxx for 2Macc 1.8 is wrongly construed.

Given these four options, the following would be the corresponding sense: (1) give us the bread we need to live, (2) give us bread for today, (3) gives us bread for the coming day, and (4) give us bread sufficient for each day. The common translation, "give us <u>this day</u> our daily bread" rests on option 2.

The standard Greek text has τὸν ἄρτον ἡμῶν τὸν ἐπιούσιον δὸς ἡμῖν σήμερον, literally "our *epiousios* bread give to us today." Many commentators, including some of the early Church Fathers, sought to understand this request in light of the giving of the manna to Israel in the wilderness (Ex 16). There, the people were instructed to gather enough bread just for the day and not to attempt to gather bread for the next day.

> Then Adonai said to Moses, "Behold, I will rain bread from heaven for you; and the people shall go out and gather a day's portion every day ((דְּבַר־יוֹם בְּיוֹמוֹ, that I may test them, whether or not they will walk in My instruction. (Ex 16:4)

The Hebrew דְּבַר־יוֹם בְּיוֹמוֹ is literally "the day's matter in its day," understood to mean "a day's portion each day." The Lxx has τὸ τῆς ἡμέρας εἰς ἡμέραν, "that of a day for a day." Since the manna was given in the morning (Ex 16:13), and since morning prayers in the 1st Century were apparently well in place, prayers which may have included something like the ninth benediction of the *Shemoneh Esreh* (prayer for good crops), many have opted for the third meaning listed above, yielding the sense "gives us bread to last the entire day."

But in light of the difficulties in deciding the precise meaning of the word *epiousios*, we should not stress too much the idea that the petition limits one to pray only for today's needs and not for future needs. Granted, Yeshua teaches not to worry about future needs (Matt 6:30-34), but this is in the context of lacking faith. Praying about future needs is rather a demonstration of faith in God's ability to provide. The primary point of this third petition is simply that we recognize and live within the reality that God is the One Who supplies our most basic needs. In our diligence to work six days a week and to honor God with the labor of our hands, we at the same time know that what we gain by our work is still from His hands as a matter of His grace.

A number of commentators, sensing the eschatological flavor introduced in the petition for God's kingdom to come, have also suggested that the request for bread might have an eschatological meaning in the sense of Lk 14:15, "Blessed is everyone who will eat bread in the kingdom of God!" Hagner[1] goes so far as to translate "Give us today the eschatological bread that will be ours in the future." But this, in my viewpoint, reads too much into the text. The ensuing petitions regarding forgiveness and testings are clearly "here-and-now." Of course, there is always a sense that in our current experiences we look forward to and long for the day of the Lord. But from a Hebraic perspective, which is surely the context of our Master's instructions, the recognition of God as the One Who brings forth food (bread) from the earth is no small matter. In our request that God supply our earthly needs, we see and confess the larger reality, that He is the God Who controls all things, including the full consummation of the kingdom.

Finally, the idea attached to this petition by some of the Church Fathers, a notion that is repeated by some modern day commentators, that the bread spoken of here relates to the eucharist, is surely unfounded.

12 And forgive us our debts, as we also have forgiven our debtors.

The structure of this petition is such that the request is conditioned: we asked that our debts would be forgiven in the same manner (ὡς, *hos*, "in the same way," "as") that we have forgiven others. The following verses (vv. 14–15) make this amply clear. If we are unwilling to forgive others, we should not expect that our heavenly Father will forgive us. The parable of the unforgiving servant (Matt 18:23–35) well illustrates this teaching. For this reason, the ability to forgive (which is the fruit of genuine love) is an essential characteristic of all true disciples of Yeshua. "By this all men will know that you are My disciples, if you have love for one another" (Jn 13:35).

The same is taught by the Sages.

> He who is merciful to others, mercy is shown to him by Heaven, while he who is not merciful to others, mercy is not shown to him by Heaven. (b.*Shabbat* 151b)

And we see it in an early Jewish work such as Ecclesiasticus (28:2–5):

> Forgive you neighbor the wrong he has done, and then your sins will be pardoned when you pray. Does a man harbor anger against another, and yet seek healing from the Lord? Does he have no mercy toward a man like himself, and yet pray for his own sins? If he himself, being flesh, maintains wrath, who will make expiation for his sins?

As noted above, the Luke parallel has the word "sins" in place of Matthew's "debts" "And forgive us our sins, for we ourselves also forgive everyone who is indebted to us" (Lk 11:4). 1Macc 15:8 also pairs the words "debt" and "forgive":

> Every debt (ὀφείλημα) you owe to the royal treasury and any such future debts shall be forgiven (ἀφίημι) for you from henceforth and for all time.

It is clear that though the word "debt" usually applies to what one owes another, it was easily used in a religious sense for "sin" because sin makes one in debt to God (Lk 7:41–43; Col 2:13–14). Note m.*Avot* 2.9:

> All the same is a loan owed to a human being and a loan owed to the Omnipresent, blessed be he, as it is said, The wicked borrows and does not pay back, but the righteous person deals graciously and hands over [what he owes] [Ps. 37:21]

Moreover, the Aramaic word חוּבָא "debt" also means "sin" or "guilt"[1] and if an Aramaic original lies behind the Greek rendering of Matthew, it is easy to see how Matthew has "debt" while Luke (writing to a non-Jewish audience) would have used "sin."[2]

Once again, both the final day of judgment (an eschatological viewpoint) as well as an application for the present time coalesces in our text. For surely there is the reality of God's forgiving our sins now (e.g., Mk 2:5; Lk 7:48; Rom 5:1) on the basis of Yeshua's atoning work and the faith that lays hold of it. But the issue of forgiveness of sins also causes us to cast our eyes forward to the final day when we will stand before God and give account (Rom 14:10; 2Cor 5:10). It is in knowing now that we are forgiven, a knowledge made firm by our ability and willingness to forgive others, that we have full assurance of our standing at the final day. And it is in our constant seeking of forgiveness at the throne of God through prayer that such assurance grows and is made firm.

13 And do not lead us into temptation, but deliver us from evil.

Note b.*Berachot* 60b:

> Bring me not into the power of sin, and not into the power of guilt, and not into the power of temptation, and not into the power of anything shameful.

This prayer has been incorporated into the daily morning prayers as well (see the *Metsudah Complete Siddur*, p. 19). The language of 2Pet 2:9 may indicate an allusion to the Lord's Prayer:

> the Lord knows how to rescue the godly from temptation, and to keep the unrighteous under punishment for the day of judgment

The word translated "temptation" (πειρασμός, *peirosmos*) may also be understood as "testing." James (1:1–3) instructs us to "consider it all joy, my brethren, when you encounter various trials (πειρασμός). Moreover, James also makes it clear that temptation to sin does not come from God:

> Let no one say when he is tempted (πειράζω), "I am being tempted by God"; for God cannot be tempted by evil, and He Himself does not tempt anyone. But each one is tempted when he is carried away and enticed by his own lust. Then when lust has conceived, it gives birth to sin; and when sin is accomplished, it brings forth death. (James 1:13–15).

How then are we to understand the petition of this prayer?

[1] Jastrow, *Lexicon*, p. 429.

[2] See the comments of Matthew Black, *An Aramaic Approach to the Gospels and Acts* (Hendrickson, 1967), p. 140.

Though we recognize that God does, at times, bring us into times of testing, He does so for our good and not to cause us to fail. Note Paul's words in 1Cor 10:13–

> No temptation (or testing, πειρασμός) has overtaken you but such as is common to man; and God is faithful, who will not allow you to be tempted (or tested, πειράζω) beyond what you are able, but with the temptation (or testing, πειρασμός) will provide the way of escape also, so that you will be able to endure it.

Here, once again, the question is whether we should understand *peirosmos* and the cognate verb *peirazo* to mean "temptation/to tempt" or "test/to test." "Testing," it seems to me, is the better option, for as we have already seen from the words of James, God does not "tempt" any one in the sense of "draw them to do evil." What Paul is saying 1Cor 10:13 is that testing is part of the human experience—it is common to all mankind. Yet such testing is not random. It falls within the overarching providence of God. As such, He does not allow a testing to come upon His any one of His children that is more than they can bear. In each case, He provides the necessary means of enduring the test.

Yet we know that such testing is allowed by the Almighty in order to perfect and sanctify those who are His.

> And not only this, but we also exult in our tribulations, knowing that tribulation brings about perseverance; and perseverance, proven character; and proven character, hope; and hope does not disappoint, because the love of God has been poured out within our hearts through the Holy Spirit who was given to us. (Rom 5:3–5)

Given this reality, it might occur to some to seek such testing. Clement of Alexandria prayed, "O Lord, put me to the test" (*Strom.* 4.7.55). But such a perspective is contrary to what God desires for His children. The human spirit with which we have been created does not naturally desire trouble, but seeks shalom. Masochism (the desire for pain) is demonically driven.

The fact that this request speaks of God "leading" (ἐισφέρω, *eisphero*) should be understood within the scope of His overarching providence. Since He sovereignly orders the affairs of men (Dan 4:35; Matt 5:45; Rom 8:28), the path of life for each person is in His hands. Here we come, once again, to the enigma of prayer itself, for if God's providence governs the affairs of men, what good is it to prayer that the determined outcome of His providence should be changed? And yet we are instructed so to pray. Somehow, in the infinite scope of His designs, our prayers are significant in the outworking of His predetermined plan.

In the Prayer, then, when we are instructed to pray "and lead us not into temptation," we should understand this to mean "do not allow our path in life to lead us into trouble." When we do find ourselves in times of testing, we recognize that God is in control and will enable us to endure whatever tribulation comes our way as we rely, by faith, upon His sovereign love. But we do not ask Him for such tribulation. Rather, we ask that He should spare us those events in life which bring pain and sorrow, bringing us instead to moments of shalom in this fallen world. Moreover, as the next phrase of the Prayer indicates, the troubles that beset this fallen world, which were introduced through the tempter himself, continue to be instigated by him. Thus, our request that we be spared such troubles is likewise a prayer against the advances of Satan himself.

but deliver us from evil – The question is whether we should understand this to mean "deliver us from *the evil one*" or simply from all manner of evil. The NIV, NET, and NRSV opt for the former, and the Greek could sustain such a translation because the word "evil" (πονηρός, *poneros*) has the article and could therefore rightly be understood as "the evil one" (cf. 13:19, 38, cp. 5:37) We may compare b.*Berachot* 16b:

> When Rabbi had finished saying his Prayer, this is what he said: "May it be pleasing before you, O Lord our God and God of our fathers, that you save us from those who are arrogant and from arrogance, from a bad man and a bad encounter, from the evil impulse and a bad associate, from a bad neighbor and from the destructive Satan, from a bad judgment and from a difficult litigant, whether a member of the covenant or not."

This has also been incorporated into the morning prayers.

Yet not all evil is to be attributed to the activity of Satan. Our own sinful nature, evidenced in our willful disobedience against God, is well capable of evil and the troubles that attend inevitable follow. And just because the Greek word *poneros* has the definite article does not necessarily mean it must be understood as "the evil one." Often in Greek, abstract nouns are found with the article. We may therefore understand this request to be more inclusive than specific, encompassing evil in its widest sense which includes the designs and activities of the enemy of our souls. When we ask that we should be delivered (ῥύομαι, *ruomai*)[1] from evil, we are confessing our own inabilities and weakness, and our utter need of divine deliverance. This is true not only in our personal striving for sanctification but also in the battle we fight against the evil one.[2]

Some have also suggested that the request to be delivered from "the evil one" could carry a strong eschatological sense, meaning that the prayer requests deliverance from the apostasy that will characterize the final tribulation and the work of the evil one in the last days (cf. Matt 24:5, 9–14). While we have noted the possible eschatological flavor interwoven throughout the Prayer, it seems more likely that the requests have primarily to do with the "here-and-now" rather than some trouble in the future. But of course, in one sense, our current struggle against the forces of evil are all part of the final battle (cf. Eph 6:12).

[For Yours is the kingdom and the power and the glory forever. Amen.] The NASB puts this final line of the Prayer in brackets to show that its textual authenticity is questioned. Most other modern English translations leave it out of the text, noting its inclusion in the later manuscripts by placing a note in the margin. The KJV and NKJV have it in the text without indicating its possible spurious nature.

This final line of the Prayer is not found in any manuscript earlier than the 5th Century, it earliest attestation being in W (Washingtonius, one of the manuscripts in the Freer collection). Except for W, the phrase is found only in 8th Century and later manuscripts. No Alexandrian texts have it, nor do most of the Western texts (e.g., D and most of the Old Latin MSS.). In addition, early patristic commentaries on the Prayer (Tertullian, Origen, Cyprian) do not include this last phrase. Most scholars believe that it was added on

[1] ῥύομαι often is used in the LXX to translate both יָשַׁע, "to save" and נָצַל, "to deliver," words that a near synonyms in many contexts of the Tanach.

[2] It is interesting to note that nowhere in the Tanach does the articular הָרָע stand for Satan. Thus, if the articular ὁ πονηρός does mean "the evil one," it does so on the basis of later usage and not the MT or the LXX. The closest one comes in Esther 7:6, speaking of Haman.

the basis of 1Chron 29:11–13 in order to adapt the Prayer for liturgical use.

> Yours, O LORD, is the greatness and the power and the glory and the victory and the majesty, indeed everything that is in the heavens and the earth; Yours is the dominion, O LORD, and You exalt Yourself as head over all. Both riches and honor come from You, and You rule over all, and in Your hand is power and might; and it lies in Your hand to make great and to strengthen everyone. Now therefore, our God, we thank You, and praise Your glorious name.

It should be noted, however, that a very similar text to that of Matthew occurs in *Didache* 8:2, which concludes the Prayer with: "for Yours is the power and the glory forever." Two versions of the Coptic (Sahidic and Fayyumic, the manuscripts of which are late) also contain the same conclusion to the Prayer (leaving out "the kingdom"). The Curetonian Syriac (manuscript dated to the 5th Century) has "For Yours is the kingdom and the glory forever," leaving out "the power." A number of other late manuscripts have various renditions of this concluding clause.

Given the data at hand, it seems warranted to conclude that Matthew did not end the Prayer with this phrase, though it seems likely that it was added (in some form) by the end of the 1st Century or early in the 2nd Century since the *Didache* includes a form of it. It also seems likely that it was added for liturgical reasons, since ending the Prayer with a request to be delivered from evil (or the evil one) would leave it on a negative note, liturgically speaking. Adding the final phrase from the wording of 1Chron 29 affirmed to the congregants that their prayer would be affective based upon the sovereign omnipotence of God.

[1] Allison-Davies, *Matthew*, 1.615, n. 54.

Davies & Allison note[1] that it was an ancient tradition (though we do not know how far back the tradition goes) that the congregation would end the recitation of the "Lord's Prayer" with "and deliver us from evil," with the Leader (priest) responsible to add his own final benediction. It is possible that this concluding benediction was eventually standardized within the liturgy and was added by scribes to the Matthew text.

14–15 For if you forgive others for their transgressions, your heavenly Father will also forgive you. But if you do not forgive others, then your Father will not forgive your transgressions.

These added verse pertain to the fifth petition of the Prayer, "forgive us our debts and we also forgive our debtors." They are not paralleled in Luke, but Mark 11:25 has "Whenever you stand praying, forgive, if you have anything against anyone, so that your Father who is in heaven will also forgive you your transgressions." None of the early Greek manuscripts have Mark 11:26, and it seems most likely that it was added by scribes in conformity to Matthew's text.

We should first note that the injunction to forgive others is cast in the plural: "If you (pl) forgive people (ἀνθρώποις, pl) your heavenly Father will forgive you (pl). But if you (pl) do not forgive people (ἀνθρώποις, pl), your heavenly Father will not forgive your (pl) transgressions." Thus, the requirement to forgive remains in a communal setting, just as is the case with the Prayer (which utilizes plurals throughout, e.g., "give us," "forgive us," "do not lead us," "deliver us"). Of course, such communal prayers are to be made personal by each congregant.

Secondly, it appears at first reading that the forgiveness afforded by God to sinners is somehow dependent upon their obedience, or that such forgiveness is won or made certain by one's own willingness to forgive others. But this is contrary to the consistent message of the Scriptures that portray God's forgiveness as a matter of His grace and not something earned (e.g., Ps 32:1–2; 79:9; Jer 31:31-34; Rom 3:24; 6:23; Eph 2:8–10; Tit 3:5). Rather, the unwillingness to forgive others hinders one's ability to seek forgiveness from God. John reminds us in his first epistle (1Jn 1:9) that forgiveness from God requires that we confess our sins. One who remains embittered against others retains in his heart an unwillingness to submit to God, and as such also refuses honestly to seek His forgiveness. "If I regard wickedness in my heart, the Lord will not hear [my prayer]" (Ps 66:18).

Moreover, the person who continually refuses to forgive others has called into question whether they have honestly experienced the forgiveness of God in their own lives. "We love Him because He first loved us" (1Jn 4:19). It is the love of God poured out in our hearts that both motivates and teaches us to love others. If we have an enduring and growing love for the Almighty, we will also have the desire and ability to love others by forgiving them as we have been forgiven. As Hagner notes:

> These verses are a forceful way of making the significant point that it is unthinkable—impossible—that we can enjoy God's forgiveness without in turn extending our forgiveness toward others.[1]

Donald Hagner, *Matthew 1–14* in *The Word Bible Commentary,* p. 152.

Paul makes this same point in Col 3:12–13:

> So, as those who have been chosen of God, holy and beloved, put on a heart of compassion, kindness, humility, gentleness and patience; bearing with one another, and forgiving each other, whoever has a complaint against anyone; just as the Lord forgave you, so also should you.

Some Thoughts on Forgiving Others

It is often the case that people refuse to take the first steps toward forgiving others because they misunderstand what forgiveness is in the first place. What exactly does it mean to forgive someone who has wronged us? In the Tanach, the words most often used to denote the act of forgiving are נָשָׂא, *nasa'*, "to lift up" (usually followed by a word denoting transgressions or sins), כָּסָה, *kasah*, "to cover," and סָלַח, *salach*, "to forgive." What is the picture of "lifting up the transgressions" of someone? We may gain some insight by noting the parallelism of Ps 32:1–

| אַשְׁרֵי נְשׂוּי־פֶּשַׁע | Blessed is the person whose transgression is lifted up, |
| כְּסוּי חֲטָאָה | whose sin is covered |

Here we have the two terms in parallel. Thus, "to lift up transgression" is to "cover it." In other words, forgiveness consists in not requiring the wrongdoer to bear the penalty of his actions. The weight of guilt is lifted from upon him. Likewise, the penalty of the sin is no longer required since in the eyes of the Judge, the sin is not seen—it is covered.

The verb סָלַח means "to forgive," but may have the sense of "strip off" or "take away" (see *KB*) in the sense of "remove the penalty" for the wrong doing.

The Greek term most often encountered that gives the meaning "to forgive" is χαρίζομαι, *charizomai*, which forms the basis for the Greek word χάρις, *charis*, "grace." To forgive someone is to act toward them in grace, to forego the need to require payment for their transgression.

What are we to derive from this in terms of defining forgiveness? In each case, the words used in the Scriptures to denote the act of forgiveness indicate a change of mind or heart on the part of the one against whom the sin has been committed. And here is the first and perhaps most important thing to realize about forgiveness: *Forgiveness consists in a change of heart of the one sinned against without reference to any change in the one who has committed the transgression.*

This has important ramifications for taking the first step in forgiving someone who has wronged us. We often are hesitant to initiate forgiveness because we erroneously think that forgiveness is impossible until the offender has changed. We think that our forgiving the offender is dependent upon that person asking to be forgiven, but this is not the case. Forgiveness is a change of heart in the one who has been wronged. And what is that change of heart? First, it is a recognition that vengeance belongs to God:

> Never pay back evil for evil to anyone. Respect what is right in the sight of all men. If possible, so far as it depends on you, be at peace with all men. Never take your own revenge, beloved, but leave room for the wrath of God, for it is written, "Vengeance is Mine, I will repay," says the Lord [Deut 32:35–36]. "But if your enemy is hungry, feed him, and if he is thirsty, give him a drink; for in so doing you will heap burning coals on his head [Prov 25:21–22]." Do not be overcome by evil, but overcome evil with good. (Rom 12:17–21)

We are enabled to have a change of heart toward someone who has wronged us when we realize and accept the fact that it is not our duty to administer punishment for the wrong doing. That duty belongs to God and those He has appointed as judges. Thus, having a change of heart that leads to forgiveness in no way negates the need for justice to be served. But recognizing that "vengeance" belongs to God makes it clear that such justice will be meted out by Him, not by the one who is wronged.

Secondly, the change of heart comes when we realize that forgiving someone who has wronged us is not dependent upon a restoration of relationship. Such a restoration is always desired and hoped for, but one can forgive fully without having to wait for the breach that has been caused to be reconciled. In other words, forgiveness consists in a change of heart on the part of the person who has been wronged whether or not the relationship to the offender is restored. This means that we can forgive those who have wronged us before they ever ask for forgiveness, and especially if they never do ask. Moreover, it is not our duty to bring the offender to repentance. It is our duty to love, exhort, and even rebuke, but none of these actions can rightly be done out of a desire to "get even" or inflict retribution. Even if our approaches to the offending party are rebuffed, we can fully forgive that person because we have agreed that God is the One Who must mete out penalties for wrong doing. Further, if we attempt to exhort or rebuke the wrong doer before we have forgiven him, our words will more than likely have little positive effect and may cause greater offense.

In Eph 4:32, Paul exhorts us to be kind to each other, tender-hearted, forgiving each other, just as God in Messiah has forgiven us. This final phrase of the verse gives us a key to the pattern of forgiveness, and may well rely upon the *logion* of our Master as found in our Matthew text. In the same way as God has forgiven us, we are to forgive others. On this basis, some may challenge what I have said about forgiveness being a separate reality from the restoration of relationship, since in God's economy of things, those He forgives inevitably come into relationship with Him through His Son, Yeshua. In other words, for God, forgiveness and relationship are inevitably tied together.

But note several things. First, it is obviously true that all whom God forgives He brings into His family and thus into a saving relationship with Himself. The greatest proof of this restoration of relationship is the gift of the indwelling Spirit. The fruit of God's forgiveness is the very dwelling of His Spirit within those He has forgiven. But this is because God has not only the purpose but also the ability to change the heart. Those who are truly His are known as such by their changed lives; their willingness to obey Him; to seek His grace; and to be conformed to the image of His Son. But secondly, we should also note that God forgave us long before we accepted His gracious gift of forgiveness. Paul writes:

> When you were dead in your transgressions and the uncircumcision of your flesh, He made you alive together with Him, having forgiven us all our transgressions, having canceled out the certificate of debt consisting of decrees against us, which was hostile to us; and He has taken it out of the way, having nailed it to the cross. (Col 2:13–14)

God did not wait for the time when we would turn to Him in faith and receive His gift of salvation before He forgave us. Paul says that in Yeshua, God cancelled out our debt of sin having "nailed it to the cross." What is more, in the infinite and eternal nature of God Who is beyond or outside of time, the death of Messiah at a point in the history of our world had been anticipated from all eternity. Paul speaks of the power of God

> who has saved us and called us with a holy calling, not according to our works, but according to His own purpose and grace which was granted us in Messiah Yeshua from all eternity (2Tim 1:9).

This means that from all eternity, God had forgiven us of our transgressions because of the inevitable sacrifice that Yeshua would offer on our behalf.

Now consider what this means to us in terms of the whole matter of forgiving others. Long before we ever turned to God in faith; long before we ever were repentant for our sins against Him; before we even had any sense of the gravity of our transgressions, God had forgiven us in Yeshua. Granted, in His sovereign wisdom and power He had planned that we should be drawn to Him, that we should seek Him and the forgiveness He offered, and that He would change our hearts to love and obey Him. But I want to focus on that period of time when we were yet rebellious against Him, when we willfully sinned and thought nothing of it; when we besmirched His image in which we were created and despised His kingship, mocking His Son and going our own sinful way. Even at that time, He had forgiven us! And though in time His sovereign power would overcome our sinful rebellion, yet His forgiveness was real *even when we were estranged from Him.* This means, as I have stated above, forgiveness can validly exist even when restoration has not taken place.

Obviously, forgiveness is a great impetus to restoration and often brings it about. But not always. Sometimes relationships are broken beyond repair, or at least beyond complete repair. But even when relationships may not restored to their fulness, forgiving the offender is not only possible, but is essential because God has commanded us to forgive those who sin against us, and such a command is not dependent upon the actions of the wrong doer—it can be fulfilled entirely by the one who has been wronged.

So to reiterate: Forgiveness is a change of heart on the part of the one who has been wronged and is not dependent upon a change in the one who has caused the offense. Nor is restoration of a former relationship necessary for forgiveness to have been fully accomplished.

The reason it is so important to recognize what forgiveness entails is because often people feel justified in remaining unforgiving toward someone who has offended them, waiting for the person to change, to repent, and to ask for forgiveness. While they wait, bitterness, which is the fruit of unforgiveness, grows and gains a foothold in the soul. Such bitterness is like leaven that eventually envelopes one's entire life, and what is more, gives an open door to the devil. Paul writes:

> Be angry, and yet do not sin; do not let the sun go down on your anger, and do not give the devil an opportunity. (Eph 4:26–27)

There is nothing wrong with righteous indignation. But all too often anger is not righteous but self-serving and the telltale sign of bitterness. Anger and bitterness are too sides of the same coin, the one more outer and the other inward. Anger shows itself in evil speech, lose of temper, and even physical violence. Bitterness nests in the soul and envelopes the heart until it turns it to stone. Worst of all, such a scenario gives the devil an opportunity, because the devil is opposed to any part of forgiveness but applauds and encourages bitterness. Where bitterness resides, the devil feels right at home. But where forgiveness is practices, he flees. "Submit therefore to God. Resist the devil and he will flee from you" (James 4:7).

Therefore, nothing need stand in the way of forgiving those who have wronged us. To obey the command of our Master, both in the Prayer itself, as well as in the verses that follow it (6:14–15) requires only our obedience. We cannot be satisfied in thinking that our requirement to forgive is dependent upon the offender admitting his or her wrong, or asking for forgiveness. Rather, forgiveness requires that we have a change of heart toward the offender, that we relinquish to God the task of retribution for wrongs committed, and that we trust Him to right the scales of justice. Moreover, in the process of changing one's heart toward one who has offended, we must take new stock in the reality of the forgiveness we have been given by God Himself. To the extent that we appreciate the forgiveness we have received and the great sacrifice given to secure our forgiveness, to that extent we will be enabled to forgive those who sin against us. And in doing so, we show forth the very reality of our standing in grace, for in the manner in which we forgive others, we also show that God has forgiven us.

16 Whenever you fast, do not put on a gloomy face as the hypocrites do, for they neglect their appearance so that they will be noticed by men when they are fasting. Truly I say to you, they have their reward in full.

Having given His disciples a teaching on prayer, our Master turns to the subject of fasting which has an obvious connection to prayer. We should understand that His remarks relate to personal and private fasting, though some principles may carry over to corporate fasting as well.

In the Tanach, the only prescribed fast is that required on Yom Kippur, and though the Torah text itself does not name fasting as the manner in which one is to afflict one's soul (וְעִנִּיתֶם אֶת־נַפְשֹׁתֵיכֶם), the parallel to Is 58:3ff (which is the *haftarah* for Yom Kippur) seems to strengthen the idea that "afflicting one's soul" (עָנָה, *'anah*) means "to fast" (צוּם, *zum*) since in v. 3 the two terms are parallel. Zechariah (7:5; 8:15) also mentions corporate fasts that were apparently observed by the exilic community. These fasts are mentioned in b.*Rosh HaShanah* 18b as well. The fast of the fourth month (9th of Tammuz) related to the date when the walls of Jerusalem were breached by Nebuchadnezer (2Ki 25:3), the fast of the fifth month (9th of Av) mourned the destruction of the Temple (2Ki 25:8f); the fast of the seventh month (3rd of Tishri), the anniversary of the assassination of Gedaliah, governor of Jerusalem (2Ki 25:25), and the fast of the tenth month (10th of Tevet), the day the siege of Jerusalem began (2Ki 25:1).

Here, Yeshua presumes that people will engage in fasting, "When you fast…." It was apparently customary, according to Pharisaic *halachah*, to fast on Mondays and Thursdays, and this is generally how *Didache* 8.1 is understood (though "hypocrites" need not refer to Jews as over against Christians):

> But do not let your fasts coincide with those of the hypocrites. They fast on Monday and Thursday, so you must fast on Wednesday and Friday.

Earlier in Matthew's Gospel, we learned of Yeshua's fast for 40 days before His wilderness temptation (4:2). Later in the Gospel (9:14–15), Yeshua's disciples are confronted by the disciples of Yochanan for their lack of fasting in accordance with the prevailing *halachah*. Yeshua's answer is that it is inappropriate to fast in the presence of a bridegroom, but that once the bridegroom is gone, His disciples will fast. It would appear from this notice that the fasting normally done by the disciples of John and the Pharisees was understood to be a sign of mourning, something which was inappropriate in the presence of a bridegroom lest his joy be diminished.

The idea that fasting was an appropriate to express mourning is evidenced by the rabbinic prohibitions for Yom Kippur:

> On the Day of Atonement it is forbidden to eat, drink, bathe, put on any sort of oil, put on a sandal, or engage in sexual relations. But a king and a bride wash their faces. And a woman who has given birth may put on her sandal, the words of R. Eliezer. And sages prohibit. (m.*Yoma* 8.1)[1]

It is not difficult to see how fasting as a sign of mourning could have been misused by those who wanted to make a public display of their personal piety. But fasting for public notice was to fast for the wrong reasons.

For a historical survey of fasting in the early Judaisms, see George F. Moore, *Judaism in the First Centuries of the Christian Era*, 3 vols. (Harvard, 1937), 2.257ff.

[1]Contrary to some, the rabbinic materials do not entirely forbid anointing one's head or face when fasting. In m.*Ta'anit* 1.4–5 we read: "[If] the seventeenth day of Marheshvan came and rain did not fall, individuals began to fast a sequence of three fasts [Monday, Thursday, Monday]. They eat and drink once it gets dark. And they are permitted to work, bathe, anoint, put on a sandal, and have sexual relations."

Apparently Yeshua fasted before the Temptation as a preparation for His soul in light of the battle He was to face. And fasting in order to gain a more unfettered singlemindedness in prayer is surely a private matter. One does not gain greater access to God through self-afflicted suffering as the ascetics teach. Nor can one's own suffering affect any atonement for one's sins. While asceticism is foreign to the teaching of Judaism, early Gnostic teachings, which attracted both Jews and Christians in the early centuries, clearly taught the deprecation of the body as a means of attaining spiritual piety. It is possible that such early strains of nascent Gnosticism had affected the practice of fasting in Yeshua's day.

But the primary point of Yeshua's negative warnings regarding fasting is simply that it should not be done as a show to others in order to publicize one's personal piety. Of course, to attempt to flaunt one's own piety is in itself proof of a grave lack of piety.

The manner in which such "hypocrites" made a public display of their fasting was to neglect their personal appearance. They put on a "gloomy face" (σκυθρωπός, *skuthropos*). The Greek word suggests a state of sadness, as the downcast look on the disciples as they made their way toward Emmaus (Lk 24:17). Likewise, the Lxx uses the same word in Gen 40:7 where Joseph asks the cupbearer and baker who had been thrown into prison, "Why are your faces so sad today?" The hypocrites go about with the look of sadness in order to attract compassion from others.

They also "neglect their appearance." Here the Greek offers a play on words. Literally the Greek has "for they hide their faces" (ἀφανίζουσιν γὰρ τὰ πρόσωπα αὐτῶν). The word ἀφανίζω, *aphanizo*, means "to hide, darken, conceal." Did they put ash or dust upon their faces during their times of fasting? Perhaps. But the play on words is found in the next phrase: "so that they may be seen (φανῶσιν, *phonosin*) by men." They "hide" their faces so that they may be "seen." Thus, their "hiding" is hypocritical since their true motivation is to be "seen."

Yeshua's conclusion is: "they have their reward in full." In the Greek, "they have" (ἀπέχουσιν from ἀπέχω, *apexo*) is in the present tense, emphasizing that they "are, at that moment, receiving the only reward they will get,"[1] meaning that their only reward is being noticed by men, implying that God does not give them His notice.

17–18 But you, when you fast, anoint your head and wash your face so that your fasting will not be noticed by men, but by your Father who is in secret; and your Father who sees what is done in secret will reward you.

Here we have more information about those who fast in a hypocritical fashion "hide their faces." They do not wash their faces nor do they attend to their hair. In contrast, the disciples of Yeshua, during times of fasting, are to appear in public as they normally would, with proper personal grooming. The word used for "anoint" (ἀλείφω, *aleipho*) is not the word normally used for anointing someone to a special office (as a priest), which is χρίω, *xrio*, from which Χριστός, *xristos*, "Christ = Messiah = anointed One" is derived. The word used here (*aleipho*) relates to the use of perfumes or oils used in the course of personal hygiene. The point is that fasting is to be done in such a way that others will not know of it. Fasting is a private matter between the worshipper and God. In giving us these instructions, Yeshua wisely reminds us that our souls inevitably possess an admixture of motives. Even when we

[1]Hagner, *Matthew* in *The Word Bible Commentary*, Op. cit., p. 154.

are properly motivated to seek God in prayer and fasting, there remains the possibility of selfish motives, i.e., to seek the favor of men in our pursuit of God. Yet in the same manner that God hears our private prayers, so He is fully aware of our deep desire to draw close to Him. Our fasting in secret is unknown to men but is fully known to the One Who sees all things. Moreover, the reward we seek is not from men but from God, and therefore we should have no motivation to display our acts of piety beyond the secret place of His purview.

What is the reward for fasting that our Master promises? It may well be that Is 58:3ff forms the background for His words here. There, the prophet tells us that fasting has its reward in aligning our hearts and actions with the very desires of God.

> Is this not the fast which I choose, to loosen the bonds of wickedness, to undo the bands of the yoke, and to let the oppressed go free and break every yoke? Is it not to divide your bread with the hungry and bring the homeless poor into the house; when you see the naked, to cover him; and not to hide yourself from your own flesh? Then your light will break out like the dawn, and your recovery will speedily spring forth; and your righteousness will go before you; the glory of the Lord will be your rear guard. (Is 58:6–8)

When we engage in fasting for the purpose of drawing near to God in order to better understand His ways, our reward is communion with Him which provides the proper motivation and strength to obey Him. The reward of such heartfelt and genuine piety is righteous living which shows itself in love to others, particularly those in dire need.

19–21 Do not store up for yourselves treasures on earth, where moth and rust destroy, and where thieves break in and steal. But store up for yourselves treasures in heaven, where neither moth nor rust destroys, and where thieves do not break in or steal; for where your treasure is, there your heart will be also.

Once again, the teaching of Yeshua is cast in a negative admonition followed by a positive. We are not to store up treasures on earth, but we are to store up treasures in heaven. The reason given is that earthly treasures are transient while heavenly ones are permanent. To spend all of our energies on that which passes away and neglect that which remains forever is to play the part of a fool.

But Yeshua is not admonishing a life of poverty as some have interpreted His words here. It is righteous to work and from one's work to receive a proper pay so that one's needs and the needs of one's family are adequately met (cf. 1Tim 5:8). The idea of "storing up" (θησαυρίζω, *thesaurizo*) means to "safeguard something for the future" with the hope of securing a favorable outcome in the future. Once again, there is nothing wrong in doing this, and in fact, wisdom dictates that one should prepare for the future.

> Go to the ant, O sluggard, observe her ways and be wise,
> Which, having no chief, officer or ruler,
> Prepares her food in the summer
> And gathers her provision in the harvest.
> (Prov 6:6–8)

Yeshua's point is seen in His concluding statement (v. 21): "for where your treasure is, there your heart will also be." The difficulty comes when we spend so much of our time and energy to store up earthly treasures that we neglect the more important work of storing up treasures in heaven.

Yeshua contrasts earthly treasures and heavenly ones by noting that earthly treasures are easily lost: "...where moth and rust destroy, and where thieves break in and steal." In the Tanach, the moth destroys that which is feeble (Job 4:19; 13:28; Is 33:1[Lxx]; 50:9; 51:8; Hos 5:12). The word translated "rust" (βρῶσις, *brosis*) literally means "eating, consuming" and some have suggested that it represents another insect, such as a worm or locust, varieties of which were common pests in the ancient world. James 5:2-3 may well be based upon this *logion* of Yeshua:

> Your riches have rotted (σήπω) and your garments have become moth-eaten (σητόβρωτος). Your gold and your silver have rusted (κατιόω); and their rust (ἰός) will be a witness against you and will consume your flesh like fire. It is in the last days that you have stored up your treasure! (James 5:2–3)

Here, "moth-eaten" utilizes the same root as the word translated "rust" in our Matthew text. But James does go on to use the normal verb and noun for oxidation (κατιόω/ἰός) in v. 3. Perhaps the idea of *brosis* in Matthew is simply that of decay. Hagner notes that in classical Greek, the word is used of tooth-decay.[1] The point is that treasures stored up on earth are subject to forces of destruction which are very often outside of our control. This, of course, would have been all the more the case in the ancient world where families would often store their valuables in wooden boxes buried under the floors of their homes. Such conditions would have fostered quick decay and would thus have been a fitting illustration of Yeshua's words.

Likewise, to the natural forces of decay may be added the forces of evil men who would break through the mud-brick wall of a house to steal something. As secure as we might think our belongings are, they are actually subject to the incessant degenerative forces that pervade this fallen world.

In contrast, Yeshua exhorts His disciples to store up treasures in heaven where such degenerative forces, including thieves, do not exist. The Sages teach this principle by noting that wealth given away is wealth stored away. One rabbinic story will illustrate:

> Our Rabbis taught: It is related of King Monobaz[2] that he dissipated all his own hoards and the hoards of his fathers in years of scarcity. His brothers and his father's household came in a deputation to him and said to him, 'Your father saved money and added to the treasures of his fathers, and you are squandering them.' He replied: 'My fathers stored up below and I am storing above, as it says, Truth springs out of the earth and righteousness looks down from heaven. [Ps 85:2] My fathers stored in a place which can be tampered with, but I have stored in a place which cannot be tampered with, as it says, Righteousness and judgment are the foundation of his throne. [Ps 97:2] My fathers stored something which produces no fruits, but I have stored something which does produce fruits, as it is written, Say you of the righteous [*zaddik*] that it shall be well with them, for they shall eat of the fruit of their doings. [Is 3:10] My fathers gathered treasures of money, but I have gathered treasures of souls, as it is written, The

[1] Hagner, *Matthew* in *The Word Bible Commentary*, Op. cit., p. 157.

[2] King Monobaz was a convert to Judaism c. 36 CE.

fruit of the righteous [*zaddik*] is a tree of life, and he that is wise wins souls.[Prov 11:30] My fathers gathered for others and I have gathered for myself, as it says, And for you it shall be righteousness [*zedakah*]. [Deut 24:13] My fathers gathered for this world, but I have gathered for the future world, as it says, your righteousness [*zedakah*] shall go before you, and the glory of the Lord shall be your rearward.'[Is 58:8] (b.*Bava Batra* 11a, cf. t.*Peah* 4.18)[1]

[1] For additional references in the early Jewish literature, see Allison-Davies, *Matthew,* 1.631.

[2] Ibid., 1.632.

[3] Ibid.

In the *Testament of Levi* (13.5) we read: "Do righteousness, My sons upon the earth, that you may have treasure in heaven."

The manner in which one stores up treasures in heaven is through the doing of *mitzvot,* and particularly in assisting those in need as the larger context of *The Sermon* makes clear. But such blessing should not be considered as "other worldly" but as finally and fully enjoyed in the Kingdom of God, which though now only known in part, will be all encompassing in the world to come. What I mean by this is that "storing up treasures in heaven" means that in some measure, the benefit of such treasure is experienced even now.

> Both heaven and the kingdom of God could be spoken of as treasure (cf. Matt 13:44; *Gos. Thom.* 109; T. Job 26.3); and no doubt for Matthew as for Jesus before him, treasure stood not for specific rewards for specific acts but rather conjured up the kingdom of God and all its blessings....[2]

Thus, Yeshua is not negating the storing up of treasures, He is simply emphasizing the better place to store them. A life of faith which issues in humble obedience to God provides treasure in this world as well as in the world to come. Thus our motivation for obeying God is not that we should receive some greater reward in the "sweet bye-and-bye." The reward which God promises to the righteous is unending communion with Him. If in this world we do not treasure the communion we already have with the Almighty, it is almost certain that we have a wrong idea of what constitutes "treasures in heaven."

The concluding statement (v. 21) therefore draws us to the primary purpose of Yeshua's teaching about treasures: "for where your treasure is, there your heart will be also." Paul's words are closely parallel:

> Therefore if you have been raised up with Messiah, keep seeking the things above, where Messiah is, seated at the right hand of God. Set your mind on the things above, not on the things that are on earth. For you have died and your life is hidden with Messiah in God. (Col 3:1–3)

In this sense, "one's treasure tells the tale of one's heart. A person is worth what the object of his heart is worth."[3] If our highest good is to glorify God and to enjoy a growing friendship with Him, then our lives will manifest this passion. To the extent that we have singleness of heart in "fearing God and keeping His commandments" (Ecc 12:13), to that extent we will enjoy the treasures He safeguards for us, not only now, but in the world to come.

It is this singleness of heart to which Yeshua now turns in His teaching, describing in practical and clear ways the life of faith and trust which yields the rare treasure of contentment and shalom.

22–23   The eye is the lamp of the body; so then if your eye is clear, your whole body will be full of light. But if your eye is bad, your whole body will be full of darkness. If then the light that is in you is darkness, how great is the darkness!

The understanding of this saying of Yeshua must be gleaned from the idiomatic use of "good eye" and "evil eye" in the Tanach and thus in the Jewish and rabbinic literature. An "evil eye" (עַיִן רָעָה) is one who lacks generosity and who hoards things for himself. The opposite, then, is a "good eye" (עַיִן טוֹבָה), one who is generous and gives to those in need. Note the following:

> Beware that there is no base thought in your heart, saying, 'The seventh year, the year of remission, is near,' and your eye is hostile (וְרָעָה עֵינְךָ) toward your poor brother, and you give him nothing; then he may cry to the LORD against you, and it will be a sin in you. (Deut 15:9)

> The man who is refined and very delicate among you shall be hostile toward his brother (literally, his eye shall be evil toward his brother, תֵּרַע עֵינוֹ בְאָחִיו)... (Deut 28:54)

> Do not eat the bread of a selfish man (literally, evil of eye, רַע עָיִן), Or desire his delicacies (Prov 23:6)

> A man with an evil eye (רַע עָיִן) hastens after wealth and does not know that want will come upon him. (Prov 28:22)

The rabbis speak similarly:

> A good eye (עַיִן טוֹבָה) and a humble spirit and a lowly soul, they in whom are these are of the disciples of Abraham our father. (m.*Avot* 5.19)

> R. Joshua says, Envy (עַיִן רָעָה), desire of bad things, and hatred for people push a person out of the world."

We therefore understand how this saying of Yeshua follows closely on His teaching regarding the storing up of treasures. We store up treasures in heaven in numbers of ways, but one way is to be generous to others, i.e., have a "good eye."

However, the saying of our text is not so easily understood, for a number of reasons. First, we tend to read the text from our modern world without considering how the ancient man considered the function of the eye. Premodern people tended to believe that the eyes contained a fire or light, and it was this fire or light that made seeing possible.[1] Prov 15:30 speaks of the "light of the eyes" (מְאוֹר־עֵינַיִם) and Gen 48:10 speaks of the "eyes becoming dim" as indicating near blindness. In 2Sam 12:11, "broad daylight" is literally "the eyes of the sun" in the Hebrew (עֵינֵי הַשָּׁמֶשׁ). It was not until c. 1500 CE that the eye was understood as collecting and focusing light. Up until that time, the belief was that the eye generated its own light. Thus, in our text, the eye is spoken of as a "lamp" (λύχνος, *luxnos*) which is obviously a source, not a collector, of light.[2]

This being the case, the point that Yeshua is making is that the "light"

[1] Hagner disagrees and thinks that even ancient man considered the eye simply as a collector of light, *Matthew*, pp. 158–59.

[2] Note Zech 4 in which the seven lamps of the menorah are describes as the "eyes of the LORD" in v. 10.

of the "eye" shines forth in being generous, while the "eye" of the stingy person actually brings darkness. Moreover, the "eye" as a metaphor for one's generous or stingy heart is capable of representing the entire person (represented metaphorically by one's "whole body") and thus one's entire life. The person who is generous, his generosity is seen in all that he is and does. Conversely, the person who is self-absorbed and therefore stingy is so in all that he is and does. This will be emphasized in the Master's teaching about the "two masters" in v. 24.

We should also note in this regard that the word translated "clear" in the second phrase of v. 22, "so then if your eye is clear," is ἁπλοῦς (*haplous*) which means "to being motivated by singleness of purpose so as to be open and aboveboard, single, without guile, sincere, straightforward i.e. without a hidden agenda."[1] This fits well with the understanding that the "eye" is used metaphorically here of one's disposition, either of generosity or selfishness. Singleness of purpose in being a disciple of Yeshua will evidence itself in a consistent generosity toward others. For if we have become aware of the unspeakable gift of grace given to us in Yeshua, then we will most certainly strive to express a genuine generosity to others. "Freely you have received, freely give" (Matt 10:8).

Thus, the emphasis upon one's whole life having a single, overarching purpose and direction, flows perfectly into the next verse which discussing the impossibility of serving two masters.

24 No one can serve two masters; for either he will hate the one and love the other, or he will be devoted to one and despise the other. You cannot serve God and wealth.

Yeshua is not speaking here in absolute terms, for surely there are those who serve more than one master (cf. Acts 16:16). But rather what our Lord teaches, and which is an obvious and absolute truth, is that no one can serve two masters well, giving to each his rightful due, for the simple reason that each one, as a master, has the right to demand the attention of the servant at any given moment. Moreover, Yeshua has two masters well in mind: God, on the one hand, and wealth on the other. Thus, His teaching about the two masters is a continuation of His early teaching about storing up treasure (vv. 19–21) and the necessity to be generous (vv. 22–23).

The contrastive terms "love" and "hate" should not be understood so much as an emotional response to the masters, but in terms of faithful labor, "love" having its covenant sense of "loyalty" while "hate" implying a lack of loyalty and service. These two terms are paralleled in the next line with "devoted" and "despise," again, seen in the context of fulfilling one's obligation to the master.

The Greek word translated here as "wealth" is μαμωνᾶς, *mamonas*, which is a transliterated form of the Aramaic מָמוֹן or מָמוֹנָא. The etymology of this word is not certain, though some have suggest אָמַן, "to trust" as its root. The word signifies "resources, money, property, or possessions." Some have suggested that the word had already gained a pejorative sense in the 1st Century. Hengel writes that "Perhaps the early church left this Semitic loanword untranslated because they regarded it almost as the name of an idol: the service of mammon is idolatry."[2]

Here Yeshua warns us about the trap of materialism, which reminds us that the same things that impede our striving for righteousness are those

[1] So *BDAG*, ad. loc.

[2] Quoted from Allison-Davies, *Matthew*, 1.643.

which are common to all people in all generations. The snare of materialism is that one's longing for it can never be satisfied. In our affluent society, moving up the economic ladder more often than not simply results in larger homes and more possessions, which in turn require greater outlays of money and the need, therefore, to acquire greater wealth. Moreover, once a person has become use to living at a certain economic level, it is increasingly difficult to ever think of returning to something more modest. Indeed, the desire to have wealth is a master that can never be satisfied.

The simple words of our Master at the end of the Sermon apply here: "But seek first His kingdom and His righteousness, and all these things will be added to you" (v. 33), that is, all the things necessary for true happiness and fulfillment in being the servant of One Master.

Luke 12:22–31 parallels the Matthew pericope very closely, with some minor changes.

25 For this reason I say to you, do not be worried about your life, as to what you will eat or what you will drink; nor for your body, as to what you will put on. Is not life more than food, and the body more than clothing?

Yeshua now goes on to exhort His talmidim to the positive duty of faith and trust in God. Having shown that a true disciple's perspective is not to store up treasures on earth but rather to store up treasures "in heaven" by fulfilling the *mitzvah* of charity (being generous to others, especially those in need) with a view to serving God in life's affairs, the question would naturally be raised as to how one is to provide for one's own needs. "For this reason" (διὰ τοῦτο, literally "On account of this") thus refers back to the immediate context of vv. 19–24, and specifically to the whole enterprise of serving only one Master (v. 24) which summarizes the entire outlook of a true disciple.

I say to you – Throughout the sermon, Yeshua sets forth His teaching as authoritative, both in terms of the content of His words as well as in the *halachah* that derives from them. As the Master, His words are not optional—they are to be the guiding principles for His talmidim.

do not be worried – The Greek word is μεριμνάω (*merimnao*) which means "to be apprehensive, have anxiety, be anxious, be (unduly) concerned" (*BDAG*, ad loc) and is a key word in our text (used six times). The KJV "take no thought" is misleading in our modern English, for Yeshua requires His disciples, in this very context, "to consider" the issue at hand by noting how God provides even for the birds (v. 26) and how the flowers of the field prove His faithfulness (v. 28). This issue of one's own needs and how they will be met is not, therefore, to be neglected or relegated to something unworthy of thought and planning. Even the petition for daily food in the Prayer indicates that considerations about one's own needs is expected.

Nor does the translation "do not be worried" quite tell the whole story, for it could imply in modern English that one's future needs should not be a concern at all ("Don't worry about it!", like שׁוּם דָּבָר in modern Hebrew), which could give rise to carelessness, apathy, indifference, laziness, and self-indulgence, all of which are unbecoming of a disciple of the Master Yeshua. For our Messiah has already taught that we should guard even the smallest stroke of the Torah (5:17–20), and the Torah commands that we work six days of the week (Ex 20:9, "six days you shall labor and do all your work"). As noted earlier (see comments on vv. 19–21 above), Paul requires that a man provide for his family (1Tim 5:8) because to do so befits one who claims to be a believer in Yeshua. Diligence in providing for the future is a matter of godly wisdom.

Rather, the word implies the sense of "anxiety," of mental anguish over the future which no one but God can control. Note the ESV: "do not be anxious about your life," which gives the proper sense. Anxiety, in this sense, marks both a lack of faith in God's ability to provide as well as a misplaced sense of one's own ability to control future events. If we have prayed that He would provide our daily bread, then we must trust that He will do so by giving us the strength and ability to complete the day's work. But if we have prayed for His provision, then to live in anxiety about tomorrow is to lack faith that He has heard our prayer and will answer in accordance with His wise and merciful will.

Yeshua teaches us not to be anxious about "your life" (τῇ ψυχῇ ὑμῶν), literally "with regard to your soul." In Hebrew, נֶפֶשׁ, *nefesh*, "soul" can be used to denote a person in general (e.g., Gen 46:15; Lev 24:17). It can also be used as a reflexive pronoun, meaning "oneself" (e.g., Num 30:5–12). Thus, if this is a semitism, we might translate "do not be anxious yourself." But the parallel to "body" (σῶμα, *soma*) in the next phrase should probably alert us to the use of ψυχή, *pseuxe*, "soul" meaning "life." We are not to be overcome with anxiety over how we will sustain our lives. In living according to the wise disciplines of God's instructions, we leave our lives in His hands and trust that He will provide all that is needed to sustain our lives for the days He has allotted to us.

as to what you eat or what you will drink – Some manuscripts leave out "what you will drink" (ἢ τί πίητε, ℵ, *f¹*, vg, syᶜ, saᵐˢˢ) but other early manuscripts, including citations by Church fathers, include it (B, W, *f¹³*, 33, saᵐˢˢ, Or, Hierᵐˢˢ). But it is possible that its absence is the result of homoioteleuton, since φάγητε ("to eat") and πίητε ("to drink") have the same ending. It is also possible that it was added to conform this verse to v. 31 which has both "to eat" and "to drink." The Lukan parallel lacks "to drink."[1] It is difficult to decide on the basis of either external (manuscript) evidence or internal matters. The Nestle-Aland Greek text puts it in brackets to indicate the committee was undecided on the matter. But in either case, the basic meaning of the verse is not altered. Eating and drinking often form a kind of *merism* meaning "food in general," which is how the parallel line at the end of the verse reads: "is not the soul [life] more than food?"

nor for you body, as to what you will put on – The essentials for life, as far as the Apostle Paul is concerned, are food and clothing: "If we have food and covering, with these we shall be content" (1Tim 6:8), a teaching which might be based on this *logion*. Nakedness in the Tanach bespeaks not only shame (as in the case of Adam and Chavah) but also abject poverty. Job describes the poor in this way:

> They spend the night naked, without clothing, and have no covering against the cold. (Job 24:7)
> They [those who power] cause the poor to go about naked without clothing, and they take away the sheaves from the hungry. (Job 24:10)

Is not life more than food, and the body more than clothing? – The point Yeshua is making in this rhetorical question is that one's existence (the life [soul], the body) entails far more than food and clothing, as necessary as these are. If God is the very Giver of life (cf. Jn 5:21), then surely He is able

[1] The DuTillet and the Münster both include "to drink" but the Shem Tov (Even Bohan) does not. Once again, the Shem Tov is aligned with the Vulgate.

to provide all things necessary to sustain life. If we spend all of our energy in anxiety over how we will obtain the necessities for life, we may miss the purpose of our lives in the process.

In m.*Avot* 2.7 Hillel is reported as saying: "Lots of meat, lots of worms; lots of property, lots of worries…." But if more possessions bring more care, the opposite is also true: less possessions also brings more care. The love of money can equally be the bane of the wealthy and the impoverished, proving that more money or buying power does not overcome the anxiety against which our Master teaches. It is not the getting of more that overcomes such anxiety but the getting of faith in one's heavenly Father Who promises to provide.

> … just as one must serve either God or mammon, so must one either be sustained by anxiety or by faith.[1]

26 Look at the birds of the air, that they do not sow, nor reap nor gather into barns, and yet your heavenly Father feeds them. Are you not worth much more than they?

Yeshua now gives a fitting example of God's faithfulness in providing our needs. He asks us to consider birds. Luke's account has "ravens," but for Matthew's Jewish audience, the unclean raven (Lev 11:15) may have been avoided (though note Ps 147:9). He also uses the Greek equivalent of הַבִּיטוּ אֶל, "to look to something" (cf. Is 51:1, 2, 6), ἐμβλέψατε εἰς rather than Luke's κατανοήσατε ("give attention to").[2] This analogy finds parallel in the rabbinic literature:

> R. Simeon b. Eleazar says, "Have you ever seen a wild beast or a bird who has a trade? Yet they get along without difficulty. And were they not created only to serve me? And I was created to serve my Master. So is it not logical that I should get along without difficulty? But I have done evil and ruined my living." (m.*Qiddushin* 4.14, cp. *Exodus Mechilta* on 16:14)

Thus, Yeshua's illustration is well within the rabbinic teachings and argues from the lesser to the greater. If God provides for the birds of air which were not created in God's image and thus not given the privilege of ruling over the earth (Gen 1:28), how much more is He willing and able to provide for those who bear His image (cf. Matt 10:31).

27 And who of you by being worried can add a single hour to his life?

Here we find the second time μεριμνάω (*merimnao*, "to be anxious") is used, reminding us of the main theme of this pericope.

The primary interpretive issue is how we are to understand the words ἡλικία (*helikia*, "life time, life span, height") and πῆχυς (*pexus*, "arm, cubit"). Is Yeshua talking about adding inches to one's height (so KJV, NKJV, "can add one cubit unto his stature") or time to one's life span (so NASB, NIV, ESV, CJB)? The word *helikia* usually means "age" (so in Classical Greek) but by analogy also "height" in that as one becomes older, one also grows in height. The word *pexus* means "cubit," which was the span of the arm, usually 18 inches but it could also be as long as 25 inches. Those who opt for the

---

[1] Allison-Davies, *Matthew*, 1.647.

[2] The Münster has רְאוּ אֶת-עוֹפוֹת. The DuTillet and Shem Tov both have הַסְתַּכְּלוּ בְּעוֹף. Lachs (p. 132) erroneously speaks of καταμάθετε "to examine, look carefully," as occurring in v. 26, but it actually is found in v. 28. The verb used in v. 26 (ἐμβλέπω) is a common word for "observing" or "looking."

sense of adding one's height press the literally meaning of this word. But it could just as well be used here metaphorically (cf. Ps 39:5 "You have made my life a few handbreadths"), and it seems most likely that this is the case. For the point of the saying is that one cannot add even a very small measure (cf. Lk 12:26, If you cannot do the least of these things…"), and the idea of adding 18 inches to one's height hardly seems a small matter!

Thus, the point is that we cannot guarantee tomorrow—our lives are in the hands of the Almighty. Those who live with anxiety over the future hope to lengthen their lives but in reality only spoil the time allotted to them. Therefore, such anxiety is foolish and accomplishes nothing. Ironically, modern medical science has proven that stress, worry, and anxiety actually shorten one's life by disabling the immune system and overtaxing vital organs. Stress and anxiety also adversely affect eating and sleeping which contribute to poor health.

28–30 And why are you worried about clothing? Observe how the lilies of the field grow; they do not toil nor do they spin, yet I say to you that not even Solomon in all his glory clothed himself like one of these. But if God so clothes the grass of the field, which is alive today and tomorrow is thrown into the furnace, will He not much more clothe you? You of little faith!

Yeshua now adds an illustration to bolster His previous words about clothing. In the same way that the birds of the air are fed by God's hand, so the flowers of the field are adorned in beauty by the Creator's care. We find in both of these analogies a sacred motivation for the study of nature.

Once again the key word is "worry" or "to be anxious" (*merimnao*). In the same way that one should not fret about tomorrow's food, so one should not be anxious over how one's other basic life's needs will be met. As Allison-Davies point out, Yeshua turns a common motif of the Tanach in a surprising way. Throughout the Tanach, the grass and flower of the field are symbols of the transitory nature of life:

> …All flesh is grass, and all its loveliness is like the flower of the field. The grass withers, the flower fades, when the breath of the Lord blows upon it; Surely the people are grass. (Is 40:6–7, cf. Job 8:12; 14:2; Ps 37:2; 90:5–6; 102:11; 103:15–16; Is 37:27, cp. James 1:9–11)

Yet in Yeshua's analogy, the flower of the field is put forth as a symbol of enduring beauty maintained by the hand of God. Moreover, the beauty of the flower (regardless of whether the word means "lily" or some other kind) exceeds that of Solomon's raiments, which must have been lavish owing to his legendary wealth. In rabbinic literature, Solomon's lavish meals are used as a measure of true wealth (m.*Bava Metzia* 7.1; t.*Ta'anit* 4.13; b.*Eruvin* 40b–41a). If therefore the flower of the field, having done nothing of itself to obtain such beautiful adornments, exceeds the glorious fineries available to the world's richest man, and such attainments are necessarily from God, certainly He is able and willing to cloth His own children. Even more, the flower of the field enjoys a very short existence, being cut down in the harvest or wilting at the change of seasons. If God takes care to adorn such transitory figures, surely He will care for His chosen ones. Once again, the argument is from the lesser to the greater (*kal v'chomer*).

You of little faith! – This phrase is actually one word in the Greek, ὀλι-γόπιστος, *oligopistos* (*oligos*, "little, small" + *pistos*, "faith"). The word is a favorite of Matthew (Matt 6:30; 8:26; 14:31; 16:8) and is found elsewhere in the Apostolic Scriptures only in Luke's parallel to our text (Lk 12:28). Outside of the Apostolic Scriptures, the word is found primarily in references to the Gospels (see *BDAG* ad loc). In the rabbinic literature we meet the phrase קְטַנֵּי אֲמָנָה, "little ones of faith," as in b.*Berachot* 24b: "One who says the Tefil-lah so that it can be heard is of the small of faith," The meaning is that one who feels he must pray loudly in order for God to hear lacks proper faith. An even closer parallel to our Master's teaching is found in b.*Sota* 48b:

> R. Eliezer the Great declares: whoever has a piece of bread in his bas-ket and says, "What shall I eat tomorrow?" belongs only to them who are little in faith" (מִקְּטַנֵּי אֲמָנָה)

Interestingly, every time *oligopistos* "one of little faith" is used in Mat-thew, it is addressed to the disciples, so it does not mean "one who lacks faith" but one who, though he believes, is not willing to exercise faith to the extent that he should.

It is true that the initial faith that a person possesses to trust in God and His Messiah Yeshua for eternal salvation is a gift from God and not some-thing produced by the person himself. Paul is clear about this in Eph 2:8–9,

> For by grace you have been saved through faith; and that not of your-selves, it is the gift of God; not as a result of works, so that no one may boast.

The demonstrative "that" most likely refers to the entire first clause, meaning that the salvation and the faith by which it is obtained are both a gift from God and not something manufactured by the one who believes. Thus, Paul specifically states in Rom 4:5 that believing is not a work.

Yet once the initial gift of faith is given, it remains the duty of the be-liever to grow in his faith or to enlarge his faith. So it is said of Abraham that he did not "become weak" in faith, but rather "grew strong in faith" (Rom 4:19–20). The believer, born from above through the gift of his initial faith, is given the ability and opportunity to enlarge his faith by trusting God in all of life's vicissitudes. It is the consistent attendance to the means of grace given to us by God that cause our faith to grow. These means of grace include: knowing Him through the Scriptures, prayer, assembling together for mu-tual encouragement and edification, and the doing of the *mitzvot*.

31–32 Do not worry then, saying, 'What will we eat?' or 'What will we drink?' or 'What will we wear for clothing?' For the Gentiles eagerly seek all these things; for your heavenly Father knows that you need all these things.

The Master here summarizes His previous teaching by repeating the main verbs or ideas: eat, drink, wear.[1] The disciples of Yeshua are not to have anxiety over these matters and as such, are to be seen as distinct from the Gentiles (here meaning "unbelievers, pagans," cf. 6:7) who are entirely taken up with the pursuit of ("eagerly seek") these mundane matters. While the unbelievers focus their entire lives upon that which will pass away, the

---

[1] In v. 25 uses ἐνδύω for "wearing clothes" while v. 31 has περιβάλλω, "to put on clothes," but the meaning is the same.

talmidim of Yeshua are able to serve one Master because they rely upon Him to supply their daily needs. It is this singular focus in life that enables the follower of Yeshua truly to enjoy life rather than living under the cloud of anxiety over what tomorrow might bring.

Notice how, once again, this is a life of faith. Trusting God for tomorrow's needs means accepting and living in the reality that He already knows what tomorrow holds, and that He has the needs of His people well in focus with a purpose to meet those needs. It is the goodness of God that forms the bedrock for faith.

33 But seek first His kingdom[1] and His righteousness, and all these things will be added to you.

Here is the capstone of our Master's teaching about the practical faith that marks His true disciples. This faith has a single-hearted focus: God's kingdom and His righteousness.

What does it mean to "seek" His kingdom? We should note first that the word "seek" (ζητέω, *zeteo*) is a present imperative and may therefore be understood to mean "keep on seeking." This tells us that the command of Yeshua does not mean to "initially find" the kingdom of God, but that the word "seek" means in this case "to enter into, submit to, and participate in" those activities that pertain to God's kingdom. The addition of the word "first" (πρῶτος, *protos*) means that this seeking is to be "above all else," not first in a series.

Some have seen in this command a purely eschatological sense, meaning that one is to pray for the coming of the kingdom (as in the Prayer: "may Your kingdom come") or in some manner strive to bring in the eschatological reign of the Messiah. But as we have already noted, the kingdom of God/Heaven is presented in Matthew as having already arrived in the person of Yeshua, its present reality guaranteeing its eschatological victory. It is better, then, and especially since "righteousness" is added to the objects sought, to understand the kingdom to be the rule of God as expressed both in the life of the individual disciple as well as in the community of believers to which he or she belongs. Seeking the kingdom of God means having a single focus in all of life's activities so that God's rule and kingship is seen, known, and appreciated by others.

Coupled with the kingdom is "His righteousness." Righteousness here is not equated to "justification," as though Yeshua is giving a call for sinners to be saved. Remember that what governs all of the ethical teaching in the Sermon is the statement of 5:20, that unless one's righteousness exceeds that of the Scribes and Pharisees, they will not enter the kingdom of Heaven. Thus, righteousness in this verse refers to the very character of the kingdom in that it is comprised of citizens who emulate the righteousness of the King. In seeking to enter into the kingdom, to submit to the King, and to participate in those activities that pertain to the kingdom, what governs all of this is the righteousness seen in Yeshua's own life of obedience and submission to the Father. Kingdom life is, then, the pursuit of this righteousness, that is, to walk in the footsteps of the Messiah, and in doing so to live "sensibly, righteously and godly in the present age" (Tit 2:12). The heart of the Master's disciple has this single focus in all of life's activities.

But in having this single focus, one should not think that he or she has accepted a life of poverty. God is not extolled or exalted by poverty. Surely

[1]Some manuscripts add "God" – "But seek first the kingdom of God," while a few have "kingdom of heaven." Internal evidence would suggest that it was easier for scribes to add "of God" than to delete it. The manuscript evidence is evenly waited. Because of this, "of God" (τοῦ θεοῦ) is put in brackets within the NA27 text.

those who are impoverished may glorify God in very real and absolute ways, but they do so in spite of their poverty, not because of it. The promise Yeshua makes is that if, by faith, one puts the kingdom of God and His righteousness as the single priority of life, "all these things will be added unto you." This is not a prescription for prosperity in the sense of gaining wealth or worldly treasures. What is promised is that the necessities of life need not usurp one's life energies. Living and working with the kingdom of God and His righteousness in mind means that one can leave the anxiety of tomorrows problems in the hands of the Almighty and trust that He will supply one's needs. Thus, all things necessary to continue to seek God's kingdom and His righteousness will be made readily available to the person who lives by faith.

34 So do not worry about tomorrow; for tomorrow will care for itself. Each day has enough trouble of its own.

Yeshua leaves us with a pithy proverb, once again turned in such a way to fit His current teaching purpose. Taken by itself, it could appear to be a pessimistic statement of life in the fallen world: "trouble comes every day whether you like it or not, and there's nothing you can do about it." But in the context of the Sermon, the meaning is well understood. Do not have anxiety about tomorrow, let tomorrow have its own anxiety. Concern yourself about the duties of today, and trust God for provision and strength needed for the future.

The rabbinic materials have similar proverbs:

> "I am that I am." The Holy One, blessed be He, said to Moses, Go and say to Israel, I was with you in this servitude, and I shall be with you in the servitude of other kingdoms. He said to Him, Lord of the universe, sufficient is the evil in the time thereof. (b.*Berachot* 9a)

> Do not fret over tomorrow's troubles, for you know not what a day may bring forth. Tomorrow may come and you will be no more and so you will have grieved over a world that is not yours. (b.*Sanhedrin* 100b, cp. b.*Yevamot* 63b)

James reminds us that our plans for the future, even the immediate future, ought always to be framed within a recognition and acknowledgement of God's providential control. We plan to go into town tomorrow, but if we stop to consider reality, we may not have tomorrow as we think we do.

> Instead, you ought to say, "If the Lord wills, we will live and also do this or that." (James 4:15)

Thus, life as Yeshua's disciple, which is life in the kingdom of Heaven, must be characterized by a growing faith in the One Who holds all things in the council of His own will, and Who brings about His purposes in heaven and upon the earth. Trusting in the God of Israel through His Messiah means that one is able to live with the kingdom of God and His righteousness as the single focus of life, a life in which anxiety about the future can be safely set aside in view of God's power and love.

Chapter Seven
Commentary

The teaching of Yeshua in The Sermon continues in this chapter, now with the emphasis upon how the disciples of Yeshua are to treat others. The opening two verses of the first paragraph (vv. 1–5) are cast in the 2nd person plural, "you," but vv. 3–5 are in the singular. Some have suggested that this indicates a piecing together of several *logia* of Yeshua by Matthew (the same occurs in Luke's parallel). But it may be that the opening verses reiterate a common, well-known saying or principle, while the following verses give us Yeshua's direct application of this principle to His own disciples.

1–2 Do not judge so that you will not be judged. For in the way you judge, you will be judged; and by your standard of measure, it will be measured to you.

It is not uncommon to hear people refer to this saying of our Lord as an indication that all forms of judgment on the part of His disciples are forbidden. But this cannot be the case for a number of reasons. First, the Greek word "to judge," κρίνω (*krino*) has a wide range of meanings. It can mean "to judge," but also "to condemn" as well as "to discern." Surely Yeshua's words cannot be taken to deny the rightful duty of a court to render judgment. Moreover, in this very context, Yeshua Himself renders judgment, in some cases, severe judgment. In v. 6 He refers to some people as "dogs" and "pigs," a clear judgment on their spiritual condition. In vv. 15–20 He speaks of "false prophets," again making a clear judgment of their prophetic activities. In John 7:24 Yeshua commands His followers to "judge with righteous judgment." Paul likewise expects believers to whom he writes to be discerning and to make judgments. In Gal 1:8–9, he requires that the Galatians receive no one if their message differs from the Gospel they had already received, which means he intends them to judge what they are taught against the standard of the Apostolic Gospel. He writes to the Philippians: "Beware of the dogs, beware of the evil workers, beware of the false circumcision" (Phil 3:2), which likewise would entail judging the words and actions of others. Thus, our Lord does not here prohibit making wise and discerning judgments of what others do or say.

What He is teaching against is a judgmental attitude by which one would usurp the authority of God Himself. In calling His disciples to a righteousness that exceeds that of the Scribes and Pharisees (5:20), He does not authorize them to become judge and jury, condemning others for their lack of righteousness. Such judgment belongs to God alone (cf. Rom 14:10).

It is with God as the final and ultimate Judge in mind that the opening phrase should be understood. He teaches us that we dare not usurp the place of God as Judge, for if we do, we will answer to Him. We might paraphrase: "Do not usurp the place of God as judge so that you will not be judged yourself by God." For those who have genuinely experienced the love and mercy of God will likewise be willing to show love and mercy to others. In the same that God will forgive in accordance with how we forgive others (Matt 6:12, 14), so God will judge us in the manner that we judge others. Moreover, one who sets himself up as a judge will not be able to plead ignorance of the law when he stands before the Judge.

We may note a similar teaching in the words of the Sages:

> By that same measure by which a man metes out [to others], they mete out to him. (m. *Sota* 1:7)

> Our rabbis have taught on Tannaite authority: To him who gives one's fellow the benefit of the doubt they give the benefit of the doubt. And there was the case of someone who came down from Upper Galilee and was employed by someone in the South for three years. On the eve of the Day of Atonement he said to him, "Pay me my wages so that I can go and feed my wife and children." He said to him, "I don't have any ready cash." He said to him, "Then pay me in produce." He said to him, "I don't have any." "Give me land." "I don't have any." "Give me cattle." "I don't have any." "Give me pillows and blankets." "I don't have any." So he tossed his things over his shoulder and went home depressed. After the festival the householder took the man's salary in hand and with it three loaded asses, one bearing food, another drink, the third, various goodies, and he went to the man's house. After they had eaten and drunk, he gave him his salary. He said to him, "When you said to me, 'Give me my wages,' and I said to you, 'I don't have any ready cash,' of what did you suspect me?" "I thought that you might have come upon a real bargain to buy with the cash." "And when you said to me, 'Give me cattle,' and I said to you, 'I don't have cattle,' of what did you suspect me?" "I thought that it might have been hired out to third parties." "When you said to me, 'give me land,' and I said to you, 'I don't have any land,' of what did you suspect me?" "I thought that it might have been sharecropped by a third party." "And when I said to you, 'I don't have produce,' of what did you suspect me?" "I thought that they might not be tithed." "And when I said to you, 'I don't have pillows and blankets,' of what did you suspect me?" "I thought that you might have sanctified all your property to Heaven." He said to him, "By the Temple service! That's just how things were. I vowed all my property [to others] on account of my son, Hyrcanus, who does not engage in Torah study, and when I went to my fellows in the South, they released me from my vow, and you, just as you gave me the benefit of the doubt, may the Omnipresent give you the benefit of the doubt." (b.*Shabbat* 117b)

Thus, the positive side of our Lord's prohibition is found in Prov. 10:12, "Hatred stirs up strife, but love covers all transgressions" (cf. 1Pet 4:8). Having a judgmental approach to life, one seeks to find the faults in others. If, however, one's approach is governed by love, one seeks to diminish or even cover the faults of others. Just as the rabbinic tale describes give another person the "benefit of the doubt," so Paul describes love as "believing all things." A judgmental attitude presumes the worse; an attitude governed by love hopes for the best. Joshua b. Perahiah says, "Set up a master for yourself. And get yourself a fellow disciple. And give everybody the benefit of the doubt." (m. *Avot* 1.6).

3–5 Why do you look at the speck that is in your brother's eye, but do not notice the log that is in your own eye? Or how can you say to your brother, 'Let me take the speck out of your eye,' and behold, the log is in your own eye? You hypocrite, first take the log out of your own eye, and then you will see clearly to take the speck out of your brother's eye.

Here Yeshua is specifically speaking of inter-community relationships as His use of "brother" implies. Matthew uses this term to denote either one's family relation or one's fellow believer.

The use of "speck" (κάρφος, *karphos*) meaning "twig, speck, splinter" is put in contrast to "log" (δοκός, *dokos*), "beam or log" in order to show the unfairness of those who are critical of others but who refuse to take criticism themselves. Quite often, those who are known for their critical spirits have well known faults of their own.

The metaphor of having a log or beam in one's eyes, meaning something that is obvious to others, to which the person himself is oblivious, is used by the rabbis as well:

> It has been taught [on Tannaite authority]: Said R. Tarfon, "I should be surprised if there is anyone left in this generation who accepts rebuke. If one says to someone, 'Remove the chip from your eye,' the other party responds, 'Take the beam from your eye'!" (b.*Arakin* 16b)

> And said R. Yohanan, "What is the meaning of the verse, 'And it came to pass in the days of the judging of the judges' (Rut. 1:1)? It was a generation that sat in judgment on its judges. The judge would say to a man, 'Remove the splinter from between your teeth,' and he would reply, 'Take the log from between your eyes.' If the judge said, 'Your silver is dross,' he would reply, 'So your liquor is watered down.'" (b.*Bava Batra* 15b)

Once again, the words of our Master do not prohibit taking the speck out our brother's eye— they only instruct us to do it after careful self-examination and removal from ourselves of that which might be even more egregious. If our true desire is to aid our brother by removing the speck in his eye, then we will be motivated by love to make sure that our approach to him is the best possible. Nothing is more irksome than to be reproved by someone whose life is marked by flagrant disregard for God's ways. A chain-smoking instructor at a seminar on how to quit smoking will hardly be heeded.

Moreover, it may often be the case that once a person removes the log from his own eye, what he thought was a speck in his brother's eye appears much differently. Someone whose life is encumbered with sin will, more often than not, have less than sterling abilities to access the right or wrong of others. It is often the case that those who are guilt-ridden seek to degrade others in order to build themselves up. If, however, a person comes honestly do deal with his own failings, he will look at others with far less critical eyes.

That this whole matter of not judging others while one has clear faults himself was undoubtedly a well rehearsed topic among the Jewish communities of the 1st Century, it is still possible that Paul's words in 1Cor 11:31, "But if we judged ourselves rightly, we would not be judged," are based upon this teaching of Yeshua.

6 Do not give what is holy to dogs, and do not throw your pearls before swine, or they will trample them under their feet, and turn and tear you to pieces.

[1]see Hagner, *Matthew 1–14* in *The Word Bible Commentary*, p. 172.

[2]See Allison-Davies, *Matthew*, 1.674-75; Carson, *Matthew*, on 7:6.

[3]Ibid.

Some commentators[1] take this verse to be an independent *logion* of Yeshua without connection to the former or following contexts. At first it may appear to be this way, since there seems to be no verbal or even content parallels. Interestingly, the Didache (9.5) appears to quote this verse as substantiation for disallowing participation at the Eucharist by unbaptized persons. It seems better, however, to see this stern commandment of our Lord as connected with His previous instructions on judging, as a corrective to those who might misunderstand and think that Yeshua was condemning all manner of judgment and wise discernment.[2]

> Disciples exhorted to love their enemies (5:43-47) and not to judge (v.1) might fail to consider the subtleties of the argument and become undiscerning simpletons. This verse guards against such a possibility.[3]

In the ancient world, "dogs" were not normally taken as pets, but roamed the streets in packs eating from refuse piles. As a result, "dog" became a degrading term of reproach. English "cur" and "Cynic" (which literally means "dog-like") derive from this metaphor (in Classical Greek, the word for "dog" is κύνας, *kunas*. The word we have here, in the Koine, is κύων, *kuon*). In the Tanach, "dog" is sometimes used of a pagan, male prostitute (Deut 23:18). It is also used of Gentiles (Mat 15:26–7 = Mk 7:27–28; cp. 1Enoch 89:42–9). Paul refers to the "false circumcision" as "dogs" (Phil 3:2). Peter (2Pet 2:22) quotes Prov 26:11 and combines the metaphor of "dogs" with "swine" to describe false prophets:

> It has happened to them according to the true proverb, "A dog returns to its own vomit," and, "A sow, after washing, returns to wallowing in the mire."

Thus, since swine were used as the a primary metaphor of all this is unclean, combining the two (dogs and swine) forms a fitting parallel, as does "holy" and "pearls." The obvious point of the saying is that something of high value should not be wasted by giving it to those who would neither appreciate it nor use it correctly.

The question, of course, relates to (1) what is not to be given ("holy"/"pearls") and (2) from whom it is to be withheld ("dogs"/"swine"). As noted above, early in Christian literature, the dogs/swine metaphor was taken to describe "unbelievers." Many have suggested, however, that "holy/pearls" stands for the Gospel message, and "dogs/swine" stand for Gentiles. This interpretation rests on the repeated instructions of Yeshua to His disciples that they were to go only to the lost sheep of Israel and not to the Gentiles (Matt 10:6; 15:24).

Some have suggested that the Greek misunderstands an Aramaic word, *qedasa*, meaning "ring" and read it as *qedosh*, "holy," thus producing "what is holy" and missing the parallel to Prov 11:22, "As a ring of gold in a swine's snout So is a beautiful woman who lacks discretion." But seeking to interpret this verse by supposed emendations to the text is dubious, and besides, the picture given is of swine who trample the pearls underfoot because they would rather have morsels of slop for food. In a similar way, the dogs, only wanting food, turn on the one who would give them something else, even if it were of far greater value.

Interpreting "what is holy" (τὸ ἅγιον, *to hagion*) to mean "the Gospel of the Kingdom" may find support in the similar use of pearls in 13:45–46. There, a man sells all he has in order to purchase fine pearls. The point is that the Gospel of the Kingdom is of great value, worthy of one's whole life.

However, to interpret "dogs/swine" as meaning that Yeshua forbade giving the Gospel to Gentiles is contrary not only to His own teaching, that Gentiles would become part of God's people (Matt 8:11), but would undermine His direct command to the Twelve to go and make disciples of the Gentiles (Matt 28:19). Rather, the "dogs/swine" metaphor is better understood as standing for those people (and perhaps even communities of people) who, having heard the Gospel, refuse to have any part in it, and even overtly work to destroy its message. Lachs[1] notes that in the rabbinic literature, the designation "dogs" is used in some cases specifically of the Samaritans. Likewise, the designation "swine" (or even "wild bore") is used of Romans. In the time of Yeshua, these two groups were the most antagonistic against the general Jewish community, and therefore formed a ready literary motif for those who were "enemies" in general.

Thus, what seems most likely is that Yeshua is warning His disciples to be fully discerning and wise in their mission of preaching the Gospel of the Kingdom. They should "wring their hands" over those cities that refused their message, but should leave them, shaking of the dust of their feet (cf. Matt 10:14; Mark 6:11; Luke 9:5; 10:11), and go to other places where the message of the Gospel would be received and have its due affect. In the post-resurrection era, we see this was a lesson the disciples had well learned (Acts 13:34–51; 18:5–6; 28:17–28; Tit 3:10–11).

In learning to forgive and to be open-hearted; to live in such a way as to give others the benefit of the doubt; the disciples were still have wisdom and discernment. They would be doing the Master's work in an often hostile environment, and they needed to be as wise a serpents while, at the same time, being gentle as doves (Matt 10:16).

This is a lesson we must also learn. Much time can be wasted attempting to persuade those whose hearts are hardened against the Gospel. This does not mean that we give up giving such people the Gospel, but we should recognize that once the seed has been sown, some of the soil upon which it has landed will never bring forth fruit. The increase is in God's hands, and we must be wise to discern when our sowing in one place is finished and it is time to move to another part of the field. We may remember the wisdom of Prov 9:8, "Do not rebuke a mocker or he will hate you; rebuke a wise man and he will love you."

7–8 Ask, and it will be given to you; seek, and you will find; knock, and it will be opened to you. 8 "For everyone who asks receives, and he who seeks finds, and to him who knocks it will be opened.

What Yeshua is requiring of His disciples in The Sermon may appear impossible. Forgiving as a characteristic of one's life; forsaking treasures on earth in favor of treasures "in heaven;" having an open rather than critical spirit; and giving others the benefit of the doubt, while at the same time be-

[1]Tobias Lachs, *A Rabbinic Commentary on the New Testament*, pp. 138–39.

[1] A quote from Broadus given by Carson, *Matthew,* on 7:7–8.

[2] b.*Megillot* 12b.

[3] Mid. Rab. *Lev* 21.5.

ing able to discern those who are self-serving and obstinate, and not wasting one's time with what cannot be changed, all seems like a daunting task. Yeshua therefore turns our attention to the necessity of prayer. "One may be a truly industrious man, and yet poor in temporal things; but one cannot be a truly praying man, and yet poor in spiritual things."[1]

The three successive imperatives (all in the present tense) are: ask, seek, and knock, repeated in the parallel line for emphasis. The present tense of each would emphasize that these are to be the on-going activity of the disciple of Yeshua: "keep on asking, keep on seeking, and keep on knocking." Those who follow Him and do His bidding are to be known as those who ask, seek, and knock. Moreover, while in the previous verse it is clear that not all will receive the Gospel of the Kingdom, here, anyone who approaches God in this way of asking, seeking, and knocking, will be welcomed, heard, and helped.

Similar metaphors are found in the rabbinic literature, where one stands at the gates of knowledge (whether of study in Torah or the teachings of the Sages) and seeks to enter in, or one approaches the Almighty in prayer and "enters into" the presence of God. Thus, Mordecai the son of Kish indicates that he knocked at the gates of mercy and they were opened to him.[2]

> R. Bennas said: A man should always immerse himself in Mishnayot, for if he knows, it will be opened for him, and if in Talmud, Talmud, and if in Aggadah, Aggadah.[3]

James reminds us that when we ask but do not receive, it is because we have asked with selfish motives (James 4:2–3). The asking, seeking, and knocking our Master describes is of one who earnestly wants to come before the King with requests that honor His glory.

We should not seek to differentiate meanings between "ask," "seek," and "knock." These all pertain to the same enterprise of prayer, though the added words may give us a better sense of the heart of the pray-er. Seeking denotes earnest sincerity, while knocking may evoke the sense of active, diligent pursuit of that which is sought.

We should also note the passive verbs which emphasize the divine prerogative in supplying the requests of the pray-er: "it will be given," "it will be opened." When we come to God in prayer, we do so without an sense that we have somehow obligated Him to meet our requests. We come recognizing that whatever we have, and whatever we may receive, is the gift of His grace and the outworking of His mercies. We come before the King fully aware of His grandeur and might, yet at the same time knowing that He has bid us come. Here, Yeshua reminds His disciples that they have an open invitation to enter the gates of mercy, and to bring their requests before the One Who alone is able to do all things.

Therefore, James reminds us that "we have not because we ask not" (James 4:2). What a pity that anyone should neglect such a privilege, to ask, seek, and knock at the very doorway of Heaven!

9–11 Or what man is there among you who, when his son asks for a loaf, will give him a stone? Or if he asks for a fish, he will not give him a snake, will he? If you then, being evil, know how to give good gifts to your children, how much more will your Father who is in heaven give what is good to those who ask Him!

Yeshua now gives an illustration from common human experience in order to emphasize the truth of His previous statements. For in consideration of the holy transcendence of God, one might perceive Him as less than anxious to answer those who "ask," "seek," and "knock." The reality, however, is that for those who are members of Yeshua's kingdom, the Father treats them as His dear children. The argument, then, proceeds from the lesser to the greater: if human fathers, themselves beset by sin, still naturally strive to give their children what is best, how much more will the heavenly Father, who is entirely holy (and thus Whose motives are never tainted with selfishness), always give to His children out of the bounty of His goodness.

Matthew pairs "loaf" (ἀρτός, *artos*, which denotes "bread" in general, but like לֶחֶם, *lechem*, can stand generally for "food") with "stone" (λίθος, *lithos*) and "fish" (ἰχθύς, *ichthus*) with "serpent" (ὄφις, *ophis*). Luke (11:11–12) begins with the "fish"/"serpent" comparisons, but has "egg" (ᾠόν, *oon*) paired with "scorpion" (σκορπίος, *skorpios*) instead of "bread"/"stone" as Matthew has it. It may be that Yeshua taught this same lesson about prayer on a number of occasions, utilizing different illustrations. That Matthew employs both "bread" and "fish" may be a *leitmotif* for the upcoming miracle of the loaves and fish (Matt 14:17f; 15:32f). Likewise, "bread" compared to "stone" may hearken back to the desert Temptation in which Satan suggests that stones could be turned into bread (Matt 4:3).

The obvious point of the comparisons is that what is requested is good food, and what is compared is unusable for food, either because it is unpalatable (as a stone) or because it is prohibited (being unclean). In other words, when a child requests food, a father does not give what could not, or should not, be eaten.

But the comparison is heightened by the fact that earthly fathers who do good for their children, do so in spite of the fact that they have, themselves, mixed motives. Surely it is the heart of every good father to give what is best to his children. But the reality is that an earthly father may be burdened with his own selfish desires which, if not overcome, may derail him from acting in full selflessness toward his children. Lachs, presenting the common view of rabbinic Judaism, considers Yeshua's words that attribute evil to mankind in general as being outside of a Jewish perspective:

> The emphasis on the concept that man is evil from brith, born in sin, and the like, is of a later theological development

[1]Lachs, *A Rabbinic Commentary on the New Testament*, p. 142.

[2]See my further thoughts on the subject in *Paul's Epistle to the Romans*, vol. 1 (TorahResource, 2005), pp. 66-69.

While this is true of later rabbinic Judaism, most likely in reaction to the Christian doctrine of "original sin," it cannot be demonstrated from the earliest strata of Jewish literature. Even the rabbinic literature of the post-destruction era affirms the presence of the *yetzer hara*, "evil inclination" as part and parcel of human nature. Moreover, the Tanach is clear on this issue: mankind, following in the sin of Adam, is corrupted with a sinful nature (Ps 14:1–3; 51:5; 53:1–3; Ecc 7:20, cp. Rom 3:9–18[2]).

The emphasis, then, is upon the absolute goodness of God and His covenant relationship with those He has chosen, a relationship cast in the common motif of family. Genuine prayer presupposes the goodness of God, for one would hardly pray to a god who was known to be capricious and evil. When we seek God's favor, we do so because we believe in the fundamental goodness of God. That being the case, we may always trust that He will give to us that which is good for us in the all-wise counsel of His own love and wisdom. But once again, the emphasis is upon our need to ask Him. In the enterprise of prayer, God desires that in our asking we come to recognize time and again that He is the One Who provides not only our needs but also our joy and happiness.

This promise of God's willingness to answer our prayers must not be construed as a guarantee that all for which we ask will necessarily be given. We are again reminded of the words of James, who teaches us that when we ask but do not receive, it because we have asked in order to fulfill our own desires, not those of our Father (James 4:3). We therefore constantly are to incorporate into our prayers the underlying condition of God's will. "If it is pleasing to You" ought to preface all of our requests.

12 In everything, therefore, treat people the same way you want them to treat you, for this is the Torah and the Prophets.

It might appear at first, from the word "therefore" (οὖν, *oun*), that these words of our Master apply directly to the previous verses, in which case the meaning would be "in the same way that the Father in heaven is benevolent to you, so you be benevolent to others." Or "if you expect to receive good things for your heavenly Father, have the same attitude toward others when they ask you for something." But it is more likely that these words, well known as the "Golden Rule," form a conclusion to the whole Sermon which began in 5:17, for in repeating the all-inclusive term "Torah and Prophets," Yeshua here offers a fitting "book end" (*inclusio*) with the former "Torah and Prophets" of 5:17. Even as the Ten Words encompass "love for God" and "love for one's neighbor," so 5:17 when paired with 7:12 emphasize both realities.

Yeshua was not the first to offer this succinct summation of true Torah observance in loving one's neighbor as oneself. Hillel, in his famous interchange with a Gentile who was seeking to learn Torah, said: "What is hateful to you, do not do to anyone else. This is the whole Torah; all the rest is commentary. Go and learn it" (b.*Shabbath* 31a).[1] We find this principle in other rabbinic sources as well:

> R. Eliezer says: "Let the honor of your fellow be as dear to you as your own [honor]. (m.*Avot* 2.10)

> R. Joshua says: "A grudging eye...put[s] a man out of the world. What is this? This teaches that even as a man looks out for his own home, so should he look out for the home of his fellow. And even as no man wishes that his wife and children be held in ill repute, so should no man wish that his fellow's wife and children be held in ill repute. (*Avot de Rabbi Nathan* 1.16)[2]

It is interesting to note that while the rabbinic references cast this axiom in the negative, Yeshua puts it in the positive. In doing so, He includes not only those things that we should not do in relation to our fellowman, but

[1]Interestingly, this same "negative Golden Rule" is found in the D manuscript at Acts 15:29 as one member of the prescriptions drawn up by the Jerusalem Council for Gentile believers. Note also *Didache* 1.2 which also casts the "Golden Rule" in the negative. Likewise, Targum Yerushalmi on Lev 19:18 glosses the Golden Rule.

[2]Quoted from Lachs, *A Rabbinic Commentary on the New Testament*, p. 144.

also those things we should do. In other words, casting the Rule in positive terms includes not only acts of commission but also acts of omission. The disciples of Yeshua are both to refrain from ill treatment of their fellow and also to seek their good.

The fact that living in accordance with the "Golden Rule" *is the Torah and Prophets* (οὗτος γάρ ἐστιν ὁ νόμος καὶ οἱ προφῆται) means that one's intention to live in accordance with the Torah must necessarily involve loving one's neighbor. Once again, the principle of love is at the heart of Yeshua's *halachah*. But this tells us yet another thing: the motivation for treating one's neighbor as one hopes to be treated is not primarily utilitarian, as though I get what I want when I treat others properly. While in some measure this may be the reality of things, the motivation for the disciple of Yeshua so to treat their neighbor is to honor God by obeying His Torah. Here we discover the obvious linkage between the first and second halve of the Ten Words. For only when we have honestly set ourselves to loving God are we properly motivated to love our neighbors. This is not to negate the fact that even improper motivations may yield genuine help for one's neighbor, but the point is, that in the immediate context of the Sermon, Yeshua is teaching us how our righteousness could exceed that of the scribes and Pharisees. And in the Golden Rule, cast in positive terms, we find the concluding statement: our obedience to the Torah, our practical righteousness, will be seen as superior only when our actions towards others are motivated by a genuine and growing love for God. When this is the case, our love will be governed not only by compassion but also by wisdom.

13–14 Enter through the narrow gate; for the gate is wide and the way is broad that leads to destruction, and there are many who enter through it. For the gate is small and the way is narrow that leads to life, and there are few who find it.

Having given the general summation of the Sermon, Yeshua now appeals to His disciples to commit themselves to His message. He does so by presenting four warnings, each in the form of a pair: two gates or ways (13–14), two trees (15–20), two claims (21–23), and two builders (24–27).[1]

The teaching of the "Two Ways" forms the opening of the *Didache* which also incorporates the Golden Rule in its negative formulation:

> There are two ways, one of life and one of death, and there is a great difference between these two ways. Now this is the way of life: first, "you shall love God, who made you;" second, "your neighbor as yourself;" and "what ever you do not wish to happen to you, do not do to another." (*Didache* 1.1–2)

The contrasting picture of a wide and narrow gate (Luke has "door," 13:24) offer a number of possible emphases. The wide gate accommodates a crowd and stands for the way that is easy and common. One who is looking to "follow the crowd" will likewise look for the wide gate. It is also natural to think that a large crowd bespeaks something of high value. Moreover, a large gate would be easy to find. In contrast, the narrow gate may require waiting, giving way to others, it may be more difficult to find, and carrying one's load through it may take more work. In short, the broad gate appears to offer far more advantages than the narrow gate. But the point is not the

[1]Carson, *Matthew*, on 7:13–14.

gate itself, but the destination to which it leads. The broad gate leads to death while the narrow gate leads to life, but in an ultimate sense, for Yeshua is speaking in eschatological terms, life being eternal life and death, eternal death. Thus, these "gates" represent two distinct patterns of living: those who are unrighteous enter the broad gate and those who are righteous, the narrow gate. But there is more to the example than this, for in the context of the Sermon, the broad gate exemplifies the majority while the narrow gate speaks of the minority. In the context of the 1st Century Judaisms, the Pharisees would constitute the majority, and their view of "righteousness" would therefore be the broad gate. In contrast, Yeshua's own teaching regarding what constituted righteousness, i.e., a righteousness that exceeds that of the scribes and Pharisees, would clearly have been in the minority, and therefore would constitute the narrow gate. The point is clear: the masses may present a compelling case for their way of "righteousness" and may even be convinced that they are on the path of life, but the gate they enter leads to destruction. Conversely, the path of life leading through the narrow gate may be far more difficult and unpopular, but those upon it know their true destination, for they have heard the words of the Master.

15–20 Beware of the false prophets, who come to you in sheep's clothing, but inwardly are ravenous wolves. You will know them by their fruits. Grapes are not gathered from thorn bushes nor figs from thistles, are they? So every good tree bears good fruit, but the bad tree bears bad fruit. A good tree cannot produce bad fruit, nor can a bad tree produce good fruit. Every tree that does not bear good fruit is cut down and thrown into the fire. So then, you will know them by their fruits.

The second warning, which follows well on the heels of the first, deals with the presence of false prophets. If the broad gate is naturally the most appealing, being the choice of the majority, then it stands to reason that there would be many teachers attempting to draw people into it. Conversely, for those who choose the narrow gate, they may often be confronted by false prophet or teachers trying to persuade them otherwise.

The mention of "false prophets" (ψευδοπροφήτης, *pseudoprophetes*) may be broad enough to include "false teachers," for there is evidence that in the 1st Century, itinerate teachers went about under the guise of having received special revelation from God. The *Didache* likewise warns against false prophets and apostles, apparently considering them to be the same:

> Now concerning the apostles and prophets, deal with them as follows in accordance with the rule of the Gospel. Let every apostle who comes to you be welcomed as if he were the Lord. But he is not to stay for more than one day, unless there is need, in which case he may stay another. But if he stays three days, he is a false prophet. And when the apostle leaves, he is to take nothing except bread until he finds his next night's lodging. But if he asks for money, he is a false prophet. (11:3–5)

The text goes on to warn specifically about a prophet whose life does not match the truth, labelling such as a false prophet (11:7–12).

Much debate has taken place over who the false prophets were within Matthew's community. Some suggest that they were Pharisees, others that they were Gnostics, and still others, that they were members of Yeshua communities who disagreed with the teachings of the Apostles. Some suggest that Yeshua's words did not particularly apply to the day in which He spoke them, but warned about the coming of false prophets in the eschaton. It seems almost certain, however, that Yeshua was addressing a current problem, for in the very next paragraph (7:21–23), there are those who claim: "did we not prophesy in Your name," indicating an on-going activity with in the believing community. Moreover, the false prophets present themselves within the believing community as sheep when, in fact, they are wolves. Thus, they appear to be true followers of Yeshua, to be part of His flock, when they are not.

The later rabbinic literature shows that the post-destruction Sages considered the prophetic era to have ceased with death of Haggai, Zechariah, and Malachi:

> With the death of the last prophets, Haggai, Zechariah, and Malachi, the Holy Spirit departed from Israel. (b.*Sanhedrin* 11a)

Others marked the end of prophecy with the destruction of the Temple:

> R. Abdimi of Haifa said: 'From the day that the Temple was destroyed, prophecy was removed from the prophets and given to the Sages.' R. Yochanan said: 'From the day the Temple was destroyed, prophecy was removed from the prophets and given to fools and children. (b. *Bava Batra* 12b)

These rabbinic notices may, in fact, be a polemic against the followers of Yeshua who claimed to have prophets endowed with the Holy Spirit.[1]

In the Tanach, the test of a prophet was two-fold. If his prophecy comes true (i.e., he gives a sign or wonder) and then he leads the people into idolatry, he is to be regarded as a false prophet and put to death (Deut 13:1ff); or, if his prophecy did not come true, he was to be disregarded, i.e., his words were not to be followed (Deut 18:20–22). However, the test which Yeshua gives relates to the life of the prophets themselves. They were to be judged on the basis of their "fruit," on the analogy that "Grapes are not gathered from thorn bushes nor figs from thistles." One who is a true prophet will live a life of righteousness befitting members of Yeshua's kingdom. Likewise, a good tree bears good fruit, meaning that the fruit is edible. A bad tree, which probably means a tree for which no care is given, brings forth inedible fruit. Thus, one looks at the fruit of the tree to determine whether it is good or bad, and similarly, one looks at the life of a prophet or teacher to determine whether he is worthy or unworthy. The test of the prophet, as far as Yeshua is concerned, is whether their lives conform to the righteous standards of the kingdom, with love being the governing factor.

Might this indicate that the "prophet" in the early communities of The Way was viewed in a different category than the prophets of ancient Israel? It is possible.[2] It may be significant that while the writing of the Tanach is almost universally attributed to prophets, not one of the authors of the Apostolic Scriptures claims to have the prophetic office. It might appear from this that the authority accorded to the writing prophets of Israel was taken up by the Apostles of Yeshua, not by the prophets of the early communities of The Way. If this were the case, then the prophets within the various communi-

[1] See Lachs, *A Rabbinic Commentary on the New Testament*, p. 147.

[2] See Wayne Grudem, *The Gift of Prophecy in 1Corinthians* (Univ Press of America (1982), pp. 43ff.

ties of the followers of Yeshua, while possessing a certain level of authority, were not viewed as having the same authority as Israel's ancient prophets. Or to put it simply: the prophets during the Apostolic Era were not those who were endowed with enacting divinely ordained *halachah* as were the Apostles.

Yeshua indicates in our text that the punishment meted out to false prophets within the believing community awaited the judgment of God Himself, and perhaps the judgment of the eschaton: "Every tree that does not bear good fruit is cut down and thrown into the fire." This language sounds very much like that of the final judgment, words previously uttered by Yochanan the Baptizer (cf. 3:10) in the context of "the wrath to come" (3:7). Surely the communities of The Way were to deal with known false prophets when they were discovered, but it does not appear that the severe penalty ascribed to the false prophets in the Torah was in view. This in itself might indicate that the role of the prophet in the early communities of the believers was understood as different than those prophets of old sent to Israel. Indeed, it may have been that the promise of a "prophet like Moses" (Deut 18:18–19) was applied to Yeshua specifically, and that as a result, others were not considered to have the prophetic authority that rightly belonged only to Him.

Whatever the case, the prophets were to be judged carefully, making sure that their lives matched their message. Those who bore bad fruit, meaning that they lived contrary to the ways of righteousness as taught by Yeshua, were not be received or listened to. Their message was a false message intended to deceive rather than enlighten; to lead the people to destruction rather than to life.

Once again, the emphasis of our Master is upon actions rather than merely on words. How often the people of God have been led astray by someone with glowing words! This teaching of our Master should be carefully heeded among the communities of our day. Teachers who come into a community without first proving their "metal" through demonstration of life should be held with reserve. Moreover, this teaching of Yeshua should encourage us all the more to seek teachers from within the community rather than outside of it. For when a teacher's life has been proven through a careful and consistent conformity to righteous living, his words will have power and effect.

21–23 Not everyone who says to Me, 'Lord, Lord,' will enter the kingdom of heaven, but he who does the will of My Father who is in heaven will enter. Many will say to Me on that day, 'Lord, Lord, did we not prophesy in Your name, and in Your name cast out demons, and in Your name perform many miracles?' And then I will declare to them, 'I never knew you; depart from Me, you who practice lawlessness.'

The contrast of the "broad gate" and the "narrow gate," the former leading to destruction and the latter, to life, is here put forward to the eschaton and the day of judgment. Even as Yeshua is the Good Shepherd guarding His flock, and warning them of wolves in sheep clothing, so here He gives a divine warning to those who are self-deceived into thinking that their deeds of grandeur for the show of others will earn them entrance into the kingdom. What they lack is the understanding that their righteousness must exceed that of the Scribes and Pharisees, but in the end, they are judged as practicing lawlessness. In all of their activity, they have neglected the most important part—demonstrating love for God by loving their fellowman. While this is not made explicit in Yeshua's words at this point, when one compares the judgment scene of 25:31ff, it is clear that those who are accursed are those who failed to help those in need:

> Then He will also say to those on His left, 'Depart from Me, accursed ones, into the eternal fire which has been prepared for the devil and his angels; for I was hungry, and you gave Me nothing to eat; I was thirsty, and you gave Me nothing to drink; I was a stranger, and you did not invite Me in; naked, and you did not clothe Me; sick, and in prison, and you did not visit Me.'

Several obvious things link our text with the eschatological blessing and judgment portrayed in chapter 25. The same address, "Lord, Lord" is found in 25:11 as it is here. Likewise, "I never knew you; depart from Me" is paralleled by the words in 25:42, "Depart from Me, accursed ones, into the eternal fire which has been prepared for the devil and his angels."

For the concept of entering into the "kingdom of heaven," see the previous excursus on "The Kingdom of Heaven," (pp. 84f). The fact that the verb "will enter" (εἰσερχόμαι, *eiserchomai*) is in the future tense signals the fact that Yeshua is here referring to final salvation in the last day. This is likewise emphasized by the phrase "on that day" (v. 22) which refers to the day of judgment.

The primary and summary judgment is that only those who "do the will of My Father who is in heaven" will enter the kingdom. From this it is obvious that those who are rejected have not done the will of the Father. This is reiterated at the close of the paragraph by the parallel phrase, "you who practice lawlessness." Thus, to do the will of the Father is to live "lawfully," summed up by the Golden Rule (v. 12) which "is the Torah and the Prophets."

Not everyone who says to Me, 'Lord, Lord" – What first arrests our attention is that Yeshua is Himself the Divine Judge. Indeed, all judgment has been given into His hand: "For not even the Father judges anyone, but He has given all judgment to the Son…" (John 5:22). Here we have the use of "Lord" (κύριος, *kurios*) as an address to Yeshua, which, though it may have simply meant "Master" or "Teacher" to those of Yeshua's immediate audience, carried a much higher connotation when coupled with His stated role as the Divine Judge. Following the resurrection, the followers of Yeshua recognized that the use of "Lord" bespoke His divine nature and absolute unity with the Father. Indeed, in the Christological hymn of Phil 2, the "name which is above every name" is stated to be "Lord"—"…every tongue will confess that Yeshua Messiah is Lord" (2:11). While some suggest that such a "high Christology" is imported into Matthew from a later stage in emerging Christianity, the use of "Lord" here is rather the proof of Yeshua's own self-realization as the Messiah, that "Son of Man" portrayed in Dan 7:13f Who reigns as Sovereign over the kingdoms of the earth. The repeated "Lord, Lord" would indicate the urgency of the appeal being made.

The urgency of the appeal is that those who are being judged as unworthy believe they have received an unjust verdict. The stunning reality is that these are not few but "many" (πολλοὶ, *polloi*) who rest in their false security. The very fact that they appeal the verdict makes it appear as though they had no idea of their precarious state until it was too late. They had lived under the false presumption that their religious activities had gained them a sure entrance into the kingdom of heaven.

Who do these people represent? First, it is clear that they are those who call Yeshua "Lord" – "Many will say to *Me* on that day, 'Lord, Lord.'" Secondly, their activities are done in Yeshua's name: prophecy, exorcisms, and miracles. Thirdly, they are quite certain that "you who practice lawlessness" is not a characteristic they share. It would appear probable that Yeshua continues to speak of the "false prophets" (cf. vv. 15–20). In that warning, the false prophet is not known by his *words* but by his *deeds*. Here, the *deeds* might even appear to be worthy, but such an assessment utilizes the wrong standard for judgment. Even as the false prophet is to be *known* by his deeds (fruit), so here Yeshua declares "I never knew you," making a pointed play on the word "know."

But it seems hardly probable that Yeshua is addressing a phenomenon that was occurring in His day, for it seems hardly possible that "many" were falsely prophesying "in His name." Rather, we see here Yeshua's "prophetic self-consciousness"[1] in which He speaks of the last days when He would sit as Judge with ultimate authority.

If indeed those who are rejected are the false prophets who have fooled themselves and the people, then we might rightly ask by what power they could have performed such miraculous deeds. Here we must remember that Satan is the grand counterfeiter who mimics the miraculous power of God in order to deceive. Just as the magicians of Egypt were able to produce (by whatever means) the duplicate miracle of turning a staff into a snake and back to a staff again; just as they were able to duplicate the miracle of turning water into blood (Ex 7); just as the false prophet of Deut 13:1 performs signs and wonders but then seeks to lead the people into idolatry; so the false prophets who work under the guise of Yeshua's name are able to produce signs and wonders. But they are not to be reckoned as true prophets simply because they perform miracles in Yeshua's name. It is a life of righteousness that authenticates a true prophet.[3]

How easily the people of God are persuaded by outward acts of grandeur! But such will not be the case in the courtroom of Yeshua. His words are penetrating and final: "Then I will declare (ὁμολογέω, *homologeo*) to them...." The word translated "declare" might just as well be translated "confess" (note the KJV, "Then I will profess unto them..."). This word is found in legal settings and denotes the irreversible verdict of the Judge.[2] Yeshua sends forth His verdict, based not on some external law but on the eternal, unchangeable Torah which He Himself encompasses. When He pronounces the verdict, He does so as the Living Torah.

I never knew you – While the previous warning against the false prophets teaches us that a person is *known* by their fruits, by which we should understand "properly judged" by their fruits, Yeshua declares that He *did not* know them. By this He could not be saying that He was unaware or unable to judge their fruits, but rather He uses the word "know" in a covenant sense, to describe the close relationship of covenant partners (cp. Amos 3:2). This brings into the picture another element of what it means to live righteously, to surpass the righteousness of the scribes and Pharisees: such can only be accomplished by those who are in covenant relationship with Yeshua. It is by knowing Him, or rather being known by Him (cf. Gal 4:9) that the Torah is written, not merely on stones or parchment, but on the heart, by which a person is enabled to actually live out the Torah as God intends. It is

---

[1] Allison-Davies, *Matthew*, 1.713, referencing Bultman.

[2] Ibid., p. 717; cp. Matt 10:32.

[3] Note Didache 11:8, "But not everyone who speaks in a spirit is a prophet, except he have the behavior of the Lord."

impossible to surpass the righteousness of the scribes and Pharisees unless one has a genuine covenant relationship with God through His Messiah, Yeshua, a relationship that is afforded to all who truly believe.

Thus, Yeshua, in His declaration, comes to the pivotal issue: while the "many" seek to establish their *bona fide* claim for entrance into the kingdom based upon what they have done ("did we not prophesy…did we not cast out demons…did we not do miracle"), Yeshua lays the foundation for salvation on what He has done—"I never knew you." Eternal life is not won by our deeds but by the work of our Savior on our behalf. It is His knowing us (in that covenant sense of the word "know") that causes us to know Him. "We love because He first loved us" (1Jn 4:19).

This sense of "knowing" to which Yeshua refers also informs the biblical doctrine of God's foreknowledge (cf. Acts 2:23; Rom 8:29; 11:2; 1Pet 1:2, 20). In each of these references, God's foreknowledge does not have events as the objects but people. God foreknows people, by which we are to understand not that God has knowledge about them even before they exist (though this is certainly true) but that He has determined to enter into a covenant relationship with them from eternity. Before the chosen ones of God ever exist in time and space, He has "known" them in the sense of entering into covenant relationship with them from before time began.

> For those whom He foreknew, He also predestined to become conformed to the image of His Son, so that He would be the firstborn among many brethren; (Rom 8:29)

> Peter, an apostle of Yeshua Messiah, to those who reside as aliens, scattered throughout Pontus, Galatia, Cappadocia, Asia, and Bithynia, who are chosen according to the foreknowledge of God the Father, by the sanctifying work of the Spirit, to obey Yeshua Messiah and be sprinkled with His blood: May grace and peace be yours in the fullest measure. (1Pet 1:1–2)

The same is true of Yeshua Himself, Who is described as having a covenant relationship with the Father from eternity:

> For He was foreknown before the foundation of the world, but has appeared in these last times for the sake of you. (1Pet 1:2)

Thus, when Yeshua declares "I never knew you," He is pronouncing a guilty verdict upon those who supposed themselves to be covenant members but who never were. They believed that their acts of piety and religious acumen had assured them of a place in the world to come when all along they stood outside of the covenant.

depart from Me, you who practice lawlessness – Yeshua here quotes from Ps 6:8 [Heb 6:9], "Depart from me, all you who do iniquity…."[1] Matthew essentially uses the Lxx in the quote, though the verb "depart " is changed to ἀποχωρέω (*apochoreo*) from the Lxx's ἀφίστημι (*aphistemi*), but both words are close synonyms meaning "to depart."

> Verse 23 presupposes an implicit christology of the highest order. Jesus himself not only decides who enters the kingdom on the last day but also who will be banished from his presence. That he never knew these false claimants strikes a common biblical note, viz., how

[1]Note the clear allusion to Ps 6:4–5 in Jn 12:27.

[2]Carson, *Matthew*, on 7:23.

[1]Note the last two stanzas of Ann Ross
Cousin's Hymn, "The Sands of Time
are Sinking:"

O I am my Beloved's,
And my Beloved's mine!
He brings a poor, vile sinner
Into His house of wine;
I stand upon His merit,
I know no other stand,
Not e'en where glory dwelleth
In Immanuel's land.

The bride eyes not her garment,
But her dear bridegroom's face;
I will not gaze at glory,
But on my King of grace:
Not at the crown He giveth,
But on His pierced hand:
The Lamb is all the glory
Of Immanuel's land.

close to spiritual reality one may come while knowing nothing of its fundamental reality....[2]

Here, Yeshua describes the very kingdom of Heaven as essentially communion with Him. He does not say "depart from the kingdom" but "depart from Me." From this we may derive that the essential element of the kingdom of Heaven is to dwell with Yeshua Himself.[1]

you who practice lawlessness – The word "lawlessness" is ἀνομία (*anomia*), related to the word νόμος (*nomos*), the common word for "law" and the word most often used in the Lxx to translate תּוֹרָה, *torah*. The word *anomia* is found three more times in Matthew: 13:41; 23:28; 24:12. It is found 12 more times in the Apostolic Scriptures (Rom 4:7; 6:19[2x]; 2Cor 6:14; 2Th 2:3, 7; Titus 2:14; Heb 1:9; 10:17; 1John 3:4[2x]). Its close equivalent, ἄνομος (*anomos*) is found nine times (Luke 22:37; Acts 2:23; 1Cor 9:21; 2Th 2:8; 1Tim 1:9; 2Pet 2:8). Both words carry the general sense of "transgression," "lawless," or "violating moral or ethical standards." The Greek of this phrase is literally "the workers of lawlessness." The NASB is warranted in translating "practice lawlessness" since the present participle ἐργαζόμενοι (*ergazomenoi*) denotes an characteristic activity. Yeshua is not dismissing sinners in general, else no one could be admitted. He rather is dismissing those whose lives are characterized by lawlessness—those who live in disregard of what God has commanded.

How could it be possible that people with such a track record for performing charismatic deeds could, on the other hand, have so easily disregarded the very commandments of the God they claimed to serve? We should resist interpreting this phrase anachronistically as we might in our day, in which the majority of the Christian Church has accepted an antinomian approach to the Torah, based upon (1) a limiting of the application of Torah to ethnic Jews alone, or (2) a distinguishing between so-called "moral," "ceremonial," and "civil" laws within the Torah, of which only the "moral" laws are retained, or (3) the belief that Yeshua abolished the Torah and replaced it with His own teachings, or (4) that the Torah is simply *passe* without valid application in our modern world. We should remember that by all accounts, the anti-Torah stance of the emerging Christian Church did not occur until well after the destruction in 70 CE. So Yeshua's immediate audience would not have considered an "alternative" to Torah as did the later Christian Church. Yeshua's condemnation, then, is not so much based upon the idea that the people had entirely discounted the Torah but on their neglect of its true meaning and requirements.

Yet, as I noted above, these words of Yeshua are cast in a prophetic mode. He is describing events of the final judgment day. These words do, therefore, have a direct impact upon those of our day who have adopted a relative ethic based upon current culture and society. Moreover, nothing has ever replaced the Torah, since it is God's eternal standard for determining what is righteous and what is not. When the Torah is considered an antique that is admired but not to be used, it is certain that lawlessness will take over. The Torah is a safeguard (note the use of מִשְׁמֶרֶת, *mishmeret* usually translated "charge," as in Gen 26:5) to keep those who love God's instructions from overstepping the bounds of His will. One may always know that he or she is doing the will of the Father in heaven when they are obeying the Torah as explained and modelled by Yeshua.

In these verses, then, we have Yeshua's radical view of discipleship portrayed in a scene from the final judgment. The righteousness He requires is not necessarily demonstrated by deeds that draw the amazement of on-lookers, but is lived out in submission to His Torah—love for God demonstrated in acts of love to others.

24–27 "Therefore everyone who hears these words of Mine and acts on them, may be compared to a wise man who built his house on the rock. And the rain fell, and the floods came, and the winds blew and slammed against that house; and yet it did not fall, for it had been founded on the rock. Everyone who hears these words of Mine and does not act on them, will be like a foolish man who built his house on the sand. The rain fell, and the floods came, and the winds blew and slammed against that house; and it fell—and great was its fall.

In good rabbinic fashion, Yeshua concludes His Sermon with a parable. The metaphor He employs is well known from the Tanach. For instance, in the curses and blessings of the covenant found in Deut, one curse is "You will build a house, and you shall not dwell in it (Deut 28:30). In the wisdom of Prov, the metaphor is likewise used: "When the whirlwind passes, the wicked is no more, but the righteous has an everlasting foundation" (Prov 10:25); "The wicked are overthrown and are no more, but the house of the righteous will stand" (Prov 12:7); "The house of the wicked will be destroyed, But the tent of the upright will flourish" (Prov 14:11).

The same metaphor is found in the rabbinic materials. In *Avot de Rabbi Natan* we read:

> Elisha ben Abuyah says: One in whom there are good works, who has studied much Torah, to what my he be likened? To a person who builds first with stones and afterward with bricks: even when much water comes and collects by their side, it does not dislodge them. But one in whom there are no good works, though he studied Torah, to what may he be likened? To a person who builds first with bricks and afterward with stones: even when a little water gathers, it overturns them immediately. (24)

Note also m.*Avot* 3.18–

> R. Eleazar b. Azariah used to say: "Anyone whose wisdom is greater than his deeds-to what is he to be likened? To a tree with abundant foliage, but few roots. When the winds come, they will uproot it and blow it down, as it is said, He shall be like a tamarisk in the desert and shall not see when good comes but shall inhabit the parched places in the wilderness (Jer. 17:6). But anyone whose deeds are greater than his wisdom-to what is he to be likened? To a tree with little foliage but abundant roots. For even if all the winds in the world were to come and blast at it, they will not move it from its place, as it is said, He shall be as a tree planted by the waters, and that spreads out its roots by the river, and shall not fear when heat comes, and his leaf shall be green, and shall not be careful in the year of drought, neither shall cease from yielding fruit (Jer. 17:8)."

In Luke's parallel (6:47), he adds "coming to Me" to the opening phrase: "Everyone who comes to Me and hears My words and acts on them, I will show you whom he is like…." Matthew more than likely considers the idea of "coming to Me" to be included in the Hebraic understanding of "hears," which means far more than simply to hear an audible sound. It means "to give attention to" in preparation of acting upon what is heard.

The lesson of the parable is obvious: a wise man not only recognizes that today's actions impact tomorrow's consequences, but knowing this to be the case, he does what is right today in order to be ready for tomorrow. The foolish man, giving no thought to the future, just does what is easiest and requires the least effort in order to meet the present needs. Failing to plan for winter rains, the foolish man builds a house that can only stand if there are no storms. But it is inevitable that the storms will come. Conversely, the wise man builds on a solid foundation so that his house will withstand the storm's tempest.

The parts of the parable match the emphasis of the Sermon. Building the house represents one's life, and particularly one's service for Yeshua in anticipation of the coming kingdom. The rock foundation (note Luke's explanation that the man dug down to find rock, Lk 6:48) upon which the wise man builds his house is the teaching of Yeshua and His view of what constitutes righteousness. The sand upon which the foolish man built his house stands for the teachings of others who contradicted Yeshua and gave their own ideas of how righteousness could be obtained. The storm represents the final judgment when the righteousness of all will be assessed.

We may draw a number of interesting lessons from the parable. First, both men are engaged in the same work—they both are building a house, meaning they both see themselves as striving to enter the kingdom. Secondly, the only thing that distinguishes their respective houses is the foundation or lack thereof. This means that until the storm (judgment) comes, both houses seem to be of equal worthy and dependability. Thirdly, when the storm (judgment) does come, the house of the wise man stands while the house of the fool is destroyed. The primary point of the parable, however, is not that the wise man invested more work to make his house secure or that the foolish man was lazy. Rather, the point of the parable is simply that what will make the difference in the judgment day is the foundation. Those who understand and take heed to Yeshua's words are building their house upon a rock. Those who do not, will be rejected from entering into the kingdom of Heaven, a rejection that ultimately ends in their full and final demise.

Very significant is the fact that twice Yeshua refers to "these words of Mine" as being the basis for one's final salvation. In doing so, He puts His words or teaching as essential for having a place in the world to come.

[1]Carson, *Matthew,* on 7:24–27.

> A wise person represents those who put Jesus' words into practice; they too are building to withstand anything. Those who pretend to have faith, who have a merely intellectual commitment, or who enjoy Jesus in small doses are foolish builders. When the storms of life come, their structures fool no one, above all not God.[1]

28 When Yeshua had finished these words, the crowds were amazed at His teaching; for He was teaching them as one having authority, and not as their scribes.

While the Sermon is directed specifically to those who were Yeshua's disciples, it must have been spoken in the midst of a crowd that listened. Their reaction to the teaching was one of amazement, since He spoke with personal authority. Surely Yeshua upheld the Torah (5:17-20), but unlike

Israel's ancient prophets who constantly came to the people with "Thus says Adonai…," Yeshua never opens His teaching with such words. Rather, He regularly introduces His teaching with "I say to you…" and those who hear and heed *His words* are the ones who enter into the kingdom. In taking such authority upon Himself, He stands in stark contrast to the rabbinic tradition of always basing one's teaching upon the wisdom of the former generation. For instance, in y.*Pesachim* 6.1.33a, it is noted that Hillel "discoursed of the matter all the day, but they did not receive his teaching until he said, 'Thus I heard from Shemaiah and Abtalion.'"[1] Yeshua, without in any way disregarding the Torah as the foundation for God's revealed truth, stood before the people as the Incarnate Word, the Torah personified in the very Son of God. Surely the quoting of Scripture as proof of one's argument (as the Scribes did) is noble and proper. But appealing to the Scriptures rightly gives notice of one's lesser authority. When Yeshua appealed to His own authority in the phrase "I say to you," He was not usurping the authority of the Scriptures, nor changing their immutable status. He simply was indicating, even if in subtle ways, that His authority was equal to the Scriptures since He was Himself the full embodiment of the Torah, the incarnate "Word of God."[2]

Even though Matthew uses this same formula to signal the end of a discourse by the Master ("When Yeshua had finished these words/instructions/parables…", cf. 11:1; 13:53; 19:1; 26:1), it is only here that he includes the reaction of the crowd. They were amazed at His teaching since, when compared with the scribes, He taught as one having authority. The verb ἐκπλήσσω (*ekpleisso*) is a perfective form of πλήσσω (*pleisso*), meaning "to be filled with amazement to the point of being overwhelmed" (so *BDAG*). In Matthew, this verb is only used of the crowd's amazement at Yeshua's teaching (13:54; 19:25; 22:33). It was not simply that they were mildly surprised, but that they were moved and most likely unsettled because Yeshua's teaching left them with an either/or proposition presented on the basis of His claimed authority. His teaching was not given as yet another *possible* interpretation of this *halachah* or that, but as describing, in decisive and distinguishing terms, the very boundaries of the kingdom. Moreover, it was not merely an intellectual exercise in rhetoric, nor even a wonderful expositional teaching on matters relating to the Tanach. He had presented Himself in His teaching, and in calling the people to heed His words, He was calling them either to accept or reject His own position of authority as the crucial element in whether they would enter the kingdom or not. They were not merely exhorted to believe and accept His words, they were confronted with the eternal Word as the very object of saving faith. Thus, their amazement entailed not only a sense of wonder at the wisdom contained in Yeshua's teaching, it seems likely that there was also a sense of fright (which the verb can also denote) in that Yeshua claimed an ultimate authority in terms of the kingdom. Whereas the scribes taught from their profound knowledge of the text and the traditional interpretations attached to it, Yeshua left the crowd with the need to act upon His own words as a matter of eternal consequences.

At the end of Matthew's Gospel, Yeshua says that "all authority has been given to Me in heaven and earth" (28:18). It might appear, then, that prior to the resurrection, His authority was limited. Yet 11:27 makes it clear that Yeshua was fully aware of His divine authority prior to the resurrection. Note also John 13:3 where Yeshua was aware that the "Father had given all things into His hand." We may understand Matt 28:20 to mean that His ultimate authority was, on the basis of the resurrection, established for all to

[1] Quoted from Allison-Davies, *Matthew*, 1.726.

[2] Note Matt 24:35 (Mk 13:31; Lk 21:33) in which Yeshua, by alluding to Ps 119:89 ("Forever, O Lord, Your word is settled in heaven"), puts His words as eternal and thus equal to the Scriptures: "Heaven and earth will pass away, but My words will not pass away."

recognize as now indisputable.

The Sermon ends, then, with a sharp contrast between the scribes (some texts add "and the Pharisees"[1]) and the teachings of Yeshua. This should not be construed, however, as a contrast between Yeshua's words and the Torah, nor as an indication that Matthew's community has already separated from the synagogue into their own "Christian community." Yet it does seem clear that Matthew's community is engaged in critical dialog with the Jewish community and its leaders, and this is all the more possible if we consider that the final form of Matthew's Gospel may well have been completed in the post-destruction era (see p. 7 of the Introduction). In *Avot*, we have a the pre-destruction teaching of Simon the Just, purported to have been one of the last survivors of the Great Assembly during the Maccabean era:

> He would say: "On three things does the world stand: On the Torah, and on the Temple service, and on deeds of loving kindness."

Obviously, after the destruction of the Temple, this saying and that fundamental axiom that it embodied for the Jewish community was in dire need of revision. One of the world's pillars had been destroyed! It was to this need for redefinition that the Sages at Yavneh applied their acumen.

Doubtlessly, the communities of The Way were engaged in such a redefinition even before the destruction of the Temple, for if Simon's well known teaching represented a cornerstone for Pharisaism, the most popular Judaism of the day, it left out an essential element: the Messiah. And those who had become followers of Yeshua, including Matthew's community, were intent on showing that in an ultimate sense, all three of Simon's pillars described the person and work of Yeshua, Who is the living Torah, Who is the fulfillment of the Temple service, and Who taught and, by His life, demonstrated the meaning of "loving kindness" (גְּמִלוּת חֲסָדִים, *g'milut chasdim*).

The contrast, then, between Yeshua's teaching and that of the scribes, did not entirely exist in a different style or approach, but in explaining how a teaching such as Simon's had missed the mark by failing to appreciate the true work of the promised Messiah and how central He would be to the realization of Israel's ultimate goal and success. It was therefore this sense of having touched the very heart of the prophet's message that marked Yeshua's teaching out as different and as having an authority which the teaching of the scribes lacked. Yeshua did not teach *about* the Messiah and His role in the overall salvation of Israel, but He presented Himself as that very Messiah Whose wisdom and instruction matched the expectations of the prophets. He was to be heeded because He was the fulfillment *par excellence* of the prophet spoken of by Moses (Deut 18:18) Who spoke the divine words, not about someone else, but of Himself. When He said "I say to you" rather than "thus says Adonai," He was speaking as *the* Prophet Whose words were the very words of Adonai, not by delegated authority, but on the basis of the authority He personally possessed.

Made in the USA
Columbia, SC
09 June 2021